CliffsTestPrep®

Officer Candidate Tests

CliffsTestPrep®
Officer Candidate Tests

by

By Fred N. Grayson, M.A., 1st Lt. USAF (Ret'd)

Contributing Authors

Mark Weinfeld

Sharon Shirley

Michael Hamid

WILEY

Wiley Publishing, Inc.

About the Author

As an independent book developer and publisher, Fred N. Grayson has published hundreds of books in conjunction with many major publishers. In addition, he has also written and/or coauthored dozens of books in the test preparation field.

Publisher's Acknowledgments

Editorial

Project Editor: Suzanne Snyder

Acquisitions Editor: Greg Tubach

Copy Editor: Kelly Henthorne

Technical Editor: Brian Proffitt

Composition

Proofreader: Cindy Ballew

Wiley Publishing, Inc. Composition Services

CliffsTestPrep® Officer Candidate Tests

Published by:
Wiley Publishing, Inc.
111 River Street
Hoboken, NJ 07030-5774
www.wiley.com

Copyright © 2004 Wiley, Hoboken, NJ

Published by Wiley, Hoboken, NJ
Published simultaneously in Canada

Library of Congress Cataloging-in-Publication Data

Grayson, Fred N.

Officer candidate tests / by Fred N. Grayson ; contributing authors, Mark Weinfeld ... [et al.].— 1st ed.

p. cm. — (CliffsTestPrep)

ISBN 978-0-7645-6824-4

1. United States—Armed Forces—Examinations. 2. United States—Armed Forces—Officers. I. Weinfeld, Mark. II. Title. III. Series.

U408.5.G7324 2004

355'.0076—dc22

2004012356

ISBN: 0-7645-6824-8

Printed in the United States of America

10 9 8 7 6

1B/QR/QV/QW/IN

WILEY

Table of Contents

Introduction

Good Luck!

This may seem an odd way to begin an introduction—something more suited until the end. But assuming that you have made the decision to apply for Officer Candidate School (or Officer Training School), wishing you good luck is the appropriate way to begin. To become an officer in the U. S. Armed Services is a major step in your career.

The purpose of our military is to provide a strong national defense throughout a broad range of career opportunities. The military provides training and work experience for more than 2.5 million people. More than 1.4 million people serve in the active Army, Navy, Marine Corps, and Air Force, and more than 1.1 million serve in their reserve components and the Air and Army National Guard. The Coast Guard is now part of the U.S. Department of Homeland Security.

The military distinguishes between enlisted and officer careers. Enlisted personnel, who make up about 85 percent of the Armed Forces, carry out the fundamental operations of the military in areas such as combat, administration, construction, engineering, health care, and human services. Officers, who make up the remaining 15 percent of the Armed Forces, are the leaders of the military, supervising and managing activities in every occupational specialty of the Armed Forces.

Military Career Areas

The career areas offered by the military for officers are almost unlimited and in many cases replicate those found in civilian life—except, of course, for careers such as combat officers and other areas that may put you "in harms way."

Combat specialty officers plan and direct military operations, oversee combat activities, and serve as combat leaders. This category includes officers in charge of tanks and other armored assault vehicles, artillery systems, special operations forces, and infantry. Combat specialty officers normally specialize by the type of unit that they lead. Within the unit, they may specialize by the type of weapon system. Artillery and missile system officers, for example, direct personnel as they target, launch, test, and maintain various types of missiles and artillery. Special-operations officers lead their units in offensive raids, demolitions, intelligence gathering, and search-and-rescue missions.

Engineering, science, and technical officers have a wide range of responsibilities based on their areas of expertise. They lead or perform activities in areas such as space operations, environmental health and safety, and engineering. These officers may direct the operations of communications centers or the development of complex computer systems. Environmental health and safety officers study the air, ground, and water to identify and analyze sources of pollution and its effects. They also direct programs to control safety and health hazards in the workplace. Other personnel work as aerospace engineers to design and direct the development of military aircraft, missiles, and spacecraft.

Executive, administrative, and managerial officers oversee and direct military activities in key functional areas such as finance, accounting, health administration, international relations, and supply. Health services administrators, for instance, are responsible for the overall quality of care provided at the hospitals and clinics they operate. They must ensure that each department works together to provide the highest quality of care. As another example, purchasing and contracting managers negotiate and monitor contracts for the purchase of the billions of dollars worth of equipment, supplies, and services that the military buys from private industry each year.

Health-care officers provide health services at military facilities, on the basis of their area of specialization. Officers who assist in examining, diagnosing, and treating patients with illness, injury, or disease include physicians, registered nurses, and dentists. Other health-care officers provide therapy, rehabilitative treatment, and additional services for patients. Physical and occupational therapists plan and administer therapy to help patients adjust to disabilities, regain independence, and return to work. Speech therapists evaluate and treat patients with hearing and speech problems. Dietitians manage food service facilities and plan meals for hospital patients and for outpatients who need special diets. Pharmacists manage the purchase, storage, and dispensation of drugs and medicines. Physicians and surgeons in this occupational group provide the majority of medical services to the military and their families. Dentists treat diseases and disorders of the mouth. Optometrists treat vision problems by prescribing eyeglasses or contact lenses. Psychologists provide mental health care and also conduct research on behavior and emotions.

Media and affairs officers oversee the development, production, and presentation of information or events for the public. These officers may produce and direct motion pictures, videotapes, and television and radio broadcasts that are used for training, news, and entertainment. Some plan, develop, and direct the activities of military bands. Public information officers respond to inquiries about military activities and prepare news releases and reports to keep the public informed.

Protective service officers are responsible for the safety and protection of individuals and property on military bases and vessels. Emergency management officers plan and prepare for all types of natural and human-made disasters. They develop warning, control, and evacuation plans to be used in the event of a disaster. Law enforcement and security officers enforce all applicable laws on military bases and investigate crimes when the law has been broken.

Support services officers manage food service activities and perform services in support of the morale and well-being of military personnel and their families. Food services managers oversee the preparation and delivery of food services within dining facilities located on military installations and vessels. Social workers focus on improving conditions that cause social problems such as drug and alcohol abuse, racism, and sexism. Chaplains conduct worship services for military personnel and perform other spiritual duties covering the beliefs and practices of all religious faiths.

Officers in *transportation occupations* manage and perform activities related to the safe transport of military personnel and material by air and water. Officers normally specialize by mode of transportation or area of expertise, because, in many cases, they must meet licensing and certification requirements. Pilots in the military fly various types of specialized airplanes and helicopters to carry troops and equipment and to execute combat missions. Navigators use radar, radio, and other navigation equipment to determine their position and plan their route of travel. Officers on ships and submarines work as a team to manage the various departments aboard their vessels. Ships' engineers direct engineering departments aboard ships and submarines, including engine operations, maintenance, repair, heating, and power generation.

The following table indicates the various occupational groups by branch of service and the number of officers in each group.

Military Office Personnel by Broad Occupations Category and Branch of Service as of June 2003						
Occupational Group	*Army*	*Air Force*	*Coast Guard*	*Marine Corps*	*Navy*	*Total, all services*
Combat specialty	18,306	5,422	2	3,990	5,626	33,346
Engineering, science, and technical	17,368	15,902	1,715	3,044	15,413	53,442
Executive, administrative, and managerial	10,139	9,579	388	2,398	8,234	30,738
Health care	9,775	9,247	10		6,531	25,563
Human resource development	1,369	2,406	247	23	3,807	7,852
Media and public affairs	177	503	15	131	932	1,758
Protective services	2,174	1,838	172	174	855	5,213
Support services	1,500	836	0	40	1,654	4,030

Occupational Group	Army	Air Force	Coast Guard	Marine Corps	Navy	Total, all services
Transportation	12,612	19.710	3,244	6,258	12,629	54,503
Totals, by service	73,420	65,443	5,793	16,058	55,731	216,445

Benefits of a Military Career

Most commissioned officers started at Grade O-1; some with advanced education started at Grade O-2; and some highly trained officers—for example, physicians and dentists—started as high as Grade O-3. Pay varies by total years of service as well as rank. Because it usually takes many years to reach the higher ranks, most personnel in higher ranks receive the higher pay rates awarded to those with many years of service.

Salaries are based on your grade level, as follows (figures are rounded off and are based on mid-2003 figures):

	Years of Service					
Grade Level	Less than 2	Over 4	Over 8	Over 12	Over 15	Over 20
O-10						$11,874
O-9						$10,563
O-8	$7,474	$7,927	$8,468	$8,868	$9,239	$10,008
O-7	$6,210	$6,739	$7,120	$7,559	$8,468	$9,051
O-6	$4,603	$5,388	$5,641	$5,672	$6,564	$7,233
O-5	$3,837	$4,678	$4,977	$5,403	$5,991	$6,329
O-4	$3,311	$4,145	$4,637	$5,201	$5,471	
O-3	$2,911	$3,883	$4,273	$4,623		
O-2	$2,525	$3,410				
O-1	$2,183	$2,746				

In addition to receiving their basic pay, military personnel are provided with free room and board (or a tax-free housing and subsistence allowance), free medical and dental care, a military clothing allowance, military supermarket and department store shopping privileges, 30 days of paid vacation a year (referred to as leave), and travel opportunities. In many duty stations, military personnel may receive a housing allowance that can be used for off-base housing. This allowance can be substantial but varies greatly by rank and duty station. For example, in July 2003, the housing allowance for an O-4 with dependents was $961 per month; for a person without dependents, it was $836. Other allowances are paid for foreign duty, hazardous duty, submarine and flight duty, and employment as a medical officer. Athletic and other facilities—such as gymnasiums, tennis courts, golf courses, bowling centers, libraries, and movie theaters—are available on many military installations. Military personnel are eligible for retirement benefits after 20 years of service.

The Veterans Administration (VA) provides numerous benefits to those who have served at least two years in the Armed Forces. Veterans are eligible for free care in VA hospitals for all service-related disabilities, regardless of time served; those with other medical problems are eligible for free VA care if they are unable to pay the cost of hospitalization elsewhere. Admission to a VA medical center depends on the availability of beds, however. Veterans also are eligible for certain loans, including loans to purchase a home. Veterans, regardless of health, can convert a military life insurance policy to an individual policy with any participating company in the veteran's state of residence. In addition, job counseling, testing, and placement services are available.

Grade Levels

What do these grades mean? The Armed Services basically have 10 major grades, from O-1 through O-10, but in each branch of the service, there's a different name for that grade.

Grade	Army	Navy and Coast Guard	Air Force	Marine Corps	Total Employment
O-10	General	Admiral	General	General	35
O-9	Lieutenant General	Vice Admiral	Lieutenant General	Lieutenant General	126
O-8	Major General	Rear Admiral Upper	Major General	Major General	282
O-7	Brigadier General	Rear Admiral Lower	Brigadier General	Brigadier General	446
O-6	Colonel	Captain	Colonel	Colonel	11,884
O-5	Lieutenant Colonel	Commander	Lieutenant Colonel	Lieutenant Colonel	28,565
O-4	Major	Lieutenant Commander	Major	Major	44,501
O-3	Captain	Lieutenant	Captain	Captain	69,184
O-2	1st Lieutenant	Lieutenant (JG)	1st Lieutenant	1st Lieutenant	29,416
O-1	2nd Lieutenant	Ensign	2nd Lieutenant	2nd Lieutenant	28,579

Qualifications, Training, and Advancement: The Road to Becoming an Officer

Officer training in the Armed Forces is provided through the Federal service academies (Military, Naval, Air Force, and Coast Guard); the Reserve Officers Training Corps (ROTC) program offered at many colleges and universities; Officer Candidate School (OCS) or Officer Training School (OTS); the National Guard (State Officer Candidate School programs); the Uniformed Services University of Health Sciences; and other programs. All are highly selective and are good options for those wanting to make the military a career. Persons interested in obtaining training through the Federal service academies must be single to enter and graduate, and those seeking training through OCS, OTS, or ROTC need not be single. Single parents with one or more minor dependents are not eligible to become commissioned officers.

The Service Academies

Federal service academies provide a 4-year college program leading to a bachelor-of-science degree. Midshipmen or cadets are provided free room and board, tuition, medical and dental care, and a monthly allowance. Graduates receive regular or reserve commissions and have a 5-year active-duty obligation or more if they are entering flight training.

To become a candidate for appointment as a cadet or midshipman in one of the service academies, applicants are required to obtain a nomination from an authorized source, usually a member of Congress. Candidates do not need to know a member of Congress personally to request a nomination. Nominees must have an academic record of the requisite quality, college aptitude test scores above an established minimum, and recommendations from teachers or school officials; they also must pass a medical examination. Appointments are made from the list of eligible nominees. Appointments to the Coast Guard Academy, however, are based strictly on merit and do not require a nomination.

Reserve Officer Training Corp (ROTC)

ROTC programs train students in about 950 Army, approximately 70 Navy and Marine Corps, and around 1,000 Air Force units at participating colleges and universities. Trainees take 2 to 5 hours of military instruction a week, in addition to regular college courses. After graduation, they may serve as officers on active duty for a stipulated period. Some may serve their obligation in the Reserves or National Guard. In the last two years of a ROTC program, students receive a monthly allowance while attending school, as well as pay for summer training. ROTC scholarships for two, three, and four years are available on a competitive basis. All scholarships pay for tuition and have allowances for subsistence, textbooks, supplies, and other costs.

Officer Candidate School/Officer Training School

College graduates can earn a commission in the Armed Forces through OCS or OTS programs in the Army, Navy, Air Force, Marine Corps, Coast Guard, and National Guard. These officers generally must serve their obligation on active duty. Those with training in certain health professions may qualify for direct appointment as officers. In the case of persons studying for the health professions, financial assistance and internship opportunities are available from the military in return for specified periods of military service. Prospective medical students can apply to the Uniformed Services University of Health Sciences, which offers free tuition in a program leading to a doctor of medicine (M.D.) degree. In return, graduates must serve for seven years in either the military or the U.S. Public Health Service. Direct appointments also are available for those qualified to serve in other specialty areas, such as the judge advocate general (legal) or chaplain corps. Flight training is available to commissioned officers in each branch of the Armed Forces. In addition, the Army has a direct enlistment option to become a warrant officer aviator.

Each service has different criteria for promoting personnel. Generally, the first few promotions for officer personnel come easily; subsequent promotions are much more competitive. Criteria for promotion may include time in service and in grade, job performance, a fitness report (supervisor's recommendation), and the passing of written examinations. People who are passed over for promotion several times generally must leave the military.

Requirements

Certain basic requirements must be met by those interested in serving in the Armed Forces. Although they may be somewhat different for each branch of the service, you must have several basic qualifications:

1. Be at least 19 and not older than 29 for OCS/OTS
2. Be a U.S. citizen
3. Have at least a 4-year college degree from an accredited institution (or SAT, ACT Assessment, ASVAB, AFOQT, or ASTB)
4. Meet the height standard

    Males: 4'10"–6'8"

    Females: 4'10"–6.8"

    There is no minimum or maximum weight requirement for most branches of the service, although you will have to pass the physical, and your weight should be in proportion to your height on most height/weight standards.

5. Pass a complete physical. There are certain diseases or existing conditions that might disqualify an individual from being accepted, including alcoholism, drug dependency, epilepsy, and so on.
6. Be able to obtain a security clearance
7. Have no more than 10 years of active Federal Service at time of commission
8. Be single or married, but not a single parent

Keep in mind that each branch of the service has its own qualification requirements, and certain waivers may be granted, depending upon the situation. Therefore, you shouldn't be discouraged if you do not satisfy all of the preceding requirements. It's worth pursuing a waiver with the branch of the service in which you're interested.

OCS History

The OCS schools, as we know them today, began with the U.S. Army. In 1938, Brigadier General L. Singleton, then Commandant of the Infantry School, Fort Benning, Georgia, conceived the idea for the modern Officer Candidate School for Infantry. It wasn't until 1941, that the Infantry, Field Artillery, and Coastal Artillery Officer Candidate

Schools were formed. Other branches later followed with their own Officer Candidate Schools. The first Infantry OCS class began with 204 men and on September 27, 1941, graduated 171 second lieutenants.

General Omar Bradley, former Commandant of the Infantry School, is the man credited with establishing the format, discipline, and code of honor still used in OCS today. As the Commandant of the Infantry School, General Bradley emphasized rigorous training, strict discipline, and efficient organization. These tenets remain the base values of today's Officer Candidate School.

More than 100,000 candidates enrolled in 448 Infantry OCS classes between July 1941 and May 1947. Approximately 67 percent of these men received commissions. After World War II, the Department of the Army transferred Infantry OCS to Fort Riley, Kansas, as part of the Ground General School and discontinued all other Officer Candidate Schools.

On November 1, 1947, the Department of the Army discontinued the Infantry OCS program. The final class graduated only 52 second lieutenants.

However, a shortage of officers during the Korean conflict caused the Department of the Army to reopen Infantry OCS at Fort Benning in 1951 and lengthen the course from 17 to 22 weeks. The Infantry Officer Candidate School became the First Officer Candidate Battalion, Second Student Regiment. The strength of OCS increased rapidly. As one of eight branch programs, Infantry OCS included as many as 29 companies with a class graduating every week. During the Korean War, approximately 7,000 infantry officers graduated from OCS at Fort Benning. On August 4, 1953, the Department of the Army once again reduced OCS from eight to three programs: Infantry, Artillery, and Engineer.

The Army further reduced OCS to two programs, Infantry and Field Artillery, shortly before the onset of the Vietnam Conflict. During the height of the Vietnam Conflict, Infantry OCS was one of five programs and produced 7,000 officers annually from five battalions at Fort Benning. Toward the end of the conflict, the Department of the Army once again reduced OCS to two programs, Infantry and Female OCS.

In April 1973, the Army created a Branch Immaterial Officer Candidate School to replace the branch specific courses and reduced the length of the course to 14 weeks. OCS for female officer candidates remained at Fort McClellan, Alabama, until December 1976, when it merged with the branch immaterial OCS program at Fort Benning, Georgia.

Today's officer candidates enter the school from throughout the force. OCS continues to provide commissioned officers to the total force for all 16 basic branches of the Army.

On June 12, 1998 to further integrate the total force, the Army National Guard OCS Phase III candidates began training alongside their active duty counterparts at Fort Benning. Officer Candidates from the National Guard and Army Reserve conduct the final phase of training before commissioning during their two-week annual training period. More than 650 future officers were trained for the Army in the first year, with similar numbers being trained in subsequent years.

The mission of OCS remains—to train selected personnel in the fundamentals of leadership; to provide basic military skills; to instill professional ethics; to evaluate leadership candidates potential; and to commission those who qualify as second lieutenants in all 16 branches of the Army.

Information on the history of the OCS schools for other branches of the military besides the Army can be found in the sections that follow.

The Army Officer Candidate School

Enlisting with the intention to attend Officer Candidate School (OCS) is a highly competitive enlistment option that isn't available to everyone. Prospective candidates need to have a 4-year college degree and must also meet other requirements like height, weight, and medical standards. Those who are selected must successfully complete Basic Combat Training before attending OCS.

During the 14-week OCS course, candidates are trained in the skills that provide the foundation for Army leadership. After successfully completing OCS, officers attend the Officer Basic Course (OBC) for their designated career fields, where they'll receive classroom and hands-on training in career-specific skills. New OBC graduates generally begin their Army management careers as platoon leaders in the rank of Second or First Lieutenant and are stationed at installations around the world.

Air Force Officer Training School

Officer Training School is located at Maxwell AFB, Alabama, and provides a 12-week basic officer training course programmed to commission 1,000 officers annually. Additionally, OTS conducts a 4-week commissioned officer training program for more than 1,500 new judge advocates, chaplains, and medical officers each year.

The Air Force OTS was organized at Medina Annex, Lackland Air Force Base, TX, in 1959. Its predecessor, the Officer Candidates School was established in 1942 in Miami Beach, FL, and its mission was to train and commission members from the enlisted ranks. OCS moved to Lackland in the spring of 1944 and gained the additional mission of training officers directly from civilian status in September 1951. This mission was transferred to the OTS in 1962, and OCS closed its doors with its last graduation in June 1963.

Basic Officer Training Program

A 12-week program designed for college graduates interested in earning a commission in the USAF, BOT helps prepare Officer Trainees for the leadership challenges they will face in the U.S. Air Force officer corps.

Commissioned Officer Training Program

A four-week program designed for professionals who have received a direct commissioned appointment as a lawyer, chaplain, or into a corps of the medical service. The Reserve COT course is a 14-day intensive program designed for hard-to-recruit Air Force Reserve and Air National Guard medical service officers.

Navy Officer Candidate School

Navy Officer Candidate School is a 13-week officer orientation school in Pensacola, Florida. The OCS is the Navy's primary source for officers. It was established in 1951. It prepares you for the roles and responsibilities of U.S. Naval officers and teaches the basics of today's high-tech Navy. Academic and military coursework, and physical fitness training are demanding and intense to bring out your fullest potential. You can apply as early as your sophomore year in college depending on your grade point average (GPA) and overall qualifications. Your chances are greater of getting into the school if you apply before your graduate.

OCS is extremely demanding—morally, mentally, and physically. Your personal honor, courage, and commitment will be tested at OCS, and you will be challenged to live up to the highest standards of these core values. The school's curriculum will demand the most of your academic prowess. Mental training involves memorization of military knowledge, academic courses, and military inspections. Physical training (PT) begins almost immediately upon arrival at OCS. PT consists of running programs augmented by calisthenics, as well as aquatic programs (includes passing the third-class swimming test). You must be committed to the goal of earning a commission as an Ensign in the Navy before arriving at Officer Candidate School.

Marines Officers Candidate School (OCS)

This is where Marine Officer Candidates find out whether they've got what it takes to become leaders of Marines. Students immerse themselves in some of the most demanding training in the world. Testing and evaluation is ongoing for character, appearance, speech, command presence, strength, agility, coordination, endurance, and intelligence. Candidates will be assigned temporary leadership positions to gauge their abilities to lead other Marines.

The Officer Candidate School consists of The Officer Candidates Class, the Platoon Leaders Course, or the Naval Reserve Officer Training Corps. Historically, the OCS can trace its beginnings to as early as 1891, when the first formal resident school for Marine Officers; the "School of Application" at Marine Barracks, Washington, D.C was established. In the fall of 1919, the Commanding General of Quantico, Major General John A. Lejuene, established the "Marine Corps Officers Training School" and the "Marine Officers Infantry School." These two schools were subsequently combined in 1920 to become the "Marine Officers Training School." In 1963, the Officer Candidate School became the official name. The last reorganization occurred in 1977 when women officer training was placed under the cognizance of the Commanding Officer of Officer Candidates School.

The Basic Officer Course is taught at The Basic School (TBS) in Quantico, Virginia. It is a foundation of professional knowledge and skills necessary for officers to effectively command and lead Marines. Upon successful completion of OCS, candidates will have earned their commissions as Second Lieutenants in the Marines.

Newly commissioned officers will spend 21 weeks in courses on first aid, leadership, and techniques of military instruction: marksmanship, map reading, communications, infantry tactics weapons, organization and staff functions, drill, command, military law, logistics, personnel administration, and Marines history.

Coast Guard OCS

OCS is a rigorous 17-week course of instruction that prepares candidates to serve effectively as officers in the U.S. Coast Guard. In addition to indoctrinating students into a military lifestyle, OCS also provides a wide range of highly technical information necessary for performing the duties of a Coast Guard officer.

The Coast Guard's OCS program was originated in 1942 at the Coast Guard Academy in New London, CT, but was officially inaugurated in 1951. In 1959 it moved to Yorktown, VA, but then returned in 1998 to New London.

The Coast Guard is considered the oldest continuous seagoing service and has fought in almost every war since 1789. After the terrorist attacks on September 11, the president established the Department of Homeland Security in 2002. In February 2003, the Coast Guard was transferred from under the jurisdiction of the Department of Transportation to the Department of Homeland Security.

Graduates of the program receive a commission in the Coast Guard at the rank of Ensign and are required to serve a minimum of three years of active duty. Graduates may be assigned to a ship, flight training, to a staff job, or to an operations ashore billet. However, first assignments are based on the needs of the U.S. Coast Guard. Personal desires and performance at OCS are considered. All graduates must be available for worldwide assignment.

Qualifying Tests

The three major tests that you will encounter in your quest to become a commissioned officer in the U.S. Armed Services are the *Armed Services Aptitude Battery* (ASVAB), the *Air Force Officer Qualifying Test* (AFOQT), and the *U.S. Navy and Marine Corps Aviation Selection Test Battery* (ASTB). Each of these tests covers a wide range of topics. However, we have focused only on those sections of each examination that will lead to acceptance to Officer Candidate/Training Schools in each of the branches of the service. We have *not* included those sections that are applicable for pilot, navigator—or other specialized training.

Air Force Officer Qualifying Test (AFOQT)

The AFOQT measures aptitudes and is used to select applicants for officer commissioning programs, such as Officer Candidate School (OCS), Officer Training School (OTS), or Air Force Reserve Officer Training Corps (Air Force ROTC). The test assesses aptitudes required of student pilots, navigators, students in technical training, and officers in general. You will be required to complete all sections of the test regardless of the program for which you are applying. The test can be taken only twice, although that restriction might be waived. However, you will have to wait at least 180 days between tests, and the most recent AFOQT scores are the ones that count—whether you do better or worse if you take the test the second time. These scores never expire.

The complete AFOQT contains 380 test items divided into 16 subsets and requires approximately five hours to administer.

The following is a brief description of each subset:

- **Verbal Analogies:** Measures your ability to reason and see relationships between words. (25 questions/8 minutes)
- **Arithmetic Reasoning:** Measures general reasoning, one's ability to arrive at solutions to problems. (25 questions/29 minutes)
- **Reading Comprehension:** Measures your ability to read and understand paragraphs. (25 questions/18 minutes)
- **Data Interpretation:** Measures your ability to interpret data from graphs and charts (25 questions/24 minutes)

- **Word Knowledge:** Measures verbal comprehension, the ability to understand written language. (25 questions/ 5 minutes)

- **Math Knowledge:** Measures your functional ability in using learned mathematical relationships (25 questions/ 22 minutes)

- **Mechanical Comprehension:** Measures your ability to learn and reason with mechanical terms. This test has pictures of mechanisms whose functions call for comprehension. (20 questions/10 minutes)

- **Electrical Maze:** Measures your ability to choose a path from among several choices. (20 questions/10 minutes)

- **Scale Reading:** Measures your ability to read scales, dials, and meters. (40 questions/15 minutes)

- **Instrument Comprehension:** Measures your ability to determine the position of an airplane in flight from reading instruments. (20 questions/6 minutes)

- **Block Counting:** Measures your ability to "see into" a three-dimensional stack of blocks and determine how many pieces are touched by a certain numbered blocks. (20 questions/3 minutes)

- **Table Reading:** Measures your ability to read tables quickly and accurately. (40 questions/7 minutes)

- **Aviation Information:** Measures your knowledge of general aeronautical concepts and terminology (past and current). (20 questions/8 minutes)

- **Rotated Blocks:** Measures your spatial aptitude—that is, your ability to visualize and manipulate objects in space. (15 questions/13 minutes)

- **General Science:** Measures verbal comprehension in the area of science. (20 questions/10 minutes)

- **Hidden Figures:** (Template matching) Measures your perceptual reasoning using visual imagery and short-term memory. (15 questions/8 minutes)

Testing Table		
Test	*No. of Test Items*	*Time (minutes)*
Verbal Analogies*	25	8
Arithmetic Reasoning*	25	29
Reading Comprehension*	25	18
Data Interpretation*	25	18
Word Knowledge*	25	6
Math Knowledge*	25	22
Mechanical Comprehension	20	10
Electrical Maze	20	10
Scale Reading	40	15
Instrument Comprehension	20	6
Block Counting	20	3
Table Reading	30	7
Aviation Information	20	8
Rotated Blocks	15	13
General Science	20	10
Hidden Figures	15	8
TOTALS	**380**	**191 minutes**

*Tests covered in this book.

The test actually takes about 4½ hours, including breaks.

Test results are given in five areas: *Pilot, Navigator, Academic Aptitude, Verbal,* and *Quantitative (Math)*. However, the sections that are necessary for entering OCS and that are covered in this book are the Academic Aptitude (Arithmetic Reasoning, Reading Comprehension, Data Interpretation, Word Knowledge, Math Knowledge), Verbal (Verbal Analogies, Reading Comprehension, Word Knowledge), and Quantitative (Arithmetic Reasoning, Data Interpretation, Math Knowledge) sections. Following are the scoring requirements.

- **Verbal:** All candidates must achieve a minimum score of 15. This composite measures various types of verbal knowledge and abilities. The verbal composite includes subtests that measure your ability to reason and recognize relationships among words, your ability to read and understand paragraphs on diverse topics, and your ability to understand synonyms.

- **Quantitative:** All candidates must achieve a minimum score of 10. This composite measures various types of quantitative knowledge and abilities. The quantitative composite includes subtests that measure your ability to understand and reason with arithmetic relationships, interpret data from graphs and charts, and to use mathematical terms, formulas, and relationships.

- **Academic Aptitude:** No minimum score required. The Academic Aptitude score, which is a composite of math and verbal sections, is used as part of the Field Training selection process. This composite measures verbal and quantitative knowledge and abilities.

U.S. Navy and Marine Corps Aviation Selection Test (ASTB)

These tests were developed by the Bureau of Medicine and Surgery in conjunction with the Naval Aerospace Medical Institute in order to test those interested in pursuing a career in aviation. Until recently, this test had six sections, but they have eliminated the Biographical Inventory, which was to be a predictor of training attrition. However, studies indicated that this section of the test was no longer a valid predictor.

You may take this test as many times as you want, although there is a waiting period of 30 days between the first time you take the test and the second. You then must wait at least 180 days for all subsequent retests. After you pass the test, the scores are good for life. In order to become an aviator, you must pass this test.

The four sections of the test are

- **Math/Verbal (MVT):** This is a 35-minute test/37-question test of general intelligence, which includes both mathematics and verbal questions. Those who have low scores on this test tend to have difficulty in the academic portions of training.

- **Mechanical Comprehension (MCT):** This is a 15-minute/30-question test of your ability to perceive physical relationships and to solve some practical problems in mechanics.

- **Spatial Apperception (SAT):** This test measures your ability to perceive spatial relationships from differing orientations. The test has 35 questions, and you have 10 minutes to complete them. This test is given to those individuals applying for aviation training. If you are interested in becoming a Navy or Marine pilot, you can apply for pilot training once you've received your commission as an officer.

- **Aviation and Nautical (AN):** This test is a measure of your knowledge of aviation information and nautical knowledge, demonstrating an interest in Naval aviation. The test has 30 questions, and you have 15 minutes to complete them. Like the Spatial Apperception portion of the test, this test is given to those individuals applying for aviation training. For more information, please see *CliffsTestPrep Military Flight Aptitude Tests* (Wiley Publishing, Inc.).

Test Table		
Test	*No. of Test Items*	*Time (minutes)*
Math/Verbal*	37	35
Mechanical Comprehension*	30	15

Test	No. of Test Items	Time (minutes)
Spatial Apperception	35	10
Aviation and Nautical	30	15
Aviation Interest	49	15
TOTALS	**181**	**90 minutes**

Tests covered in this book.

For the OCS tests, the only section you should be concerned with the Academic Qualification Rating.

Academic Qualifications Rating (AQR) (scoring range: 1–9). These scores predict your performance in the academic portions of ground school training.

For the Navy, you must achieve an AQR score of 3, and for the Marine Corp, you must have at least a 4. However, in order to be competitive, you should have a score of 5 or higher.

The Armed Services Vocational Academic Battery (ASVAB)

The Armed Services Vocational Academic Battery (ASVAB) presents a series of individual tests to measure various academic and vocational skills.

Until 2002, the exam had 10 subtests. Two tests—Numerical Operations and Coding Speed—were eliminated and replaced by a new test, Assembling Objects, which is a form of spacial relations.

This exam is administered in three forms. One is for high school students who are planning to take the exam some time in their junior or senior year. A second form, known as the "production" version, is for those enlisting directly in the service, and the third form is a CAT ASVAB. This latter exam is a computer-based test that presents questions based on your answers. CAT stands for "computer-adaptive test" and means that the computer adapts its questions based on your answers. The first question you will get will be of medium difficulty. If you answer it correctly, the next question you get will be slightly more difficult. If your answer was incorrect, the next question will be somewhat easier, and so on. The key to scoring well on the CAT ASVAB is to focus your efforts on the earlier questions. The better you do in the beginning, the better you will do overall, because the final score is normally based on both the number of correct answers as well as the level of difficulty.

Regardless of the type of test you'll be taking, however, you should know some specifics about the test. First of all, following are the subtests:

- General Science*
- Arithmetic Reasoning*
- Word Knowledge*
- Paragraph Comprehension*
- Auto & Shop Information
- Mathematics Knowledge*
- Mechanical Comprehension
- Electronics Information
- Assembling Objects

Tests covered in this book.

Background

The ASVAB tests go back to World War II. The test was developed to help the armed services screen recruits for eligibility for the military and to classify and assign enlisted personnel. The tests were designed to provide a general measure of intellectual ability and specific aptitudes that were required by each of the branches of the military. In 1948, with the beginning of the Selective Service Act, a standard screening test was mandated, and the Army General Classification Test (at that time the primary screening test) was adopted as the model for the joint-service test. It was called the Armed Forces Qualification Test (AFQT).

Over the years, the test has undergone several changes, but in the 1960s, the Department of Defense directed the various branches of the military to come up with a standard test that would provide more accurate screening of those taking the test, and more specifically, gearing the test for high school students in the eleventh and twelfth grades. These tests then would provide scores that would be associated with success in military training programs for jobs in all military services. Students would receive academic ability and vocational aptitude scores to help them explore careers and decision-making. The ASVAB was the result of these objectives.

Currently, the ASVAB is given in about 14,000 schools and more than 900,000 students take the ASVAB each year. As we said earlier, there are different forms of the test—some just for schools, others used within the military for qualification, placement, and research (the production version). In the last year, a short form version of the exam was developed and consists of only those parts of the exam that make up the Armed Forces Qualification Test (AFQT). These consist of Arithmetic Reasoning, Mathematics Knowledge, Word Knowledge, and Paragraph Comprehension. These are the particular parts of the exam that are important for those applying for OCT/OTS.

Content of the ASVAB

Originally, you were tested on 10 different items, but the test has changed, and now there are only 9. However, the tests with which you will be concerned for OCS/OTS application are compiled into various subsets to help measure your potential for various activities. For officers, the following subsets are used to determine your abilities and eligibilities for OCT/OTS.

- **Verbal Ability Composite:** Word Knowledge plus Paragraph Comprehension measures your potential for verbal activities.
- **Math Ability Composite:** Arithmetic Reasoning plus Mathematics Knowledge measures your potential for mathematical activities.
- **Academic Ability:** Verbal Ability plus Math Ability composites measures your potential for further formal education.

The following chart provides the details and purpose of each test you will take.

Test	Time Allowed	# Test Items	Purpose
Arithmetic Reasoning	36 minutes	30	To evaluate your ability to solve arithmetic word problems.
Word Knowledge	11 minutes	35	To evaluate your ability to understand the correct meaning of words and to select appropriate synonyms where applicable.
Paragraph Comprehension	13 minutes	15	To evaluate your ability to understand and identify information from given passages.
Mathematics Knowledge	24 minutes	25	To evaluate your ability to perform mathematical computations including algebra and geometry.
TOTALS	**84 minutes**	**105 questions**	

Your ASVAB scores are compiled into various subsets to help measure your potential for various activities. The scores from the ASVAB can be used for both civilian and military careers. These scores are valid predictors of success in training programs and on-the-job performance for enlisted military occupations, 80 percent of which are applicable in civilian life. That means that even if you don't join the military, you can still use your scores to help you choose a career path.

The Final Step

Final words before you begin. The tests should not be that difficult for a college student. They require a bit of knowledge and a lot of skill. This book will help you develop those skills while adding some knowledge about the types of questions you will encounter on whichever examination you plan to take. All of the service branches will look at these test scores in conjunction with your SAT or ACT scores, as well as your college transcript and any extracurricular activities in which you've been involved. Office Candidate School/Officer Training School is, however, much more difficult than the tests you will take. You will develop personal discipline. You will learn to follow orders unlike those you have encountered in the past, although if you've played college sports, you may have learned some of this discipline and following orders from your coaches. Our motto, when I attended OTS in the Air Force was, "cooperate and graduate." You will learn to function as a group, relying on the person next to you to help you through the rough spots.

The journey through these programs is not long, but they may be academically and physically arduous. In the end, however, it will be worth it—the day you receive your commission, throw your hat into the air, and become an officer in one of the branches of the Armed Forces of the United States. And again, we wish you good luck.

PART I

SUBJECT AREA REVIEW

Verbal and Reading Review

Analogies

An analogy is a comparison of two proportions or relations. In standard usage—and for many of the military exams—you will encounter several types of analogies.

Why are analogies important? Understanding analogies exhibits your ability to recognize relationships between words. It helps you develop a more complete ability to use words, images, and expressions, both in your spoken words and in your writing. As a future officer in the military, it's important for you to be articulate, now and when you are commanding others.

Each question presents two words that have some type of relationship; you are asked to select the choice that best completes the analogy, which is similar to the relationship presented in the original pair of words. There are two formats for the questions. For example, look at the following:

FORK is to EAT as PEN is to

- **A.** INK
- **B.** PENCIL
- **C.** WRITE
- **D.** LETTER
- **E.** BOOK

You first must ask yourself what the relationship is between FORK and EAT. A fork is used to eat. Thus, the next pair demonstrates a similar relationship—a PEN is used to WRITE. The correct answer is **C.**

Here's another sample question.

PLUM is to FRUIT as STEAK is to

- **A.** MEAL
- **B.** DINNER
- **C.** VEAL
- **D.** COW
- **E.** BEEF

Although many of these choices sound correct, let's analyze them. A plum is fruit. A steak can be a meal, but not necessarily the entire meal. A steak can be dinner, but it can also be lunch. A steak is not veal, so that's incorrect. A steak comes from a cow, but it's only part of a cow. The most obvious answer would be **E,** BEEF. This answer establishes the same relationship between PLUM and FRUIT as STEAK and BEEF.

The second format of analogy questions that you will encounter is as follows:

PREMIER is to COUNTRY as

- **A.** TEACHER is to LEARNING
- **B.** PRINCIPAL is to SCHOOL
- **C.** PRESIDENT is to CABINET
- **D.** SOLDIER is to SAILOR
- **E.** POLICEMAN is to CRIME

The correct answer is **B,** PRINCIPAL is to SCHOOL. The PREMIER is the leader of the COUNTRY, and the PRINCIPAL is the leader of the SCHOOL. If you look at the other choices, you can see the differences in relationships when compared to the original pair. The teacher's job is to help the students learn, and he or she is surely in charge of students, but that is not the direct relationship. The President chooses the Cabinet, but the Cabinet is only a small part of the country. Soldier to Sailor and Policeman to Crime are different relationships entirely.

Keep in mind that the relationship between the words is the most important aspect when answering an analogy question. *It is more important than the actual meanings of the words*. Try to establish the relationship immediately as you read the question. How are the two words related? Are they the same? Are they part of a group? Are they antonyms? It is often helpful to paraphrase the relationship.

For example, you might encounter the following:

> FISH is to OCEAN as HORSE is to
>
> A. OATS
> B. RACETRACK
> C. STABLE
> D. GALLOP
> E. FIELD

You would paraphrase this by saying, "A FISH lives in the OCEAN; therefore, a HORSE lives in the STABLE." The correct answer is **C.** Although some horses may live in the field, city horses may live only in a stable. (Questions usually require you to be fairly specific.) By paraphrasing the original pair, you help yourself in identifying the correct answer.

Here's one that requires even more specific attention.

> BAT is to BASEBALL, as
>
> A. PASS is to FOOTBALL
> B. CLUB is to GOLF
> C. BALL is to TENNIS
> D. SPIKES is to SLIDE
> E. CARDS is to POKER

You would say, "A BAT is used in BASEBALL." Then again, A CLUB is used in GOLF, a BALL is used in TENNIS, and CARDS are used in POKER. You can eliminate the PASS since this is not an *object* used in the game. SPIKES is to SLIDE is an entirely different relationship—you wear SPIKES in a game, but they are not necessarily used to SLIDE. How do you narrow down your choices? You do this by becoming more specific. You would now paraphrase this by saying "A BAT is used to hit a ball in the game of BASEBALL." Choice **B** now becomes the logical selection, because a CLUB is used to hit a ball in the game of GOLF.

Make sure that you start by eliminating those choices that do not express a clear relationship to the original pair. This will make selecting the correct pair somewhat easier by narrowing down the number of choices. Also be careful of choices with similar words that might be included just to trip you up. If the choice sounds too similar to the original pair, it's probably incorrect and is being used by the test-developer as a "distracter."

Classification of Analogies

Dozens of different types of analogies exist, defined based on their relationships. However, we'll just cover a few of the major types, because these are the most common types of questions you'll find on the test.

Synonyms

As you should know, synonyms are words that have similar meanings and are usually from the same part of speech.

DOWDY is to DRAB as

- **A.** QUIET is to DEN
- **B.** SAFETY is to STELLAR
- **C.** OBJECTIVE is to DISPASSIONATE
- **D.** PETTY is to ELEPHANTINE
- **E.** RECREATION is to TOYS

The correct answer is **C.** A synonym for **dowdy** is **drab.** One who is **objective** is **dispassionate.**

Antonyms

Antonyms are words that have opposite meanings.

HAPPY is to SAD as RIGID is to

- **A.** FAULTY
- **B.** TIGHT
- **C.** CONSERVATIVE
- **D.** ALTRUISTIC
- **E.** FLEXIBLE

The correct answer is **E. Rigid** means still and unyielding. The opposite is **flexible.**

Function

What is the purpose, or function, of the relationship?

HAMMER is to NAIL as

- **A.** CAR is to WHEEL
- **B.** GLUE is to TUBE
- **C.** KNIFE is to SHARP
- **D.** SCISSORS is to PAPER
- **E.** PEN is to INK

The correct answer is **D.** The function of a **hammer** is to hit a **nail,** and the function of a **scissors** is to cut **paper.**

Part to Whole

In this type of analogy, the first word in the pair is part of the second word. It can also be used in an opposite manner.

DANCERS is to TROUPE as

- **A.** SINGERS is to CHORUS
- **B.** WRITERS is to BOOKS
- **C.** SENATORS is to REPRESENTATIVES
- **D.** TEACHERS is to PROFESSORS
- **E.** PILOTS is to JETS

Dancers are part of a **troupe,** and **singers** are part of a **chorus.** The correct answer is **A.** If you analyze each of the answers, you'll see that although the first and second choices are related, they are not parts-to-whole relationships.

Definition

This is similar to synonyms. The first word is the definition of the second word.

SANCTUARY is to REFUGE as

A. CAVE is to BEAR
B. VAULT is to VALUABLES
C. TRIUMPH is to CONTEST
D. STRIATION is to STRIPE
E. CARNIVORE is OMNIVORE

The correct answer is **D.** A **striation** is **stripe.** None of the other choices are definitions of each other.

Type

One word in the pair represents a type of the second word. For example, MAPLE is a type of TREE, SEDAN is a type of CAR, and ROBIN is a type of BIRD.

ARGON is to GAS as

A. BOOK is to LIBRARY
B. GESSO is to PAINT
C. HEART is to PACEMAKER
D. PAUPER is to MONEY
E. COMPUTER is to KEYBOARD

The correct answer is **B. Gesso** is a type of **paint.** These are sometimes known as "Member and Class" analogies.

Dozens of other types of analogies actually exist—some very sophisticated and some fairly simple. To learn how to solve analogies, you must spend the time on the practice problems, study the material presented previously, and try to identify the types of pairs in each question. Analyze them and take your time with these questions in order to be familiar with the different types of analogies and to be able to recognize them quickly when you take the test.

Analogy Practice Questions

Try these practice questions.

1. TOOL is to DRILL as POEM is to

   A. SONG
   B. MACHINE
   C. SONNET
   D. BIRD
   E. NOVEL

2. TALK is to SHOUT as DISLIKE is to

   A. SCREAM
   B. DETEST
   C. FRIGHTEN
   D. CONTRIBUTE
   E. ADMIRE

3. CONDUCTOR is to ORCHESTRA as SHEPHERD is to

   A. FILM
   B. CANINE
   C. CONTROL
   D. FLOCK
   E. GENERAL

4. OBSTINATE is to COMPLIANT as OBLIVIOUS is to

   A. CONSCIOUS
   B. CAREFREE
   C. FORGETFUL
   D. INTUITIVE
   E. NATURAL

5. BOUQUET is to VASE as GARBAGE is to

   A. URN
   B. ABDOMEN
   C. CENTERPIECE
   D. SEWER
   E. CARTON

6. TENSION is to STRESS as VIRUS is to

   A. LIVING
   B. DISEASE
   C. BACTERIA
   D. IMMUNITY
   E. MORBIDITY

7. BAROMETER is to PRESSURE as CALIPERS is to

   A. CUTTING
   B. HEIGHT
   C. CONSTANCY
   D. THICKNESS
   E. PLIERS

8. MISER is to MONEY as GLUTTON is to

   A. FOOD
   B. ENVY
   C. LITERATURE
   D. PUNISHMENT
   E. NUTRIENTS

9. PRIDE is to HUMBLE as HUMOR is to

   A. INTELLECTUAL
   B. ENERGETIC
   C. SOMBER
   D. SERVILE
   E. LUDICROUS

10. CANDID is to TRUTHFUL as CONTENTIOUS is to

    A. HARMONIOUS
    B. QUARRELSOME
    C. COHERENT
    D. MENDACIOUS
    E. UNPLEASANT

11. COWARD is to COURAGE as

    A. CYNIC is to DOUBT
    B. REVELER is to CHEER
    C. MISER is to GENEROSITY
    D. THINKER is to CONTEMPLATION
    E. PARTNER is to COOPERATION

12. IMPECUNIOUS is to WEALTH as

    A. ALACRITY is to SPEED
    B. MYSTIQUE is to MYSTERY
    C. ACERBITY is to BITTERNESS
    D. IGNORANT is to UNDERSTANDING
    E. POMPOUS is to SHOW

13. BIASED is to IMPARTIALITY as

    A. APATHETIC is to EMOTION
    B. STEADFASTNESS is to SOLIDITY
    C. INCONGRUITY is to DISORGANIZATION
    D. FORTUITOUS is to LUCK
    E. HONEST is to INTEGRITY

14. SHOVEL is to DIG as

    A. WASP is to STING
    B. BROOM is to FLY
    C. WOUND is to HEAL
    D. DETERGENT is to CLEAN
    E. CLIMB is to MOUNTAIN

15. POKER is to PROD as

    A.   PEN is to WRITE
    B.   ATTRACT is to SMELL
    C.   STILTS is to CRAWL
    D.   CAUTION is to SUCCEED
    E.   ACTIVATE is to LEVER

Analogy Answers and Explanations

1. C. An example of a kind of tool is a **drill,** and an example of a kind of **poem** is a **sonnet.**

2. B. An intense form of **talk** is to **shout,** and in intense form of **dislike** is to **detest.**

3. D. The function of a **conductor** is to lead an **orchestra,** and the function of a **shepherd** is to lead a **flock.**

4. A. The opposite of **obstinate** is **compliant,** and the opposite of **oblivious** is **conscious.**

5. D. A location for a **bouquet** is a **vase,** and a location for **garbage** is a **sewer.**

6. B. An effect of **tension** is to cause **stress,** and an effect of a **virus** is to cause **disease.**

7. D. The function of a **barometer** is to measure **pressure,** and the function of **calipers** is to measure **thickness.**

8. A. The desire of a **miser** is **money,** and the desire of a **glutton** is **food.**

9. C. To lack **pride** is to be **humble,** and to lack **humor** is to be **somber.**

10. B. A synonym of **candid** is **truthful,** and a synonym of **contentious** is **quarrelsome.**

11. C. A **coward** suffers from a lack of **courage,** and a **miser** lacks **generosity.**

12. D. A person who is **impecunious** is poor, and therefore lacks **wealth.** A person who is **ignorant** lacks **understanding.**

13. A. A **biased** individual lacks **impartiality,** and an **apathetic** person lacks **emotion.**

14. D. **Detergent** is characteristically used to **clean,** and a **shovel** is characteristically used to **dig.**

15. A. A **poker** is used for **prodding,** and a **pen** is used for **writing.**

Reading Comprehension and Paragraph Comprehension

The Word Knowledge review in the following section will help you develop and test your understanding of vocabulary. This is important to help you express yourself clearly. However, reading comprehension is vital in understanding what you have read. It is important for you on several levels. First, you need to have the right skills to correctly answer these types of questions on the Officer Training School (OCS) exams. That's the primary purpose of this book—to help you score as high as possible when you apply for OCS.

Second, you need to have the ability to fully comprehend what you read for your career in the military. How can you function at the highest level, commanding others, if you don't understand regulations? How can you succeed if you don't understand written orders?

Third, it's important to understand what you read in your daily life, outside of the military. How do you learn about what's going on in the world? You read newspapers and magazines, but unless you are able to interpret what you read, you will be limited to the brief overviews you will garner from radio and/or television news reports.

This section reviews the basics of reading comprehension based on the various tests that are given in the military for those applying for OCS. Of course, not only do you want to do well on the exams, but you want to master reading comprehension for day-to-day functioning.

Answering Reading Comprehension Questions

You will find Reading Comprehension and/or Paragraph Comprehension questions on the AFOQT and the ASVAB exams. They are both similar in approach. You'll also find similar questions—Sentence Comprehension—on the ASTB exam. Although somewhat shorter in approach, these questions still test your reading comprehension.

You will be asked to demonstrate your ability to understand what you have read. Sometimes, you will be asked about the content of the passage, and the correct answer repeats words or phrases from the passage. Some questions have an answer that repeats the content of the passage in different words. For these questions, the correct answer is a paraphrase of material in the passage. Some questions ask you to make an inference. To *infer* is to make a conclusion based on the information in the passage, although the passage itself does not state this conclusion. There also may be questions about the meaning of words in the passage, but you are not expected to know the meaning of the word before reading the passage. You can determine the correct answer choice by seeing how the word is used.

Unless it is otherwise stated, the correct answer is based on something that is in the passage. Although you might know something additional about what appears in the passage, you should limit your answer choice to information presented in the passage. The questions do not expect you to bring in other material. Answer choices that are true statements may be provided, but if they are not in the passage, they are not the correct choice. You may even know that something in the passage is untrue. Even so, if that statement is given as an answer choice, it may be correct according to the passage.

As you read the passage to get a general idea of the subject, focus on the first and last sentence of each paragraph. These sentences often contain the most important idea in the paragraph, and one of them may state the paragraph's main idea. Look for words indicating how ideas are related. Words like *but* or *however* indicate contrasts. Often, words and phrases relating to causes and effects, such as *because, therefore,* and *as a result,* are material about which there will be questions.

Read each question and all four of the answer choices. Eliminate any choices that seem obviously incorrect. If one answer seems to be correct, reread the portion of the passage that it is about, and if this still seems to be the correct choice, select that answer. If none of the answers seem appropriate, reread the passage to see whether you can eliminate choices or find information to determine the correct answer.

If you still are uncertain about an answer, do not spend more time on that question. Because there is normally no deduction for wrong answers, choose the answer that seems most likely, even if you are unsure. You can return to these questions if you have time to do so.

Some people find it easier to skim over the questions before reading the passage. This gives them an idea of what to look for while they read. As you take the practice tests in this book, try this method to see whether it makes it easier for you to answer the questions.

The Directions

Following is a typical set of directions.

Directions: This is a test of your ability to understand what you read. In this section, you will find one or more paragraphs of reading material followed by incomplete statements or questions. You are to read the paragraph and select one of the four lettered choices that best completes the statement or answers the question. When you have selected your answer, fill in the correct numbered letter on your answer sheet.

From a building designer's standpoint, three things that make a home livable are the client, the building site, and the amount of money the client has to spend. According to this statement, to make a home livable

A. the prospective piece of land makes little difference.
B. it can be built on any piece of land.
C. the design must fit the owner's income and site.
D. the design must fit the owner's income.

The correct answer is **C.** The passage states both the building site and the amount of money the client has to spend are part of what makes a home livable.

Test-Taking Strategies

The ASVAB test requires that you answer 15 questions in a 13-minute period. You will be presented with a paragraph followed by a question with four choices from which to choose the correct answer. The AFOQT test presents 25 questions in 18 minutes, and you have five choices from which to select the best answer. On the ASTB exam, you'll also encounter Sentence Comprehension questions that are essentially reading comprehension. Each question on the ASTB exam provides four choices from which to choose.

You cannot spend a long time on any single question. If one of the answers immediately appears to you to be correct, quickly check the passage to see whether your answer is accurate and select that answer on the answer sheet. If you are not certain which answer is correct, first eliminate choices that you are sure are not correct. Then glance at the passage and decide which of the remaining possibilities is the best answer. If you find the question difficult to understand and do not have any idea about which answer is correct, go on to the next question. Return to the difficult questions after you have completed as many of the other questions as you can.

Be sure that your answers are based *only on the information that is given in the passage*. Sometimes, you may have more information about a subject than is given in a passage. You may find a statement in a passage that you do not think is correct. This section tests your reading ability, however, not your general knowledge about the subject of the passage. Do not choose an answer that you think is correct based on what you know about the subject of the passage. Only choose answers that are based on information in the passage.

Some test takers find it helpful to read the question before reading the passage. As you work on the practice questions in this chapter, try that method, as well as the method of reading the passage first and then the question. You should be able to decide which of these two methods makes it easier for you to determine the correct answer.

A sure way to do well on this section is to improve your general reading ability. Reading teachers agree that the best way to improve reading skills is to read as much as possible. The passages on this test use the kind of information you are likely to find in newspapers and magazines as well as in books. Practice reading all three kinds of material will be helpful when taking this test.

Kinds of Questions

You will encounter several different types of questions on most reading comprehension tests, regardless of whether you're answering a short passage or longer paragraphs. Following are samples and explanations of each type of question you will encounter on either of these different exams. These are followed by practice questions with the answers explained.

Identifying Stated Facts

These questions require that you read carefully for facts in a passage. Do not choose an answer that adds information not contained in the passage and be sure that your answer states all the information in the passage about the question. Look for an answer that uses exactly the same wording as a part of the passage.

A ballad is a type of poem that tells a story. It is written in groups of four lines. The lines rhyme in a set pattern. Often, ballads tell stories about death, or ghosts, or other supernatural beings. Sometimes, ballads tell love stories. To be a ballad, a poem must

A. tell a story.
B. contain a love story.
C. be only four lines long.
D. tell stories about death.

Explanation: The correct answer is **A.** It is stated in the first sentence of the passage. Choices **B** and **D** are only sometimes true of ballads. Choice **C** is not true according to the passage's second sentence.

Here is another practice question for you to try. Complete the last sentence.

The laws of the United States include rules and customs about the display of the U.S. flag. The flag should be displayed only from sunrise to sunset. It may be displayed at night if it is lighted so that it can be seen. It should be displayed at or near every place where voting is held on election days. It should never touch the ground or the floor. It should never be used for advertising purposes. The flag should never be displayed

A. from sunrise to sunset.
B. at night.
C. above the ground or floor.
D. for advertising purposes.

Explanation: The correct answer is **D.** It uses the same words that appear in the passage. You probably have seen advertisements that show the American flag. According to the passage, those advertisements violate rules about the display of the flag. Choices **A** and **C** are opposite statements from what the paragraph says. The second sentence says the flag *may* be displayed at night, so **B** is not a correct choice.

Identifying Reworded Facts

When you answer these questions, look for information in the answer that states the same facts that the passage states, even though the wording is different. The answer means the same thing as the statement in the passage, even though the words are not exactly the same.

In certain areas, water is so scarce that every attempt is made to conserve it. For instance, on an oasis in the Sahara Desert, the amount of water necessary for each date palm has been carefully determined. How much water is each tree given?

A. No water at all
B. Water on alternate days
C. Exactly the amount required
D. Water only if it is healthy

Explanation: The correct answer is **C.** The passage states "the amount of water necessary for each date palm has been carefully determined." "The amount required" means the same as "necessary."

Here is a practice question for you to try.

Liaison can refer to a person who communicates information between groups. The press secretary to the President of the United States is a *liaison* between the President and journalists. A manufacturing engineer is a *liaison* between a product's designers and the workers involved in making the product. The word *liaison* means someone who

A. argues for a point of view.
B. analyzes political issues.
C. helps groups understand each other.
D. designs products.

Explanation: The correct answer is **C.** To "communicate information between groups" is a way of helping them understand each other. **A** is not correct because it states the *liaison* only represents one point of view. Choices **B** and **D** are suggested by the examples in the paragraph, but they do not define *liaison*.

Determining Sequence of Events

The *sequence of events* means the order in which events occur. When a question asks about the order of events, look for key words that tell about time. These are words and phrases with which you are familiar such as soon, then, before, after, later, next, previously, lastly, to begin, in a little while, shortly, after an hour. These key words in the passage point to the answer to the question.

To check the engine oil on a car, lift the hood of the car. Be sure that it is propped open securely. Locate the dipstick, a rod that goes into the engine. Remove the dipstick to check the oil. Then see whether the oil comes up to the line marked on the dipstick. If it does, the engine is full. Next look at the condition of the oil. It should be light brown and clear, not dark or gritty looking. After replacing the dipstick, add or change oil if necessary. Finally, close the hood, and you're ready to drive. After removing the dipstick,

A. see whether the engine is full.
B. check the condition of the oil.
C. replace the dipstick.
D. close the hood.

Explanation: The correct answer is **A.** According to the passage, this is the first thing to do after removing the dipstick. Choices **B, C,** and **D** are introduced by "next," "after" and "finally," words showing these acts occur later in the order of events.

Antarctica is now a continent of ice and rocks. It was not always so. Millions of years ago, Antarctica, South America, Australia and New Zealand formed a supercontinent near the equator. Then, moving oceanic plates began to split the supercontinent apart. First, Antarctica, still attached to Australia, drifted south. Later, Antarctica separated from Australia and moved farther south until it rested over the South Pole. When did Antarctica come to rest over the South Pole?

A. When it was part of a supercontinent.
B. When it was attached to Australia.
C. After it began to drift to the south.
D. After it separated from Australia.

Explanation: The correct answer is **D.** According to the passage, choices **A, B,** and **C** list events that occurred before Antarctica came to rest over the South Pole.

Identifying Main Ideas

The main idea of a paragraph is a general statement that tells what the passage is about. It is a broad general statement. The other information in the paragraph is specific. It provides support for the main idea by explaining it or giving details and examples to illustrate or prove the main idea. An example of a general statement would be a sentence like "Green vegetables provide nutrients necessary for good health." Specific details supporting this could be spinach contains iron, and broccoli has large quantities of B vitamins.

Sometimes, the main idea of the paragraph is stated. A stated main idea is called the paragraph's topic sentence. This most often is the paragraph's first sentence, but the main idea can also be stated at the end of the paragraph. It is unusual for the main idea to be stated in the middle of a paragraph, but sometimes a paragraph is written that way.

When a paragraph states a main idea, the correct answer to the question may present that idea in slightly different words. Sometimes, a writer chooses not to write a sentence stating the main idea. If so, the reader must decide what the main idea is by seeing what general statement could be made by adding up the specific information in the passage. When you do this, you are inferring the main idea.

In the 50 years between the end of the Civil War and the beginning of World War I, the United States changed from a rural nation to a power in the modern world. The country expanded to include all the territory between the Atlantic and the Pacific oceans. The population grew, partly as a result of immigration. The economy became increasingly industrial. Increased production of goods led to more trade with other nations. The main idea of this passage is that

A. immigration increased the country's population.
B. international trade increased.
C. the country became a powerful modern nation.
D. the country's territory expanded.

Explanation: The correct answer is **C.** It is a general statement. All of the other choices are specific details that demonstrate the growth of the country.

Toothpaste can be used to clean chrome faucets and make them shiny. A few tablespoons of white vinegar mixed with water in a spray bottle create an excellent cleaner for windows or mirrors. And, wet tea leaves will take the sting out of a burn. The main idea of this paragraph is

A. some ordinary products have surprising uses.
B. cleaning products don't have to be expensive.
C. vinegar and water mixed create a glass cleaner.
D. tea is a refreshing beverage.

Explanation: The correct answer is **A.** It makes a general statement that the three sentences in the paragraph are examples of. Choice **B** describes an idea implied by the paragraph's first two sentences, but it does not apply to the third sentence. Choices **C** and **D** are specific details, not general statements, and although **D** may be true, this idea is not stated in the paragraph.

Drawing Conclusions

These questions ask you to decide what you can conclude from information that is in the passage, although the passage does not directly state a conclusion. You can infer the conclusion from the information in the passage. The passage presents separate pieces of information, and drawing a conclusion requires that you see what these pieces of information imply. The passage does not tell you what the answer to the question is. Whatever is directly stated in the passage is not a conclusion. You determine the conclusion based on the logical relationships of information in the passage.

Twenty-five percent of all household burglaries can be attributed to unlocked windows or doors. Crime is the result of opportunity plus desire. To prevent crime, it is each individual's responsibility to

A. provide the desire.
B. provide the opportunity.
C. prevent the desire.
D. prevent the opportunity.

Explanation: The correct answer is **D.** The first sentence states 25 percent of burglaries result from leaving doors and windows unlocked. This is an *opportunity* for burglars. The second sentence tells you that crime is made up of not only opportunity but also the criminal's *desire* to commit a crime. Choice **B,** providing opportunity, is the opposite of preventing crime. Choices **A** and **B** are actions an individual cannot be responsible for in another person. The only logical conclusion, therefore, is that individuals can help to prevent crime by preventing the opportunity.

In a survey taken in July of residents of Metropolis, 44 percent approve of the mayor's job performance, 52 percent disapprove, and 4 percent have no opinion. In a similar survey one year ago, 51 percent approved, 39 percent disapproved, and 10 percent had no opinion. Based on this information, you can conclude

A. the mayor's popularity increased.
B. the mayor's popularity decreased.
C. the mayor took an action the residents did not like.
D. the mayor took an action the residents approved of.

Explanation: The correct answer is **C.** Choices **A** and **B** state in different words facts given in the passage about the change in the mayor's approval rating, but they are not conclusions. You logically can conclude there was a cause for the change. Since the approval rating declined, the cause would have to be an action the residents did not like.

Determining Purpose

Questions about purpose ask you to decide what the passage aims at or intends to do. A paragraph may be written to provide information or explanations. The reader thinks "Now I know something I didn't know before." The passage may give directions or instructions. The reader learns how to do something. The writer may want to persuade the reader to agree with what the passage says. A reader may agree or disagree with the main idea of the passage. This kind of writing is known as an argument.

In determining the purpose of a passage, consider how the sentences relate to each other. If the passage provides reasons for agreeing with a statement, it is probably an argument. If the sentences list a series of steps occurring in a process, the passage usually gives instructions. If the sentences present a series of facts, the passage's purpose is to inform or explain.

This medicine may be taken on an empty stomach or with food. Do not drive a car or operate heavy machinery after taking this medication, because it may make you sleepy. Take one pill each morning until all the pills have been taken. If you forget to take a pill, do not take two pills the following day. The purpose of this passage is to

A. argue against taking two pills in one day.
B. explain how the medicine may affect you.
C. give instructions about how to take the medicine.
D. inform the reader how the medicine will help cure symptoms.

Explanation: The correct answer is **C. A** is not correct because "do not take two pills" is not an idea with which you can agree or disagree. Although the passage says the medication may make you sleepy, the rest of the passage does not explain how the medicine will affect you, so **B** is not a correct choice. **D** is incorrect because nothing in the passage discusses how the medicine works.

As far as genes are concerned, those of chimpanzees and human beings are nearly 99 percent identical. The bonobo, a species related to chimpanzees, also has this genetic similarity. The genes of monkeys and orangutans are not as similar to human genes. Scientists are trying to find out which genes differ in humans and chimpanzees and how they are different. The author of this passage wants to

A. inform readers about animal and human genes.
B. explain why chimpanzee and human genes differ.
C. argue for learning about genes.
D. argue against experiments using animals.

The correct answer is **A**. **B** is incorrect because causes for the differences are not stated in the paragraph, so it does not explain why the genes differ. The passage does not give reasons for learning about genes. Therefore, **C** is incorrect. **D** is incorrect because the passage does not say anything about experiments on animals.

Identifying Technique

Authors can organize a brief passage or paragraph using different techniques. Questions about technique ask you to identify the basis of the passage's structure. Key words connecting sentences in the passage can help you to identify its technique.

If a passage tells a story of events in time order, using words or phrases like "first," "soon after" "then," "next," or "after a few minutes," its structure is based on narrative technique. Some paragraphs use description. What is known through the five senses makes up the passage's content. Descriptive paragraphs use the technique of organizing details spatially. Words and phrases like "on," "next to," "in front of," "over," "under" and "to the right [or left]."

Paragraphs that show how things are similar use comparison as a technique. Paragraphs that show how things are different use contrast as a technique. Some paragraphs use both comparison and contrast. Words and phrases like "similarly," "also," "likewise," and "in the same way" show comparison. "But," "yet," "however," and "on the other hand" indicate contrasts.

Paragraphs based on cause give information about why things, events, or ideas happen. Paragraphs based on effects give information about the results of events or ideas. Some paragraphs discuss both causes and effects. Words and phrases like "because," "for this reason," and "since" show organization based on cause. "As a result," "so," "therefore," "thus," and "consequently" indicate effects.

Today's professional golfers often hit the ball farther than golfers did in the past. One reason is that they spend time physically conditioning themselves. Therefore, they are strong. Golf clubs made of materials developed for modern technology are light, so they are easy to swing. Using computers, engineers design the surface of golf balls to make them travel great distances in the air. The organizing technique of this paragraph is best described as

A. comparison and contrast.
B. description.
C. narration.
D. cause and effect.

Explanation: The correct answer is **D**. Although the first sentence is a comparison, the rest of the paragraph gives reasons that the ball is hit farther and shows how these causes produce the effect of greater distance.

The Boston Tea Party was not the first protest against British taxes by the American colonists. A tax had been placed on sugar in 1764. Then, in 1765, the Stamp Act taxed legal documents and newspapers. These taxes were removed after the colonists stopped buying British goods. Two years later, the British put new taxes on lead, paper, glass, and tea. After further protests, all but the tax on tea were removed. Finally, in 1773, the colonists tossed boxes of tea overboard from ships in Boston Harbor to protest this tax. The organizing technique of this paragraph is

A. description.
B. contrast.
C. narration.
D. cause and effect.

Explanation: The correct answer is **C.** The first date mentioned is 1764, and the last is 1773, so time has passed. Time indicators like "then," "after," and "two years later" confirm that the passage's technique is narration.

Determining Mood and Tone

The mood and tone of a passage consist of the emotions suggested by its content. To answer questions about mood and tone, think about the words in the passage. Are they associated with things that make people feel happy, like a bright sunny day or a special birthday party? Or, are they words related to events that usually make people sad, like illness or gloomy weather? Is the language strong and harsh, suggesting that the writer of the passage is angry? Are there exclamation points to indicate excitement? If the passage is a description, think about how you would feel if you were in the place that was described or were watching the events described. If a person is described, what facts about that person indicate how the person feels?

Through the open window, she saw that the tops of the trees were breaking out in little green buds that would soon be leaves. The rain had cleaned the air, and she felt a warm breeze signaling the end of winter. Patches of blue sky showed through the clouds, and she heard birds singing. The mood of this passage could best be described as

A. fearful.
B. hopeful.
C. disgusted.
D. comical.

Explanation: The correct answer is **B.** The clean air, the green buds, the blue sky, the warm air, and the singing birds are all descriptive details connected to springtime. Spring is the season when things that have stopped growing during the winter begin to grow again, so it is associated with life and hope. Although the passage is happy, it is not funny, so **D** would not be a good answer.

It was a dark and stormy night. The rain rattling on the roof sounded like skeletons dancing. Then I heard a strange sound outside the front door. What could it be? Who would go out in such a storm? I approached the door slowly, and opened it just a crack. I could see nothing. Cautiously, I opened the door another inch or two. But, still I saw nothing. A gust of wind—or something—I don't know what —caught the door and opened it fully. With trembling hands, I slammed the door shut to keep out the wind. The tone of this passage is

A. angry.
B. frightened.
C. thoughtful.
D. unhappy.

Explanation: The correct answer is **B.** Storms often create a spooky mood. Words like "slowly" and "cautiously" as well as the description of the sound of the rain and being unable to see anything when the door is opened add to the tone of fright. The speaker's trembling hands in the last sentence also indicate fear.

Reading Comprehension and Paragraph Comprehension Practice Questions

This sample test contains all of the different types of questions discussed in this chapter, but the questions are not in the same order as the preceding descriptions.

Directions: This is a test of your ability to understand what you have read. In this section, you will find one or more paragraphs of reading material followed by incomplete statements or questions. You are to read the paragraph and select one of four lettered choices that best completes the statement or answers the question. When you have selected your answer, fill in the correct numbered letter on your answer sheet.

1. In January 2002, a person buys a car that comes with a three year or 36,000 mile free replacement guarantee on the engine and transmission. In June 2005, the car has 34,300 miles on it. The transmission fails.

   According to the situation described in the paragraph, the car dealer will

   A. put in a new transmission.
   B. give the person a new car.
   C. not fix the transmission at no cost.
   D. not replace the car's engine.

2. A sonnet is a specific type of poem. It has 14 lines. The lines must rhyme in a set pattern. Sometimes, the last six lines of a sonnet contrast with the first eight lines. Many sonnets are love poems.

   To be a sonnet, a poem must

   A. be a love poem.
   B. present a contrast.
   C. have fewer than 14 lines.
   D. rhyme in a specific way.

3. When many people want to buy a product, the price will probably go up. In the summer, Americans travel more than they do at other times of year. They may take planes or trains, and many families drive to their vacation spots.

   From the information in the paragraph, you can conclude that

   A. gasoline prices will rise in the summer.
   B. gasoline prices will rise in the winter.
   C. gasoline prices will go down in the summer.
   D. gasoline prices will not change in any season.

4. When you send a document to someone by electronic means, you are faxing it. The word "fax" comes from the word *facsimile*. Earlier ways of making facsimiles included photocopying and photographing. The oldest facsimiles were handwritten versions of original texts.

   The word *facsimile* means

   A. an electronic copy.
   B. an exact copy.
   C. any document.
   D. a photocopy.

5. The U.S. Supreme Court is the highest court in the nation. Its nine judges review cases from other courts. They decide whether these courts have ruled in a way that agrees with the U.S. Constitution. But, they cannot make new laws. Their decision is based on a majority vote of the nine judges.

   The main idea of this paragraph is that

   A. The U.S. Constitution is the basis for our laws.
   B. The Supreme Court is the highest court in the United States.
   C. The Supreme Court cannot make new laws.
   D. The Supreme Court's decisions are based on a majority vote.

6. Most cars today have automatic transmissions. But, it is useful to know how to shift gears in a car with a standard transmission. Press the clutch pedal in with your left foot. Then use the shift lever to choose the proper gear. Release the clutch pedal while gently applying pressure to the gas pedal.

   The last thing to do when shifting gears is to

   A. step on the gas.
   B. release the clutch.
   C. use the shift lever.
   D. press down on the clutch.

7. Recycling household waste is very important. Space for landfills where garbage is dumped is becoming scarce. Putting waste in the oceans causes pollution. Recycling is a way for cities to make money by selling recyclable items. And, recycling items helps to saves natural resources.

The author's purpose in this passage is to

A. explain what recycling is.
B. tell a story.
C. show a contrast.
D. argue for recycling.

8. Jackrabbits are not rabbits but members of the hare family. Hares are larger than rabbits, and they have longer ears. Newborn rabbits are naked and helpless, but infant hares are covered with fur and aware of their surroundings.

Hares and rabbits are contrasted by describing all of the following except

A. their size.
B. length of ears.
C. what color they are.
D. newborn rabbits and hares.

9. Superman originated as a character in a comic book in the 1930s. Then a radio program called *The Adventures of Superman* was created. Later, Superman became part of going to the movies. Short episodes were shown each week in theaters in addition to a feature film. When television became part of American life, it, too, had a weekly program about Superman. In the 1980s several full-length films about Superman appeared.

From this passage, you can conclude

A. Superman is a great hero.
B. Superman has been popular for a long time.
C. Superman has often appeared in films.
D. Superman began in comic books.

10. People may think of pizza as a snack food. But, it is nutritious. The crust, made of a kind of bread, provides carbohydrates. The tomatoes contain Vitamin C and provide fiber. The cheese is a good source of calcium, which is needed for healthy bones.

Pizza is healthful because it

A. includes a good source of calcium.
B. tastes good.
C. is a snack food.
D. can be ordered in a restaurant or bought frozen to bake at home.

11. The space shuttle is coming in for a landing. Over a loudspeaker, the waiting spectators hear "STS 42 is now over Brandenburg, making its turn for the coast." They quickly stand, look up, turn their eyes skyward. They hear the sonic boom and stare at the sky even more closely. There it is! First, it is only a speck. Then, the crowd applauds and cheers as they see it approaching earth.

The spectators who watch the shuttle land feel

A. fear.
B. anger.
C. happiness.
D. excitement.

12. When people are in a group, they may not react to an emergency the same way they would if they were alone. One reason may be that each person thinks someone else has already done something. Or, seeing no one else speak, a person may feel nothing needs to be done. A third possibility is that the person does not want to draw attention to himself or herself.

This passage explains

A. differences between individuals and people in groups.
B. the effects of being part of a group.
C. causes for behavior in a group.
D. how people react to an emergency.

13. In 1963, Martin Luther King, Jr., led a protest march in Birmingham, Alabama. Because he did not have a permit to hold the march, he was arrested. Then eight clergymen wrote a letter that was published in the local newspaper. The letter opposed protest marches as a way to end racial problems. While King was in jail, he wrote a reply to that letter. It has been reprinted many times since then under the title "Letter from Birmingham Jail."

King wrote the letter

    A. before the protest march.

    B. when he was arrested.

    C. while he was thinking about racial problems.

    D. after he read the clergymen's letter.

14. King was arrested because

    A. the clergymen wrote a letter.

    B. he did not have a permit to hold the march.

    C. there were racial problems in Birmingham.

    D. he was put in jail.

15. People sometimes say they will return back to a place they have visited. Since *return* means the same thing as *go back to*, the expressions *return back* is *redundant*.

The word *redundant* could be used to describe which one of the following phrases?

    A. cooperate together

    B. walk slowly

    C. review again

    D. add information

Reading Comprehension and Paragraph Comprehension Answers and Explanations

1. C. Because the car is more than three years old, the free replacement guarantee will not apply. **A** is not correct because it does not tell whether the customer will have to pay for the work. No information in the paragraph suggests that **B** would be what would happen. Although **D** may be a true statement, the situation in the paragraph does not describe any problem with the engine.

2. D. Choices **A** and **B** are statements that describe some but not all sonnets according to the paragraph. **C** is incorrect because the paragraph states that a sonnet has 14 lines.

3. A. The paragraph states that Americans travel more in the summer. You can conclude that if they travel more, they will use more gasoline. And, the paragraph states that when people want to buy more of a product, the price goes up.

4. B. Answers **A** and **D** are examples of facsimiles; they do not define the word. **C** is incorrect because the paragraph indicates that ways of making facsimiles are ways of making copies.

5. A. A main idea is a general statement. The other choices are specific facts.

6. A. The paragraph is written in the order of things to do, and this is the last action mentioned in the paragraph.

7. D. The paragraph explains why recycling is a good idea. The paragraph is not a story (choice **B**) and does not have a contrast (choice **C**). It does not tell what recycling is, so **A** is incorrect.

8. C. All of the other choices are discussed in the paragraph.

9. B. The paragraph discusses Superman from the 1930s to the 1980s, so one can conclude that he has been popular for a long time. Choices **C** and **D** are facts stated in the paragraph. Most people would agree with choice **A,** but it is not part of the information in the paragraph.

10. A. It is the only choice that states a fact about why pizza is a nutritious food.

11. D. The details in the paragraph about standing up, staring at the sky, the exclamation "there it is," and the applause and cheering show that the spectators are excited.

12. C. Because the paragraph gives reasons, it is explaining causes. Although the first sentence of the paragraph is a contrast, the paragraph does not explain the contrast, so **A** is an incorrect choice.

13. D. Because King's letter was a reply to the clergymen, he had to have written it after he read the letter.

14. B. This fact is stated in the second sentence of the paragraph.

15. A. From the paragraph, you can infer that a *redundant* expression is one in which both words have the same meaning. *Cooperate* means *work together,* so it is an example of a redundant expression. Choice **C** may look appropriate because *review* means look at again, but something can be reviewed more than one time.

Word Knowledge Review

Word Knowledge appears on the ASVAB, AFOQT, and the ASTB exams. The formats of the exams differ slightly, however. It's important to understand that a strong vocabulary and sense of how to use words is important in any career field or in school. Applying for Officer Candidate School—regardless of the service branch—is an important step in your military career. You should be aware of the importance of words, their meanings, and their interpretations. Whether you are applying directly from school, or you already serve in the Armed Forces, the greater your abilities and knowledge in this area are, the better your chances for success—on the exams and in OCS.

The Word Knowledge section of the ASVAB presents questions in two different formats; both formats test your knowledge of synonyms, words that have the same or nearly the same meaning. In the first type of question, synonyms, the test presents an underlined word and then asks you to choose the word or phrase that has the same or nearly the same meaning. The second type of question, word-in-context presents a sentence. You must find the word or phrase that has a nearly identical meaning as the underlined word in the context of the sentence.

On the AFOQT exam, you are given a word and then asked to find the synonym from five choices (A–E). On the ASTB, two different types of questions test your vocabulary knowledge. The first type of question is a sentence with a missing word, and you are asked to choose the missing word from among four choices (A–D). The second type of question is a little more complex. You are given a brief quotation that contains a word that is used incorrectly. You are asked to select from a choice of five words, the word that would replace the incorrect word and would correctly convey the meaning of the quotation.

Kinds of Questions

Let's look at the different question types you will encounter on the exams. There are two different forms of the question. The first type of questions is found on the ASVAB exam.

Rapid most nearly means

- **A.** slow.
- **B.** shameful.
- **C.** quick.
- **D.** gently.

C is the correct answer. The word **quick** means the same as the word **rapid.**

Following is the second question form.

He was asked to **cease** his activities.

- **A.** increase
- **B.** stop
- **C.** begin
- **D.** slow down

B is correct. The word **stop** is the same as the boldface word **cease.**

You can find the next type of question on the AFOQT.

CIRCUMVENT

- **A.** get over
- **B.** go under
- **C.** get through
- **D.** go around
- **E.** go easily

The correct answer is **D,** to get around. There's no trick to this type of question. It requires, however, a strong vocabulary (*circum = around, vent = go*). It's not much different than the ASVAB type question.

The next type of question is from the ASTB. This question format consists of a sentence in which one word is omitted. Select the choice that best completes the sentence.

Paul was able to _____ the complainer with a look of contempt.

- **A.** squelch
- **B.** offend
- **C.** assail
- **D.** expel

The correct answer is **A.** To squelch is to silence. This satisfies the meaning of the sentence.

The final type of question is also from the ASTB and is a little more complex. The following quotation contains a word that has been misused. It is not in keeping with the meaning of the quotation. You must first determine which word is incorrect, and then select, from the choices given, the word that would be more appropriate for that quotation.

"Even while their components vary from culture to culture, rites of adulteration convey status in a new social grouping on the participants."

- **A.** maturity
- **B.** ceremony
- **C.** initiation
- **D.** consumption

The correct answer is **C.** The word **adulteration** is incorrect. It means to make something impure by adding a foreign substance. **Initiation,** which means the process of being admitted to something, fits the meaning of the sentence.

All of these questions really just require you to understand the vocabulary. This last type of question, however, requires a little more thought process on your part. You are required to first identify the word that is misused and then substitute the correct word.

Ways to Improve Your Vocabulary

The ability tested in the Word Knowledge portion of all three of these tests is your command of the language—in other words, your vocabulary. Of course, by this point in your life you might think that you have learned all of the words you will ever learn or that it will be impossible to improve your vocabulary. On the contrary! If you are diligent and put your mind to it, you can improve your vocabulary in several ways. Here are three that will definitely help:

- Read, read, read. Pick up a newspaper, a magazine, or a novel and make note of words you do not understand. Make a list or put them on note cards. First, try to figure out the meaning of the words by looking at the context in which they are used. Make an educated guess. If you are still not sure, look up the meaning of the words and write the words and their meaning out in a notebook or on note cards. Then try to make up your own sentences using the words.

- Learn a new word every day or every other day. You can get into the habit of looking up a new word in the dictionary every day. Write the word and its definition on a piece of paper. Then write a sentence using the word. This will help you visualize it. Don't pick words that are too technical or specialized (such as medical/scientific terms or proper names). Try using this new word in conversation.

- Words are made up, generally, of prefixes, roots, and suffixes. Many prefixes and roots have a Latin or Greek origin. If you can familiarize yourself with some of these, you will find that you can arrive at the meaning of some words by breaking them down. The following section will offer you some common prefixes, roots, and suffixes to help you tackle words you are unfamiliar with in the Word Knowledge section.

Prefixes

In order to break down words you do not understand or to help you recognize why a word means what it means, you should become familiar with prefixes. Prefixes are parts of words that come at the beginning of a word and that can affect its meaning.

As an example, look at the word *synonym*. This word is made up of the prefix *syn* plus the root *nym*. If you knew that the prefix syn means *with/together* or *same* and the root *nym* means *name* or *word,* then you could conclude that the word *synonym* means *same word*. And, that's what it means!

Look at another example. The word *circumvent* is made up of the prefix *circum* plus the root *vent*. If you knew that the prefix circum means *around* and the root *vent* means *go* or *come,* then you could conclude the word *circumvent* means *go around*.

What follows is a list of common prefixes that you often will find at the beginning of certain words. Following the prefix, you will find the meaning of the prefix and a word using the prefix (with a rough definition in parentheses following the word). Try including a word of your own in the space provided for each prefix. If you cannot come up with your own word, refer to a dictionary for help.

Prefix	Meaning	Word (Definition)	Your Example
ab-	away from	abnormal (away from normal)	
ad-	to, toward	adjoin (join to)	
a-, an-	not, without	apathy (without feeling)	
anti-	against	antiviolence (against violence)	
ambi-	both	ambidextrous (both hands)	
bene-	good	benign (good or harmless)	
circum-	around	circumvent (go around)	
con-	with, together	connect (come together)	
contra-	against	contradict (speak against)	
com-	with, together	communion (coming together)	
de-	down, away	descend (move down)	
dis-	apart, not	discontent (not content)	
e-	out of, from	eject (throw out)	

Prefix	Meaning	Word (Definition)	Your Example
ex-	out of, from	exclude (leave out)	
hyper-	over	hyperactive (overactive)	
hypo-	under	hypodermic (below the skin)	
inter-	between	interconnected (connected between)	
il-	not	illegal (not legal)	
in-	not	indiscreet (not discreet)	
in-	into	ingest (take into the body by mouth)	
im-	not	impossible (not possible)	
im-	into	imbibe (drink in)	
ir-	not	irrational (not rational)	
mal-	bad, evil	malign (speak badly of)	
ob-	against	obstruct (build against)	
omni-	all	omniscient (knows all)	
peri-	around	periscope (view around)	
post-	after	postgraduate (after graduation)	
pre-	before	precede (go before)	
pro-	for, forward	proceed (move forward)	
re-	again, back	reconvene (get together again)	
retro-	back	retrogression (step back)	
se-	away from	seduce (lead away)	
sub-	under	subhuman (below human)	
sur-, super-	over, above	supersonic (above sound)	
sym-, syn-	together, with	sympathy (feeling with or for)	
trans-	across	Transatlantic (across the Atlantic)	

Roots

Along with prefixes, roots are central to the meanings of words. If you familiarize yourself with some common roots, then you may be able to better recognize certain words or at least get a general feel for several words. By studying the following list of roots, you will be better equipped to break down many words and make sense of them.

Following you will find a root, its meaning, a word using the root and a space in which you can write another word that uses the same root.

Root	Meaning	Word (Definition)	Your Example
ami, amic	love	amicable	
anthrop	human, man	anthropology	
arch	chief or leader	patriarch	

Root	Meaning	Word (Definition)	Your Example
auto	self	autobiography	
aud	sound	audible	
brev	short	brief	
bio	life	biography	
cap	take, seize	capture	
ced	yield, go	intercede	
corp	body	corporal	
cred	believe	credible	
culp	guilt	culpable	
chron	time	synchronize	
crac, crat	rule, ruler	democracy	
dic	speak, say	dictate	
duc, duct	lead	deduce	
demo	people	democracy	
equ	equal	equity	
grad, gress	step	progression	
graph	writing, printing	biography	
ject	throw	inject	
luc	light	elucidate	
log	study of	geology	
mono	one	monotone	
man	hand	manual	
min	small	minority	
mit, miss	send	emit	
mort	death	mortal	
mut	change	mutate	
nym	word or name	pseudonym	
nov	new	renovate	
pac	peace	pacify	
pel, puls	push	compel	
pot	power	potent	
port	carry	portable	
path	feeling	apathy	

Root	Meaning	Word (Definition)	Your Example
phil	like, lover of	philosophy	
quer, quis	ask	query	
scrib	write	manuscript	
sed	sit	sedentary	
sent	feel	sensory	
sequ	follow	sequel	
son	sound	unison	
spir	breathe	inspire	
tang, tact	touch	tangible	
vac	empty	vacant	
ven	come, go	intervene	
ver	truth	verify	
vert	turn	introvert	
vit	life	revitalize	
voc	call	evocative	

Suffixes

Suffixes come at the end of words and usually change the part of speech (noun, adjective, adverb, and so on) of words, which also subtly changes the meaning. Becoming familiar with suffixes may help you get a sense of the meaning the word is *conveying,* even if you are not sure of what the definition of the word is exactly.

Look at a word with different suffixes to see how the part of speech or the meaning can change. For example, the word *sedate* means to calm or relax. The following sentences contain words that are made up of the root word sedate but have different suffixes attached:

- The doctor prescribed a sedat*ive* [something that sedates] to calm her nerves.
- The speech was delivered sedate*ly* [in a sedate manner].
- The dog was under sedat*ion* [in a state of sedation] for the long trip.
- Many office workers live a sedent*ary* [relating to nonactive] lifestyle.

As you can see, in each of the sentences, the word *sedate* means generally the same thing, but the part of speech changes. However, you can get a sense of *how* the word changes if you know what the suffixes mean.

What follows is a list of common suffixes that you may encounter at the ends of certain words. Try applying these suffixes at the ends of words you know (or words from the preceding lists) to see how the part of speech or the meaning of the word changes.

Suffix	Meaning	Your Example
-able, ible	capable of or susceptible to	
-ary	of or relating to	
-ate	to make	

Suffix	Meaning	Your Example
-ian	one relating to or belonging to	
-ic	relating to or characterized by	
-ile	relating to or capable of	
-ion	action or condition of	
-ious	having the quality of	
-ism	quality, process, or practice of	
-ist	one who performs	
-ity	state of being	
-ive	performing or tending to	
-ize, ise	to cause to be or become	
-ly	resembling or in the manner of	
-less	without	
-ment	action or process or the result	
-ology	study of	
-y, -ry	state of	

Strategies for Scoring Well

With the prefixes, roots, and suffixes you have studied at this point, you should be ready to answer the following practice questions. These practice questions consist of 40 questions in the three formats that you will encounter on the AFOQT and the ASTB exams. Regardless of which test you plan to take, it would be extremely helpful to answer all three types of questions. They all test your knowledge of vocabulary, and your ability to select the correct word. Upon completion of the practice questions, you should check your answers with the answer key that follows and look at the explanations.

Word Knowledge Practice Questions

Directions: The AFOQT Word Knowledge test has 25 questions and will test your ability to understand written language. For each question, choose the answer that means the same as the capitalized word.

Although this is not an actual test, it would be helpful if you were to answer these questions under simulated conditions.

1. GRAPHIC

    A. unclear
    B. detailed
    C. large
    D. childish

2. INDISPENSABLE

    A. trashy
    B. ridiculous
    C. necessary
    D. uninvited

3. CONCOCT

    A. make up
    B. throw away
    C. go through
    D. walk around

4. SONIC

    A. relating to the sun
    B. relating to the moon
    C. relating to sound
    D. relating to the earth

5. ASSIMILATE

    A. to take in
    B. to make fun of
    C. to rob of
    D. to ignore

6. DEGRADATION

    A. happiness
    B. anger
    C. celebration
    D. poverty

7. CONTRADICT

    A. to talk about
    B. to see the future
    C. to fall down
    D. to speak against

8. SEQUENTIALLY

    A. sensibly
    B. randomly
    C. in order
    D. out of order

9. CULPRIT

    A. a shy person
    B. a shallow waterway
    C. the guilty party
    D. the most qualified person

10. OMNIPOTENT

    A. all-knowing
    B. all-seeing
    C. all-hearing
    D. all-powerful

11. SUBMISSIVE

    A. meek
    B. not intelligent
    C. kind
    D. strong

12. DEMEANING

    A. boring
    B. humiliating
    C. colorful
    D. ignorant

13. FLUCTUATE

    A. remain the same
    B. follow a downward course
    C. follow an upward course
    D. change

14. RENOVATE

    A. destroy
    B. restore
    C. return
    D. go around

15. INTERCEDE

    A. to bring something to an end
    B. to act as a judge
    C. to act as mediator
    D. to laugh at something

Directions: The following questions from the ASTB consist of sentences in which one word is omitted. For each question, select the lettered choice that best completes the thought expressed in the sentence.

16. The committee voted to _____ the membership requirements, but the board of directors overruled the vote, and the requirements remained in place.

    A. consider
    B. remember
    C. rescind
    D. enhance

17. He tried to budget his funds, but his _____ for gambling led him into debt.

    A. talent
    B. predilection
    C. consideration
    D. distaste

18. After the cake collapsed in the oven, the cook decided the recipe needed to be _____.

    A. increased
    B. fermented
    C. consolidated
    D. amended

19. Pouring water on burning grease will not put out the fire; instead it will _____ the danger.

    A. quench
    B. improve
    C. exacerbate
    D. expiate

20. The casserole of potatoes, made without salt, pepper, or spices, tasted _____.

    A. savory
    B. complex
    C. necrotic
    D. insipid

21. Loudly and repeatedly, the suspect _____ protested, "I didn't do it."

    A. vehemently
    B. contentedly
    C. simply
    D. graciously

22. Advertisements use hidden persuasion; _____ and manipulation create a demand for products.

    A. guile
    B. simplicity
    C. candor
    D. mischief

23. Because the plot was familiar and the dialogue commonplace, the critics called the film _____.

    A. exciting
    B. creative
    C. banal
    D. awkward

24. The game was tied, the potential winning run was at bat, and the fans became _____, jumping up from their seats, stamping their feet, and cheering.

    A. angry
    B. frenetic
    C. disillusioned
    D. outspoken

25. The defendant sat _____ in the witness chair, neither moving nor showing any facial expressions.

    A. stupidly
    B. softly
    C. solidly
    D. stolidly

26. Country music songs often describe people at the _____ of their lives; their dogs run away, their spouses leave them, and their pickup trucks break down.

    A. pyramid
    B. sample
    C. nadir
    D. confluence

27. Having a _____ of acting talent, she was not selected for the leading role in the play.

    A. modicum
    B. plenitude
    C. quality
    D. similarity

28. So many factors were involved in the decision that he could find no way out of the _____.

    A. mine
    B. solution
    C. quandary
    D. question

29. The attorney tried to be _____ in drawing up the contract; nevertheless, some of its terms were unclear.

    A. hyperactive
    B. conscientious
    C. punctilious
    D. legitimate

30. Slavery is the _____ of destroying human dignity.

    A. negation
    B. epitome
    C. institution
    D. practice

Directions: The following questions from the ASTB consist of quotations that contain one word that is incorrectly used because it is not in keeping with the meaning that each quotation is evidently intended to convey. Determine which word is incorrectly used. Then select from the lettered choices the word that, when substituted for the incorrectly used word, would best help to convey the intended meaning of the quotation.

31. "When a reader tells me my novel makes a political statement, I am distressed, because such a remark complies literature with propaganda."

    A. corrupts
    B. communicates
    C. concocts
    D. confounds

32. "His baseball-oriented parents, his work ethic, and his reluctant competitive nature made it possible for Cal Ripken, Jr., the best shortstop of his era, to break the record for consecutive games played."

    A. relentless
    B. persuasive
    C. moderate
    D. contest

33. "Applicants for insurance disclose personal information to our company; state and federal laws regulate the uses of this information for any purpose; and, therefore, we instruct our employees to understand the importance of restraining the confidentiality of personal information supplied by you to our company."

    A. permitting
    B. maintaining
    C. complicating
    D. forwarding

34. "Arguments, in the academic sense of the term, provide a device for exploring a controversy or dispute, a tool for isolating issues in contention, and a way to evaluate different possible outcomes; furthermore, they shape and mangle each arguer's position."

    A. manipulate
    B. clarify
    C. reply
    D. obscure

35. "In ancient cultures, natural phenomena such as thunder and lightning storms and eclipses of the sun or the moon were believed to be omens that some great event or disaster was studied."

    A. motivated
    B. famous
    C. imminent
    D. reclusive

36. "United States Supreme Court decisions are presented in a written document known as an opinion, which includes the Court's ruling and the reasoning of the majority of the justices; any justice in the minority may write a rebuking opinion."

A. consoling
B. dissenting
C. condemned
D. motive

37. "E-mail allows communication to be processed at a time convenient to the calculator rather than requiring immediate attention, which may interrupt other work priorities."

A. vendor
B. administrator
C. messenger
D. recipient

38. "A useless plan for improving elementary education must take into consideration not only the standards pupils should meet, but also the resources available to schools."

A. revolting
B. willful
C. viable
D. noble

39. "While Supreme Court decisions have rejected the view that all conduct engaged in to express an idea can be labeled speech, it has held that some conduct may be sufficiently persuaded by the element of communication to fall under the First Amendment's protection of speech."

A. criticized
B. distanced
C. negated
D. pervaded

40. "To study mistakes and errors in logic can be instructive, because the recognition and correction of these errors helps one to understand the principles of reasoning on which such exacerbating activities depend."

A. remedial
B. determinate
C. notice
D. philosophical

Word Knowledge Answers and Explanations

Use the following answer key to check your answers. You will find a brief explanation of each answer.

1. B. Graphic (graph = written or drawn) means described in vivid detail or clearly drawn out, so detailed would most closely mean graphic.

2. C. Indispensable literally means not dispensable (able to be thrown away). So, if something is indispensable, it is necessary; you cannot do away with it.

3. A. Concoct means to create or come up with, like in the sentence "The two boys concocted a plan to skip school." Concoct most closely means to make up.

4. C. Sonic means relating to sound (son = sound).

5. A. Assimilate means to absorb or take in. If a group of individuals successfully assimilates, then they have converged and incorporated into one group.

6. D. Degradation is a state of poverty or squalor. It literally means "a step down" (de = down, grad = step).

7. D. Contradict literally means to speak against (contra = against, dict = speak).

8. C. Sequentially means items are arranged in order or in a sequence (sequ = follow).

9. C. The culprit is the person who is guilty (culp = guilt).

10. D. Omnipotent literally means all-powerful (omni = all, pot = power).

11. A. A submissive (sub = under, miss = send) person is one who is meek and passive, not aggressive.

12. B. Demeaning (de = down) means something that puts one down or is humiliating.

13. D. Fluctuate (fluc = change) means to change, go up and down, not constant.

14. B. Renovate means to restore or to make new again (re = again, nov = new).

15. C. Intercede means to go between (inter = within, ced = go) or to mediate.

16. C. The word **rescind** means to repeal; to revoke.

17. B. The word **predilection** means inclination toward; preference for.

18. D. The word **amended** means changed.

19. C. The word **exacerbate** means to make worse; to increase the severity.

20. D. The word **insipid** means dull; lacking excitement or flavor.

21. A. The word **vehemently** means with great force.

22. A. The word **guile** means trickery; deceit; cunning.

23. C. The word **banal** means predictable; trite.

24. B. The word **frenetic** means wildly excited.

25. D. The word **stolidly** means showing little or no emotion; impassive.

26. C. The word **nadir** means the lowest point.

27. A. The word **modicum** means a small amount.

28. C. The word **quandary** means dilemma; perplexity.

29. D. The word **punctilious** means extremely careful; precisely observing rules.

30. B. The word **epitome** means perfect example; embodiment.

31. D. The word **complies** is incorrect. The writer is distressed, so the quotation intends to convey the idea that literature should not be thought of as propaganda. **Confounds,** which means fails to distinguish between, best expresses the sentence's meaning.

32. A. The word **reluctant** is not correct. A reluctant person is unwilling to do something. **Relentless,** which means steady and persistent, describes the kind of person who could break a record.

33. B. The word **restraining** is incorrect because to restrain means to put limits on. The quotation is intended to reassure people that information will be kept confidential. Therefore, **maintaining** is the word that would convey the intended meaning.

34. B. The word **mangle,** meaning to ruin, is incorrect. The quotation is about the advantages of argument. Replacing **mangle** with **clarify** expresses that idea.

35. C. The word **studied** is incorrect. The idea of the sentence is that these phenomena were about to occur, which is what the word **imminent** means.

36. B. The word **rebuking,** which means scolding, is incorrect. A justice in the minority disagrees with the majority. The word **dissenting** means disagreeing.

37. D. The word **calculator** is incorrect. The meaning of the sentence is that the person who receives the e-mail, the **recipient,** will not have to interrupt other tasks.

38. C. The word **useless** is incorrect. The sentence intends to convey what the requirements for a good plan would be. The word **viable,** meaning capable of success or effective, best conveys that meaning.

39. D. The word **persuaded** is incorrect. The sentence's intended meaning is that some conduct deserves the same protection as speech. This is conduct that is **pervaded** by elements of communication. Pervaded means to be present throughout.

40. A. The word **exacerbating,** meaning to make worse, is incorrect. **Remedial,** which means to correct or to find a remedy for, describes the recognition and correction of errors.

This section reviews all the skills you need to do well on the math portions of the ASVAB, AFOQT, and the ASTB tests, including plenty of examples. Also try the practice problems to make sure that you've got a handle on these types of questions.

Arithmetic Reasoning

Several basic arithmetic and mathematics sections appear on the AFOQT, AFAST, and ASTB exams. For example, the AFOQT exam includes the sections "Arithmetic Reasoning" and "Mathematics Knowledge." The ASTB exam has a combined "Math and Verbal" section. The following is a brief review of arithmetic and mathematics, covering some basic information that will come in handy on any of these tests.

Although you might not have to know everything that we present in this section, it would be a good idea to review most of this material. In addition, take all the arithmetic and mathematics tests in this book to get a better understanding of what you know and what you might need to study.

The Numbers of Arithmetic

In this section, you will cover the basics of Arithmetic. You will find that this information is necessary in all of the tests that you will take. Naturally, these are the basics of arithmetic and the building blocks of mathematics, so your understanding of this material is important. This section includes review material on Whole Numbers, Fractions, Decimals, Percents and Interest, Arithmetic Operations, Arithmetic Word Problems, Ratio and Proportion Problems, and Measurement Problems.

Whole Numbers

The numbers 0, 1, 2, 3, 4, and so on are called *whole numbers*. The whole number system is a *place value* system—that is, the value of each digit in a whole number is determined by the place it occupies. For example, in the number 6,257, the 6 is in the thousands place, the 2 is in the hundreds place, the 5 is in the tens place, and the 7 is in the ones place.

The following table contains a summary of whole number place values:

Ones	1
Tens	10
Hundreds	100
Thousands	1,000
Ten-thousands	10,000
Hundred-thousands	100,000
Millions	1,000,000
Ten millions	10,000,000
Hundred millions	100,000,000
Billions	1,000,000,000

For example, the number 5,124,678 would be read five million, one hundred twenty-four thousand, six hundred and seventy-eight.

> Write the number thirty million, five hundred seven thousand, three hundred twelve.

30,507,312

> Write in words the number 34,521.

Thirty-four thousand, five hundred twenty-one

Rounding Whole Numbers

When you need only an approximate value of a whole number, the following procedure can be used to round off the number to a particular place:

Procedure for Rounding Whole Numbers:

1. Underline the digit in the place being rounded off.
2. If the digit to the right of the underlined digit is less than five, leave the underlined digit as it is. If the digit to the right of the underlined digit is equal to five or more, add one to the underlined digit.
3. Replace all digits to the right of the underlined digit with zeros.

Rounding whole numbers often helps you determine the correct answer to a multiple choice question more quickly.

> Round off the number 34,521 to the nearest hundred.

Because we are rounding to the nearest hundred, begin by underlining the digit in the hundreds place, which is a five:

34,521

Now, look to the right of the underlined digit. Because the number to the right of the five is two, leave the five as it is, and replace all digits to the right of the five with zeros.

34,500 is rounded to the nearest hundred.

> Round off the number 236,789 to the nearest ten-thousand.

Because we are rounding to the nearest ten-thousand, begin by underlining the digit in the ten-thousands place, which is three:

236,789

Now, look to the right of the underlined digit. Because the number to the right of the three is six, increase three by one, obtaining four, and replace all digits to the right of this four with zeros.

240,000 is rounded to the nearest ten-thousand.

Fractions

A fraction is made up of two numbers, separated by a line that is known as a fraction bar. Typically, a fraction is used to represent a part of a whole. For example, in the following diagram, note that five out of eight pieces of the diagram are shaded:

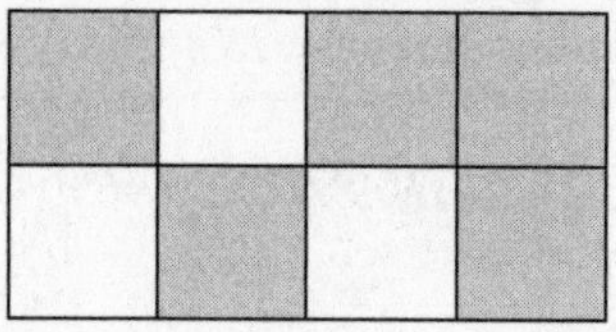

In this case, the fraction $\frac{5}{8}$ could be used to represent the fact that five of the eight equal pieces have been shaded. In the same way, the fraction $\frac{3}{8}$ could be used to represent the fact that three of the eight pieces have been left unshaded.

When the number on the top is *less than* the number on the bottom, fractions are said to be *proper*. Thus, the fractions $\frac{2}{9}$, $\frac{5}{8}$, and $\frac{3}{7}$ are proper fractions. The value of a proper fraction is always less than one.

When the number on the top is either *equal to or greater than* the number on the bottom, fractions are called *improper.* For example, the fractions $\frac{5}{2}$, $\frac{7}{4}$, and $\frac{11}{5}$ are improper. If the number on the top is greater than the number on the bottom, the value of the fraction is greater than one. If the number on the top and the number on the bottom are equal, such as in $\frac{8}{8}$, the value of the fraction is equal to one.

A *mixed number* is a whole number together with a fraction, such as $7\frac{1}{2}$ or $3\frac{5}{8}$. The mixed number $7\frac{1}{2}$ represents the number seven plus the fraction $\frac{1}{2}$. As you see later, every improper fraction can be written as a mixed number and vice versa.

> Classify the following numbers as proper fractions, improper fractions, or mixed numbers: $\frac{8}{9}$, $\frac{9}{6}$, $5\frac{2}{3}$, $\frac{6}{4}$, and $\frac{112}{113}$.

The numbers $\frac{8}{9}$ and $\frac{112}{113}$ are proper fractions; the numbers $\frac{9}{6}$ and $\frac{6}{4}$ are improper fractions; and $5\frac{2}{3}$ is a mixed number.

Decimals

The numbers 10, 100, 1,000, 10,000, and so on, are called the *powers of 10.* Fractions like $\frac{7}{10}$, $\frac{59}{100}$, and $\frac{323}{1000}$, which have powers of 10 on the bottom, are called *decimal fractions* or *decimals.*

Decimals typically are written using a shorthand notation in which the number on the top of the fraction is written to the right of a dot, called a *decimal point.* The number on the bottom of the fraction is not written but is indicated in the following way: If the number to the right of the decimal point contains one digit, the number on the bottom of the fraction is 10, if the number to the right of the decimal point contains two digits, the number on the bottom of the fraction is 100, and so on. Therefore, $\frac{7}{10} = .7$, $\frac{59}{100} = .59$, and $\frac{323}{1000} = .323$. The decimal .7 is read "point seven" or "seven tenths." In the same way, .59 is read "point fifty-nine" or "fifty-nine hundredths."

> Write the following fractions using decimal notation: $\frac{3}{10}$, $\frac{157}{1000}$, and $\frac{7}{100}$.

$$\frac{3}{10} = .3,\ \frac{157}{1000} = .157, \text{ and } \frac{7}{100} = .07$$

Note that in the last example, a 0 must be placed between the decimal point and the 7 to indicate that the number on the bottom is 100.

> Write the following decimals as fractions: .7, .143, and .079.

$$.7 = \frac{7}{10},\ .143 = \frac{143}{1000}, \text{ and } \frac{79}{1000}$$

A number that consists of a whole number and a decimal is called a *mixed decimal.* The number 354.56, for example, represents the mixed number $354\frac{56}{100}$.

> Write the following mixed numbers as mixed decimals: 76.3, 965.053.

$$76.3 = 76^3/_{10}, \ 965.053 = 965^{53}/_{100}$$

Percents

A *percent* is a fraction whose bottom number is 100. Percents (the word percent means *per hundred*) often are written using a special symbol: %. For example, $^{67}/_{100}$ can be written as 67%, and $^3/_{100}$ can be written as 3%. Note that, just as every percent can be written as a fraction, every percent can also be written as a decimal. For example, $51\% = {^{51}/_{100}} = .51$ and $7\% = {^7/_{100}} = .07$.

A quick way to rewrite a percent as a decimal is to move the decimal point two places to the left and drop the percent sign. Thus, 35% = .35. In a similar way, to write a decimal as a percent, move the decimal point two places to the right and put in a percent sign. Thus, .23 = 23%.

> Write the following decimals as percents: .23, .08, and 1.23.

$$.23 = 23\%, \ .08 = 8\%, \text{ and } 1.23 = 123\%$$

> Write the following percents as decimals: 17%, 2%, and 224%.

$$17\% = 17, \ 2\% = .02, \text{ and } 224\% = 2.24$$

Arithmetic Operations

Addition, subtraction, multiplication, and division are called the *fundamental operations of arithmetic*. To solve the word problems that are asked on the "Arithmetic Reasoning" section of the AFOQT test, you need to be able to add, subtract, multiply, and divide whole numbers and decimals. In this section, the techniques of doing this are reviewed.

Addition of Whole Numbers

When numbers are added, the result is called the *sum*. The first step in adding whole numbers is to line them up, placing ones under ones, tens under tens, hundreds under hundreds, and so on. Then, add each column of numbers, beginning with the ones and moving to the tens, hundreds, thousands, and so on. If the sum of the digits in any column is 10 or more, write down the last figure of the sum as a part of the answer, and then carry the other figures into the next column.

For example, suppose that you are asked to add 37, 64, and 151. Begin by lining up the numbers in columns as shown:

$$\begin{array}{r} 37 \\ 64 \\ +151 \\ \hline \end{array}$$

Now, add the digits in the units column: 7 + 4 + 1 = 12. Because this number is more than 10, write the 2 below the units column in the answer and carry the one over to the tens column.

$$\begin{array}{r} {}^1 \\ 37 \\ 64 \\ +151 \\ \hline 2 \end{array}$$

Now, add the 1 (that you carried over) to the other digits in the tens column: $1 + 3 + 6 + 5 = 15$. Put the 5 below the tens column and carry the remaining 1 to the hundreds column:

$$
\begin{array}{r}
{}^{1\ 1}37 \\
64 \\
+151 \\
\hline
52
\end{array}
$$

Because $1 + 1 = 2$, the final answer would be 252:

$$
\begin{array}{r}
{}^{1\ 1}37 \\
64 \\
+151 \\
\hline
252
\end{array}
$$

Add 235, 654, and 12.

$$
\begin{array}{r}
235 \\
654 \\
+\ 12 \\
\hline
901
\end{array}
$$

Addition of Decimals

Adding decimal numbers is also very straightforward. Line up the decimal points of the numbers involved and add as you normally would. Suppose, for example, that you want to add 23.31, 19, and 3.125. Begin by writing the numbers in a column, lining up the decimal points:

$$
\begin{array}{r}
23.31 \\
19. \\
+\ 3.125
\end{array}
$$

Note that the number 19 is a whole number, and, as such, the decimal point is to the right of the number; that is, 19 and 19.0 mean the same thing. If it helps you when you add these numbers, you can fill in the missing spaces to the right of the decimal points with zeros:

$$
\begin{array}{r}
23.310 \\
19.000 \\
+\ 3.125
\end{array}
$$

Now, position a decimal point in the answer directly below the decimal points of the numbers in the problem:

$$
\begin{array}{r}
23.310 \\
19.000 \\
+\ 3.125 \\
\hline
.
\end{array}
$$

Finish by adding as described previously:

$$
\begin{array}{r}
23.310 \\
19.000 \\
+\ 3.125 \\
\hline
45.435
\end{array}
$$

Some problems on the test ask you to add money. Of course, to add money, just line up the decimal points, as shown previously, and add the money. For example, expenses of $32.25, $52.35, and $97.16 would lead to a total expense of

$$
\begin{array}{r}
\$23.25 \\
\$52.35 \\
+\$97.16 \\
\hline
\$172.76
\end{array}
$$

Add 23.56, 876.01, 34, and .007.

$$
\begin{array}{r}
23.56 \\
876.01 \\
34 \\
+\quad .007
\end{array}
$$

If you like, before doing the addition, you can put in some zeros so that all the numbers have the same number of digits:

$$
\begin{array}{r}
23.560 \\
876.010 \\
34.000 \\
+\quad .007 \\
\hline
933.577
\end{array}
$$

If Brian buys three items priced at $3.45, $65.21, and $143.50, how much has he spent?

To find the answer to this problem, you need to add the three amounts spent:

$$
\begin{array}{r}
\$\ 3.45 \\
\$\ 65.21 \\
+\$143.50 \\
\hline
\$212.16
\end{array}
$$

Subtraction of Whole Numbers

When two numbers are subtracted, the result is called the *difference*. The first step in subtracting two whole numbers is to line them up, placing ones under ones, tens under tens, hundreds under hundreds, and so on. Then, subtract each column of numbers, beginning with the ones and moving to the tens, hundreds, thousands, and so on. If, in any step, the digit on the top is smaller than the digit on the bottom, add 10 to the digit on top by borrowing 1 from the figure directly to the left. If the sum of the digits in any column is 10 or more, write down the last figure of the sum as part of the answer and then carry the other figures into the next column.

Take the following problem as an example:

$$
\begin{array}{r}
567 \\
-382
\end{array}
$$

The first step is, of course, to subtract 2 from 7. Because 7 is bigger than 2, no borrowing is necessary, so this step is easy:

$$
\begin{array}{r}
567 \\
-382 \\
\hline
5
\end{array}
$$

Now, you need to subtract the numbers in the tens column. Note that 6 is smaller than 8, so you need to borrow 1 from the 5 to the left of the 6. This makes the 6 into 16, and, by borrowing the 1 from the 5, it becomes 4, as shown:

$$\begin{array}{r} \overset{4}{\cancel{5}}67 \\ -382 \\ \hline 5 \end{array}$$

Next, you can subtract the 8 from the 16, which leaves 8. Finally, in the hundreds column, subtracting the 3 from the 4 leaves us with 1:

$$\begin{array}{r} \overset{4}{\cancel{5}}67 \\ -382 \\ \hline 185 \end{array}$$

Remember that if you would like to check the answer to a subtraction problem, you can add the difference (that is, the answer) to the number you are subtracting and see whether you get the number from which you subtracted. Because 185 + 382 = 567, you know that you have the correct answer.

Subtract 534 from 893.

$$\begin{array}{r} 8\overset{8}{\cancel{9}}3 \\ -534 \\ \hline 359 \end{array}$$

Subtraction of Decimals

Just as with addition of decimals, begin by lining up the decimal points of the two numbers involved. Then, place a decimal point for the answer directly below the decimal points of the two numbers. For example:

$$\begin{array}{r} 265.01 \\ -127.5 \\ \hline \end{array}$$

When performing a subtraction, it certainly helps to write in extra 0s so that both numbers have the same number of digits to the right of the decimal point.

$$\begin{array}{r} 265.01 \\ -127.50 \\ \hline 137.51 \end{array}$$

Of course, to subtract monetary amounts, line up the decimal points and subtract as usual. For example:

$$\begin{array}{r} \$324.56 \\ -\ \$34.07 \\ \hline \$290.49 \end{array}$$

Jimmy pays a $14.51 dinner charge with a $20 bill. How much change does he receive?

Simply subtract $14.51 from $20.

$$\begin{array}{r} \$20.00 \\ -\$14.51 \\ \hline \$5.49 \end{array}$$

Multiplication of Whole Numbers

When two numbers are multiplied, the result is called the *product*. The first step in multiplying whole numbers is to line the number up, placing ones under ones, tens under tens, hundreds under hundreds, and so on. Now, consider two possible cases:

Case 1. If the number on the bottom of your multiplication contains a single digit, multiply every digit in the number on top by this digit. Start on the right, and move to the left. If, at any time, the result of a multiplication is a number that contains more than one digit, write down the ones digit of the number and carry the tens digit over to the next column, to be added to the result of the multiplication in that column.

For example, suppose that you need to multiply 542 by 3. Write the problem down as shown:

$$
\begin{array}{r}
542 \\
\times\ \ \ 3 \\
\hline
\end{array}
$$

Begin by multiplying 3 by 2 and write the result, which is 6, below the 3:

$$
\begin{array}{r}
542 \\
\times\ \ \ 3 \\
\hline
6 \\
\end{array}
$$

Next, multiply the 3 on the bottom by the 4 on the top. The result is 12. Write the ones digit from the 12 below the 4 in the problem and carry the tens digit, which is 1, over to the next column:

$$
\begin{array}{r}
\overset{1}{5}42 \\
\times\ \ \ 3 \\
\hline
26 \\
\end{array}
$$

Finally, multiply the 3 by the 5. The result of 15 should be added to the 1 that was carried from the previous column:

$$
\begin{array}{r}
\overset{1}{5}42 \\
\times\ \ \ 3 \\
\hline
1,626 \\
\end{array}
$$

Case 2: If the number on the bottom contains more than one digit, begin as you did previously and multiply every digit on the top by the ones digit of the number on the bottom. Write the result in the usual spot. Then move over to the tens digit of the number on the bottom and multiply each number on the top by this number. Write the result below your previous result, but position the ones digit of the result below the number by which you are multiplying. Continue on to the hundreds digit, multiplying as usual, but position the ones digit of the result below the hundreds digit of the number on the bottom. Continue until you have multiplied the number on top by every digit on the bottom. Finish by adding together all the "partial products" you have written.

The following example illustrates the process discussed previously. To multiply 542 by 63, set up the problem as shown:

$$
\begin{array}{r}
542 \\
\times\ 63 \\
\hline
\end{array}
$$

Begin exactly as you did in the preceding example, multiplying the 542 by 3. After doing this, you should have written

$$
\begin{array}{r}
542 \\
\times\ \ 63 \\
\hline
1,626 \\
\end{array}
$$

Now, multiply the 542 by the 6 in the tens digit of the number on the bottom. Note that the result of this multiplication is 3,252. Also note how this number is positioned:

$$
\begin{array}{r}
542 \\
\times\ 63 \\
\hline
1626 \\
3252 \\
\hline
\end{array}
$$

Be very careful when multiplying to line up the numbers correctly. As the last step, add the 1,626 to the 3,252, as shown:

$$
\begin{array}{r}
542 \\
\times\ 63 \\
\hline
1626 \\
3252 \\
\hline
34{,}146
\end{array}
$$

Multiply 234 by 16.

$$
\begin{array}{r}
234 \\
\times\ 16 \\
\hline
1404 \\
234 \\
\hline
3{,}744
\end{array}
$$

Multiplication of Decimals

When we discussed addition and subtraction with decimals, we saw that the very first step in finding the answer is to correctly position the decimal point of the answer. When multiplying numbers with decimals, the procedure is almost exactly the opposite. Begin by ignoring the decimal points in the numbers you are multiplying and figure out the answer as if the numbers involved were whole numbers. After you have done this, you can figure out where the decimal point in the answer goes.

To figure out where the decimal point in the answer goes, you need to do a little bit of counting. Begin by counting the total number of digits to the right of the decimal points in the two numbers you were multiplying. However many digits you count when you do this should also be the number of digits to the right of the decimal point in the answer.

A few examples make this procedure very clear. You previously solved the problem:

$$
\begin{array}{r}
542 \\
\times\ 63 \\
\hline
1626 \\
3252 \\
\hline
34{,}146
\end{array}
$$

Now, suppose that instead the problem had been:

$$
\begin{array}{r}
5.42 \\
\times\ 6.3 \\
\end{array}
$$

Note that the number on the top contains two digits to the right of the decimal point and that the number on the bottom contains one digit to the right of the decimal point. To start, multiply as you normally would, ignoring the decimal points:

$$
\begin{array}{r}
5.42 \\
\times\ \ 6.3 \\
\hline
1626 \\
3252 \\
\hline
34146
\end{array}
$$

5.42 Two digits to the right of the decimal point
× 6.3 One digit to the right of the decimal point
34146 Decimal point needs to be positioned

Now, because you have a total of 2 + 1 = 3 digits to the right of the decimal point in the two numbers you are multiplying, you need to have three digits to the right of the decimal point in the product:

$$
\begin{array}{r}
5.42 \\
\times\ \ 6.3 \\
\hline
1626 \\
3252 \\
\hline
34.146
\end{array}
$$

5.42 Two digits to the right of the decimal point
× 6.3 One digit to the right of the decimal point
34.146 Three digits to the right of the decimal point in the answer

That's all there is to it! What if the problem had been instead:

$$
\begin{array}{r}
5.42 \\
\times\ \ .63
\end{array}
$$

In this case, you have a total of four digits to the right of the decimal point in the two numbers you are multiplying. Thus, the answer is not 34.146, but rather 3.4146.

Note that if you are multiplying an amount of money by a whole number, you can use the preceding process. Of course, when you do this, you have a total of two digits to the right of the decimal point in the two numbers you are multiplying, so the answer ends up looking like money—that is, it has two digits to the right of the decimal point.

Multiply 23.4 by 1.6.

$$
\begin{array}{r}
23.4 \\
\times 1.6 \\
\hline
1404 \\
+234 \\
\hline
37.44
\end{array}
$$

23.4 One digit to the right of the decimal point
×1.6 One digit to the right of the decimal point
37.44 Two digits to the right of the decimal point in the answer

> John buys four calculators, each of which costs $3.51. What is the total cost of the four calculators?

$$
\begin{array}{r}
\$3.51 \\
\times\ \ \ \ 4 \\
\hline
\$14.04
\end{array}
$$

$3.51 Two digits to the right of the decimal point
× 4 No digit to the right of the decimal point
$14.04 Two digits to the right of the decimal point in the answer

Division of Whole Numbers

When one number is divided into another, the result is called the *quotient*. Division is probably the most complicated of the four fundamental arithmetic operations, but it becomes easier when you realize that the procedure for division consists of a series of four steps, repeated over and over. The four steps are illustrated in the following sample problems.

Suppose, for example, that you are asked to divide 7 into 245. Begin by writing the problem in the usual way:

$$7\overline{)245}$$

Now, for the first step, determine the number of times that 7 goes into 24. Because 7 goes into 24 three times (with something left over), begin by writing a 3 above the 4 in the division:

$$7\overline{)245}^{\,3}$$

As a second step, multiply the 3 by the 7 to obtain 21 and write this product below the 24:

$$\begin{array}{r} 3 \\ 7\overline{)245} \\ 21 \end{array}$$

The third step is to subtract the 21 from the 24. When you do this, you get 3, of course. This should be written below the 21, as shown:

$$\begin{array}{r} 3 \\ 7\overline{)245} \\ -21 \\ \hline 3 \end{array}$$

The final step in the four-step process is to "bring down" the next digit from the number into which you are dividing. This next (and last) digit is 5, so bring it down next to the 3:

$$\begin{array}{r} 3 \\ 7\overline{)245} \\ -21 \\ \hline 35 \end{array}$$

Now, the entire procedure starts over again. Divide 7 into 35. It goes in 5 times, so put a 5 next to the 3 in the solution.

$$\begin{array}{r} 35 \\ 7\overline{)245} \\ -21 \\ \hline 35 \end{array}$$

When you multiply and subtract, note that you end up with 0. This means that you have finished, and the quotient (answer) is 35:

$$\begin{array}{r} 35 \\ 7\overline{)245} \\ -21 \\ \hline 35 \\ -35 \\ \hline 0 \end{array}$$

The procedure for dividing by two-digit numbers (or even larger numbers) is essentially the same but involves a bit more computation. As an example, consider the following problem:

$$23\overline{)11408}$$

Note that 23 does not go into 11, so you have to start with 114. To determine how many times 23 goes into 114, you are going to have to estimate. Perhaps you might think that 23 is almost 25, and that it seems as if 25 would go into 114 four times. So, try 4. Write a 4 on top, and multiply, subtract, and bring down in the usual way:

$$
\begin{array}{r}
4 \\
23\overline{)11408} \\
-92 \\
\hline
220
\end{array}
$$

Continue, as before, by trying to estimate the number of times 23 goes into 220. If you try 9, things continue rather nicely:

$$
\begin{array}{r}
49 \\
23\overline{)11408} \\
-92 \\
\hline
220 \\
-207 \\
\hline
138
\end{array}
$$

As a final step, estimate that 23 goes into 138 six times:

$$
\begin{array}{r}
496 \\
23\overline{)11408} \\
-92 \\
\hline
220 \\
-207 \\
\hline
138 \\
-138 \\
\hline
0
\end{array}
$$

If at any step you make the incorrect estimate, modify your estimate and start over. For example, suppose that in the last step of the preceding example, you had guessed that 23 would go into 138 seven times. Look what would have happened:

$$
\begin{array}{r}
497 \\
23\overline{)11408} \\
-92 \\
\hline
220 \\
-207 \\
\hline
138 \\
-161
\end{array}
$$

Because 161 is larger than 138, it means that you have over estimated. Try again, with a smaller number.

Divide 12 into 540.

$$
\begin{array}{r}
45 \\
12\overline{)540} \\
-48 \\
\hline
60 \\
-60 \\
\hline
0
\end{array}
$$

Remember that division problems can always be checked by multiplying. In this case, because $12 \times 45 = 540$, you know that you have the right answer.

Division with Decimals

Recall that when you added and subtracted with decimals, you began by positioning the decimal point for the answer and then added or subtracted as usual. When you are dividing a whole number into a decimal number, the idea is similar; begin by putting a decimal point for the quotient (answer) directly above the decimal point in the number into which you are dividing. Then divide as normal. So, for example, if you need to divide 4 into 142.4, begin as shown:

$$4 \overline{)142.4}$$ *Note the decimal point positioned above the decimal point in* 142.4

Now, divide in the usual way:

```
        35.6
    4) 142.4
      −12
        22
       −20
         24
        −24
          0
```

That's all that there is to it.

A dinner bill of $92.80 is shared equally between four friends. How much does each friend pay?

To find the answer, you need to divide $92.80 by 4.

```
        23.20
    4) 92.80
      −8
       12
      −12
        08
       −8
        00
       −0
         0
```

Arithmetic Word Problems

The arithmetic sections of the AFOQT and ASTB might present word problems that involve arithmetic calculations. If you have learned how to do the computations discussed previously, the hardest part of these word problems is to determine which of the arithmetic operations is needed to solve the problem.

Basic One-Step and Two-Step Problems

Some of the word problems on the test involve only a single computation. Others are multiple-step problems in which several computations need to be performed. Examples of both types of problems are shown. Following these examples are some special types of problems that also appear on the test.

> Brett earned \$235.25 during his first week on a new job. During the second week, he earned \$325.50; during the third week he earned \$275.00; and during the fourth week he earned \$285.75. How much did he earn over the course of the four weeks?

It should be obvious that, in this problem, all you need to do is add the weekly payments to find the total.

$$\begin{array}{r} \$225.25 \\ \$325.50 \\ \$275.00 \\ \underline{\$285.75} \\ \$1,111.50 \end{array}$$

> An office building is 540 feet high, including a 23-foot antenna tower on the roof. How tall is the building without the antenna tower?

It should be clear that, in this problem, you need to remove the 23-foot tower from the top of the building by subtracting. This is a one-step problem:

$$\begin{array}{r} 540 \\ -23 \\ \hline 517\,\text{ft.} \end{array}$$

The building is 517 feet tall without the antenna tower.

> Brett has a job that pays him \$8.25 an hour. If during the first week he works 21 hours and during the second week he works 19 hours, how much money has he earned over the course of the two weeks?

This is an example of a two-step problem. One way to find the answer is to find how much he made each week by multiplying and then to add the two weekly totals:

$$\begin{array}{cc} \text{Week 1} & \text{Week 2} \\ \$8.25 & \$8.25 \\ \times21 & \times19 \\ \hline \$173.25 & \$156.75 \end{array}$$

Because \$173.25 + \$156.75 = \$330, Brett earned \$330.

Perhaps you have noticed an easier way to solve the problem. If you begin by adding the number of hours he worked each week, you get 19 + 21 = 40 as a total. Then, you need only to multiply \$8.25 by 40 to get the answer.

> At a restaurant, the bill for dinner is \$137.50. Bill contributes \$20 to the bill and then leaves. The rest of the bill is split evenly between the remaining five people. How much does each person contribute?

This is another two-step word problem. After Bill leaves, \$137.50 − \$20 = \$117.50 remains to be paid. This has to be divided by the five people that remain.

$$
\begin{array}{r}
23.50 \\
5 \overline{)117.50} \\
-10 \\
\hline
17 \\
-15 \\
\hline
25 \\
-25 \\
\hline
00 \\
-0 \\
\hline
0
\end{array}
$$

Clearly, each person needs to pay $23.50.

Percent and Interest Problems

These tests also contain some problems that involve working with percents and interest. Typically, these problems involve finding percents of numbers. You need to remember two things: First, the way to find a percent of a number is by multiplying, and second, before multiplying you should write the percent as a decimal.

Several examples of this type of problem follow.

> A family spends 26% of its monthly income on their mortgage. If their monthly income is $2,400, how much do they spend on their mortgage each month?

This problem asks us to find 26% of $2,400. To do this, write 26% as .26 and then multiply.

$$
\begin{array}{r}
\$2400 \\
\times .26 \\
\hline
14400 \\
+4800 \\
\hline
624.00
\end{array}
$$

$\times\ .26$ *Two digits to the right of the decimal point*

624.00 *Two digits to the right of the decimal point in the answer*

Thus, the monthly expenditure for the mortgage is $624.00.

> Bob invests $5,500 in an account that pays 9% annual interest. How much interest does he earn in one year?

This is another one-step percent word problem. For this problem, you need to find 9% of $5,500. Begin by writing 9% as a decimal, which is .09 (Note carefully that 9% is equal to .09, not .9.) Then multiply to finish the problem:

$$
\begin{array}{r}
\$5,500 \\
\times .09 \\
\hline
495.00
\end{array}
$$

$\times\ .09$ *Two digits to the right of the decimal point*

495.00 *Two digits to the right of the decimal point in the answer*

He earns $495 in interest in one year.

> Bob invests $5,500 in an account that pays 9% annual interest. How much money is in the account at the end of one year?

Note that this problem is based on the preceding one but includes an extra step. After determining how much interest is in the account at the end of the year, this amount needs to be added to the $5,500 to obtain $5,500 + $495 = $5,995.

Ratio and Proportion Problems

Another type of word problem that might appear on these tests involves ratios and proportions.

A ratio is a comparison of two numbers. For example, a school might say that its student-teacher ratio is eight to one. This means that, for every eight students at the school, there is one teacher. Another way to look at this ratio is that, for every one teacher, there are eight students.

You might have seen a ratio written with a colon between the two numbers, like 8:1. A ratio can also be written as a fraction, like $\frac{8}{1}$. When it comes to solving word problems involving ratios, it is usually best to write the ratios as fractions so that you can perform computations with them.

In the preceding ratio, you were comparing a number of people (students) to a number of people (teachers). When a ratio is used to compare two different kinds of quantities, it is called a *rate*. As an example, suppose that a car drives 300 miles in 5 hours. Then you can write the rate of the car as $\frac{300\,\text{miles}}{5\,\text{hours}}$. If you divide the number on the bottom into the number on the top, you get the number 60 and then can say that the rate of the car is $\frac{60\,\text{miles}}{1\,\text{hour}}$ or 60 miles per hour. Sixty miles per hour is also known as the speed of the car.

When you divide the number on the bottom of a ratio or a rate into the number on the top, the result is what is known as a *unit ratio* or a *unit rate*. Often, solving ratio problems hinges on computing a unit ratio or rate. The techniques of working with ratios and rates are illustrated in the following problems.

> A supermarket customer bought a 15-ounce box of oatmeal for $3.45. What was the cost per ounce of oatmeal?

The rate of cost to ounces is given in the problem as $\frac{\$3.45}{15\,\text{ounces}}$. To find the *unit cost,* divide $3.45 by 15 ounces.

$$
\begin{array}{r}
.23 \\
15\overline{)3.45} \\
-30 \\
\hline
45 \\
-45 \\
\hline
0
\end{array}
$$

Therefore, the cost is 23 cents per ounce.

> A supermarket sells a 15-ounce box of oatmeal for $3.45. At the same rate, what would be the cost of a 26-ounce box of oatmeal?

This type of problem is what is known as a proportion problem. In a proportion problem, you are given the rate at which two quantities vary and asked to find the value of one of the quantities given the value of the other. A good way to approach a problem of this type is by first finding the unit rate and then multiplying. Note that in the preceding problem we found the unit rate of the oatmeal; it was 23 cents per ounce. The cost of 26 ounces, then, is 23 cents times 26:

$$
\begin{array}{r}
.23 \\
\times\ 26 \\
\hline
138 \\
+\ 46 \\
\hline
5.98
\end{array}
$$

Thus, 26 ounces costs $5.98.

A bus travels at a constant rate of 45 miles per hour. How far can the bus go in 5½ hours?

Previously, you saw that the rate of a vehicle is equal to its distance divided by its time. In the same way, the distance that the vehicle travels is equal to its rate multiplied by its time. You might remember from previous math classes that this formula is written $d = r \times t$, meaning distance = rate × time.

It is easier to solve this problem if you write 5½ as its decimal equivalent 5.5. Then, you simply need to multiply 45 by 5.5 to find the distance:

$$\begin{array}{r} 45 \\ \times\ 5.5 \\ \hline 225 \\ +225 \\ \hline 247.5 \end{array}$$

Thus, the car goes 247.5 miles in 5½ hours.

Measurement Problems

Some of the problems on the exams involve working with measurements and geometric shapes. Two concepts that you should be familiar with are *perimeter* and *area*.

The perimeter of a figure is the distance around it—that is, the sum of the lengths of its sides. Perimeter is measured in units of length, such as inches, feet, or meters. The area of a figure is the amount of surface contained within its boundaries. Area is measured in square units, such as square inches, square feet, or square meters.

Two important geometric figures of which you should know how to find the perimeter and area are the rectangle and the square.

A rectangle is a figure with four sides. The opposite sides are the same length. For example, the following figure depicts a rectangle with a measurement of four inches by three inches:

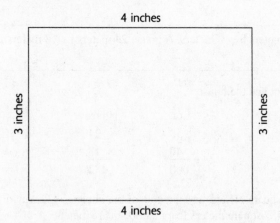

The perimeter of a rectangle is given by the formula $P = 2l + 2w$, which means that, to find the perimeter of a rectangle, you need to add together two lengths and two widths. If the rectangle is four inches by three inches, then its perimeter is $P = 3 + 3 + 4 + 4 = 18$ inches.

The area of a rectangle is given by the formula $A = l \times w$, which means that the area is the length times the width. In this case, the area would be 3 inches × 4 inches = 12 square inches. By the way, a square inch is simply a square that is an inch long on all 4 sides. If you look again at the preceding picture of the rectangle, you can see that it can be thought of as consisting of 12 squares that are each an inch on all sides. That is what is meant when we say that the area is 12 square inches.

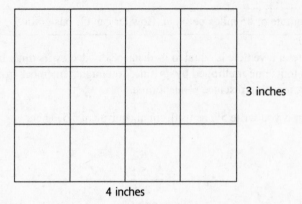

3 inches

4 inches

A square is a rectangle with 4 equal sides. In the case of a square, the formulas for the perimeter and the area of a rectangle take a simpler form. The perimeter of a square is $P = 4s$, where s is the length of the side, and the area is $A = s \times s$. For example, in the following figure, the perimeter of the rectangle is 20 feet because 4×5 feet = 20 feet. The area is 5 feet $\times$ 5 feet = 25 square feet.

It also helps to know some common measurement conversions, such as 12 inches are in a foot and 3 feet (or 36 inches) are in a yard.

The following examples are based on the concepts discussed previously.

> A small bag of fertilizer covers 20 square feet of lawn. How many bags are needed to cover a lawn that is 4 yards by 3 yards?

The most direct way to handle this problem is to change the measurements of the lawn to feet because that is how the capacity of the bag of fertilizer is measured. A lawn that is 4 yards by 3 yards is 12 feet by 9 feet. Thus, its area is 12 feet $\times$ 9 feet = 108 square feet. Now, to determine the number of bags needed, you need to divide 20 into 108. When you do this division, you get the answer 5.4 bags. Because you obviously cannot purchase 5.4 bags, you would need 6 bags to cover the lawn.

> A lot of land measures 50 meters by 40 meters. A house 24 meters by 18 meters is built on the land. How much area is left over?

Begin by finding the area of the lot and the house:

	Lot	House
	50	24
	$\times$ 40	$\times$ 18
	2000	432

Thus, the area of the lot is 2,000 square meters, and the area of the house is 432 square meters. To determine how much area is left, you need to subtract 432 square meters from 2,000 square meters:

$$2,000 - 432 = 1,568 \text{ square meters is left over.}$$

Mathematics Knowledge

Number Theory

Number theory involves the relationships and properties of numbers or integers—any of the natural numbers, the negatives of these numbers, or zero. In this section we will cover Factors, Prime Numbers, Multiples, Exponents, Square Roots, The Order of Operations, Operations with Integers, and Operations with Fractions.

Factors

Remember that earlier we defined *whole numbers* as the set of numbers 0, 1, 2, 3, 4, 5 and so on. Now, we are going to look at some of the properties of whole numbers and then of the set of numbers called the *integers*.

To begin, a *factor* of a given whole number is any number that can be used in a multiplication that results in the given whole number. For example, consider the whole number 24. Both 6 and 4 are factors of 24 because $6 \times 4 = 24$. Further, both 2 and 12 are factors of 24 because $2 \times 12 = 24$. Technically, both 1 and 24 are also factors of 24 because $1 \times 24 = 24$.

To determine whether a particular number is a factor of a given whole number, divide the number into the given whole number. If no remainder exists, the number is a factor.

> Is 8 a factor of 72?

To determine whether 8 is a factor of 72, divide 8 into 72. Because it goes in evenly (9 times), 8 is a factor of 72.

> If 13 is a factor of 91, determine another factor other than 1 and 91.

You know that 13 is a factor of 91, so you know that if you divide 13 into 91 it goes in evenly. If you do this division, you get:

$$13 \overline{)91} ^{7}$$

Thus, $13 \times 7 = 91$, so 7 is another factor of 91.

Common Factors

A number that is a factor of two different whole numbers is called a *common factor*, or a *common divisor*, of those numbers. As the following examples show, two given whole numbers might have no common factors (other than, of course, 1), or they might have one or more. If two numbers have several common factors, the largest one is called the *greatest common factor*.

> Find all the common factors and the greatest common factor of 36 and 48.

The factors of 36 are 1, 2, 3, 4, 6, 9, 12, 18, and 36.
The factors of 48 are 1, 2, 3, 4, 6, 8, 12, 16, 32, and 48.
The common factors of 36 and 48 are 1, 2, 3, 4, 6, and 12.
The greatest common factor is 12.

Find all the common factors of 35 and 66.

The factors of 35 are 1, 5, 7, and 35.
The factors of 66 are 1, 2, 3, 6, 11, 22, 33, and 66.
The only common factor is 1.

Prime Numbers

Obviously, every number has at least two factors: the number itself and 1. Some other numbers have additional factors as well. For example, the number 14 not only has 1 and 14 as factors, but also 2 and 7 because $2 \times 7 = 14$.

Numbers that have no additional factors other than themselves and 1 are known as *prime numbers*. An example of a prime number is 13. Although 1 and 13 divide evenly into 13, no other whole numbers divide evenly into 13.

By definition, the smallest prime number is 2. The first 10 prime numbers are:

2, 3, 5, 7, 11, 13, 17, 19, 23, 29

To determine whether a number is prime or not, you need to find out whether any whole numbers (other than the number itself and 1) divide evenly into the number.

> Which of the following numbers are prime: 33, 37, 39, 42, 43?

33 is not prime because $33 = 3 \times 11$.

37 is prime; it has no factors other than 1 and 37.

39 is not prime because $39 = 3 \times 13$.

42 is not prime because $42 = 2 \times 21$ or 6×7, and so on.

43 is prime; it has no factors other than 1 and 43.

A number that is not prime is called a *composite* number. Any composite number can be *prime factored;* that is, it can be written as a product of prime numbers (excluding 1) in one and only one way. For example, 35 is a composite number and can be prime factored as 5×7. The number 12 is also composite. Note that 2×6 is a factorization of 12, but is not the prime factorization because 6 is not prime. The prime factorization of 12 would be $2 \times 2 \times 3$. The quickest way to prime factor a number is to break the number up as a product of two smaller numbers and then to break these two numbers up, until you are left with only prime numbers. The following example illustrates this process.

> Prime factor the number 150.

By inspection, you can see that 150 can be factored as 15×10. This is not the prime factorization, however, as neither 15 nor 10 is prime. The number 15, however, can be further broken down as $15 = 3 \times 5$, and both 3 and 5 are prime. The number 10 can be further broken down as $10 = 2 \times 5$, and both 2 and 5 are prime. Therefore, the number 150 can be prime factored as $3 \times 5 \times 2 \times 5$. When prime factoring numbers, it is standard to rearrange the factors so that the numbers are in increasing order. Therefore, the prime factorization of 150 can best be expressed as $2 \times 3 \times 5 \times 5$.

> What are the prime factors of 54?

You can begin by writing 54 as, for example, 2×27. The number 2 is prime, but 27 is not, so it can be further factored. Because 27 is 3×9, you get $54 = 2 \times 3 \times 9$. Now, 3 is prime, but 9 is not, so we need to factor the 9. The only way to do this is $9 = 3 \times 3$, so the prime factorization of 54 is $2 \times 3 \times 3 \times 3$. Thus, the prime factors of 54 are 2 and 3.

Multiples

A multiple of a given whole number is a number that results from the multiplication of the given whole number by another whole number factor. For example, the multiples of 7 are 7, 14, 21, 28, 35, 42, 49, and so on because $7 = 7 \times 1$, $14 = 7 \times 2$, $21 = 7 \times 3$, and so on.

A *common multiple* of two numbers is a number that is a multiple of both of the numbers. For example, 32 is a common multiple of 8 and 16 because it is a multiple of both 8 and 16. Should you ever need to find a common multiple of two numbers, one quick way to find one is to multiply the two numbers together. For example, a common multiple of 4 and

10 would be $4 \times 10 = 40$. Note, however, that 40 is not the smallest common multiple of 4 and 10 because 20 is also a common multiple.

The smallest common multiple of two numbers is called the *least common multiple* (LCM). A quick way to find the LCM of two numbers is to write out the first several multiples of each number and then find the smallest multiple that they have in common. The following examples show how to do this.

Find the first 8 multiples of 11.

To answer this question, you need to compute 11×1, 11×2, 11×3, and so on. The first 8 multiples would be 11, 22, 33, 44, 55, 66, 77, and 88.

Find the least common multiple of 3 and 8.

The first several multiples of 3 are 3, 6, 9, 12, 15, 18, 21, 24, and 27.

The first several multiples of 8 are 8, 16, 24, and 32.

Clearly, the LCM is 24, which in this case is the same as the product of 3 and 8.

Find the LCM of 6 and 9.

The first several multiples of 6 are 6, 12, 18, 24, and 30.

The first several multiples of 9 are 9, 18, 27, and 36.

Clearly, the LCM is 18, which in this case is less than $6 \times 9 = 54$.

Exponents

As you saw previously, the numbers used in multiplication are called *factors*. Whenever the same factor is repeated more than once, a special shorthand, called *exponential notation,* can be used to simplify the expression. In this notation, the repeated factor is written only once; above and to the right of this number is written another number that is called the *exponent,* or *power,* indicating the number of times the base is repeated.

For example, instead of writing 7×7, you can write 7^2. This expression is read "seven to the second power," or more simply, "seven squared," and it represents the fact that the seven is multiplied by itself two times. In the same way, $5 \times 5 \times 5 \times 5$ can be written as 5^4, which is read "five to the fourth power," or simply "five to the fourth."

Recall that previously, you prime factored the number 150 and obtained $2 \times 3 \times 5 \times 5$. It is more common (and a bit simpler) to write this prime factorization using exponential notation as $2 \times 3 \times 5^2$.

What is the value of 3^5?

Based on the preceding definition, 3^5 represents $3 \times 3 \times 3 \times 3 \times 3 = 243$.

Simplify the expression $a \times a \times a \times a \times b \times b \times b \times b \times b \times b \times b$ by using exponential notation.

Because you have four factors of a and seven factors of b, the expression is equal to $a^4 \times b^7$.

Prime factor the number 72 and write the prime factorization using exponential notation.

Begin by prime factoring the number 72. One way to do this is as follows:

$72 = 2 \times 36 = 2 \times 6 \times 6 = 2 \times 2 \times 3 \times 2 \times 3 = 2 \times 2 \times 2 \times 3 \times 3$. Then, writing this using exponents, you get $2^3 \times 3^2$.

Square Roots

The *square root* of a given number is the number whose square is equal to the given number. For example, the square root of 25 is the number that yields 25 when multiplied by itself. Clearly, this number would be 5 because $5 \times 5 = 25$. The square root of 25 is denoted by the symbol $\sqrt{25}$.

The square roots of most numbers turn out to be messy, infinite nonrepeating decimal numbers. For example, $\sqrt{2}$ is equal to 1.414213562.... When such numbers appear on the test, you are able to leave them in what is known as *radical form*—that is, if the answer to a problem is $\sqrt{2}$, you can express the answer as $\sqrt{2}$, without worrying about its value.

Certain numbers, however, have nice whole-number square roots. Such numbers are called *perfect squares*. You should certainly be familiar with the square roots of the first 10 or so perfect squares. They are shown in the following table:

Perfect Square	Square Root
1	$\sqrt{1} = 1$
4	$\sqrt{4} = 2$
9	$\sqrt{9} = 3$
16	$\sqrt{16} = 4$
25	$\sqrt{25} = 5$
36	$\sqrt{36} = 6$
49	$\sqrt{49} = 7$
64	$\sqrt{64} = 8$
81	$\sqrt{81} = 9$
100	$\sqrt{100} = 10$

From time to time, you might be asked to find the *cube root* of a number. The cube root is defined in a way similar to that of the square root. For example, the cube root of eight is the number that when multiplied by itself three times, is equal to eight. Clearly, the cube root of eight would be two because $2 \times 2 \times 2 = 8$. A special notation also exists for the cube root. The cube root of eight is written as $\sqrt[3]{8}$. Therefore, $\sqrt[3]{8} = 2$.

Just as perfect squares have nice whole-number square roots, *perfect cubes* have whole-number cube roots. You don't really have to learn many of these, as they become large very quickly, but it is helpful to know the cube roots of the first five perfect cubes. The following table gives the values for these numbers.

Perfect Cube	Cube Root
1	$\sqrt[3]{1} = 1$
8	$\sqrt[3]{8} = 2$
27	$\sqrt[3]{27} = 3$
64	$\sqrt[3]{64} = 4$
125	$\sqrt[3]{125} = 5$

> What is the value of $\sqrt{81} \times \sqrt{36}$?

Because $\sqrt{81} = 9$ and $\sqrt{36} = 6$, $\sqrt{81} \times \sqrt{36} = 9 \times 6 = 54$.

> What is the value of $12\sqrt{49}$?

To begin, you must know that $12\sqrt{49}$ is shorthand for $12 \times \sqrt{49}$. Because $\sqrt{49} = 7$, $12\sqrt{49} = 12 \times 7 = 84$.

The Order of Operations

Whenever a numerical expression contains more than one mathematical operation, the order in which the operations are performed can affect the answer. For example, consider the simple expression $2 + 3 \times 5$. On one hand, if the multiplication is performed first, the expression becomes $2 + 15 = 17$. On the other hand, if the addition is performed first, the expression becomes $5 \times 5 = 25$. To eliminate this ambiguity, mathematicians have established a procedure that makes the order in which the operations need to be performed specific. This procedure is called the *Order of Operations*, and is stated here:

1. Perform all operations in parentheses or any other grouping symbol.
2. Evaluate all exponents and roots.
3. Perform all multiplications and divisions in the order they appear in the expression, from left to right.
4. Perform all additions and subtractions in the order they appear in the expression, from left to right.

Note that the Order of Operations consists of four steps. A common acronym to help you remember these steps is PEMDAS: parentheses, exponents, multiplication and division, addition and subtraction. If you choose to memorize this acronym, be careful. The expression PEMDAS might make it appear as if the Order of Operations has six steps, but it actually has only four. In the third step, all multiplications and divisions are done in the order they appear. In the fourth step, all additions and subtractions are done in the order they appear. The following examples make this clear.

> Evaluate the expression $18 - 6 \div 3 \times 7 + 4$.

Resist the temptation to begin by subtracting 6 from 18. Because this expression contains no parentheses and no roots, begin by starting on the left and performing all multiplications and divisions in the order they occur. This means that the division must be performed first. Because $6 \div 3 = 2$, you obtain:

$$18 - 6 \div 3 \times 7 + 4 = 18 - 2 \times 7 + 4$$

Next, do the multiplication:

$$18 - 2 \times 7 + 4 = 18 - 14 + 4$$

Finally, subtract and then add:

$$18 - 14 + 4 = 4 - 4 = 0$$

> Evaluate $14 - 2(1 + 5)$.

To begin, the operation in parentheses must be performed. This makes the expression $14 - 2(6)$. Now, remember that a number written next to another number in parentheses, such as $2(6)$, is a way of indicating multiplication. Because multiplication comes before subtraction in the Order of Operations, multiply $2(6)$ to get 12. Finally, $14 - 12 = 2$.

> Evaluate $5^3 - 3(8 - 2)^2$.

The first operation to perform is the one in parentheses, which gives us $5^3 - 3(6)^2$.

Next, evaluate the two exponents: $125 - 3(36)$. Now multiply and then finish by subtracting: $125 - 108 = 17$.

Operations with Integers

When you include the negatives of the whole numbers along with the whole numbers, you obtain the set of numbers called the *integers*. Therefore, the integers are the set of numbers:

. . . –4, –3, –2, –1, 0, 1, 2, 3, 4, . . .

The ellipses to the left and right indicate that the numbers continue forever in both directions.

Up to this point, when you have talked about adding, subtracting, multiplying, and dividing, you have always been working with positive numbers. However, on one of these tests, you are just as likely to have to compute with negative numbers as positive numbers. Therefore, take a look at how mathematical operations are performed on positive *and* negative numbers—that is, how mathematical operations are performed on *signed* numbers.

Adding Positive and Negative Numbers

Two different circumstances must be considered as you discuss how to add positive and negative numbers. The first circumstance is how to add two signed numbers with the same sign. If the numbers that you are adding have the same sign, add the numbers in the usual way. The sum, then, has the same sign as the numbers you have added. For example, $(+4) + (+7) = +11$. This, of course, is the usual positive number addition you are used to.

> Consider $(–5) + (–9) = –14$.

In this problem, because the signs of the two numbers you are adding are the same, simply add them $(5 + 9 = 14)$. The result is negative because both numbers are negative. It might help to think of positive numbers as representing a gain and negative numbers as representing a loss. In this case, $(–5) + (–9)$ represents a loss of 5 followed by a loss of 9, which, of course, is a loss of 14.

Now, what if you have to add two numbers with different signs? Again, the rule is simple. Begin by ignoring the signs and subtract the two numbers: the smaller from the larger. The sign of the answer is the same as the sign of the number with the larger size.

For example, to compute $(+9) + (–5)$, begin by computing $9 – 5 = 4$. Because 9 is bigger than 5, the answer is positive, or +4. You can think of the problem in this way: A gain of 9 followed by a loss of 5 is equivalent to a gain of 4.

On the other hand, to compute $(–9) + (+5)$, begin in the same way by computing $9 – 5 = 4$. This time, however, the larger number is negative, so the answer is –4. In other words, a loss of 9 followed by a gain of 5 is equivalent to a loss of 4.

> Consider $(+6) + (–8) + (+12) + (–4)$.

Two ways can be used to evaluate this expression. One way is to perform the additions in order from left to right. To begin, $(+6) + (–8) = –2$. Then, $(–2) + (+12) = +10$. Finally, $(+10) + (–4) = +6$.

The other way to solve the problem, which might be a bit faster, is to add the positive numbers, then add the negative numbers, and then combine the result. In this case, $(+6) + (+12) = +18$; $(–8) + (–4) = –12$, and finally, $(+18) + (–12) = +6$.

Subtracting Positive and Negative Numbers

The easiest way to perform a subtraction on two signed numbers is to change the problem to an equivalent addition problem, that is, an addition problem with the same answer. To do this, you need to change the sign of the second number and add instead of subtract. For example, suppose that you need to compute $(+7) – (–2)$. This problem has the same solution as the addition problem $(+7) + (+2)$ and is, therefore, equal to +9. Take a look at the following samples that help clarify this procedure:

> Determine the value of $(-7) - (+2)$.

To evaluate this, make it into an equivalent addition problem by changing the sign of the second number. Therefore, $(-7) - (+2) = (-7) + (-2) = -9$.

In the same way, you see that $(-7) - (-2) = (-7) + (+2) = -5$.

> Find the value of $(-7) - (+4) - (-3) + (-1)$.

Begin by rewriting the problem with all subtractions expressed as additions:

$$(-7) - (+4) - (-3) + (-1) = (-7) + (-4) + (+3) + (-1)$$

Now, just add the four numbers in the usual way:

$$(-7) + (-4) + (+3) + (-1) = (-11) + (+3) + (-1) = -8 + (-1) = -9.$$

Multiplying and Dividing Positive and Negative Numbers

An easy way to multiply (or divide) signed numbers is to begin by ignoring the signs and multiply (or divide) in the usual way. Then, to determine the sign of the answer, count up the number of negative signs in the original problem. If the number of negative signs is even, the answer is positive; if the number of negative signs is odd, the answer is negative. For example, $(-2) \times (+3) = -6$ because the original problem has one negative sign. However, $(-2) \times (-3) = +6$ because the original problem has two negative signs.

What about the problem $(-4) \times (-2) \times (-1) \times (+3)$? First of all, ignoring the signs and multiplying the four numbers, we get 24. Because the problem has a total of three negative signs, the answer must be negative. Therefore, the answer is -24.

Division works in exactly the same way. For example, $(-24) \div (+6) = -4$, but $(-24) \div (-6) = +4$.

> Find the value of $\dfrac{(-6)(+10)}{(-2)(-5)}$.

The easiest way to proceed with this problem is to evaluate the number on the top and the number on the bottom separately and then divide them. Because $(-6)(+10) = -60$, and $(-2)(-5) = +10$, you have $\dfrac{(-6)(+10)}{(-2)(-5)} = \dfrac{-60}{+10} = -6$.

> $(-5)(-2)(+4) - 6(-3) =$

The multiplications in this problem must be done before the subtractions. Because

$$(-5)(-2)(+4) = 40, \text{ and } 6(-3) = -18, \text{ we have:}$$

$$(-5)(-2)(+4) - 6(-3) = 40 - (-18) = 40 + 18 = 58.$$

Negative Numbers and Exponents

Be a little bit careful when evaluating negative numbers raised to powers. For example, if you are asked to find the value of $(-2)^8$, the answer is positive because you technically are multiplying eight -2s. For a similar reason, the value of $(-2)^9$ is negative.

Also, you must be careful to distinguish between an expression like $(-3)^2$ and one like -3^2. The expression $(-3)^2$ means -3×-3 and is equal to $+9$, but -3^2 means $-(3^2)$, which is equal to -9.

Evaluate $-2^4 - (-2)^2$.

Evaluating the exponents first, you get $-2^4 - (-2)^2 = -16 - (4) = -16 + -4 = -20$.

Find the value of $\dfrac{(-3)^3 + (-2)(-6)}{-5^2 + (-19)(-1)}$

Again, determine the values of the top and bottom separately and then divide. To begin, $(-3)^3 = -27$, and $(-2)(-6) = +12$, so the value on the top is $-27 + 12 = -15$. On the bottom, you have $-25 + 19 = -6$. Therefore,

$$\frac{(-3)^3 + (-2)(-6)}{-5^2 + (-19)(-1)} = \frac{-15}{-6} = \frac{15}{6} = 2.5$$

Operations with Fractions

In the "Arithmetic Reasoning" section, we discussed how to write a fraction as a decimal and vice versa. One thing that we did not discuss in that section was how to perform arithmetic operations on fractions. It is now time to review how to do this.

You probably remember learning a procedure called *reducing* or *simplifying* fractions. Simplifying a fraction refers to rewriting it in an equivalent form, with smaller numbers. As an easy example, consider the fraction $\frac{5}{10}$. This fraction can be simplified by dividing the top and bottom by the number 5. If you do this division, you get $\frac{5}{10} = \frac{5 \div 5}{10 \div 5} = \frac{1}{2}$. Thus, $\frac{5}{10}$ and $\frac{1}{2}$ have the same value, but $\frac{1}{2}$ is in simpler form.

In general, to simplify a fraction, you need to find a number that divides evenly into both the top and bottom and then do this division. Sometimes, after you divide by one number, you might notice another number by which you can further divide. As an example, suppose that you want to simplify $\frac{12}{18}$. The first thing that you might notice is that the top and bottom can be divided by 2. If you do this division, you get the fraction $\frac{6}{9}$. Now, this fraction can be further divided by 3, and if you do this division, you get the fraction $\frac{2}{3}$. Because no other numbers (except 1, of course) can divide evenly into the top and bottom, you have reduced the fraction to its *lowest terms*. If a problem on one of the tests has a fractional answer, you should always reduce the answer to its lowest terms.

Just as you can reduce a fraction to lower terms by dividing the top and bottom by the same number, you can raise a fraction to *higher terms* by multiplying the top and bottom by the same number. For example, consider the fraction $\frac{3}{4}$. If you multiply the top and bottom by 2, you get $\frac{6}{8}$. If you instead multiply the top and bottom by 5, you get $\frac{15}{20}$. The fractions $\frac{6}{8}$ and $\frac{15}{20}$ are two different ways to write $\frac{3}{4}$ in higher terms. As you see in the next section, it is often necessary to raise fractions to higher terms to add and subtract them.

Express the fraction $\frac{12}{15}$ in lowest terms.

It is easy to see that the number 3 can be divided evenly into both the numerator and the denominator. Performing this division, you get $\frac{12}{15} = \frac{12 \div 3}{15 \div 3} = \frac{4}{5}$, which is in lowest terms.

Rewrite the fraction $\frac{2}{3}$ as an equivalent fraction with a denominator of 21.

To change the denominator of 3 to 21, you need to multiply by 7. Because you need to perform the same operation to the numerator as well, you would get $\frac{2}{3} = \frac{2 \times 7}{3 \times 7} = \frac{14}{21}$.

Adding and Subtracting Fractions

You probably recall that the number on the top of a fraction is called the *numerator,* and the number on the bottom of a fraction is called the *denominator.* If two fractions have the same denominator, they are said to have *common denominators.*

Adding or subtracting two fractions with common denominators is easy. Simply add the numerators and retain the common denominator. For example,

$$\frac{2}{9} + \frac{5}{9} = \frac{7}{9}$$

$$\frac{7}{8} - \frac{5}{8} = \frac{2}{8} = \frac{1}{4}$$

Note that, in the subtraction problem, you get a fraction that can be simplified, and you perform the simplification before finishing.

If you need to add or subtract two fractions that do not have the same denominator, you need to begin by raising them to higher terms so that they do have a common denominator. The first step in this process is determining a common denominator for the two fractions. For example, suppose that you are asked to add $\frac{3}{4} + \frac{1}{3}$. You need to find a common denominator for 4 and 3. Actually, an infinite number of common denominators exist for 4 and 3. Some of them would be 24, 36, and 48. Although you can work with any of these denominators, it is easiest to work with the smallest one, which in this case is 12. This number is called the *least common denominator* of 4 and 3, and it is actually the same number as the least common multiple (LCM), which has already been discussed. Thus, the least common denominator can be found by using the same process you used to find the LCM previously.

When you know the least common denominator (LCD), you need to multiply the top and bottom of each fraction by the appropriate number to raise the denominators to the LCD. For example,

$$\frac{3}{4} + \frac{1}{3} = \frac{3}{3} \times \frac{3}{4} + \frac{4}{4} \times \frac{1}{3} = \frac{9}{12} + \frac{4}{12} = \frac{13}{12}$$

Note that the answer, $\frac{13}{12}$, is an improper fraction. Any improper fraction can also be written as a mixed number by dividing the denominator into the numerator and writing the remainder as the numerator of a fraction with the original denominator. In this case, 12 goes into 13 one time with a remainder of one, so $\frac{13}{12} = 1\frac{1}{12}$, which is another way to write the answer to the question.

Note that this process can also be reversed. So, for example, the mixed number $2\frac{1}{5}$ can be written as an improper fraction. The denominator is the same, that is, 5, and the numerator is the denominator times the whole number plus the numerator; that is, $5 \times 2 + 1 = 11$. Therefore, $2\frac{1}{5} = \frac{11}{5}$. Often, when performing operations on mixed numbers, it is helpful to write them as improper fractions. The upcoming examples illustrate this.

Add $2\frac{3}{5} + 3\frac{1}{7}$.

You can proceed in two ways. You can write both mixed numbers as improper fractions and add, but it is quicker to just add the whole number part, $(2 + 3 = 5)$, and the fractional part, $\frac{3}{5} + \frac{1}{7} = \frac{21}{35} + \frac{5}{35} = \frac{26}{35}$. The answer, then, is $5\frac{26}{35}$.

> Find the value of $\frac{3}{7} - \frac{1}{2}$.

The LCD is 14. Thus, $\frac{3}{7} - \frac{1}{2} = \frac{6}{14} - \frac{7}{14} = \frac{-1}{14}$.

Multiplying and Dividing Fractions

Multiplying fractions is actually a bit easier than adding or subtracting them. When multiplying, you don't need to worry about common denominators: Just multiply the numerators, then multiply the denominators, and then simplify if possible. For example, $\frac{2}{3} \times \frac{4}{5} = \frac{2 \times 4}{3 \times 5} = \frac{8}{15}$. That's all you need to do!

To understand the procedure for dividing fractions, you first need to understand a term. The *reciprocal* of a number is the number that is obtained by switching the numerator and the denominator of the number. For example, the reciprocal of $\frac{3}{8}$ is $\frac{8}{3}$. To find the reciprocal of a whole number, such as 7, visualize the 7 as the fraction $\frac{7}{1}$. The reciprocal, then, is $\frac{1}{7}$.

Now, the easiest way to divide two fractions is to change the division to a multiplication with the same answer. In fact, if you change the second fraction to its reciprocal and multiply, you get the correct answer! For example, $\frac{4}{5} \div \frac{3}{4} = \frac{4}{5} \times \frac{4}{3} = \frac{16}{15} = 1\frac{1}{15}$.

> What is the value of $2\frac{2}{3} \times 1\frac{4}{5}$?

Before you can multiply these mixed numbers, you need to write them as improper fractions:

$$2\frac{2}{3} \times 1\frac{4}{5} = \frac{8}{3} \times \frac{9}{5} = \frac{72}{15} = 4\frac{12}{15} = 4\frac{4}{5}$$

> Evaluate $2\frac{2}{5} \div 6$

Begin by writing the problem as $\frac{12}{5} \div \frac{6}{1}$. Then,

$$\frac{12}{5} \div \frac{6}{1} = \frac{12}{5} \times \frac{1}{6} = \frac{12}{30} = \frac{2}{5}$$

Algebraic Operations and Equations

In this section we will cover the basics of algebra, including Numerical Evaluation, Solving Equations, Solving Word Problems, Multiplication with Exponents, Factoring, and Simplifying Algebraic Expressions.

Numerical Evaluation

Algebra is a generalization of arithmetic. In arithmetic, you learned how to perform mathematical operations (such as addition, subtraction, multiplication, and division) on different types of numbers, such as whole numbers, decimals, percents, and fractions. Algebra extends these concepts by considering how to perform mathematical operations on symbols standing for numbers and how to use these techniques to solve a variety of practical word problems.

In algebra, you refer to numbers that have a definite value as *constants*. For example, the numbers 17, -3, $\frac{2}{3}$, $\sqrt{41}$, 5.123, and 12% are constants. Symbols standing for numbers are called *variables* because, until you specify further, they can take on any value. For example, in the expression $3x + 13y + 29$, the numbers 3, 13, and 29 are constants, and the symbols x and y are variables. As the following examples show, when you are given the values of all variables in an expression, you can find the value of the expression.

> If $a = 4$ and $b = -3$, find the value of the expression $a^3 - b$.

When evaluating numerical expressions, it is crucial to remember the Order of Operations and to pay careful attention to plus and minus signs. Begin by substituting the values of a and b in the given expression and then carefully evaluate as in the previous section:

$$a^3 - b = (4)^3 - (-3) = 64 + 3 = 67$$

> If $x = 3$, and $y = 2$, find the value of $\frac{24 - 2x}{-6y}$.

$$\frac{24 - 2x}{6y} = \frac{24 - 2(3)}{-6(2)} = \frac{24 - 6}{-12} = \frac{18}{-12} = -\frac{3}{2}$$

> The formula for the perimeter of a rectangle is $P = 2l + 2w$, where l represents the length of the rectangle and w represents the width. What is the perimeter of a rectangle with length 21 and width 15?

$$P = 2l + 2w = 2(21) + 2(15) = 42 + 30 = 72$$

Solving Equations

An *equation* is a mathematical expression that contains an equal sign. For example, $10 = 4 + 6$ is an equation and is always true. Alternately, $10 = 5 + 4$ is also an equation, but it is always false.

An equation that contains a variable, such as $2x + 1 = 7$, might or might not be true depending on the value of x. *Solving an equation* refers to finding the value of the unknown that makes both sides of the equation equal. Note that the number three makes both sides of the equation equal. Therefore, you say that three *solves* the equation, or that three is the *solution* of the equation.

Some equations, like the preceding one, are easy to solve by just looking at them. Others are so complicated that you need an organized series of steps to solve them. In this section, we examine how to do this.

The principal for solving equations is, essentially, to rewrite the equation in simpler and simpler forms (without, of course, changing the solution), until the solution becomes obvious. The simplest equation of all, of course, would be an equation of the form $x = a$, where x is the variable and a is some number. Whenever you are given an equation that is more complicated than $x = a$, the idea is to change the equation so that it eventually looks like $x = a$, and you can read the answer right off.

Now, what can you do to change an equation? The answer is simple: almost anything you want as long as you do the same thing to both sides. To start, you can add or subtract the same number to or from both sides, multiply both sides by the same number, or divide both sides by the same number (as long as that number isn't zero). The following examples demonstrate this procedure with some very simple equations; after this, you will look at some more complicated ones.

> Solve for x in the equation $x + 7 = 20$.

Even though you can easily solve this equation in your head, pay attention to the procedure, as it will help you when we get to more complicated equations. Remember that the easiest possible type of equation is one of the form $x = a$. The equation that you have isn't quite like that; it has a $+7$ on the left side that you would like to get rid of. Now, how can you get rid of an addition of 7? Easy; you just subtract 7 from both sides:

$$
\begin{aligned}
x + 7 &= 20 \\
-7 &= -7 \\
\hline
x &= 13
\end{aligned}
$$

So, the solution to this equation is $x = 13$.

> Solve for y in the equation $9y = 72$.

In this equation, you have a 9 multiplying the y that you would like to get rid of. Now, how can you undo a multiplication by 9? Clearly, you need to divide both sides by 9:

$$\frac{9y}{9} = \frac{72}{9}$$

$y = 8$ is the solution.

The equations in the two preceding examples are called one-step equations because they can be solved in one step. Some examples of equations that require more than one step to solve follow. The procedure is the same; keep doing the same thing to both sides of the equation until it looks like $x = a$.

> Solve for t in the equation $4t - 3 = 9$.

In this equation, you have a few things on the left hand side that you would like to get rid of. First of all, undo the subtraction of 3 by adding 3 to both sides.

$$\begin{array}{rcr} 4t - 3 & = & 9 \\ +3 & = & +3 \\ \hline 4t & & 12 \end{array}$$

Now, you need to undo the multiplication by four, which can be done by dividing both sides by 4:

$$\frac{4t}{4} = \frac{12}{4}$$
$$t = 3$$

Note that you can check your answer to any equation by substituting the answer back into the equation and making certain that both sides are equal. For example, you know that you did the preceding problem correctly because

$$4(3) - 3 = 9$$
$$12 - 3 = 9$$
$$9 = 9$$

> Solve for p in the equation $15p = 3p + 24$.

This problem puts you in a situation that you have yet to encounter. The variable p appears on both sides of the equation, but you only want it on one side. To get this into the desired form, subtract $3p$ from both sides:

$$\begin{array}{rcr} 15p = & 3p + 24 \\ -3p & -3p \\ \hline 12p & & 24 \end{array}$$

Now, you have an equation that looks a bit better. It is easy to see that if you divide both sides by 12, you end up with the answer $p = 2$.

A few more examples for you to practice will follow. Before we get to them, it will be helpful if you refamiliarize yourself with a very important mathematical property called the *Distributive Property*.

Consider, for example, the expression $7(2 + 3)$. According to the Order of Operations, you should do the work in parentheses first, and, therefore, $7(2 + 3) = 7(5) = 35$. However, note that you get the same answer if you "distribute" the 7 to the 2 and the 3 and add afterward:

$$7(2 + 3) = 7(2) + 7(3) = 14 + 21 = 35$$

The Distributive Property tells you that you can always use this distribution as a way of evaluating an expression. Algebraically, the Distributive Property tells you that $a(b + c) = ab + ac$. The following examples incorporate the Distributive Property into the solving of equations.

Solve for c: $3(c - 5) = 9$.

Before you can get the c by itself on the left, you need to get it out of the parentheses, so distribute:

$$3c - 15 = 9$$

The rest is similar to what you have already done. Add 15 to both sides to get:

$$3c = 24$$

Now divide by 3 to get:

$$c = 8$$

Solve for q: $5q - 64 = -2(3q - 1)$.

As in the preceding example, you must begin by eliminating the parentheses, using the Distributive Property:

$$5q - 64 = -6q + 2$$

Now, add $6q$ to both sides:

$$11q - 64 = +2$$

Next, add 64 to both sides:

$$11q = 66.$$

Finally, dividing both sides by 11 gives you the answer: $q = 6$.

Solving Word Problems

Many problems that deal with practical applications of mathematics are expressed in words. To solve such problems, it is necessary to translate the words into an equation that can then be solved. The following table lists some common words and the mathematical symbols that they represent:

Words	Mathematical Representation
a equals 9, a is 9, a is the same as 9	$a = 9$
a plus 9, the sum of a and 9, a added to 9, a increased by 9, a more than 9	$a + 9$
9 less than a, a minus 9, a decreased by 9, the difference of a and 9, a less 9	$a - 9$
9 times a, the product of 9 and a, 9 multiplied by a	$9a$ (or $9 \times a$)
The quotient of a and 9, a divided by 9, 9 divided into a	$\frac{a}{9}$
1/2 of a 50% of a	$\frac{1}{2} \times a$ $50\% \times a$

Now, when you are given a word problem to solve, begin by translating the words into an equation and then solve the equation to find the solution.

> If 5 increased by 3 times a number is 21, what is the number?

Call the number x. Then, the problem statement tells you that:

$$5 + 3x = 21$$

Subtract 5 from both sides:

$$3x = 15$$

Divide by 3:

$$x = 5$$

Thus, the number is 5.

> Brian needs $54 more to buy new hockey gloves. If new gloves cost $115, how much money does he already have to spend on the gloves?

Let m represent the amount of money that Brian has to spend on the gloves. Then, you have an easy equation: $m + 54 = 115$. If you subtract 54 from both sides, you get $m = 61$. Brian already has $61 to spend on the gloves.

> Edgar bought a portable compact disc player for $69 and a number of discs for $14 each. If the total cost of his purchases (before tax) was $167, how many compact discs did he buy?

Start by letting d represent the number of discs he bought. Then, the cost of the player plus d discs at $14 each must add up to $167. Therefore, $14d + 69 = 167$.

Subtract 69 from both sides: $14d = 98$

Divide both sides by 14: $d = 7$

Edgar bought 7 discs.

Multiplication with Exponents

Consider the problem $x^3 \times x^5 = ?$ If you think about it, you realize that if you compute $x^3 \times x^5$, you end up with eight xs multiplied together. Therefore, $x^3 \times x^5 = x^8$. This indicates the general rule for multiplication of numbers with exponents: $x^n \times x^m = x^{m+n}$. In other words, to multiply two numbers with exponents, add the exponents and keep the common base.

This rule can be extended to other types of multiplication. For example, if you need to multiply $x(x + 3)$, you can use the distributive property to obtain:

$$x(x + 3) = x^2 + 3x$$

Now, how would you multiply something like $(x + 2)(x + 5)$? Basically, you need to take each of the terms in the first expression—that is, the x and the 2—and distribute them to both of the terms in the second expression. Doing this, you end up with

$$(x + 2)(x + 5) = x^2 + 5x + 2x + 10 = x^2 + 7x + 10.$$

Multiply $2x(x^2 - 3x)$. Begin by distributing as you did previously:

$$2x(x^2 - 3x) = 2x(x^2) - 2x(3x)$$

Now, perform the indicated multiplications:

$$2x(x^2) - 2x(3x) = 2x^3 - 6x^2$$

Multiply $(2x + 7)(3x - 4)$.

As in the preceding example, begin by distributing the $2x$ and the 7 to the other terms:

$$(2x + 7)(3x - 4) = 2x(3x) - 2x(4) + 7(3x) - 7(4)$$

Now, perform the multiplications and combine terms where possible:

$$2x(3x) - 2x(4) + 7(3x) - 7(4) = 6x^2 - 8x + 21x - 28 = 6x^2 - 13x - 28$$

Factoring

Earlier in this chapter, we talked about factoring whole numbers; for example, 35 can be factored as $35 = 5 \times 7$. As you can see, the word *factoring* refers to taking a mathematical quantity and breaking it down into a product of other quantities.

Certain algebraic expressions can be factored, too. Earlier in this chapter, you saw how to perform two types of multiplication. In the first, you used the distributive property to perform multiplications such as $x(x + 3) = x^2 + 3x$. To use the correct vocabulary, the x at the front of this expression is called a *monomial* (one term); whereas the expression $x + 3$ is called a *binomial* (two terms). Thus, you have used the distributive property to help multiply a monomial by a binomial. You also saw how to multiply two binomials, for example:

$$(2x + 7)(3x - 4) = 6x^2 - 13x - 28$$

The process of taking the results of these multiplications and breaking them back down into their component factors is also called factoring. It is not difficult to factor, but it does often require a bit of trial and error.

For example, if you are asked to multiply the expression $2x(x - 7)$, you would get:

$$2x^2 - 14x$$

If you were given $2x^2 - 14x$ and asked to factor it, you would basically need to undo the distribution process and get the expression back to what it originally was.

To do this, begin by looking at the expression $2x^2 - 14x$ and try to find the largest common monomial factor—that is, the largest monomial that divides into both $2x^2$ and $14x$ evenly. Clearly, in this problem, the largest common factor is $2x$. You then place the $2x$ outside a set of parentheses. Finish by dividing the $2x$ into each of the two terms ($2x^2$ and $14x$) and write the resulting terms inside the parentheses. This leaves you with

$$2x(x - 7)$$

You have successfully factored the expression.

> Factor $2a^2b - 8ab$.

The largest common monomial factor in this expression is $2ab$. If you divide $2a^2b$ by $2ab$, you get a. If you divide $8ab$ by $2ab$, you get 4. Thus, putting the $2ab$ outside of the parentheses, and the a and 4 on the inside, you get $2ab(a - 4)$.

Note that it is easy to check whether you have factored correctly or not by multiplying the expression, and seeing whether you get the original expression back.

It is also possible to factor certain *trinomial* (three term) expressions into two binomials. Consider a simple example: If you were asked to multiply $(x + 2)(x + 3)$, you would get $x^2 + 5x + 6$. Now, what if you were given the expression $x^2 + 5x + 6$ and asked to factor it back down to the two binomials it came from?

To begin, make two sets of parentheses and note that you can position xs in the first position of each set because the first terms of each binomial multiply to give the x^2 in $x^2 + 5x + 6$. Therefore, to begin

$$x^2 + 5x + 6 = (x \quad)(x \quad)$$

Because both signs in $x^2 + 5x + 6$ are positive, you can position plus signs within the parentheses:

$$x^2 + 5x + 6 = (x + \quad)(x + \quad)$$

Now, what are the last entries in each binomial? Well, you know that whatever you put in these spots must multiply to get six, so the possibilities would be one and six, or two and three. The correct entries, however, must add up to five to get the correct middle term. Thus, it must be two and three, and you get $x^2 + 5x + 6 = (x + 2)(x + 3)$. You can check the answer by multiplying:

$$(x + 2)(x + 3) = x^2 + 3x + 2x + 6 = x^2 + 5x + 6$$

As you can see, factoring a trinomial into two binomials requires a bit of trial and error. The following examples give you a bit more practice with this.

Factor $x^2 - 8x + 12$.

You begin as before, by making two sets of parentheses and entering first terms of x in each:

$$x^2 - 8x + 12 = (x \quad)(x \quad)$$

Now, the two last entries must multiply to get +12 but add to get –8, so that you get the correct middle term. Proceed by trial and error, and it does not take long to determine that the two numbers that work are –2 and –6. The factorization is $x^2 - 8x + 12 = (x - 2)(x - 6)$.

Factor $x^2 - 49$.

This one might look a bit tricky, but actually it is rather easy. Begin, as before, by writing:

$$x^2 - 49 = (x \quad)(x \quad)$$

Now, the last two entries must multiply to get 49 and add to get 0, so that the middle term is, essentially, 0. Clearly, this works with +7 and –7. Thus, $x^2 - 49 = (x + 7)(x - 7)$.

Simplifying Algebraic Expressions

Earlier in this chapter, we talked about simplifying fractions. If, for example, the answer to a problem turns out to be $\frac{15}{20}$, it should be simplified to $\frac{3}{4}$. In the same way, certain algebraic expressions can be simplified as well. For example, consider the algebraic fraction $\frac{x^2 - 16}{3x + 12}$. To simplify this expression, begin by factoring the expressions on the top and on the bottom: $\frac{x^2 - 16}{3x + 12} = \frac{(x+4)(x-4)}{3(x+4)}$. Now, the common factor of $x + 4$ can be divided from the top and bottom, yielding a simplified fraction of $\frac{x-4}{3}$.

You can perform mathematical operations on algebraic fractions in much the same way as you can perform mathematical operations on fractions that contain only numbers. Consider this example:

Add $\frac{x+1}{4x+6} + \frac{x+2}{4x+6}$.

Because these two fractions have the same denominator, you can add them in the usual way:

$$\frac{x+1}{4x+6} + \frac{x+2}{4x+6} = \frac{x+1+x+2}{4x+6} = \frac{2x+3}{4x+6}$$

Now, finish by factoring the expression on the bottom and dividing:

$$\frac{x+1}{4x+6} + \frac{x+2}{4x+6} = \frac{x+1+x+2}{4x+6} = \frac{2x+3}{4x+6} = \frac{2x+3}{2(2x+3)} = \frac{1}{2}$$

Multiply $\dfrac{x^2 - 7x + 6}{x^2 - 1} \times \dfrac{x + 1}{x - 6}$.

Begin by factoring as much as possible, then multiply, and cancel:

$$\frac{x^2 - 7x + 6}{x^2 - 1} \times \frac{x + 1}{x - 6} = \frac{(x-6)(x-1)}{(x-1)(x+1)} = \frac{x+1}{x-6} = \frac{(x-6)(x-1)(x+1)}{(x+1)(x+1)(x-6)} = 1$$

Divide $\dfrac{a^2 - b^2}{5} \div \dfrac{a^2 + ab}{5a - 5}$

Begin by changing this to a multiplication problem by reciprocating the second fraction. Then factor and cancel:

$$\frac{a^2 - b^2}{5} \div \frac{a^2 + ab}{5a - 5} = \frac{a^2 - b^2}{5} \times \frac{5a - 5}{a^2 + ab} = \frac{(a+b)(a-b)}{5} \times \frac{5(a-1)}{a(a+b)} = \frac{(a+b)(a-b)5(a-1)}{5a(a+b)} = \frac{(a-b)(a-1)}{a}$$

Geometry and Measurement

On the Mathematics Knowledge section of the AFOQT, you are asked some questions that require a basic knowledge of geometry. These facts are presented in the following section.

Angle Measurement

You measure angles in degrees, which you indicate with the symbol °. By definition, the amount of rotation needed to go completely around a circle one time is 360°.

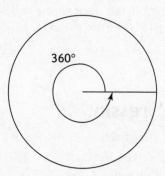

You can measure every angle by determining what fraction of a complete rotation around a circle it represents. For example, an angle that represents ¼ of a rotation around a circle would have a measurement of ¼ of 360° = 90°. The following diagram depicts a 90° angle. *AB* and *AC* are the sides of the angle, and the point *A* is the vertex.

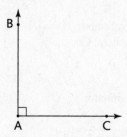

Angles that measure less than 90° are called *acute* angles, and angles that measure more than 90° are called *obtuse* angles. The following diagram depicts an acute angle of 60° as well as an obtuse angle of 120°.

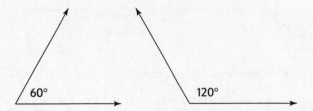

Note that an angle with the size of ½ a revolution around the circle has a measure of 180°. In other words, a straight line can be thought of as an angle of 180°.

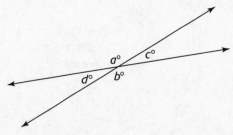

Two angles whose measures add up to 90° are called *complementary* angles, and two angles whose measures add up to 180° are called *supplementary* angles. In the following diagram, angles 1 and 2 are complementary, and angles 3 and 4 are supplementary. As the diagram shows, whenever a straight angle is partitioned into two angles, the angles are supplementary.

Another very important fact about angles relates to what are known as *vertical* angles. As the following diagram shows, when two lines intersect, four angles are formed. In this situation, the angles that are across from each other are called *vertical* angles. All vertical angles are equal, so $a° = b°$, and $c° = d°$.

In the following diagram, what is the value of a?

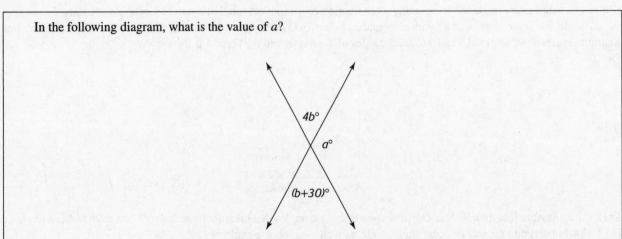

Begin by noting that the angles labeled $4b$ and $b + 30$ are vertical angles, and, therefore, have the same measure. In this case, you can set the two angles equal and solve the resulting equation for b:

$$4b = b + 30$$
$$3b = 30$$
$$b = 10$$

Now, if $b = 10$, then $4b = 40$. Because the angle labeled $a°$ is supplementary to this angle, a must be equal to $140°$.

In the following diagram, what is the value of x?

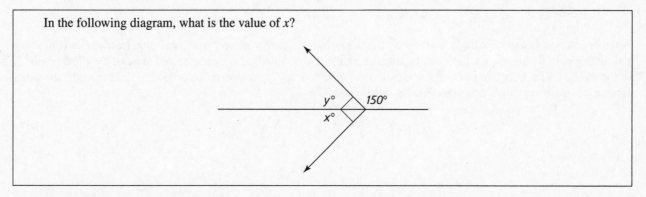

Begin by noting that the angle labeled y is supplementary to the angle labeled $150°$, and is, therefore, equal to $30°$. Next, note that the angle labeled x is complementary to that $30°$ angle, and is, therefore, equal to $60°$.

Properties of Triangles

A triangle is a geometric figure having three straight sides. One of the most important facts about a triangle is that, regardless of its shape, the sum of the measures of the three angles it contains is always $180°$. Of course, then, if you know the measures of two of the angles of a triangle, you can determine the measure of the third angle by adding the two angles you are given and subtracting from 180.

Some triangles have special properties that you should know about. To begin, an *isosceles* triangle is a triangle that has two sides of the same length. In an isosceles triangle, the two angles opposite the equal sides have the same measurement. For example, in the following figure, $AB = BC$, and therefore the two angles opposite these sides, labeled $x°$, have the same measure.

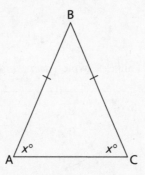

A triangle that has all three sides the same length is called an *equilateral* triangle. In an equilateral triangle, all three angles also have the same measure. Because the sum of the three angles must be $180°$, each angle in an equilateral triangle must measure $180° \div 3 = 60$. Therefore, in the following equilateral triangle, all three angles are $60°$.

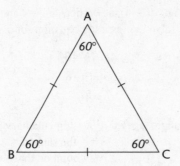

Another extremely important triangle property relates to what are known as *right* triangles—that is, triangles containing a right angle. In such triangles, the side opposite the right angle is called the *hypotenuse* and must be the longest side of the triangle. The other two sides of the triangle are called its legs. Therefore, in the following right triangle, the side labeled c is the hypotenuse, and sides a and b are the legs.

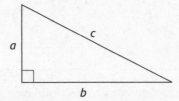

The three sides of a right triangle are related by a formula known as the *Pythagorean theorem*. The Pythagorean theorem states that the square of the hypotenuse is equal to the sum of the squares of the legs of the triangle, or, using the notation in the preceding diagram, $a^2 + b^2 = c^2$.

The importance of this result is that it enables you, given the lengths of two of the sides of a right triangle, to find the length of the third side.

> In triangle XYZ, angle X is twice as big as angle Y, and angle Z is equal to angle Y. What is the measure of angle X?

Because the measure of angle X is twice as big as angle Y, you can say that the measure of angle X is equal to $2Y$. Because it must be true that $X + Y + Z = 180$, you can write:

$$2Y + Y + Y = 180$$
$$4Y = 180$$
$$Y = 45$$

If the measure of angle Y is 45°, the measure of angle X, which is twice as big, must be 90°.

> In the following triangle, what is the length of a?
>
>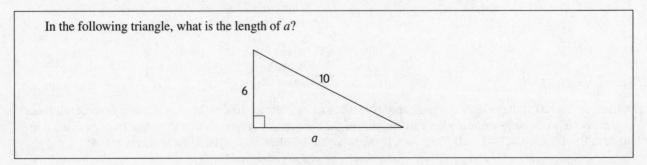

The triangle is a right triangle, so you can use the Pythagorean theorem to find the length of the missing side. Note that the hypotenuse is 10, one of the legs is 6, and you are looking for the length of the other leg. Therefore,

$$a^2 + 6^2 = 10^2$$
$$a^2 + 36 = 100$$
$$a^2 = 64$$
$$a = 8$$

Properties of Circles

A circle is a closed figure, consisting of all the points that are the same distance from a fixed point called the *center* of the circle. A line segment from the center of the circle to any point on the circle is called a *radius* of the circle. A line segment from one point on a circle, through the center of the circle, to another point on the circle is called a *diameter* of the circle. As you can see in the following diagram, the length of a diameter of a circle is always twice the length of a radius of a circle.

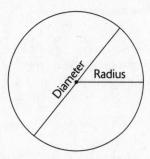

Perimeter and Area

To find the perimeter of a triangle, you need to add the lengths of the three sides. The area of a triangle is given by the formula Area = ½ *bh,* where *b* represents the length of the base of the triangle, and *h* represents the height of the triangle. The height of a triangle is defined as the length of a line segment drawn from a *vertex* (corner) of the triangle to the base, so that it hits the base at a right angle.

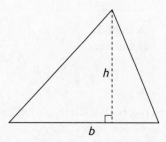

Formulas for the perimeter, which is more commonly known as the *circumference,* and the area of circles are based on the length of the radius and include the symbol π, which represents a number that is approximately equal to 3.14.

The circumference of a circle is given by the formula $C = 2\pi r$, where r is the radius of the circle. The area of the circle is given by the formula $A = \pi r^2$. Unless you are told otherwise, when answering problems involving the circumference or area of a circle, you can leave the answer in terms of π, as in the following problem.

> What is the circumference of a circle whose area is 36π?

The area of a circle is πr^2, so you have $\pi r^2 = 36\pi$. This means that $r^2 = 36$, so $r = 6$.

Now, the circumference of a circle is $2\pi r$, so the circumference in this case would be $2\pi(6) = 12\pi$.

What is the area of the shaded part of the following rectangle?

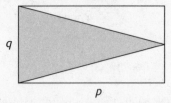

The shaded area is a triangle, so you can use the formula $A = \frac{1}{2}bh$ to find its area. The width of the rectangle, labeled q, is also the base of the triangle. You can see that the length of the rectangle, labeled p, is equal to the height of the triangle. Therefore, the area of the shaded region is $\frac{1}{2}pq$.

Coordinates and Slope

Points in a plane can be located by means of a reference system called the coordinate system. Two number lines are drawn at right angles to each other, and the point where the lines cross is considered to have a value of zero for both lines. Then, positive and negative numbers are positioned on the lines.

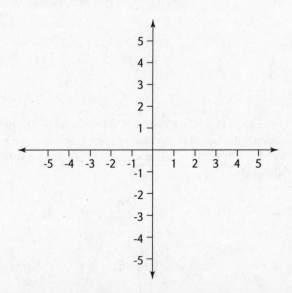

The horizontal line is called the *x-axis*, and the points on this axis are called *x-coordinates*. The vertical line is called the *y-axis*, and the points on this axis are called *y-coordinates*. Points on the plane are identified by first writing a number that represents where they lie in reference to the *x*-axis and then writing a number that expresses where they lie in reference to the *y*-axis. These numbers are called the coordinates of the point. The coordinates of a variety of points are shown in the following diagram:

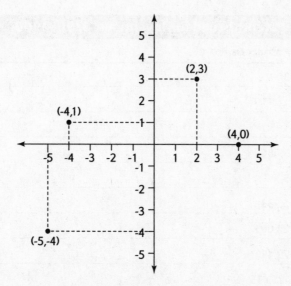

Any two points on a plane determine a line. One of the important characteristics of a line is its steepness, or *slope*. The slope of a line can be determined from the coordinates of the two points that determine the line. If the coordinates of the two points are (x_1, y_1) and (x_2, y_2), the formula for the slope is $\frac{y_2 - y_1}{x_2 - x_1}$. In other words, to find the slope of a line, find two points on the line and divide the difference of the y-coordinates by the difference of the x-coordinates.

> Find the slope of the line that goes through the points (9, 5) and (3, –2).

The slope of the line can be computed as $\frac{y_2 - y_1}{x_2 - x_1} = \frac{5 - (-2)}{9 - 3} = \frac{5 + 2}{6} = \frac{7}{6}$.

Data Interpretation and Table Reading

Data interpretation involves reading and analyzing tables, charts and graphs, and table reading tests your ability to select appropriate material by rows and columns. Let's analyze each of them one at a time.

Data Interpretation

The questions on this section of the AFOQT exam should be fairly simple, as are the table reading questions. Following are some examples of the types of data you will be asked to analyze.

Patents Issued for Inventions, 1790–1900	
Period	*Patents Issued*
1790–1800	309
1801–10	1,093
1811–20	1,930
1821–30	3,086
1831–40	5,519
1841–50	5,933
1851–60	23,065
1861–70	79,459
1871–80	125,438
1881–90	207,514
1891–1900	220,608

In what period was the greatest increase in the number of patents issued over the previous period?

A. 1790–1800
B. 1801–10
C. 1831–40
D. 1841–50
E. 1851–60

The correct answer is **E.** Do you understand why that is correct? If you analyze each of the answers, you should be able to determine the correct answer. Choice **A** is incorrect because you have no information before 1790–1800. You cannot, therefore, determine the increase from the previous period. Choice **B** shows an increase of about three times the previous period. (You don't always have to perform mathematics in these tables or graphs. You often can determine the answer just by looking at the choices.) Choice **C** also is incorrect. The growth from the previous period is less than double. Choice **D** does not indicate much growth at all from the previous period. Choice **E**, the correct answer, is almost four times the previous period.

Answer another question based on this table.

In what period was there the least amount of growth from the previous period?

A. 1801–10
B. 1811–20
C. 1821–30
D. 1831–40
E. 1841–50

Again, let's analyze each answer. To find the answers, subtract the previous period from the current period. You are only going to estimate here.

- **A.** From 1790–1800 to the next period, about 700 more patents were issued. (1,093 – 309 = 784)
- **B.** From 1801–10 to the next period, just over 800 more patents were issued. (1,930 – 1,093 = 837).
- **C.** From 1811–20 to the next period, more than 1,100 more patents were issued. (3,086 – 1,930 = 1,156)
- **D.** From 1821–30 to the next period, about 2,400 more patents were issued. (5,519 – 3,086 = 2,433)
- **E.** From 1831–40 to the next period, about 400 more patents were issued. (5,933 – 5,519 = 414)

The correct answer, therefore, is **E**.

Line graphs and bar graphs are essentially comparisons. In a line graph, you are asked to read and analyze the information based on different styles or widths of lines. The information is present on the horizontal and vertical axes. A bar graph is not as accurate as a table, but it gives you a quick, visual comparison of the data.

The following is an example of another type of question you will encounter.

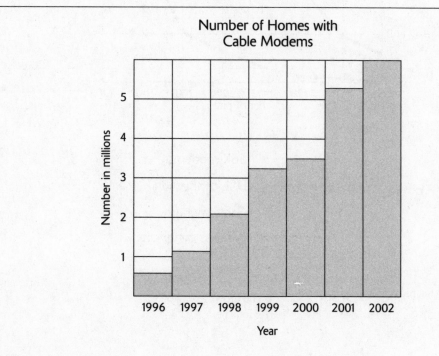

In what year was there the greatest amount of growth over the previous year?

- **A.** 1997
- **B.** 1998
- **C.** 2000
- **D.** 2001
- **E.** 2002

A quick look at the graph shows that the greatest amount of growth was from 2000 to 2001. You can see that visually by the bars. At the same time, by looking along the left, you can also see that about 3.2 million homes had cable modems in 2000 and 5.2 million homes had cable modems in 2001. This is an increase of 2 million. None of the other bars indicate that type of growth.

Look at one other type of graph—a line graph.

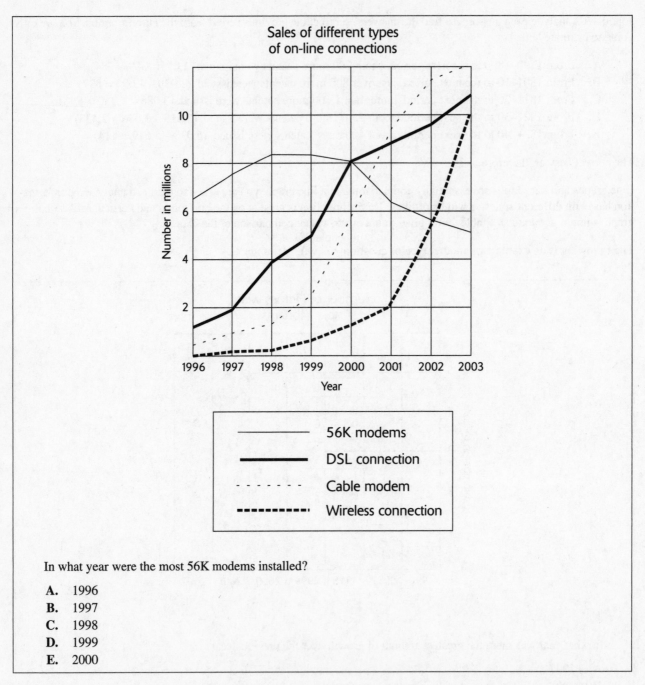

Sales of different types
of on-line connections

56K modems

DSL connection

Cable modem

Wireless connection

In what year were the most 56K modems installed?

A. 1996
B. 1997
C. 1998
D. 1999
E. 2000

If you follow the thin line that indicates 56K modems on the scale and then trace it across the graph, starting at about 6.8 million, you'll see that sales peaked in 1998 with a little more than 8 million sold. The correct answer is **C.**

How many more DSL connections were sold in 2001 compared to cable modems? (See previous graph.)

A. 1 million
B. 1.5 million
C. 2 million
D. 2.5 million
E. 3 million

The correct answer is **C**, 2 million. Find the number of cable modems sold in 2000. Trace the light dotted line to 2000. It ends on 6 million. Now find the DSL connections, which is indicated by the bold line. That ends at 8 million. The difference is 2 million.

Answering these types of questions involves some arithmetic and requires strong reading skills. You have to know what the question is asking, and you have to be aware of what is being illustrated graphically. When you find the bars, numbers or lines that you are asked to deal with, you then can do the math.

Table Reading

The second type of question that appears on the AFOQT is table reading. This portion of the test is designed to measure your ability to read tables quickly and accurately. Like the earlier material, it involves less mathematics.

Tables normally present you with columns of information, and the data corresponds to the rows and columns. There are always units such as numbers, years, dollars, and even people. You have to compare the items on both the X and Y axes to find the answers. Look at a typical table.

Player	At Bats	Runs	Hits	Walks	Strike Outs	Average	Annual Salary (millions $)
Johnson rf	4	0	1	0	0	.255	$2.7
Smith 3b	3	0	0	0	1	.231	$5.6
Hernando cf	3	0	0	1	1	.255	$6.0
Lubitz 1b	4	0	1	0	1	.291	$8.8
MacDonald lf	3	3	2	1	0	.294	$5.5
Philips dh	4	0	0	0	1	.246	$8.0
Auerhaan 2b	4	0	1	0	0	.306	$2.0
Augustine c	3	0	0	1	0	.275	$3.3
Borger ss	3	1	1	0	1	.248	$4.1
Totals	31	4	6	3	5		$46.0

Which player had the most hits?

A. Johnson
B. Lubitz
C. MacDonald
D. Auerhaan
E. Borger

Find the Hits column along the top and match it to the player along the left side. The correct answer is MacDonald, with 2 hits—choice **C.** All the other players had only one hit.

Of those players who had hits, which player has the highest average?

A. Johnson
B. Lubitz
C. MacDonald
D. Auerhaan
E. Borger

This time you have to analyze each player. Find the players with hits and follow across to the Average column to find the answer.

Johnson's average is .255.

Lubitz's average is .291.

MacDonald's average is .294.

Auerhaan's average is .306.

Borger's average is .248.

Thus, the correct answer is Auerhaan, choice **D.**

A second form of table reading question might appear on the tests. In these questions you are presented with a table of numbers, with X values running along the top and Y values running along the side. You will be asked to select the answer that occurs where the two axes intersect.

Y-Values		X-Values								
		-4	-3	-2	-1	0	+1	+2	+3	+4
	+4	16	18	20	22	24	27	29	31	33
	+3	17	19	21	23	25	26	28	30	32
	+2	18	20	22	24	26	28	30	32	34
	+1	19	21	23	25	27	29	30	33	35
	0	20	22	24	27	29	31	33	35	36
	-1	22	23	25	28	30	32	34	36	37
	-2	24	25	26	29	31	33	36	37	38
	-3	26	27	28	30	32	34	37	39	40
	-4	28	29	30	31	33	36	38	40	42

For each question, determine the number that can be found at the intersection of the row and column.

This is how the questions will appear. Try the first one and analyze it.

	X	Y	A	B	C	D	E
1.	−1	+2	22	23	24	25	26

To find the answer, locate the X values along the top and find −1. Then trace down the column until you find +2 in the Y-value row. Where they intersect, you'll find the number 24. That is the correct answer. You will have an answer sheet in which you can fill in the choice, **C.** Try the following and circle the correct answer.

	X	Y	A	B	C	D	E
2.	+1	−2	31	33	35	37	40
3.	+2	+4	18	22	25	29	30
4.	−4	−3	26	27	28	30	32
5.	0	−2	29	30	31	32	33

The correct answers are:

2. B, 33

3. D, 29

4. A, 26

5. C, 31

Now that you have an idea of the types of questions you'll encounter, take the time to answer all the following practice questions. If you have any problems with them, go back and reread this chapter. Make sure that you read the questions carefully so that you don't misinterpret what is being asked of you and as a result, misread the tables or charts.

Data Interpretation and Table Reading Practice Questions

Answer questions 1–5 based on the following table showing the number of games won by each of five teams in each month of a seven-month season.

Number of Games Won

Month	Team 1	2	3	4	5
April	11	10	10	12	16
May	12	12	17	15	11
June	15	13	13	14	13
July	10	17	13	14	10
August	11	12	14	12	15
Sept.	14	11	12	11	16
Oct.	14	16	12	13	17

1. How many games did team 4 win in the first three months of the season?

   A. 38
   B. 40
   C. 41
   D. 43
   E. 44

2. In the month of August, team 5 won how many more games than team 1?

   A. 4
   B. 5
   C. 6
   D. 11
   E. 15

3. In which month did team 3 win one game more than team 4?

   A. May
   B. June
   C. August
   D. September
   E. October

4. If there are no ties and team 1 played 28 games each month, in which month did team 1 win more games than they lost?

   A. June
   B. July
   C. August
   D. September
   E. October

5. What was the total number of games won by all five teams in June?

   A. 59
   B. 64
   C. 68
   D. 72
   E. 73

Answer questions 6–10 based on the following table of earned interest.

Interest Earned in One Year

Interest Rate in Percent	Principal in Dollars					
	1000	1100	1200	1300	1400	1500
1¼	12.50	13.75	15.00	16.25	17.50	18.75
1¾	17.50	19.25	21.00	22.75	24.50	26.25
2¼	22.50	24.75	27.00	29.25	31.50	33.75
2¾	27.50	30.25	33.00	35.75	38.50	41.25
3¼	32.50	35.75	39.00	42.25	45.50	48.75
3¾	37.50	41.25	45.00	48.75	52.50	56.25
4¼	42.50	46.75	51.00	55.25	59.50	63.75

6. If Lauren invested $1,400 at 2¼ and Evan invested $1,200 at 3¼%, what would be the combined earnings of Lauren and Evan in one year?

A. $57.50
B. $63.00
C. $70.50
D. $80.00
E. $82.50

7. How much more interest is earned on $1,500 invested at 2¼% than on $1,000 invested at 2¾%?

A. $6.25
B. $6.50
C. $6.75
D. $7.00
E. $7.25

8. John, a senior citizen, withdraws his interest earnings at the end of each year. He deposits $1,000 for one year at 4¼% and withdraws the $42.50 interest at the end of the year. The following year he is only able to get a rate of 3¼% on his $1,000. How much money does he earn that year?

A. $9.75
B. $32.50
C. $42.25
D. $50.00
E. $74.75

9. What is the minimum interest rate you could get on $1,300 to be sure of earning at least $36.00 in interest?

A. 2¼%
B. 2¾%
C. 3¼%
D. 3¾%
E. 4¼%

10. How much interest is earned in one year on $4,800 at 2¾%?

A. $33.00
B. $50.00
C. $66.00
D. $103.00
E. $132.00

Answer questions 11–15 based on the following circle graph that shows the breakdown of elementary school students by grade level.

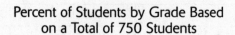

Percent of Students by Grade Based
on a Total of 750 Students

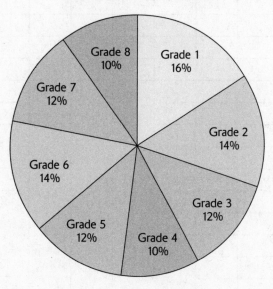

11. How many students are in grade 5?

A. 12
B. 63
C. 87
D. 90
E. 150

12. The total number of students in grades 1 and 3 is the same as the total number of students in which of the following grades?

A. 2 and 7
B. 4, 7 and 8
C. 4, 5 and 7
D. 2 and 6
E. 5 and 6

13. How many more students are in grade 2 than in grade 8?

A. 4
B. 24
C. 30
D. 46
E. 48

14. How many students are in grades 5 and 6 combined?

A. 195
B. 260
C. 305
D. 350
E. 375

15. If 30 students in grade 1 transfer to a different school and no other students enter or leave any of the other grades, what is the new percent of students in grade 3?

A. 9%
B. 9.5%
C. 10%
D. 12%
E. 12.5%

Answer questions 16–20 based on the following bar graph showing the distances covered by the drivers of the ABC Taxi Company in a one-week period.

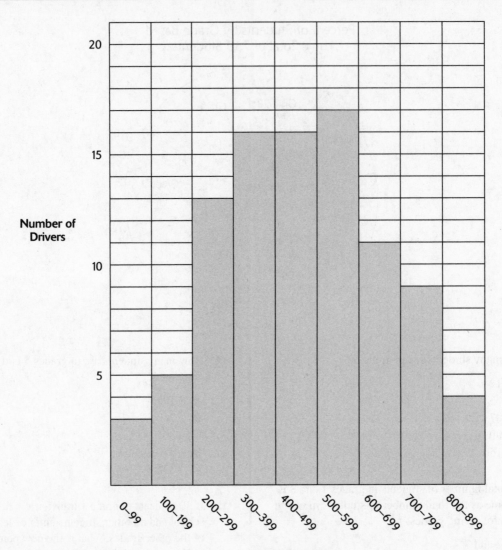

16. What is the total number of drivers?

    A. 17
    B. 45
    C. 63
    D. 94
    E. 99

17. How many drivers drove at least 700 miles?

    A. 4
    B. 5
    C. 9
    D. 11
    E. 13

18. How many drivers drove less than 300 miles?

    A. 13
    B. 16
    C. 21
    D. 28
    E. 32

19. How many drivers drove at least 600 but less than 700 miles?

    A. 11
    B. 9
    C. 8
    D. 4
    E. 2

20. If the records of six more drivers are discovered and they belong in the 100–199 range, what would be the percent of total drivers in that range?

A. 5
B. 11
C. 13
D. 16
E. 17

Answer questions 21–25 based on the following line graph showing average weekly salaries at three different companies.

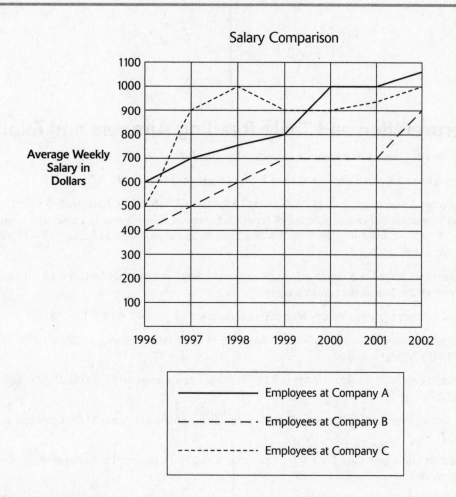

Salary Comparison

21. Which of the following statements is true for the time period from 1997–1999?

A. The average salary at Company C was less than at Company A.
B. The average salary at Company B was greater than at Company A.
C. The average salary at Company B was greater than at Company C.
D. The average salary at Company C was greater than at Company B.
E. The average salary at Company A was greater than at Company C.

22. In which time period was there no increase in the average salary at Company A?

A. 1999–2000
B. 1999–2001
C. 2000–2001
D. 2000–2002
E. 2001–2002

23. When was the average salary at Company B greater than at Company A?

    A. 1996–1998

    B. 1997–1999

    C. 1998–2000

    D. 1999–2002

    E. Never

24. What is the difference between the average salaries at Company A and Company B in 1999?

    A. $100

    B. $300

    C. $500

    D. $700

    E. $800

25. The greatest one-year increase in salary occurred at which company and in which time period?

    A. At Company A from 1999–2000

    B. At Company A from 2001–2002

    C. At Company C from 1996–1997

    D. At Company C from 1997–1998

    E. At Company B from 1998–1999

Data Interpretation and Table Reading Answers and Explanations

  1. C. The number of games won by team 4 in April, May, and June: $12 + 15 + 14 = 41$.

  2. A. In August, team 5 won 15 games and team 1 won 11 games. $15 - 11 = 4$.

  3. D. In May, team 3 won 17 games and team 4 won 15 games. $17 - 15 = 2$. In June, team 3 won 13 games and team 4 won 14 games. You cannot subtract 14 from 13. In August, team 3 won 14 games and team 4 won 12 games. $14 - 12 = 2$. In September, team 3 won 12 games and team 4 won 11 games. $12 - 11 = 1$. This is the correct answer.

  4. A. If 28 games are played in a month and team 1 won 15 games in June, they lost $28 - 15 = 13$ games. Because 15 is greater than 13, June is the correct answer.

  5. C. The total number of games won by all 5 teams in June $= 15 + 13 + 13 + 14 + 13 = 68$.

  6. C. If Lauren invested $1,400 at $2\frac{1}{4}\%$, she would earn $31.50. If Evan invested $1,200 at $3\frac{1}{4}\%$, he would earn $39.00. $31.50 + $39.00 = $70.50.

  7. A. The interest earned on $1,500 at $2\frac{1}{4}\%$ is $33.75. The interest earned on $1,000 at $2\frac{3}{4}\%$ is $27.50. $33.75 - $27.50 = $6.25.

  8. B. John's earnings the first year do not affect his earnings in subsequent years. $1,000 invested at $3\frac{1}{4}\%$ earns $32.50.

  9. C. Any interest rate higher than $2\frac{3}{4}\%$ earns more than $36.00 on a principal investment of $1,300. The question asks for the minimum rate, which is $3\frac{1}{4}\%$.

10. E. $4,800 is four times as much as $1,200 and, therefore, earns four times as much interest. $4 \times $33.00 = $132.00.

11. D. The school has 750 students and 12% of them are in grade 5. 12% of $750 = .12 \times 750 = 90$.

12. D. Sixteen percent of the students are in grade 1, and 12% of the students are in grade 3. Therefore, $16\% + 12\% = 28\%$ of the students are in grades 1 and 3. For choice **A** we need to add the percentages for grades 2 and 7: $14\% + 12\% = 26\%$. For choice **B** we need to add the percentages for grades 4, 7, and 8: $10\% + 12\% + 10\% = 32\%$. For choice **C** we need to add the percentages for grades 4, 5, and 7: $10\% + 12\% + 12\% = 34\%$. For choice **D** we need to add the percentages for grades 2 and 6: $14\% + 14\% = 28\%$. This is the correct answer.

13. C. The school has 750 students and 14% of them are in grade 2. 14% of 750 = .14 × 750 = 105. Ten percent of the students are in grade 8. 10% of 750 = .10 × 750 = 75. To determine how many more students are in grade 2, subtract: 105 – 75 = 30.

14. A. Twelve percent of students are in grade 5 and 14% of students are in grade 6. 12% + 14% = 26%. Because 750 students are in the school, we need to calculate 26% of 750 = .26 × 750 = 195.

15. E. The school has 750 students, and 12% of them are in grade 3. 12% of 750 = .12 × 750 = 90. After 30 students leave the school, 750 – 30 = 720 students remain. We need to determine what percent 90 is of 720: 90 ÷ 720 = .125 = 12.5%.

16. D. The number of drivers who drove 0–99 miles is 3. The number of drivers who drove 100–199 miles is 5. The number of drivers who drove 200–299 miles is 13, and so on. 3 + 5 + 13 + 16 + 16 + 17 + 11 + 9 + 4 = 94.

17. E. At least 700 miles means 700 or more miles. 9 + 4 = 13.

18. C. Less than 300 miles includes the first three bars of the graph. 3 + 5 + 13 = 21.

19. A. At least 600 but less than 700 means the 600–699 bar. The correct answer is 11.

20. B. The total number of drivers indicated on the graph is 94, as explained in question 16. If 6 more drivers are added to the graph, there are 94 + 6 = 100 drivers. If all 6 are added in the 100–199 range, there are 5 + 6 = 11 drivers in this range. You need to determine what percent 11 is of 100: 11 ÷ 100 = .11 = 11%.

21. D. In the time period from 1997–1999, the line representing the average salary at Company C is higher on the graph than the lines representing either of the other two companies. Therefore, the average salary at Company C was greater than at Company B, and choice **D** is the correct answer.

22. C. No increase in average salary is indicated when the line in the line graph is horizontal. For Company A this occurs from 2000–2001.

23. E. For the average salary at Company B to be greater than the average salary at Company A, the line representing Company B has to be higher than the line representing Company A. This never happens.

24. A. In 1999, the average salary at Company A was $800, and the average salary at Company B was $700. $800 – $700 = $100.

25. C. The increase at Company A from 1999–2000 is $1,000 – $800 = $200. Choice **A** = $200. The increase at Company A from 2001–2002 is $1,050 – $1,000 = $50. Choice **B** = $50. The increase at Company C from 1996–1997 is $900 – $500 = $400. Choice **C** = $400. The increase at Company C from 1997–1998 is $1,000 – $900 = $100. Choice **D** = $100. The increase at Company B from 1998–1999 is $700 – $600 = $100. Choice **E** = $100. The largest value is $400, choice **C**.

Scale Reading

The "Scale Reading" test is Part 9 of the Air Force Officer Qualifying Test (AFOQT). It is a test of your ability to read scales, dials, and meters. You are given a variety of scales with various points indicated on them by numbered arrows. You are to estimate the numerical value indicated by each arrow and then choose your answer. Look at the following sample items from the official AFOQT handbook.

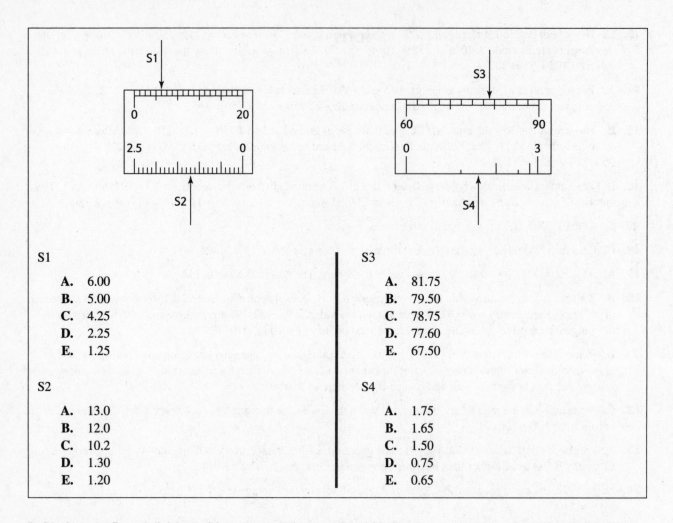

S1

A. 6.00
B. 5.00
C. 4.25
D. 2.25
E. 1.25

S2

A. 13.0
B. 12.0
C. 10.2
D. 1.30
E. 1.20

S3

A. 81.75
B. 79.50
C. 78.75
D. 77.60
E. 67.50

S4

A. 1.75
B. 1.65
C. 1.50
D. 0.75
E. 0.65

In S1, there are five subdivisions of four steps each between 0 and 20. The arrow points between the long subdivision markers representing 4 and 8. Because it points to the marker that is one step to the right of subdivision marker 4, it points to 5.00. This is choice **B** in sample item S1.

In S2 the scale runs from right to left. There are five subdivisions of five steps each, so each step represents .1, and the arrow points to the marker representing 1.20. This is choice **E** in sample item S2.

In S3 the arrow points between two markers. You must estimate the fractional part of the step as accurately as possible. Because the arrow points halfway between the markers representing 77.5 and 80.0, it points to 78.75. This is choice **C** in sample item S3.

In S4 each step represents .5, but the steps are of unequal width with each step being two-thirds as wide as the preceding one. Therefore, the scale is compressed as the values increase. The arrow is pointing to a position halfway between the marker representing .5 and 1.0, but because of the compression of the scale, the value of this point must be less than 0.75. Actually it is 0.65, which is choice **E** in sample item S4.

All that's required of you is to read the scales and determine which selection is the correct one. You have 10 minutes in which to answer 40 questions. As with all tests, the more you practice, the better you become. Keep in mind, also, that your score is based on the number of correct answers. Because you do not lose any points for incorrect answers, answer all the questions, whether you think you know the answer or not.

Scale Reading Practice Questions

Following are several more questions that will help you review for this section of the AFOQT. Time yourself. It should only take a couple of minutes to answer all 10 questions.

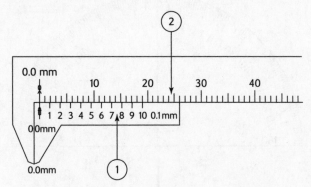

1.
A. 7.5mm
B. 7.8mm
C. 8.5mm
D. 17.5mm
E. 107.5mm

2.
A. 240mm
B. 245mm
C. 24mm
D. 24.5mm
E. 25.5mm

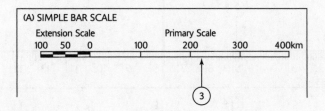

3.
A. 200km
B. 225km
C. 250km
D. 300km
E. 375km

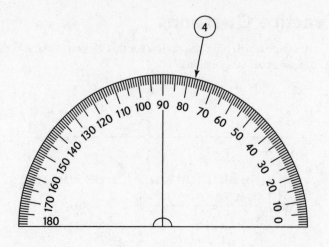

4.

    A. 80.5

    B. 80.4

    C. 77.0

    D. 75.7

    E. 75.2

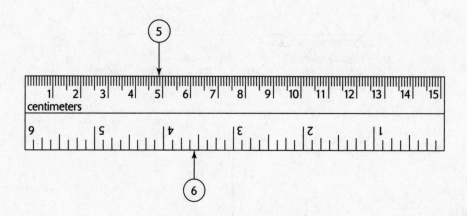

5.

    A. 47.0cm

    B. 48.0cm

    C. 48.5cm

    D. 50.2cm

    E. 50.2cm

6.

    A. 3.45

    B. 3.50

    C. 3.80

    D. 3.60

    E. 3.95

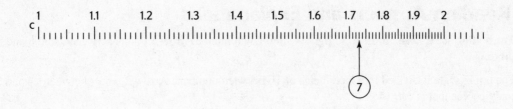

7.

   A. 172
   B. 173
   C. 17.3
   D. 1.73
   E. .173

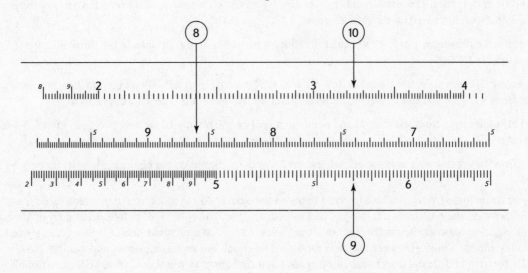

8.

   A. 9.40
   B. 8.52
   C. 8.70
   D. 5.10
   E. 5.00

9.

   A. 5.2
   B. 5.7
   C. 52.0
   D. 55.2
   E. 57.0

10.

   A. 322
   B. 47.60
   C. 32.20
   D. 8.40
   E. 3.22

Scale Reading Answers and Explanations

1. A. The bottom scale reads from left to right in single increments. Arrow 1 points between 7 and 8 and is, therefore, 7.5.

2. D. The upper scale is divided into increments of 10 between numbers. Arrow 2 points between 24 and 25. The only choice that is correct is 24.5.

3. B. On the Bar Scale, the arrow is closer to the 200 mark, and the only choice would be 225.

4. C. The numbers run from right to left with 10 increments between numbers. Arrow 4 points to 77 on the scale. Make sure that you always check to determine in which directions the numbers run.

5. C. On the centimeter scale, arrow 5 points to a number just in between 48 and 49. The only choice is 48.5.

6. D. On the inches scale, each minor tick represents an eighth of an inch, and between them, although not marked, would be 1/16 inches. The arrow points to between $3\frac{4}{8}$ and $3\frac{5}{8}$. Therefore, you would have to say the answer was $3\frac{9}{16}$, 3.5625, or 3.6, based on the choices given.

7. D. The scale runs from 1 to 2 with smaller increments between. Arrow 7 points to the third tick after 1.7. Thus, the answer is 1.73.

8. C. Arrow 8 on the slide rule points to Row C1 that runs from right to left. The larger numbers run in whole increments (1, 2, 3, and so on) and are divided in half by the number 5. The answer points to 8.6.

9. B. This scales runs from left to right and points to a spot on the bottom of the row two ticks after 5.5—thus, the answer is 5.7.

10. E. Arrow 10 points to the very top scale between 3.2 and 3.3. Based on the choices given, it can only be 3.22.

How did you do on these? Were you able to "read between the lines?" Always look to see in which directions the numbers run. Sometimes, they run from left to right, and sometimes, they run from right to left, depending on the scale. In addition, the spacing between the numbers is not always even, as it is on a standard ruler. On many gauges and other types of scales, the hash marks between numbers might not be equal. Furthermore, some gauges might have several different scales running in different directions. Just pay attention to them, and you should have very little trouble.

Mechanical Comprehension

A thorough knowledge of the mechanical world is necessary in order to successfully complete numerous everyday tasks. From understanding how engines operate to using tools to build and repair existing structures to providing support against various external forces, understanding a few general principles will provide a solid base from which a more specific understanding can be gained.

This section is designed to present you with various physical concepts ranging from the application of forces and properties of materials to fluid dynamics and compound machines. Although the material in this section has been divided into subsections for convenience, several of the ideas presented will apply to more than one type of problem.

Strategies for Scoring Well

There is more to doing well on any test than simply understanding the material. For tests such as the ASVAB, AFOQT, AFAST, and ASTB, you have a distinct advantage in that you know the exact format of the test before the test begins. Presented here are some suggestions to help maximize your performance.

- Do not spend too much time on any one question. (This is the most important suggestion and can be applied to other sections.) After you read the question, if you know the answer, select the correct answer and move on. If, however, you are unsure of the correct answer, then determine whether you can omit any answers. That is, cross out any answers you know are wrong. At this point, if you know the answer from the choices left, select it. If you are still unsure of the correct answer, then move to another question. Sometimes, it just takes a few moments for the correct answer to pop into your head.

- While reviewing for the exam, make notes on the items that give you trouble. Writing down what you are trying to learn, even if you are just copying it out of the study guide, serves to reinforce the information. This, too, will be helpful in sections other than Mechanical Knowledge.

- For the Properties of Materials section, understand how liquids and solids respond to outside stimuli, specifically forces and temperature. Be familiar with the way that mass, volume, and density, are related. Finally, be able to combine these two ideas to understand what types of material are best suited for specific applications.

- For the Structural Support section, try to visualize whether or not the configuration in question is well balanced. In other words, will it be able to have external forces applied to it without falling over or otherwise changing its orientation?

- For the fluid dynamics section, determine whether a high viscosity or low viscosity fluid would be more appropriate. Be certain to understand that a fluid maintains equal pressure throughout (as long as the height remains the same), while an applied force can be magnified by increasing the area over which it acts.

- For the Mechanical Motion section, be sure to understand the concepts of position, speed, velocity, and acceleration. Know how to apply these concepts to both linear motion and circular motion. Also, be aware that friction is present in all mechanical systems. Understand the consequences of the friction for each situation being considered.

- For both the Simple and Compound Machines sections, be able to visualize in your head a diagram of the machine. Be completely aware of which parts are required to remain stationary as well as which parts are required to be mobile. Be familiar with the mechanical advantage for the various machines, and understand that in order to gain one thing another must be lost. In linear motion, you gain force, but you lose distance. In circular motion, you gain torque, but you lose speed.

Test Formats

Although the content of all of the exams is similar, the primary differences lie in the number of questions given and the number of question choices.

The ASVAB *Mechanical Comprehension* Exam has 25 questions, each with four choices (A, B, C, and D). In the AFOQT, Part 7 is also called *Mechanical Comprehension*. You are given 20 questions with five choices (A, B, C, D, and E) each from which to choose the correct answer. The questions include both text questions and questions accompanied by an illustration.

The AFAST section of the examination called *Mechanical Functions Test* also has 20 questions. However, you are given only three choices for each question (A, B, and C). In addition, each question is accompanied by an illustration, and you must choose the correct answer based on that illustration. Finally, the ASTB exam section is called *Mechanical Comprehension Test*. It has 30 questions with only two choices (A and B). These questions are also accompanied by illustrations.

Properties of Materials

Many different types of materials are encountered on a daily basis. Almost all of these are better suited for specific uses while not so appropriate for others. For example, wood and metal are more appropriate when a rigid, sturdy structure is desired (as with a bookcase, sturdy door, or large crate to transport heavy objects). Cardboard and plastic would be used for smaller containers designed to hold lighter material. This section explores in detail the differences between various materials that determine their usefulness in various situations.

Consider first the weight of a given material. This can be considered as a measure of how much force is needed to move (or support) a given amount of this material. At first thought, most people would say that iron is heavy while paper is light. This statement by itself is false and needs to be more specific. This can be seen immediately by considering that it is possible to have five pounds of iron on one table and 10 pounds of paper on an adjacent table.

The detail that is missing is that the density of the material must also be considered. *Density* is defined as the ratio of the mass (or weight) of an object to the volume that it occupies. In other words, if two objects take up the exact same amount of space (if they have the same volume), the one that weighs more has a higher density.

It is important, however, to make sure that the weight of a material and the density of a material are not confused with the strength of a material. While, for the most part, a material that is heavier will also be stronger, this is not always the case. The strength of a material can best be considered as its ability to maintain its shape as external forces on the material are increased. The challenge to create materials that are lightweight (have a lower density) while retaining a high strength is important to transportation (such as airplanes) and many other applications.

Another important property for materials is that they expand (take up more volume) and contract (take up less volume) when exposed to a change in temperature. As a general rule, a substance will expand when it is heated, and it will contract when it is cooled. This general rule applies to solids, liquids, and gases. Different solids, as well as different liquids, will expand and contract at varying rates. In other words, one solid may expand noticeably more when exposed to a specific temperature change than another solid. Gases, on the other hand, have a more uniform expansion rate. In other words, most gases will expand by the same amount when exposed to a similar change in temperature.

For example, the following materials are listed in order of increasing expansion under a similar temperature change. That is, the materials at the beginning of the list will expand and contract more than those at the bottom of the list.

lead—aluminum—brass—copper—concrete—glass

Water is an interesting exception to the general rule. Recall that water boils at 100 degrees Centigrade and freezes at 0 degrees Centigrade. When the temperature of water drops anywhere in the range between 4 degrees centigrade and 100 degrees centigrade, its volume decreases (the water is contracting). However, when the temperature of water drops anywhere in the range between 4 degrees Centigrade and 0 degrees Centigrade, its volume increases (the water is expanding). A direct consequence of this is that water has its greatest density at 4 degrees Centigrade.

Another property of materials to be considered is *absorption*. Absorption refers to the ability of the material to pick up and retain a liquid with which it comes in contact. For example, sponges and paper towels are very good at picking up and retaining liquid. Thus, they are considered to be very good at absorbing the liquids with which they come in contact.

Some materials do not absorb liquid very well. One example is the coating used on the hulls of boats. Other materials can absorb a large quantity of liquid but require a considerable amount of time to do so. Wood (such as a fallen tree or a nontreated piece of lumber) would be such an example.

Now it is time to discuss a concept that requires a bit more explanation, namely, the *center of gravity*. This is important in determining structural support, among other things. The simplest definition for the center of gravity is that it is the point on the object where the object can be balanced. In other words, it is the point where gravity exerts the same force on either side of the balance point so that the object does not fall.

Consider the following diagram, which shows two objects and their respective centers of gravity. The first object is considered to be uniform, and the second is considered to be nonuniform. Following the diagrams are several thoughts and examples to explain the process used to find the center of gravity.

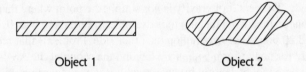

Object 1   Object 2

The first step is to define a rigid, uniform body. *Rigid* means that it is solid and does not alter its shape easily due to external forces. *Uniform* means that its volume and density is constant from one end of the body to the other. A meter stick would be an example of a uniform body. Any automobile that you see on the road would be an example of a nonuniform body.

The center of gravity for a uniform body is at its geometric center. In other words, remember that a meter stick is 100 centimeters in length. Therefore, the center of gravity for the meter stick will be at the point marked 50 centimeters, which is midway between the two ends of the meter stick. If you have a piece of treated lumber (like a 5 or 6 foot long two-by-four), the center of gravity would be midway between the two ends of the piece of lumber (this is an enlarged version of the meter stick). For nonuniform bodies, determining the location of the center of gravity requires a bit more analysis. In order to understand the process fully, it is best to build up using several examples.

Consider two golf balls that, for all intents and purposes, can be considered completely identical to each other. Now place these golf balls on a table some distance apart (use 80 centimeters for this example). The center of gravity between the two golf balls will be on the line that connects the centers of the two golf balls and the same distance from each golf ball. In other words, the center of gravity will be directly between the two golf balls and 40 centimeters away from either golf ball. This type of example works for any two identical objects.

Now think about having two objects that are not identical. Consider placing an object that weighs 10 pounds 3 meters away from an object that weighs 20 pounds. The center of gravity is no longer midway between the two objects and will be closer to the object that is heavier (with two objects of different weights, the center of gravity will *always* be closer to the heavier object). Use the following diagram to help determine and understand the location for the center of gravity between these two objects.

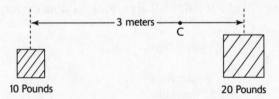

The object on the left weighs 10 pounds, and the object on the right weighs 20 pounds. The distance between the two objects is 3 meters. Notice that this distance is measured from the centers of the objects and is not the distance from the right-hand side of the 10-pound object to the left-hand side of the 20-pound object. The center of gravity is located at the point marked C and is two meters from the 10-pound object and one meter from the 20-pound object.

Justification: The ratio of the weights of the two objects must equal the inverse ratio of the respective distances of the center of gravity from the two objects. In other words, let x be the distance between the 10-pound object and the center of gravity. Let y be the distance between the 20-pound object and the center of gravity. Then the following equation must be true:

$$\frac{20}{10} = \frac{x}{y}$$

This equation can be written as

$$20 \times y = 10 \times x$$

It is also known that $(x + y)$ must be equal to 3. This is because the distance between the two objects is 3 meters. Combining these two pieces of information leads to the conclusion that x must equal 2 meters and y must equal 1 meter.

Now consider a nonuniform body. The center of gravity is *not* simply the point where there is an equal weight of material on either side. This can be understood from the previous example, where there was 10 pounds of material on one side of the center of gravity and 20 pounds of material on the other side. Problems that require determining the precise location for the center of gravity for nonuniform bodies are beyond the scope of the ASVAB, but a general understanding of the principles mentioned here will be helpful in theoretical questions regarding this matter.

If the volume of an object is increased while its weight remains the same, then the density of the object

A. increases.
B. decreases.
C. remains the same.
D. cannot be determined.

The answer is **B.** Recall that density is equal to mass (weight) divided by volume. By keeping the weight unchanged and increasing the volume, you are effectively increasing the denominator of a fraction. This causes the value of the fraction to decrease.

From the beginning of spring until the end of spring, it would be expected for the segments of a bridge to

A. expand.
B. contract.
C. remain the same size.
D. cannot be determined.

Remember that, generally, objects expand when heated and contract when cooled. Also note that, generally, the average temperature increases from the beginning of spring to the end of spring. Thus, the correct answer to this problem is **A.**

Two identical basketballs are placed 50 centimeters apart. How far from the first basketball is the center of gravity?

A. 15 centimeters
B. 20 centimeters
C. 25 centimeters
D. 30 centimeters

The answer is **C.** Recall that the center of gravity between two identical objects is midway between the objects.

There are two crates of supplies in a room. Some of the supplies from the first crate are moved into the second crate. What happens to the center of gravity between the two crates?

A. Nothing, it remains where it was originally.
B. It moves closer to the first crate.
C. It moves closer to the second crate.
D. Cannot be determined.

The answer is **C**. This is a slightly trickier question. Recall that the center of gravity is located closer to the heavier object. By moving supplies from the first crate to the second crate, the second crate is becoming heavier than it was originally, and the first crate is becoming lighter than it was originally. As a result, the center of gravity moves closer to the second crate.

Structural Support

The majority of the information needed to understand structural support has been outlined in the previous text. Specifically, *structural support* deals with combining the concepts of strength, density (weight), expansion, and center of gravity. The general idea is to take a given amount of materials and use it to provide effective support for a large weight.

For a first example, consider the structural support required for a tall building. A sturdy foundation must be used that can support the weight of the building and all the furniture and people that will eventually occupy the building. Also, a solid skeletal structure must be built that will be able to separate and support the individual floors, walls, and other building components. Finally, the building must be constructed in such a way that it can withstand the forces associated with the various winds that will be acting on the building.

Now consider bridges. They must be able to support the constant flow of traffic across the top of the bridge. If the bridge crosses a large body of water, the supports must be able to withstand the pressures exerted by the water.

On a smaller scale, consider the average table. It has four legs that are placed, for the most part, with one leg at each of the four corners of the table (if the table is round, the legs are spaced evenly around the perimeter of the table). This is done for two reasons. First, the center of gravity for the table lies inside the four legs, so that the table will not topple over (if all four legs were along the same side of the table, it would not be able to stand). The other reason is so that the weight of the table plus whatever is placed on top of the table will be shared fairly evenly by the legs.

Consider a square table with four legs placed at the corners as described. The center of gravity for the top of the table will be in the center of the table, an equal distance away from each leg. As a result, each leg will support the same amount of weight. Now, imagine that a heavy box is placed in the exact center of the table. Each leg of the table will still support the same amount of weight, because the center of gravity is still the same distance from each leg. However, if the box is placed closer to one leg in particular (call this Leg A), then that leg will support a larger weight than any of the three remaining legs. This is because the center of gravity has been moved so that it is closest to Leg A. This is the same basic theory that is used in the construction of buildings and bridges, but on a much larger and more intricate scale.

The other point to remember is that materials (solids especially) expand and contract when exposed to a change in temperature. Any structure must be able to withstand the internal forces that accompany such structural changes.

When figuring out the wind force on the side of a building, the most important characteristic of the building to consider is its

A. height.
B. width.
C. area.
D. foundation.

The answer is **C**. Remember that the force from the wind becomes greater as the area of the building increases. Thus, although the height and width are important, it is their product (the area) that is of primary concern.

> A large number of circular pieces of wood, each of different size (radius), need to be stacked. It would be best to stack them
>
> **A.** with the larger radius toward the bottom.
> **B.** with the larger radius toward the top.
> **C.** in the order they are found.
> **D.** does not matter.

The answer is **A**. The wood pieces on the bottom need to support more weight than the wood pieces on top. By placing a smaller piece atop a larger piece, the entire smaller piece receives support. This would not be the case if the larger piece were placed atop the smaller piece.

> A bridge is being built on the hottest day of the year. The surface that vehicles will drive on consists of several concrete slabs with a small space between each slab. Compared with building the bridge on a much colder day, the spaces
>
> **A.** should be separated more.
> **B.** should be separated less.
> **C.** should be the same.
> **D.** cannot be determined.

The answer is **B**. Remember that materials expand when they are heated. Thus, there should be very little space between the slabs on the hot day so that when it cools down the slabs won't be overly far apart.

> Consider the following four configurations for two supports, a rigid uniform beam, and various loads. Which configuration will be the most stable?
>

The correct answer is **B**. Convince yourself that this is true by comparing the positions of the supports relative to the center of gravity for the board as well as the position of the added load relative to the supports.

Fluid Dynamics

There are a few differences between the ways that a solid behaves and the ways that a fluid behaves. Some of the more general differences will be outlined here. First, however, a few terms need to be defined.

The first term is *viscosity,* which can be considered as the relative ease with which a fluid will flow. In other words, engine oil has a high viscosity because it flows easily while molasses has a low viscosity because it flows quite slowly. If the two liquids were allowed to flow down an incline, the oil would reach the bottom of the incline first. The second term is compressibility. Liquids are very difficult to compress—much more so than solids. This is one of the two main characteristics of liquids that lead to hydraulics.

The other characteristic is the way that liquids transfer a force from one region to another region. In a closed container filled with liquid, the pressure of the liquid will be the same at all points that are at the same height.

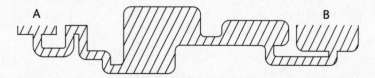

This means that in the preceding diagram, the pressure at point A is the same as the pressure at point B. Notice first that the liquid is open to the atmosphere at points A and B and that the remainder of the container is closed. Also notice that neither the shape nor the height of the rest of the container has any bearing on the fact that the pressure is the same at points A and B. Remember that pressure is defined as the force *per unit area*. In other words, because the area at point B is larger than the area at point A, a small force exerted at point A results as a larger force at point B. This is a simple definition for the process of hydraulics. The ratio of the force applied at point A to the force exerted at point B is equal to the ratio of the area at point A to the area at point B.

Remember two main ideas about hydraulics. It is very difficult to compress a liquid, and the pressure (not the exerted force) remains the same throughout the liquid. The reason that specific liquids are chosen to use in hydraulic mechanisms is that they flow easily and are more resistant to being compressed.

A force is applied at one end of a hydraulic jack. The area at the other end of the jack is five times the area where the force is applied. How much larger is the exerted force than the applied force?

A. Twice as large
B. One fifth as large
C. Five times as large
D. Half as large

The answer is **C**. Remember that the ratio of the applied force to the exerted force is the same as the ratio of the areas. Also remember that the force is greater where the area is greater.

Choose the best answer. A hydraulic jack works because

A. liquids are incompressible.
B. liquids maintain the same pressure in a closed system.
C. Both A and B
D. None of the above

The answer is **C**. This is one of the key concepts in hydraulics—liquids are incompressible and they maintain the same pressure in a closed system.

Mechanical Motion

When discussing the motion of an object, you need to consider several aspects. In order to understand these concepts, it is best to develop them from very basic ideas. These ideas can be combined to understand more complicated situations.

First consider the difference between speed and velocity. *Speed* is defined as the total distance traveled divided by the total time required to travel that distance. Velocity is defined as the total *displacement* divided by the time in which this displacement occurs. Consider the example in the following paragraph, which relates to the figure that follows.

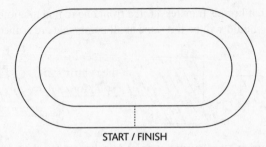

START / FINISH

A racetrack is shaped in an oval and has a total length of one mile. Now consider that a car drives around this track 10 times and does so in exactly six minutes. The total distance traveled is 10 miles. The speed is found using

$$speed = \frac{10 \; miles}{6 \; minutes} = \frac{100 \; miles}{60 \; minutes} = 100 \; miles \; per \; hour$$

Thus, the speed of the car is 100 miles per hour. However, the velocity of the car is 0! Why is this true? Because after the car has gone around the track 10 times it returns to where it started. Thus, its *displacement* is 0. Remember that displacement is merely the distance between the starting point and the finishing point, regardless of the path traveled between the two points.

The acceleration of an object is defined as the change in the speed (or velocity) of the object divided by the amount of time required for that change to take place. In other words, consider a person that is walking at a speed of 3 feet every second. Now consider that this person's speed changes to 4 feet every second. The person is said to have accelerated their speed (they are traveling faster than they were before). Had the person slowed to a speed of 2 feet every second, they would have decelerated (slowed down).

These ideas can be applied to machines as well as moving particles. Instead of thinking about a car going around a track, think of a machine that is doing work. If the machine begins to do the work faster, then the machine has accelerated the rate at which it is doing work. In other words, the machine has increased the speed with which it is doing the work. Similarly, if the machine begins to do the work more slowly, then the machine has decelerated the rate at which it is doing work. The machine has decreased the speed with which it is doing the work.

Now it is time to develop the concept of friction. There are two types of friction, referred to as static friction and kinetic friction. *Static friction* tends to keep things from moving. When pushing against a very heavy object on the floor that is not secured to the floor yet still does not move because it is so heavy, it is static friction between the object and the floor that is keeping the object from moving. *Kinetic friction* tends to slow moving objects. Kinetic friction is the reason why an object sliding across the floor will eventually come to rest.

Consider any type of engine that has moving parts. These parts interact with one another as well as with stationary parts of the engine. This produces kinetic friction, which tends to slow the speed of the engine. In this case, the friction is referred to as *internal friction*. This is because the interaction of the moving parts of the engine tends to decrease the speed with which the engine can operate.

When approaching a steep hill in a car, the accelerator must be depressed further in order to maintain the same speed up the hill that the car had on level ground before reaching the hill. Which of the following statements is true?

A. The engine is doing the same amount of work.
B. The engine is doing more work.
C. The engine is doing less work.
D. Cannot be determined.

The answer is **B.** This question is a bit trickier than most. Even though the speed of the car has not changed, the speed of the engine has. The engine has increased its speed to compensate for the extra work needed to go up the hill.

Centrifuges

A *centrifuge* is a machine that is designed to spin very rapidly in order to separate a liquid from a solid that is dissolved within the liquid. A container holding the mixture is placed in the centrifuge, and then it accelerates to a high rate of rotation very quickly. After spinning for an amount of time, the solid forms on the inner portion of the container that is farthest from the center of the centrifuge.

To understand why this happens, consider a car traveling straight on a level road. The car comes to a moderately sharp left-hand turn. As the car goes around the turn, the passengers lean toward the right side of the car. Are the people being pushed to the right?

No—the car is turning to the left, and the passengers are merely trying to continue in a straight line.

The same thing is happening in the centrifuge. The container is spinning rapidly while the liquid and solid within the container are trying to continue in a straight line. This causes the solid within the container to collect on the portion of the container farthest from the center.

A vehicle driving down the road approaches a right-hand turn. Which side of the vehicle should the passengers brace against if they are going to round the turn quickly?

A. The left side
B. The right side
C. Either side
D. The roof

The answer is **A.** In trying to continue in a straight line, the passengers will end up leaning toward the left side of the vehicle.

Simple Machines

Simple machines are used by nearly everyone on a daily basis in some form or another. This section specifically addresses how and why these machines are helpful. Also, the concept of mechanical advantage will be examined for some of the machines discussed. Mechanical advantage is a measure of the degree to which a specific job is made easier by the simple machine.

The first simple machine to be considered is a lever (sometimes referred to as a lever arm). A lever consists of a rigid object (this could be a board, rod, pipe, bar, and so on.) that is pivoted about a single point. In doing so, the force applied at one end of the lever is magnified at the other end of the lever.

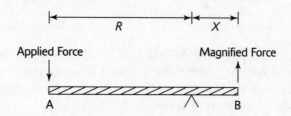

Here the applied force is at point A, and a magnified force is produced at point B. Notice that the applied force is farther away from the pivot point than the magnified force (this will always be the case). The mechanical advantage is the ratio of the distance R (from the applied force to the pivot point) to the distance X (from the pivot point to the magnified force). In other words, if the distance R is three times the distance X, then the mechanical advantage for this lever is

$$\text{mechanical advantage} = R/X = 3$$

One common example of a lever is a crowbar, also referred to as a prybar.

Another example of a simple machine is the inclined plane. This is nothing more than a flat surface that is used to move a heavy object from one height to another. A frequent application of an inclined plane is to move a heavy crate from a lower point to a higher point (loading a truck, for instance).

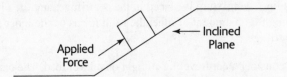

The concept of mechanical advantage does not apply directly to an inclined plane, because the applied force is not magnified by the inclined plane (remember that the applied force is magnified by the lever). Notice that the most efficient way to use the inclined plane is to have the applied force be parallel to the inclined plane. In other words, you want to push the crate up the plane, not into the plane.

Another example of a simple machine that does not magnify the applied force is a screw. A screw is used to hold together two objects.

Consider using a screw to fasten a nameplate to a wooden door. The screw is inserted into the door until the nameplate is flush against the door and the head of the screw is flush against the nameplate. The main characteristic of the screw that holds the nameplate to the door is the threads. The threads act much like the barb on a fishing hook. After the screw is inserted into the door, it cannot simply be pulled back out.

One of the more intricate simple machines is the pulley. Pulleys are very useful in that there are many diverse ways in which to combine them, depending on the task at hand. A single pulley can be used in conjunction with a rope to lift a heavy object above the ground.

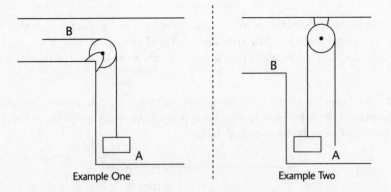

Notice that the pulley system can be arranged so that the object can be raised from point A to point B in several different ways. In the first example, the person operating the pulley is at point A lifting the object to someone else at point B. In the second example, however, the person is already at point B and uses the pulley to bring the heavy object to point B. In both of these examples, however, the applied force is equal to the exerted force.

Now consider a slight variation of the second example. In this example, the mechanical advantage is two.

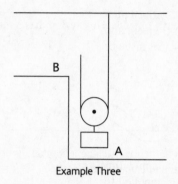

Example Three

Why is this true? Look back to the first example. In this case the person lifting the load is pulling down on the rope, and gravity is pulling down on the load. The rope supporting the pulley is actually supporting *twice* the weight of the load! In the third example, however, the person is pulling *up* on the rope, gravity is pulling down on the load, and the point where the rope is secured acts as another upward force.

As an additional point of interest, notice that in the third example the pulley is moving while in the first example the pulley is stationary. In order for any pulley system to have a mechanical advantage greater than one, there must be at least one movable pulley. In other words, it is impossible to construct a pulley system where all the pulleys are fixed (don't move) that has a mechanical advantage greater than one.

As a result, the person doing the lifting needs to exert only half of the force required in example one. However, the person must pull twice as much rope. In other words, if the person in the third example wants to lift the load 10 feet, then 20 feet of rope must be pulled through the pulley. Recalling that work is equal to force times distance, we see that the amount of work done has remained the same.

Two more things about pulley systems should be mentioned. First, it is possible to create systems with many movable pulleys that have mechanical advantages of 2, 3, or even higher. The following diagram shows a pulley system that has a mechanical advantage of 3:

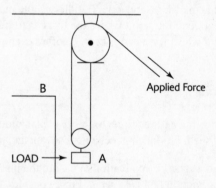

Remember, however, that in order to lift the crate 5 feet, 15 feet of rope must be pulled through the pulley system (the person lifting the crate is exerting less force but still doing the same amount of work).

The final thought is that the mechanical advantages discussed here are theoretical. In other words, the actual mechanical advantage will be slightly less. This is due mainly to friction in the pulleys and from the rope through the pulleys.

A system of pulleys designed to lift heavy objects. This system has a total of three pulleys. What is the mechanical advantage of the system?

A. 1
B. 2
C. 3
D. Cannot be determined

The answer is **D.** If all of the pulleys are fixed, the mechanical advantage will be 1. The configuration of the pulleys must be known in order to determine the mechanical advantage.

Another simple machine that is used frequently is a wedge. A *wedge* is designed to split apart a single object or separate two objects from one another. Think back to the section on levers, where we mentioned that a crowbar was a common lever. A crowbar is one method to separate two objects (two boards that have been nailed together, for example). A wedge accomplishes the same thing but works a bit differently.

The following diagram shows an example of a wedge:

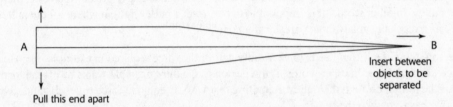

A ← → B

Insert between objects to be separated

Pull this end apart

At end A the rods are not connected. This end is used as the handles for the wedge. At end B the rods are connected and are very thin. This end is inserted between the two objects to be separated, and the handles are pulled apart. This simple machine will be more effective if the length of the wedge is long compared with the size of the objects to be separated.

The last simple machine to be discussed is the wheel and axle. For this simple machine, the force is applied by turning the wheel and is transferred through the axle to the point where the force is to be exerted. One of the most common examples of a wheel and axle is a steering wheel for a car or boat. Another example is an outdoor water faucet.

Compound Machines

Compound machines are a bit more interesting and require a bit more explanation. They normally consist of moving parts and multiple components. Some of them produce a mechanical advantage, just as simple machines do.

For our first example, consider a cam and a specific application of a cam, the piston. These compound machines are used to change linear motion into circular motion and *vice versa*. First, consider a cam where a rotating rod is used to change circular motion to linear motion.

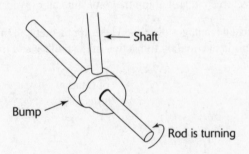

Shaft

Bump

Rod is turning

The rod turns, and as it turns so does the attached ring. Notice that the ring has a bump on it, and as this bump passes beneath the shaft, it causes the shaft to move up and down. The circular motion of the rod is used to create linear motion in the shaft.

Many, many applications of converting circular motion to linear motion can be found in the mechanical world of today. One such example is an oil pump. A more common example, however, is a piston.

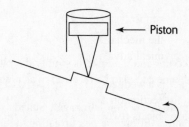

Although the appearance of the piston is slightly different, the principles involved are exactly the same. In this case, part of the rod is slightly displaced, and a second bar connects this displaced portion of the rod to the actual piston. The turning of the rod causes the piston to move up and down.

Now consider how a system of gears works. Consider the simple example in the following diagram consisting of only two gears.

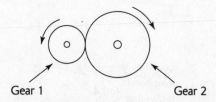

The smaller gear is designed to have 5 teeth while the larger gear is designed to have 20 teeth. This means that for every rotation of the larger gear, the smaller gear has gone through four rotations. This system of gears can be used to increase or decrease the speed of circular motion. Also notice that if the smaller gear is turning clockwise (counterclockwise), then the larger gear must be turning counterclockwise. The mechanical advantage for such a system of gears is simply the ratio of number of teeth for the gears:

$$MA = 20/5 = 4.$$

If it is desired to have both components rotate in the same direction, then a system of four gears can be used.

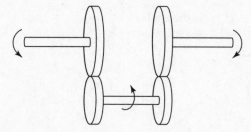

In going from the first rod to the intermediate rod, the direction of rotation changes. Then, in going from the intermediate rod to the final rod, the direction of rotation changes again or returns to what it was originally. A common application of this type of gear system is an automobile transmission.

Another compound machine is the crank. A crank consists of a rod of varying radius with a rope (or chain or other connecting device) that wraps around the larger radius portion of the rod and connects to the weight to be lifted (or moved).

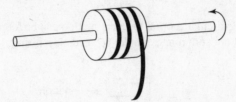

The mechanical advantage for this type of compound machine is simply the ratio of the larger radius portion of the rod to the smaller radius portion. This type of device can also be referred to as a winch.

The next compound machine requires a bit more discussion—linkages. Stated as simply as possible, linkages are capable of converting the rotating motion of a crank into a different type of rotating motion, oscillatory motion, or reciprocating motion. This is a reversible process. In other words, a linkage is also capable of taking any of the last three types of motion and using them to turn a crank.

The simplest type of a linkage is the four-bar variety.

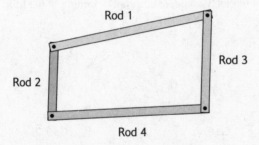

By making the four bars the appropriate length, it is possible to hold rod 1 fixed, allow rod 2 to rotate in full circular motion, and rod 3 will oscillate back and forth. A frequently used example of this system is an automobile windshield wiper. Another example that is not quite so obvious is a front-end loader. Remember that it is important to raise and lower the bucket without allowing the bucket to rotate (this keeps the material in the bucket from falling out).

The last two compound machines to be discussed are belts and chains. These serve the same purpose, to change rotational motion of one speed to rotational motion of another speed. The principle is quite similar to a system of gears, except that the rotating elements are not in contact with one another. Belts are used in automobile motors, while an example of a chain would be a bicycle. Motorcycles can be either belt driven or chain driven.

Mechanical Comprehension Practice Questions

The following questions are a representative example of the types of questions you will find on each of the four different military examinations. Answer each to the best of your ability and then check your answers with the answer key that follows.

Sample ASVAB Questions

1. When pedaling a bicycle, a chain is used to connect the gear associated with the pedals to the gear associated with the rear tire. Which of the following statements is true?

   A. Force is gained while work is lost.
   B. Torque is gained while force is lost.
   C. Speed is gained while force is lost.
   D. Speed is gained while torque is lost.

2. Which of the following compound machines would you expect to be associated with an automobile?

   A. Gear
   B. Cam
   C. Piston
   D. All of the above

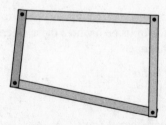

3. What type of compound machine is shown in the diagram?

   A. Piston
   B. Linkages
   C. Cam
   D. Crank

4. Five gears are connected as shown. Which of the following choices list gears that are all turning in the same direction?

   A. Gears A, C, and D
   B. Gears A, B, and D
   C. Gears A, C, and E
   D. Gears A, B, and C

5. A crank is a useful compound machine that

   A. Increases torque
   B. Decreases friction
   C. Increases speed
   D. None of these

6. In the lever shown, what is the mechanical advantage?

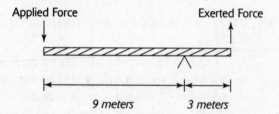

   Applied Force   Exerted Force

   9 meters   3 meters

   A. 4
   B. 3
   C. 2
   D. 1

7. A system consists of two pulleys, both of which are fixed. What is the mechanical advantage for the system?

   A. 1
   B. 2
   C. 3
   D. Cannot be determined

8. All of the following are simple machines except

   A. Pulley
   B. Cam
   C. Screw
   D. Wheel and Axle

119

Sample AFOQT Questions

In questions 9 and 10, you should neglect air resistance in order to select the correct choice.

9. A ball in freefall will have

    A. increasing speed and increasing acceleration.

    B. increasing speed and decreasing acceleration.

    C. increasing speed and constant acceleration.

    D. decreasing speed and increasing acceleration.

    E. constant speed and constant acceleration.

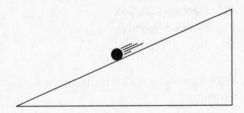

10. A ball rolling down the slope of a steep hill will have

    A. increasing speed and increasing acceleration.

    B. increasing speed and decreasing acceleration.

    C. increasing speed and constant acceleration.

    D. decreasing speed and increasing acceleration.

    E. constant speed and constant acceleration.

Questions 11 and 12 are based on the following illustration.

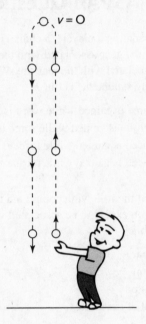

11. A ball thrown straight up will come to a full stop at the top of its path where the acceleration at that moment equals

    A. 9.8 m/s^2.

    B. zero.

    C. less than 9.8 m/s^2.

    D. more than 9.8 m/s^2.

    E. cannot be determined.

12. After the ball is thrown up and comes to full stop and starts falling down, its speed after 1 second of fall is

    A. 4.9 m/s.

    B. 9.8 m/s.

    C. 19.6 m/s.

    D. 1 m/s.

    E. 32 m/s.

Questions 13 and 14 are based on the figure that follows.

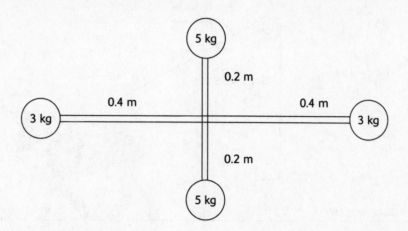

13. The rods joining the four masses shown in the preceding figure have negligible weight. Assuming that the four masses are point masses (that is, their masses are assumed concentrated at their centers of gravity), the moment of inertia of the system is

  A. 16 kg.m².
  B. 34 kg.m².
  C. 13.6 kg.m².
  D. 1.36 kg.m².
  E. 0.136 kg.m².

14. If the preceding system rotates with an angular velocity ω of 8 radians/second, what is the rotational kinetic energy of the system?

  A. 4.352 J
  B. 43.52 J
  C. 435.2 J
  D. 4352 J
  E. 0.435 J

Sample ASTB Questions

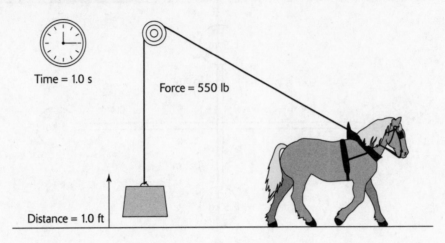

Time = 1.0 s

Force = 550 lb

Distance = 1.0 ft

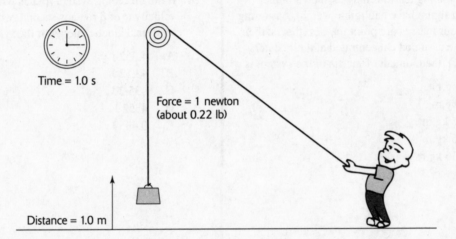

Time = 1.0 s

Force = 1 newton
(about 0.22 lb)

Distance = 1.0 m

15. In the preceding figure, who is exerting more power? The horse or the man?

    A. The horse

    B. The man

    C. Both exert the same power.

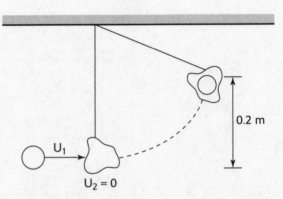

U_1

$U_2 = 0$

0.2 m

16. A 5 kg wad of clay is tied to the end of a string as shown in the figure. A 300 gm copper ball moving horizontally at velocity u_1 is embedded into the clay and causes the combination of clay and ball to rise to a height of 0.2 m. The initial velocity u_1 of the ball is nearly

    A. 6.3 m/s.

    B. 7.3 m/s.

    C. 8.3 m/s.

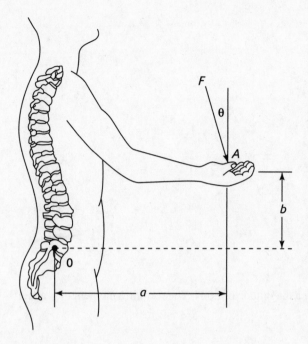

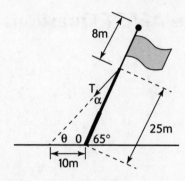

18. To raise the flagpole from the position shown in the figure, the tension force T in the cable must supply a moment about O equal to 18 KN.m. The tension T is

A. 1.5 KN.

B. 2.16 KN.

C. 9.0 KN.

17. The preceding figure shows the lower lumbar region O of the spinal cord. It is known to be the most susceptible part to damage since it provides resistance to excessive bending caused by the moment of the force F about O. If in a particular loading the distances b and a are 12 and 30 cm, respectively, the angle θ that causes the maximum bending strain is

A. 21.8°

B. 23.57°

C. 66.42°

Sample AFAST Questions

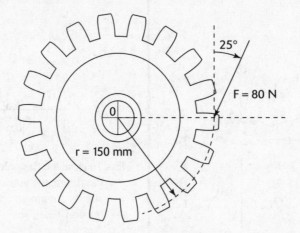

19. The force F in the diagram is applied to the gear and has a magnitude of 80 N. The resulting moment of F about the center point O is

A. 368 N.m.

B. 87 N.m.

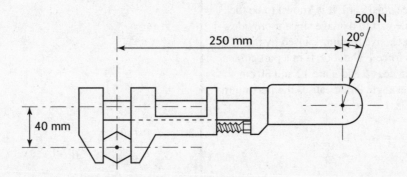

20. The moment M of the 500 N force on the handle of the monkey wrench about the center point of the bolt is

A. N.m.

B. 0.61 N.m.

Answer and Explanations

1. **D.** Remember that for linear motion the two quantities to be concerned with are *work* and *force*. For circular motion, the two quantities are *speed* and *torque*. When either of these quantities is gained, the other one is lost. For the case of pedaling a bicycle, circular motion is present.

2. **D.** The Cam is used to move the piston back and forth while the gear is part of the system that connects the drive shaft to the wheels.

3. **B.** Remember that the most common type of linkage is the four-bar variety, which is shown here.

4. **C.** Remember that adjacent gears turn in opposite directions, so every other gear turns in the same direction.

5. **A.** A crank produces circular motion, so our two properties of interest are torque and speed. A crank increases torque at the sacrifice of speed (number of rotations).

6. **B.** This is found using the ratio MA = 9/3 = 3.

7. **A.** Remember that for a system of pulleys to create a mechanical advantage greater than one that at least one of the pulleys must be mobile (capable of moving). Because both pulleys are fixed, there is no mechanical advantage.

8. **B.** A cam is a compound machine.

9. **C.** The acceleration is constant at 9.8 m/s, but the speed increases with time

10. **B.** The acceleration a equals g or 9.8 m/s for a straight downfall, but decreases to zero on the level surface at the bottom of the slope.

11. **A.** acceleration $a = g = 9.8$ m/s^2 since the ball is under the influence of gravity throughout its path.

12. **A.** The average speed is one half of the initial speed (which is zero) and the final speed after one second (which is 9.8 m/s).

13. **D.** moment of inertia I = $2[3(0.4)^2 + 5(0.2)^2] = 1.36$ kg.m^2.

14. **B.** The rotational kinetic energy $E_k = 0.5 \, I \, \omega^2 = 0.5 \, (1.36) \, (8)^2 = 43.52$ J

15. **A.** It takes 746 watts (or 746 newton.m/s) to equal I horsepower (or 550 ft.lb/s). The horse exerts 550 ft.lb/s or 1 horsepower while the man exerts 1 newton.m/s or 1 Joule/s, which is 1 watt.

16. **C.** Conservation of energy requires that the initial kinetic energy of the ball is converted to potential energy of the ball-clay combination, that is, 0.5 (0.3)u12=(5+0.3)(9.8)(0.2) or u1 = 8.32 m/s.

17. **A.** Moment about A is maximum when the force vector F is perpendicular to distance from A to B where B is the point on the hand where F is applied. Thus, $\theta = \tan^{-1}(h/b) = \tan^{-1}(12/30) = 21.8°$.

18. **B.** $\theta = \tan^{-1}[30 \, (0.866)/(12+15)] = 43.90°$. Hence $\alpha = 60° - 43.90° = 16.10°$. Since T (30) sin 16.1° = 18 KN we obtain T = 2.16 KN.

19. **B.** Taking moments about O we obtain net moment M = (0.15)(80 cos 25°) = 10.87 N.m.

20. **B.** Taking moments about the center of the bolt we obtain M = 500 (0.25) cos 20° – 500 (0.04) sin 20° = 110.61 N.m.

FULL-LENGTH PRACTICE TESTS 1

Answer Sheet for AFOQT Practice Test 1

(Remove This Sheet and Use It to Mark Your Answers)

Part 1   Verbal Analogies

1 Ⓐ Ⓑ Ⓒ Ⓓ Ⓔ	16 Ⓐ Ⓑ Ⓒ Ⓓ Ⓔ
2 Ⓐ Ⓑ Ⓒ Ⓓ Ⓔ	17 Ⓐ Ⓑ Ⓒ Ⓓ Ⓔ
3 Ⓐ Ⓑ Ⓒ Ⓓ Ⓔ	18 Ⓐ Ⓑ Ⓒ Ⓓ Ⓔ
4 Ⓐ Ⓑ Ⓒ Ⓓ Ⓔ	19 Ⓐ Ⓑ Ⓒ Ⓓ Ⓔ
5 Ⓐ Ⓑ Ⓒ Ⓓ Ⓔ	20 Ⓐ Ⓑ Ⓒ Ⓓ Ⓔ
6 Ⓐ Ⓑ Ⓒ Ⓓ Ⓔ	21 Ⓐ Ⓑ Ⓒ Ⓓ Ⓔ
7 Ⓐ Ⓑ Ⓒ Ⓓ Ⓔ	22 Ⓐ Ⓑ Ⓒ Ⓓ Ⓔ
8 Ⓐ Ⓑ Ⓒ Ⓓ Ⓔ	23 Ⓐ Ⓑ Ⓒ Ⓓ Ⓔ
9 Ⓐ Ⓑ Ⓒ Ⓓ Ⓔ	24 Ⓐ Ⓑ Ⓒ Ⓓ Ⓔ
10 Ⓐ Ⓑ Ⓒ Ⓓ Ⓔ	25 Ⓐ Ⓑ Ⓒ Ⓓ Ⓔ
11 Ⓐ Ⓑ Ⓒ Ⓓ Ⓔ	
12 Ⓐ Ⓑ Ⓒ Ⓓ Ⓔ	
13 Ⓐ Ⓑ Ⓒ Ⓓ Ⓔ	
14 Ⓐ Ⓑ Ⓒ Ⓓ Ⓔ	
15 Ⓐ Ⓑ Ⓒ Ⓓ Ⓔ	

Part 2   Arithmetic Reasoning

1 Ⓐ Ⓑ Ⓒ Ⓓ Ⓔ	16 Ⓐ Ⓑ Ⓒ Ⓓ Ⓔ
2 Ⓐ Ⓑ Ⓒ Ⓓ Ⓔ	17 Ⓐ Ⓑ Ⓒ Ⓓ Ⓔ
3 Ⓐ Ⓑ Ⓒ Ⓓ Ⓔ	18 Ⓐ Ⓑ Ⓒ Ⓓ Ⓔ
4 Ⓐ Ⓑ Ⓒ Ⓓ Ⓔ	19 Ⓐ Ⓑ Ⓒ Ⓓ Ⓔ
5 Ⓐ Ⓑ Ⓒ Ⓓ Ⓔ	20 Ⓐ Ⓑ Ⓒ Ⓓ Ⓔ
6 Ⓐ Ⓑ Ⓒ Ⓓ Ⓔ	21 Ⓐ Ⓑ Ⓒ Ⓓ Ⓔ
7 Ⓐ Ⓑ Ⓒ Ⓓ Ⓔ	22 Ⓐ Ⓑ Ⓒ Ⓓ Ⓔ
8 Ⓐ Ⓑ Ⓒ Ⓓ Ⓔ	23 Ⓐ Ⓑ Ⓒ Ⓓ Ⓔ
9 Ⓐ Ⓑ Ⓒ Ⓓ Ⓔ	24 Ⓐ Ⓑ Ⓒ Ⓓ Ⓔ
10 Ⓐ Ⓑ Ⓒ Ⓓ Ⓔ	25 Ⓐ Ⓑ Ⓒ Ⓓ Ⓔ
11 Ⓐ Ⓑ Ⓒ Ⓓ Ⓔ	
12 Ⓐ Ⓑ Ⓒ Ⓓ Ⓔ	
13 Ⓐ Ⓑ Ⓒ Ⓓ Ⓔ	
14 Ⓐ Ⓑ Ⓒ Ⓓ Ⓔ	
15 Ⓐ Ⓑ Ⓒ Ⓓ Ⓔ	

Part 3   Reading Comprehension

1 Ⓐ Ⓑ Ⓒ Ⓓ Ⓔ	16 Ⓐ Ⓑ Ⓒ Ⓓ Ⓔ
2 Ⓐ Ⓑ Ⓒ Ⓓ Ⓔ	17 Ⓐ Ⓑ Ⓒ Ⓓ Ⓔ
3 Ⓐ Ⓑ Ⓒ Ⓓ Ⓔ	18 Ⓐ Ⓑ Ⓒ Ⓓ Ⓔ
4 Ⓐ Ⓑ Ⓒ Ⓓ Ⓔ	19 Ⓐ Ⓑ Ⓒ Ⓓ Ⓔ
5 Ⓐ Ⓑ Ⓒ Ⓓ Ⓔ	20 Ⓐ Ⓑ Ⓒ Ⓓ Ⓔ
6 Ⓐ Ⓑ Ⓒ Ⓓ Ⓔ	21 Ⓐ Ⓑ Ⓒ Ⓓ Ⓔ
7 Ⓐ Ⓑ Ⓒ Ⓓ Ⓔ	22 Ⓐ Ⓑ Ⓒ Ⓓ Ⓔ
8 Ⓐ Ⓑ Ⓒ Ⓓ Ⓔ	23 Ⓐ Ⓑ Ⓒ Ⓓ Ⓔ
9 Ⓐ Ⓑ Ⓒ Ⓓ Ⓔ	24 Ⓐ Ⓑ Ⓒ Ⓓ Ⓔ
10 Ⓐ Ⓑ Ⓒ Ⓓ Ⓔ	25 Ⓐ Ⓑ Ⓒ Ⓓ Ⓔ
11 Ⓐ Ⓑ Ⓒ Ⓓ Ⓔ	
12 Ⓐ Ⓑ Ⓒ Ⓓ Ⓔ	
13 Ⓐ Ⓑ Ⓒ Ⓓ Ⓔ	
14 Ⓐ Ⓑ Ⓒ Ⓓ Ⓔ	
15 Ⓐ Ⓑ Ⓒ Ⓓ Ⓔ	

Part 4   Data Interpretation

1 Ⓐ Ⓑ Ⓒ Ⓓ Ⓔ	16 Ⓐ Ⓑ Ⓒ Ⓓ Ⓔ
2 Ⓐ Ⓑ Ⓒ Ⓓ Ⓔ	17 Ⓐ Ⓑ Ⓒ Ⓓ Ⓔ
3 Ⓐ Ⓑ Ⓒ Ⓓ Ⓔ	18 Ⓐ Ⓑ Ⓒ Ⓓ Ⓔ
4 Ⓐ Ⓑ Ⓒ Ⓓ Ⓔ	19 Ⓐ Ⓑ Ⓒ Ⓓ Ⓔ
5 Ⓐ Ⓑ Ⓒ Ⓓ Ⓔ	20 Ⓐ Ⓑ Ⓒ Ⓓ Ⓔ
6 Ⓐ Ⓑ Ⓒ Ⓓ Ⓔ	21 Ⓐ Ⓑ Ⓒ Ⓓ Ⓔ
7 Ⓐ Ⓑ Ⓒ Ⓓ Ⓔ	22 Ⓐ Ⓑ Ⓒ Ⓓ Ⓔ
8 Ⓐ Ⓑ Ⓒ Ⓓ Ⓔ	23 Ⓐ Ⓑ Ⓒ Ⓓ Ⓔ
9 Ⓐ Ⓑ Ⓒ Ⓓ Ⓔ	24 Ⓐ Ⓑ Ⓒ Ⓓ Ⓔ
10 Ⓐ Ⓑ Ⓒ Ⓓ Ⓔ	25 Ⓐ Ⓑ Ⓒ Ⓓ Ⓔ
11 Ⓐ Ⓑ Ⓒ Ⓓ Ⓔ	
12 Ⓐ Ⓑ Ⓒ Ⓓ Ⓔ	
13 Ⓐ Ⓑ Ⓒ Ⓓ Ⓔ	
14 Ⓐ Ⓑ Ⓒ Ⓓ Ⓔ	
15 Ⓐ Ⓑ Ⓒ Ⓓ Ⓔ	

Part 5   Word Knowledge

1 Ⓐ Ⓑ Ⓒ Ⓓ Ⓔ	16 Ⓐ Ⓑ Ⓒ Ⓓ Ⓔ
2 Ⓐ Ⓑ Ⓒ Ⓓ Ⓔ	17 Ⓐ Ⓑ Ⓒ Ⓓ Ⓔ
3 Ⓐ Ⓑ Ⓒ Ⓓ Ⓔ	18 Ⓐ Ⓑ Ⓒ Ⓓ Ⓔ
4 Ⓐ Ⓑ Ⓒ Ⓓ Ⓔ	19 Ⓐ Ⓑ Ⓒ Ⓓ Ⓔ
5 Ⓐ Ⓑ Ⓒ Ⓓ Ⓔ	20 Ⓐ Ⓑ Ⓒ Ⓓ Ⓔ
6 Ⓐ Ⓑ Ⓒ Ⓓ Ⓔ	21 Ⓐ Ⓑ Ⓒ Ⓓ Ⓔ
7 Ⓐ Ⓑ Ⓒ Ⓓ Ⓔ	22 Ⓐ Ⓑ Ⓒ Ⓓ Ⓔ
8 Ⓐ Ⓑ Ⓒ Ⓓ Ⓔ	23 Ⓐ Ⓑ Ⓒ Ⓓ Ⓔ
9 Ⓐ Ⓑ Ⓒ Ⓓ Ⓔ	24 Ⓐ Ⓑ Ⓒ Ⓓ Ⓔ
10 Ⓐ Ⓑ Ⓒ Ⓓ Ⓔ	25 Ⓐ Ⓑ Ⓒ Ⓓ Ⓔ
11 Ⓐ Ⓑ Ⓒ Ⓓ Ⓔ	
12 Ⓐ Ⓑ Ⓒ Ⓓ Ⓔ	
13 Ⓐ Ⓑ Ⓒ Ⓓ Ⓔ	
14 Ⓐ Ⓑ Ⓒ Ⓓ Ⓔ	
15 Ⓐ Ⓑ Ⓒ Ⓓ Ⓔ	

Part 6   Mathematics Knowledge

1 Ⓐ Ⓑ Ⓒ Ⓓ Ⓔ	16 Ⓐ Ⓑ Ⓒ Ⓓ Ⓔ
2 Ⓐ Ⓑ Ⓒ Ⓓ Ⓔ	17 Ⓐ Ⓑ Ⓒ Ⓓ Ⓔ
3 Ⓐ Ⓑ Ⓒ Ⓓ Ⓔ	18 Ⓐ Ⓑ Ⓒ Ⓓ Ⓔ
4 Ⓐ Ⓑ Ⓒ Ⓓ Ⓔ	19 Ⓐ Ⓑ Ⓒ Ⓓ Ⓔ
5 Ⓐ Ⓑ Ⓒ Ⓓ Ⓔ	20 Ⓐ Ⓑ Ⓒ Ⓓ Ⓔ
6 Ⓐ Ⓑ Ⓒ Ⓓ Ⓔ	21 Ⓐ Ⓑ Ⓒ Ⓓ Ⓔ
7 Ⓐ Ⓑ Ⓒ Ⓓ Ⓔ	22 Ⓐ Ⓑ Ⓒ Ⓓ Ⓔ
8 Ⓐ Ⓑ Ⓒ Ⓓ Ⓔ	23 Ⓐ Ⓑ Ⓒ Ⓓ Ⓔ
9 Ⓐ Ⓑ Ⓒ Ⓓ Ⓔ	24 Ⓐ Ⓑ Ⓒ Ⓓ Ⓔ
10 Ⓐ Ⓑ Ⓒ Ⓓ Ⓔ	25 Ⓐ Ⓑ Ⓒ Ⓓ Ⓔ
11 Ⓐ Ⓑ Ⓒ Ⓓ Ⓔ	
12 Ⓐ Ⓑ Ⓒ Ⓓ Ⓔ	
13 Ⓐ Ⓑ Ⓒ Ⓓ Ⓔ	
14 Ⓐ Ⓑ Ⓒ Ⓓ Ⓔ	
15 Ⓐ Ⓑ Ⓒ Ⓓ Ⓔ	

CUT HERE

AFOQT Practice Test 1

The following test contains those sections of the Air Force Officer Qualifying Tests (AFOQT) that are important for those applicants for Officer Candidate School. There are six sections that will be tested. Take these tests under simulated conditions—a quiet room and a timer. After taking the tests, give yourself a day or so before you check your answers. Use the explanations to help you understand the material. Most important, make sure that you learn and memorize the directions. On any timed exam, you can lose valuable time by wasting time trying to understand what is being asked of you. These are fairly simple directions but worth learning and understanding.

Part 1: Verbal Analogies

Time: 8 Minutes
25 Questions

Directions: This part of the test measures your ability to reason and see relationships between words. Choose the answer that best completes the analogy developed at the beginning of each question.

1. ACTOR is to STAGE

   A. PATIENT is to DOCTOR
   B. OUTSIDE is to BENCH
   C. GARAGE is to CAR
   D. TEACHER is to CLASSROOM
   E. METER is to ELECTRIC

2. TYRANT is to CRUELTY

   A. DRAWL is to SPEAKER
   B. COMPILE is to DISASSEMBLE
   C. ACCOLADE is to AWARD
   D. SYCOPHANT is to FLATTERY
   E. WAX is to CANDLE

3. SLOTH is to LAZINESS

   A. GENTEEL is to VULGAR
   B. INSOMNIAC is to SLEEPLESSNESS
   C. HACKNEYED is to UNIQUE
   D. ACCEDE is to RESPECT
   E. CRYPT is to TOMB

4. HALLOWED is to SACRED

   A. SOLDIER is to ARMY
   B. GAMUT is to PROVINCIAL
   C. LIBEL is to PRAISE
   D. NOMADIC is to WANDERING
   E. OBLIVIOUS is to KEEN

5. SANCTIMONIOUS is to SMUG

   A. ALTRUISTIC is to GREEDY
   B. LUGUBRIOUS is to MELANCHOLY
   C. GRANDIOSE is to MINISCULE
   D. RETICENT is to TALKATIVE
   E. EXACERBATE is to AMELIORATE

6. DANCER is to ENSEMBLE

   A. YOGURT is to MILK
   B. STUDENT is to CLASS
   C. MOUNTAIN is to PRECIPICE
   D. FLOCK is to SHEEP
   E. DOODLE is to NOTEBOOK

7. ANARCHIST is to DISORDER

   A. YAWN is to BOREDOM
   B. MONTH is to YEAR
   C. GOOD is to BEST
   D. PACIFIST is to PEACE
   E. CONSTELLATION is to STARS

8. DOCTOR is to HEALING

   A. PRISON is to GUARD
   B. DINOSAURS is to PALEONTOLOGIST
   C. AUTHOR is to WRITING
   D. CLAP is to HANDS
   E. PLANETS is to UNIVERSE

GO ON TO THE NEXT PAGE

9. POLICE is to LAW

   A. LION is to DEN
   B. BRUSH is to HAIR
   C. CONDUCTOR is to ORCHESTRA
   D. BOOK is to LIBRARY
   E. CLERGY is to RELIGION

10. COOL is to FRIGID

   A. SPEAKER is to ASSEMBLY
   B. BUG is to COLD
   C. WATER is to BUCKET
   D. DISLIKE is to DETEST
   E. STUNT is to GROWTH

11. CRUMB is to LOAF

   A. PAINTER is to CANVAS
   B. PUDDLE is to OCEAN
   C. SOUND is to MICROPHONE
   D. PRIDE is to FALL
   E. FEATHER is to QUILL

12. BREEZE is to GALE

   A. EYES is to FACE
   B. MALEVOLENT is to CHARITABLE
   C. HOSTILE is to ENEMY
   D. SNOWFLAKE is to BLIZZARD
   E. PUNGENT is to SMELL

13. CROISSANT is to PASTRY

   A. SCHOOL is to FISH
   B. TREE is to PEACH
   C. HAIKU is to POEM
   D. KNIFE is to CUT
   E. VENISON is to DEER

14. ROMANCE is to NOVEL

   A. BOON is to BLESSING
   B. RAP is to MUSIC
   C. CREDO is to IMMORAL
   D. FRICTION is to SANDPAPER
   E. DETERMINED is to HESITANT

15. TANKER is to SHIP

   A. INSECT is to ANT
   B. MATRIARCH is to MOTHER
   C. MINIVAN is to AUTOMOBILE
   D. COW is to VEAL
   E. DEGREE is to COLLEGE

16. WHALE is to OCEAN

   A. CONGREGATION is to CROWD
   B. POUND is to DOGCATCHER
   C. CHURCH is to STEEPLE
   D. COURT is to TENNIS
   E. BEE is to HIVE

17. PRISTINE is to UNSPOILED

   A. TAINTED is to CONTAMINATED
   B. EASE is to TAXING
   C. ARID is to DELUGED
   D. CHAMPIONED is to ABASED
   E. ANIMUS is to KINDNESS

18. BIRTH is to LIFE

   A. RODENT is to SKUNK
   B. GENTRY is to NOBILITY
   C. PROLIFERATE is to CEASE
   D. WINCE is to JOY
   E. EXPOSURE is to INFECTION

19. MEDITATION is to RELAXATION

   A. ORDER is to CHAOS
   B. SYMPTOMS is to BACTERIA
   C. HONE is to WHET
   D. SATIATION is to SATISFACTION
   E. DEXTERITY is to ACCOMPLISHMENT

20. ISOLATION is to LONELINESS

   A. SHORTEN is to NIP
   B. QUIET is to TACIT
   C. PROMOTION is to ADVANCEMENT
   D. MONOTONY is to HOMOGENOUS
   E. RUSTIC is to CITY

21. SANCTUARY is to REFUGE

    A. FINGER is to HAND
    B. IMPRISONMENT is to PUNISHMENT
    C. BANJO is to COUNTRY
    D. BALLOON is to HELIUM
    E. SADNESS is to BLUES

22. BATHING is to CLEANLINESS

    A. MEDICINE is to HARM
    B. SCHOOLING is to EDUCATION
    C. SPITE is to KINDNESS
    D. UTENSIL is to CHEF
    E. SOW is to CLOTHING

23. SMILING is to HAPPINESS

    A. EXERCISE is to RUNNING
    B. MOTORCYCLE is to TRAVEL
    C. MILK is to BREAKFAST
    D. SCOWLING is to DISPLEASURE
    E. SHOUTING is to POWER

24. HANDS is to CLOCK

    A. PIANO is to MUSIC
    B. JUSTICE is to COURT
    C. LEGS is to BODY
    D. ANNOYED is to FURIOUS
    E. CARNIVORE is to TIGER

25. QUARTER is to DOLLAR

    A. BOREDOM is to YAWN
    B. WEEK is to MONTH
    C. MONEY is to POUND
    D. CRANE is to LIFT
    E. FLOWER is to PETALS

STOP. BEFORE MOVING ON TO THE NEXT SECTION, CHECK YOUR ANSWERS IF THERE IS STILL TIME LEFT.

Part 2: Arithmetic Reasoning

Time: 29 Minutes
25 Questions

Directions: This section of the test measures your mathematical reasoning or your ability to arrive at solutions to problems. Each problem is followed by five possible answers. Select the answer that is most nearly correct.

1. There are 72 freshmen in the band. If freshmen make up $\frac{1}{3}$ of the entire band, the total number of students in the band is

    A. 24
    B. 72
    C. 144
    D. 203
    E. 216

2. Dana receives $30 for her birthday and $15 for cleaning the garage. If she spends $16 on a CD, how much money does she have left?

    A. $29
    B. $27
    C. $14
    D. $1
    E. $0.45

3. A television is on sale for 20% off. If the sale price is $800, what was the original price?

    A. $160
    B. $640
    C. $960
    D. $1,000
    E. $1,160

4. Jack earns $9.50 an hour plus 3% commission on all sales made. If his total sales during a 30-hour work week were $500, how much did he earn?

    A. $15
    B. $250
    C. $275
    D. $285
    E. $300

GO ON TO THE NEXT PAGE

5. The area of one circle is 4 times as large as a smaller circle with a radius of 3 inches. The radius of the larger circle is

A. 12 inches
B. 9 inches
C. 8 inches
D. 6 inches
E. 4 inches

6. If 400 people can be seated in 8 subway cars, how many people can be seated in 5 subway cars?

A. 200
B. 250
C. 300
D. 350
E. 400

7. An employee earns $8.25 an hour. In 30 hours, what earnings are made?

A. $240.00
B. $247.50
C. $250.00
D. $255.75
E. $257.00

8. A bread recipe calls for $3\frac{1}{4}$ cups of flour. If you only have $2\frac{1}{8}$ cups, how much more flour is needed?

A. $1\frac{1}{8}$

B. $1\frac{1}{4}$

C. $1\frac{3}{8}$

D. $1\frac{3}{4}$

E. 2

9. How many omelets can be made from 2 dozen eggs if an omelet contains 3 eggs?

A. 1
B. 3
C. 6
D. 8
E. 11

10. Two runners finished a race in 80 seconds, another runner finished the race in 72 seconds, and the final runner finished in 68 seconds. The average of these times is

A. 73 seconds
B. 74 seconds
C. 75 seconds
D. 76 seconds
E. 77 seconds

11. You use a $20 bill to buy a magazine for $3.95. What change do you get back?

A. $16.05
B. $16.95
C. $17.05
D. $17.95
E. $18.05

12. Standing by a pole, a boy $3\frac{1}{2}$ feet tall casts a 6-foot shadow. The pole casts a 24-foot shadow. How tall is the pole?

A. 14 feet
B. 18 feet
C. 28 feet
D. 41 feet
E. 43 feet

13. Rae earns $8.40 an hour plus an overtime rate equal to $1\frac{1}{2}$ times her regular pay for each hour worked beyond 40 hours. What are her total earnings for a 45-hour work week?

A. $336
B. $370
C. $399
D. $567
E. $599

14. A sweater originally priced at $40 is on sale for $30. What percent has the sweater been discounted?

A. 25%
B. 33%
C. 70%
D. 75%
E. 80%

15. A cardboard box has a length of 3 feet, a height of $2\frac{1}{2}$ feet, and a depth of 2 feet. If the length and depth are doubled, by what percent does the volume of the box change?

    A. 200%
    B. 300%
    C. 400%
    D. 600%
    E. 800%

16. Mr. Harrison earns a weekly salary of $300 plus 10% commission on all sales. If he sold $8,350 last week, what were his total earnings?

    A. $835
    B. $865
    C. $1,135
    D. $1,835
    E. $1,925

17. Tiling costs $2.89 per square foot. What is the cost to tile a kitchen whose dimensions are 4 yards by 5 yards?

    A. $57.80
    B. $173.40
    C. $289.00
    D. $520.20
    E. $640.40

18. One-eighth of a bookstore's magazines are sold on a Friday. If $\frac{1}{4}$ of the remaining magazines are sold the next day, what fractional part of the magazines remains at the end of the second day?

    A. $\frac{1}{64}$
    B. $\frac{1}{32}$
    C. $\frac{1}{8}$
    D. $\frac{7}{32}$
    E. $\frac{21}{32}$

19. Roxanne deposited $300 into a savings account earning $5\frac{1}{4}$% annually. What is her balance after one year?

    A. $15.75
    B. $315
    C. $315.25
    D. $315.75
    E. $375.15

20. One phone plan charges a $20 monthly fee and $0.08 per minute on every phone call made. Another phone plan charges a $12 monthly fee and $0.12 per minute for each call. After how many minutes would the charge be the same for both plans?

    A. 60 minutes
    B. 90 minutes
    C. 120 minutes
    D. 200 minutes
    E. 320 minutes

21. The length of a rectangle is three times its width. If the perimeter of the rectangle is 48, what is its area?

    A. 108
    B. 96
    C. 54
    D. 48
    E. 32

22. Luis collects 300 stamps one week, 420 stamps the next week, and 180 stamps the last week. He can trade the stamps for collector coins. If 25 stamps earn him one coin, how many coins can Luis collect?

    A. 27
    B. 36
    C. 50
    D. 900
    E. 925

GO ON TO THE NEXT PAGE

23. On a map, 1 centimeter represents 4 miles. A distance of 10 miles would be how far apart on the map?

- A. $1\frac{3}{4}$ cm
- B. 2 cm
- C. $2\frac{1}{2}$ cm
- D. 4 cm
- E. $4\frac{1}{2}$ cm

24. Davis donates $\frac{4}{13}$ of his paycheck to his favorite charity. If he donates $26.80, what is the amount of his paycheck?

- A. $8.25
- B. $82.50
- C. $87.10
- D. $137.50
- E. $348.40

25. Rachel ran $\frac{1}{2}$ mile in 4 minutes. At this rate, how many miles can she run in 15 minutes?

- A. $1\frac{7}{8}$
- B. 4
- C. 30
- D. 60
- E. 75

STOP. BEFORE MOVING ON TO THE NEXT SECTION, CHECK YOUR ANSWERS IF THERE IS STILL TIME LEFT.

Part 3: Reading Comprehension

Time: 18 Minutes

25 Questions

Directions: This test is designed to measure your ability to read and understand paragraphs. For each paragraph and question, select the answer that best completes the statement or answers the question based on the passage. Do not bring in outside information.

1. The United States Supreme Court is the highest court in the nation. Its nine judges review cases from other courts. They decide whether these courts have ruled in a way that agrees with the United States Constitution. But, they cannot make new laws. Their decision is based on a majority vote of the nine judges.

The main idea of this paragraph is that

- A. The United States Constitution is the basis for our laws.
- B. The Supreme Court is the highest court in the United States.
- C. The Supreme Court cannot make new laws.
- D. The Supreme Court's decisions are based on a majority vote.
- E. The Supreme Court has nine judges.

2. People sometimes say they will return back to a place they have visited. But, since *return* means the same thing as *go back to,* the expressions *return back* is *redundant.*

The word *redundant* could be used to describe which one of the following phrases?

- A. cooperate together
- B. walk slowly
- C. review again
- D. add information
- E. speak loudly

3. In the early 1900s, horticulturalist George Washington Carver developed more than 325 products from the peanut. Peanut meatloaf and chocolate covered peanuts were just two of the food items that Carver developed. However, most interestingly, Carver also engineered many unusual peanut products. For example, he formulated beauty products from peanuts such as hand lotion, shaving crème, and shampoo.

The best title for this selection is

A. Carver and Peanut Food Products
B. Carver's Many Peanut Products
C. Carver's Beauty Products from the Peanut
D. The Life of George Washington Carver
E. Carver's Unusual Products

4. Most cars today have automatic transmissions. But, it is useful to know how to shift gears in a car with a standard transmission. Press the clutch pedal in with your left foot. Then use the shift lever to choose the proper gear. Release the clutch pedal while gently applying pressure to the gas pedal.

The last thing to do when shifting gears is to

A. step on the gas.
B. release the clutch.
C. use the shift lever.
D. press down on the clutch.
E. know how to use the clutch.

5. Recycling household waste is very important. Space for landfills where garbage is dumped is becoming scarce. Putting waste in the oceans causes pollution. Recycling is a way for cities to make money by selling recyclable items. And, recycling items helps to save natural resources.

The author's purpose in this passage is to

A. explain what recycling is.
B. tell a story.
C. show a contrast.
D. argue for recycling.
E. show how to recycle.

6. Jackrabbits are not rabbits but members of the hare family. Hares are larger than rabbits, and they have longer ears. Newborn rabbits are naked and helpless, but infant hares are covered with fur and are aware of their surroundings.

Hares and rabbits are contrasted by describing all of the following except

A. their size.
B. length of ears.
C. what color they are.
D. newborn rabbits and hares.
E. infant hares.

7. In January 2002, a person buys a car that comes with a three-year or 36,000-mile free replacement guarantee on the engine and transmission. In June 2005, the car has 34,300 miles on it. The transmission fails.

According to the situation described in the paragraph, the car dealer will

A. put in a new transmission.
B. give the person a new car.
C. not fix the transmission for free.
D. not replace the car's engine.
E. replace the engine for free.

8. A sonnet is a specific type of poem. It has fourteen lines. The lines must rhyme in a set pattern. Sometimes, the last six lines of a sonnet contrast with the first eight lines. Many sonnets are love poems.

To be a sonnet, a poem must

A. be a love poem.
B. present a contrast.
C. have fewer than fourteen lines.
D. rhyme in a specific way.
E. have six lines that rhyme with the fourteen lines.

GO ON TO THE NEXT PAGE

9. When many people want to buy a product, the price will probably go up. In the summer, Americans travel more than they do at other times of the year. They may take planes or trains, and many families drive to their vacation spots.

From the information in the paragraph, you can conclude that

A. gasoline prices will rise in the summer.
B. gasoline prices will rise in the winter.
C. gasoline prices will go down in the summer.
D. gasoline prices will not change in any season.
E. gasoline prices will be lower for planes.

10. When you send a document to someone by electronic means, you are faxing it. The word *fax* comes from the word *facsimile*. Earlier ways of making facsimiles included photocopying and photographing. The oldest facsimiles were handwritten versions of original texts.

The word *facsimile* means

A. an electronic copy.
B. an exact copy.
C. any document.
D. a photocopy.
E. a photograph.

11. Superman originated as a character in a comic book in the 1930s. Then a radio program called *The Adventures of Superman* was created. Later, Superman became part of going to the movies. Short episodes were shown each week in theaters in addition to a feature film. When television became part of American life, it, too, had a weekly program about Superman. In the 1980s several full-length films about Superman appeared.

From this passage, you can conclude

A. Superman is a great hero.
B. Superman has been popular for a long time.
C. Superman has often appeared in films.
D. Superman began in comic books.
E. Superman films are popular.

12. People may think of pizza as a snack food. But, it is nutritious. The crust, made of a kind of bread, provides carbohydrates. The tomatoes contain Vitamin C and provide fiber. The cheese is a good source of calcium that is needed for the healthy bones.

Pizza is healthful because it

A. includes a good source of calcium.
B. tastes good.
C. is a snack food.
D. can be ordered in a restaurant.
E. can be baked at home.

13. The space shuttle is coming in for a landing. Over a loudspeaker, the waiting spectators hear "STS 42 is now over Brandenburg, making its turn for the coast." They quickly stand, look up, turn their eyes skyward. They hear the sonic boom and stare at the sky even more closely. There it is! First, it is only a speck. Then the crowd applauds and cheers as they see it approaching earth.

The spectators who watch the shuttle land feel

A. fear.
B. anger.
C. happiness.
D. concern.
E. excitement.

14. When people are in a group, they may not react to an emergency the same way they would if they were alone. One reason may be that each person thinks someone else has already done something. Or, seeing no one else speak; a person may feel nothing needs to be done. A third possibility is that the person does not want to draw attention to him or herself.

This passage explains

A. differences between individuals and people in groups.
B. effects of being part of a group.
C. causes for behavior in a group.
D. how people react to an emergency.
E. why people do nothing unless asked.

Questions 15–16 are based on the following passage:

In 1963, Martin Luther King, Jr., led a protest march in Birmingham, Alabama. Because he did not have a permit to hold the march, he was arrested. Then eight clergymen wrote a letter that was published in the local newspaper. The letter opposed protest marches as a way to end racial problems. While King was in jail, he wrote a reply to that letter. It has been reprinted many times since then under the title "Letter from Birmingham Jail."

15. King wrote the letter

    A. before the protest march.
    B. when he was arrested.
    C. while he was thinking about racial problems.
    D. after he read the clergymen's letter.
    E. in order to become famous.

16. King was arrested because

    A. the clergymen wrote a letter.
    B. he did not have a permit to hold the march.
    C. there were racial problems in Birmingham.
    D. he was put in jail.
    E. he wrote a letter.

17. College professors often present pedantic lectures. This fact is emphasized by yawning, sleepy students in many classrooms.

In this context, the word *pedantic* means

    A. dull.
    B. exciting.
    C. childish.
    D. inspiring.
    E. sleepy.

18. To the untrained eye, differentiating between an alligator and a crocodile is a difficult task. However, there is one main difference between these two reptiles. Alligators tend to have wide, rounded snouts while crocodiles have longer and more pointed noses.

Which of the following is implied by the preceding passage?

    A. One can never tell the difference between a crocodile and an alligator.
    B. There are no discernible physical differences in crocodiles and alligators.
    C. Most people can differentiate between crocodiles and alligators if they know about the reptiles' differing snout structures.
    D. Only experts can distinguish between crocodiles and alligators.
    E. Crocodiles have more deadly teeth than other animals.

19. Tsunamis are large waves or earthquakes caused by earthquakes or underwater landslides. The word "tsunami" is a Japanese word meaning "harbor wave" because of the destructive effects that these waves have had on coastal Japanese communities.

What is the best title for this selection?

    A. What is a Tsunami?
    B. Japanese Natural Disasters
    C. Japanese Words and Their Meanings
    D. Effects of a Tsunami
    E. Harbor Waves in Japan

20. Pyromaniacs are very rarely the setters of most criminal fires. Most people who set fires do so for insurance fraud, although others often set fires for revenge and terrorism. Very few people actually start fires because they receive strong psychological gratification from the act.

A *pyromaniac* could best be defined as

    A. a person who never sets fires.
    B. a person who is afraid of fire.
    C. a person who sets fires and receives strong psychological gratification from the act.
    D. a person who sets fires to obtain revenge.
    E. a person who needs insurance money.

GO ON TO THE NEXT PAGE

21. Mineral forms of carbon vary greatly. For example, both diamonds and graphite are forms of carbon. However, graphite is very weak and soft, and diamonds are the hardest gemstones known to man.

This passage is mainly about

A. diamonds.
B. graphite.
C. the likenesses between diamonds and graphite.
D. the difference between carbon and diamonds.
E. the varying mineral forms of carbon.

Questions 22–23 relate to the following passage.

Many environmentalists believe natural gas to be the answer to decreasing pollution produced by other traditional forms of energy. Although natural gas comes from the earth's crust like oil, it burns cleaner than oil does.

As a result, there is great emphasis from environmentalists and manufacturers on developing more vehicles that operate on natural gas rather than regular fuel. Proponents of natural gas vehicles state that such vehicles emit up to 95% less pollution than standard gasoline or diesel vehicles.

22. The principal reason for using natural gas vehicles is that they

A. are more attractive than their gasoline and diesel counterparts.
B. emit less pollution and are safer for the environment.
C. are less expensive to operate than traditional vehicles.
D. are mandated by law.
E. are not a traditional form of energy.

23. One may conclude from the above selection that

A. there is great emphasis on producing natural gas vehicles to reduce pollution.
B. traditional vehicles that operate on gasoline or diesel fuel produce very little pollution.
C. the difference in emissions between regular vehicles and natural gas vehicles is unimportant.
D. natural gas is a pollutant and should not be used to fuel vehicles.
E. natural gas is less expensive than gasoline or diesel fuel.

Questions 24–25 relate to the following passage.

Because of their reputation from myth and legend of sucking blood from animals and humans, vampire bats are viewed as heinous creatures. However, some day these greatly feared but little known animals might save lives.

Scientists have discovered that vampire bats do not suck blood from other animals. Rather, they make tiny cuts in the skin of such animals as cows. Interestingly, the bats' saliva contains a substance that aids in blood clotting. Thus, perhaps this substance might eventually be used to prevent heart attacks and strokes.

24. In this context, the word *heinous* means

A. playful.
B. friendly.
C. busy.
D. monstrous.
E. helpful.

25. The author apparently feels that

A. vampire bats are dangerous to humans.
B. vampire bats are harmful to cows.
C. vampire bats have potential in the medical field.
D. vampire bats are friendly creatures.
E. vampire bats live up to their legends.

STOP. BEFORE MOVING ON TO THE NEXT SECTION, CHECK YOUR ANSWERS IF THERE IS STILL TIME LEFT.

Part 4: Data Interpretation

Time: 24 Minutes
25 Questions

Directions: Questions 1 through 3 are based on the following table.

Total Number of Bus Accidents by Month												
	Jan	Feb	Mar	Apr	May	June	July	Aug	Sept	Oct	Nov	Dec
Number of accidents	9	7	6	5	5	9	6	7	2	5	7	11

1. How many total accidents occurred during the first quarter of the year?

- **A.** 15
- **B.** 19
- **C.** 22
- **D.** 23
- **E.** 27

2. What was the total number of accidents that occurred during the year?

- **A.** 64
- **B.** 73
- **C.** 79
- **D.** 81
- **E.** 87

3. In what month were the least number of accidents?

- **A.** April
- **B.** May
- **C.** September
- **D.** October
- **E.** December

GO ON TO THE NEXT PAGE

Questions 4–6: The graph on the left is a breakdown by grade level of the 5,000 students in Smithfield High School. The graph on the right shows the geographical location of the colleges chosen by the college-bound seniors at Smithfield High School.

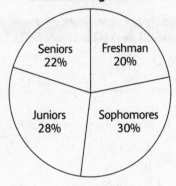

Grade-levels at Smithfield High School

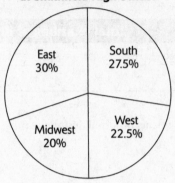

Geographical locations of colleges chosen by college-bound seniors at Smithfield High School

4. How many students are sophomores at Smithfield High School?

   A. 1100
   B. 1200
   C. 1300
   D. 1400
   E. 1500

5. If 80% of the high school seniors are college bound, what is the total number of students represented by the graph on the right?

   A. 176
   B. 270
   C. 880
   D. 1100
   E. 4000

6. If 80% of the high school seniors are college bound, how many are planning to attend colleges in the east?

   A. 150
   B. 194
   C. 264
   D. 326
   E. 458

Questions 7–10: Answer Questions 7–10 based on the circle graph that follows, showing monthly household expenditures as percents of the total monthly budget.

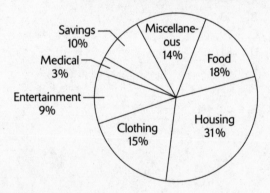

Monthly household expenditures as percent of total monthly budget

7. If clothing expenses are $192, what is the total monthly budget?

   A. $1,500
   B. $1,280
   C. $1,500
   D. $1,920
   E. $2,880

8. On which of the following groups of items is the most money spent?

   A. housing and medical

   B. food and clothing

   C. medical, entertainment, and savings

   D. clothing and miscellaneous

   E. food, medical, and entertainment

9. If the total monthly budget was $1,500, how much more money would be spent on food than put away for savings?

   A. $80

   B. $120

   C. $150

   D. $270

   E. $280

10. If $125 is spent on entertainment, how much money would be spent on food?

   A. $125

   B. $175

   C. $200

   D. $225

   E. $250

Questions 11–14: Answer Questions 11–14 based on the chart that follows, describing the rental apartments in a building.

Apartment number	Number of rooms	Number of bedrooms	Number of bathrooms	Number of closets	Eat-in kitchen	Maximum persons	Number of windows	Monthly rent
1	5	2	1	4	No	4	7	$520
2	5	3	2	6	Yes	5	7	$600
3	3	1	1	3	Yes	2	4	$460
4	4	2	1	4	Yes	4	5	$480
5	2	1	1	2	No	2	3	$400
6	4	2	1	4	Yes	4	5	$480
7	5	2	2	4	Yes	4	7	$560

11. Five people share apartment 2 and four people share apartment 6. If, in each case, they share the apartment rental evenly, which of the following is true?

   A. A renter in apartment 2 spends $24 a month more than a renter in apartment 6.

   B. A renter in apartment 2 spends $24 a month less than a renter in apartment 6.

   C. A renter in apartment 2 spends $30 a month more than a renter in apartment 6.

   D. A renter in apartment 2 spends $30 a month less than a renter in apartment 6.

   E. A renter in apartment 2 spends the same each month as a renter in apartment 6.

12. If a family of 4 needs an apartment with 2 bathrooms, what is the least amount of money they could pay each month for rent in this building?

   A. $400

   B. $460

   C. $480

   D. $560

   E. $600

GO ON TO THE NEXT PAGE

13. If a window cleaner is hired to clean all the windows in the building and he charges $7.50 per window, what will he earn?

    A. $266

    B. $285

    C. $292

    D. $304

    E. $320

14. If each monthly rental is raised 5%, which apartment will cost $546?

    A. apartment 5

    B. apartment 4

    C. apartment 3

    D. apartment 2

    E. apartment 1

Questions 15–18 are based on the bar graphs that follow, showing the heights of male and female police department applicants. All heights have been calculated to the nearest inch.

Police Department Applicants

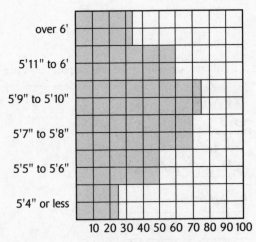

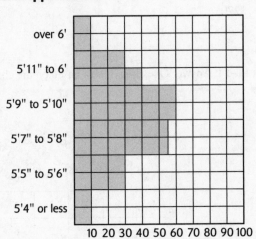

15. If 40% of the male applicants are accepted, how many are rejected?

    A. 126

    B. 132

    C. 180

    D. 189

    E. 198

16. How many male applicants are at least 5'9" tall?

    A. 60

    B. 70

    C. 75

    D. 170

    E. 200

17. How many more women are there than men in the 5'5" to 5'6" range?

    A. 10

    B. 20

    C. 40

    D. 50

    E. 60

18. Twenty-five females are added to the applicant pool, and their heights are as follows: 8 in the 5'3" to 5'4" range; 10 in the 5'7" to 5'8" range; seven in the 5'1" to 5'2" range. Which of the following statements will now be true?

   A. There are more females in the 5'1" to 5'2" range than in the 5'7" to 5'8" range.

   B. There are more females in the 5'7" to 5'8" range than in the 5'5" to 5'6" range.

   C. There is the same number of females in the 5'7" to 5'8" range as in the 5'1" to 5'2" range.

   D. There are more females in the 5'3" to 5'4" range than in the 5'5" to 5'6" range.

   E. There are fewer females in the 5'5" to 5'6" range than in the over 5'8" range.

Questions 19–22 are based on the following table, which shows average daily sales at Jumping Joe's Nightclub.

Jumping Joe's Nightclub Sales by Items Served (in Dollars)							
Time Period							
	7–8 PM	*8–9 PM*	*9–10 PM*	*10–11 PM*	*11–12 PM*	*12–1 AM*	*1–2 AM*
Club Sandwiches	35	44	72	78	68	60	24
Cold Drinks	62	67	126	155	243	96	54
Burgers	46	64	188	192	143	72	44
Salads	27	29	49	57	52	31	27
Desserts	30	35	59	77	85	71	44
Coffee/Tea	40	58	160	189	198	210	131

19. What is the difference between the greatest and least hourly sale for Burgers?

   A. 140
   B. 143
   C. 146
   D. 148
   E. 152

20. Which category exhibited the highest sales?

   A. Club Sandwiches
   B. Cold Drinks
   C. Burgers
   D. Salads
   E. Desserts

21. Which category exhibited the lowest sales?

   A. Club Sandwiches
   B. Cold Drinks
   C. Burgers
   D. Salads
   E. Desserts

22. The sales of Club Sandwiches during the hours of 8–9 PM are equal to the sales of Burgers during which time period?

   A. 9–10 PM
   B. 10–11 PM
   C. 11–12 PM
   D. 12–1 AM
   E. 1–2 AM

GO ON TO THE NEXT PAGE

Questions 23–25 are based on the line graph that follows showing calorie consumption.

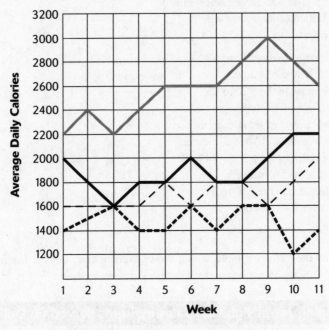

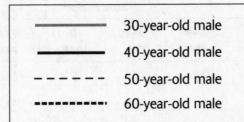

23. In which period did the 40-year-old males exhibit the greatest increase in average daily calories consumed?

    A. weeks 2–4

    B. weeks 3–5

    C. weeks 6–8

    D. weeks 7–9

    E. weeks 8–10

24. The number of calories consumed by the 30-year-old male in week 9 was how many times the number of calories consumed by the 40-year-old male in the same week?

    A. $\frac{1}{2}$

    B. $\frac{2}{3}$

    C. $1\frac{1}{2}$

    D. $1\frac{2}{3}$

    E. $1\frac{3}{4}$

25. What is the approximate number of daily calories consumed by the 50-year-old male over the 11-week period?

    A. 1,500

    B. 1,600

    C. 1,700

    D. 1,800

    E. 1,900

STOP. BEFORE MOVING ON TO THE NEXT SECTION, CHECK YOUR ANSWERS IF THERE IS STILL TIME LEFT.

Part 5: Word Knowledge

Time: 5 Minutes

25 Questions

Directions: This part of the test measures verbal comprehension involving your ability to understand written language. For each question, choose the answer that means the same as the capitalized word.

1. EXTOL

   A. stir up
   B. leave out
   C. glorify
   D. persuade
   E. send away

2. TALISMAN

   A. telegram
   B. mechanic
   C. charm
   D. juryman
   E. metal key

3. TRIVIAL

   A. boring
   B. unoriginal
   C. extreme
   D. unimportant
   E. laughable

4. VERBOSE

   A. stout
   B. ungrammatical
   C. delicate
   D. sympathetic
   E. wordy

5. INTERLOPER

   A. thief
   B. intruder
   C. translator
   D. inquirer
   E. representative

6. WAN

   A. pale
   B. humorous
   C. pleasing
   D. watchful
   E. lovesick

7. RUSE

   A. trick
   B. pause
   C. fault
   D. pattern
   E. error

8. PRUDENCE

   A. motive
   B. hatred
   C. caution
   D. distinction
   E. carefree

9. ARRAIGN

   A. debate
   B. accuse
   C. excite
   D. cancel
   E. protect

10. CUBICLE

   A. wedge
   B. puzzle
   C. tiny amount
   D. unit of measure
   E. small compartment

GO ON TO THE NEXT PAGE

11. FEASIBLE

    A. expensive
    B. foolish
    C. imaginative
    D. possible
    E. incapable

12. SQUELCH

    A. offend
    B. silence
    C. embarrass
    D. expel
    E. hire

13. QUAVER

    A. launch
    B. quicken
    C. sharpen
    D. tremble
    E. forget

14. IMPEDIMENT

    A. obstacle
    B. base
    C. spice
    D. mechanism
    E. footstool

15. BELLIGERENT

    A. unstable
    B. wealthy
    C. warlike
    D. productive
    E. docile

16. RECLUSE

    A. naturalist
    B. hermit
    C. retiree
    D. ex-convict
    E. veteran

17. CALIBER

    A. gaiety
    B. quality
    C. hope
    D. similarity
    E. politeness

18. PARADOX

    A. virtuous man
    B. equal rights
    C. seeming contradiction
    D. complicated design
    E. geometric figure

19. INANE

    A. selfish
    B. detailed
    C. personal
    D. unusual
    E. silly

20. PESSIMISTIC

    A. fearful
    B. strange
    C. gloomy
    D. disturbed
    E. disquieting

21. GRUELING

    A. exhausting
    B. surprising
    C. insulting
    D. embarrassing
    E. boring

22. DEFT

    A. critical
    B. conceited
    C. lighthearted
    D. skillful
    E. tactful

23. IDEOLOGY

    A. philosophy
    B. government
    C. goal
    D. heritage
    E. purpose

24. LACKADAISICAL

    A. delicate
    B. needy
    C. lifeless
    D. honest
    E. faulty

25. ADVENT

    A. approval
    B. opportunity
    C. welcome
    D. recommendation
    E. arrival

STOP. BEFORE MOVING ON TO THE NEXT SECTION, CHECK YOUR ANSWERS IF THERE IS STILL TIME LEFT.

Part 6: Mathematics Knowledge

Time: 22 Minutes
25 Questions

Directions: This section of the test measures your ability to use learned mathematical relationships. Each problem is followed by five possible answers. Select the answer that is most nearly correct.

1. In a standard deck of playing cards, a king of hearts is drawn and not replaced. What is the probability of drawing another king from the deck?

    A. $\frac{1}{4}$

    B. $\frac{1}{13}$

    C. $\frac{1}{17}$

    D. $\frac{3}{52}$

    E. $\frac{4}{52}$

2. How many minutes are there in one week?

    A. 10,080
    B. 1,440
    C. 420
    D. 168
    E. 24

3. If $2^{b+3} = \frac{1}{8}$, $b =$

    A. −6
    B. −3
    C. 0
    D. 2
    E. 4

4. The angles of a triangle are in the ratio 3:4:5. What is the measure of the smallest angle?

    A. 15°
    B. 30°
    C. 45°
    D. 75°
    E. 90°

5. $(3-1) \times 7 - 12 \div 2 =$

    A. 1
    B. −2
    C. 4
    D. 8
    E. 12

6. The greatest common factor of 24 and 36 is

    A. 6
    B. 12
    C. 36
    D. 60
    E. 72

GO ON TO THE NEXT PAGE

7. Solve for m: $3m - 12 = -6$

   A. −6
   B. 0
   C. 2
   D. 4
   E. 6

8. If $a = \frac{5}{2}$ then $\frac{1}{a} =$

   A. 2
   B. 5
   C. $\frac{2}{5}$
   D. $\frac{5}{2}$
   E. 7

9. Find the length of the radius in the following figure.

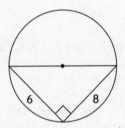

   A. 3
   B. 4
   C. 5
   D. 10
   E. 12

10. 12 is 15% of what number?

   A. 0.0125
   B. 1.8
   C. 18
   D. 36
   E. 80

11. Evaluate $3x + 7$ when $x = -3$.

   A. −2
   B. 10
   C. 16
   D. 21
   E. 30

12. What percent of $\frac{3}{4}$ is $\frac{1}{8}$?

   A. $9\frac{3}{8}\%$
   B. 12%
   C. $16\frac{2}{3}\%$
   D. 20%
   E. 25%

13. What is the area of the figure shown?

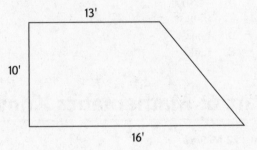

   A. 130 ft²
   B. 145 ft²
   C. 154 ft²
   D. 160 ft²
   E. 175 ft²

14. If x is a positive integer, solve $x^2 + 6x = 16$

   A. 2
   B. 4
   C. 8
   D. 10
   E. 12

15. Find the diagonal of a square whose area is 36.

   A. 6
   B. $6\sqrt{2}$
   C. 9
   D. $9\sqrt{2}$
   E. $\sqrt{9}$

16. If $a + b = 6$, what is the value of $3a + 3b$?

   A. 9
   B. 12
   C. 18
   D. 24
   E. 36

17. If $7p + 5q = -3$, find q when $p = 1$.

   A. -1

   B. -2

   C. $-\dfrac{8}{7}$

   D. $-\dfrac{2}{7}$

   E. $\dfrac{2}{7}$

18. The slope of the line shown is

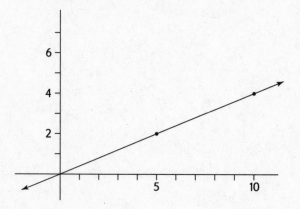

   A. $-\dfrac{2}{5}$

   B. $-\dfrac{5}{2}$

   C. $\dfrac{2}{5}$

   D. $\dfrac{5}{2}$

   E. 5

19. Simplify $\dfrac{9x^2 y^3 z - 12xy^2 z^2}{3yz}$.

   A. $3xy^2z - 4xyz$

   B. $3x^2y^2 - 12xyz$

   C. $3x^2y^2 - 4xyz$

   D. $3y^2 - 4xy^2z^2$

   E. $3y - 3xyz$

20. The value of x is

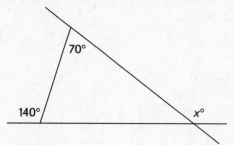

   A. $70°$

   B. $110°$

   C. $140°$

   D. $180°$

   E. $210°$

21. Subtract $(2x^3 - 3x + 1) - (x^2 - 3x - 2)$.

   A. $2x^2 + x + 1$

   B. $2x^3 - x^2 - 6x - 1$

   C. $x^3 - 6x - 1$

   D. $x^2 + 3$

   E. $2x^3 - x^2 + 3$

22. If the area of a square is 400, what is the length of its side?

   A. 20

   B. 40

   C. 100

   D. 200

   E. 400

23. Seven more than 3 times a number is equal to 70. Find the number.

   A. 10

   B. 17

   C. 21

   D. 30

   E. 210

GO ON TO THE NEXT PAGE

24. Which expression represents the volume of a cylinder whose height is equivalent to the length of the radius?

    A. πr^2

    B. πr^3

    C. $(\pi r)^2$

    D. $(\pi r)^3$

    E. $2\pi r^2$

25. How many distinct prime factors are there in 120?

    A. 2

    B. 3

    C. 4

    D. 5

    E. 12

STOP. BEFORE MOVING ON TO THE NEXT SECTION, CHECK YOUR ANSWERS IF THERE IS STILL TIME LEFT.

Answer Key for AFOQT Practice Test 1

Verbal Analogies

1. D	**10.** D	**19.** D
2. D	**11.** B	**20.** C
3. B	**12.** D	**21.** B
4. D	**13.** C	**22.** B
5. B	**14.** B	**23.** D
6. B	**15.** C	**24.** C
7. D	**16.** E	**25.** B
8. C	**17.** A	
9. E	**18.** E	

Arithmetic Reasoning

1. E	**10.** C	**19.** D
2. A	**11.** A	**20.** D
3. D	**12.** A	**21.** C
4. E	**13.** C	**22.** B
5. D	**14.** A	**23.** C
6. B	**15.** B	**24.** C
7. B	**16.** C	**25.** A
8. A	**17.** D	
9. D	**18.** E	

Reading Comprehension

1. A	**10.** B	**19.** A
2. A	**11.** B	**20.** C
3. B	**12.** A	**21.** D
4. A	**13.** E	**22.** B
5. D	**14.** C	**23.** A
6. C	**15.** D	**24.** D
7. C	**16.** B	**25.** C
8. D	**17.** A	
9. A	**18.** C	

Data Interpretation

1. C	10. E	19. D
2. C	11. E	20. B
3. C	12. D	21. D
4. E	13. B	22. E
5. C	14. E	23. E
6. C	15. D	24. C
7. B	16. D	25. C
8. A	17. A	
9. B	18. D	

Word Knowledge

1. C	10. E	19. E
2. C	11. D	20. C
3. D	12. B	21. A
4. E	13. D	22. D
5. B	14. A	23. A
6. A	15. C	24. C
7. A	16. B	25. E
8. C	17. B	
9. B	18. C	

Mathematics Knowledge

1. C	10. E	19. C
2. A	11. A	20. B
3. A	12. C	21. E
4. C	13. B	22. A
5. D	14. A	23. C
6. B	15. B	24. B
7. C	16. C	25. B
8. C	17. B	
9. C	18. C	

AFOQT Practice Test 1 Answers and Explanations

Verbal Analogies

1. **D.** An actor acts on the stage. A teacher teaches in the classroom.

2. **D.** An attribute of all tyrants is that they practice cruelty to achieve their ends. An attribute of all sycophants is that they practice flattery to achieve their ends.

3. **B.** To be a sloth is to be lazy and to be an insomniac is to be sleepless.

4. **D.** Something that is hallowed is always sacred. Someone who is nomadic is always wandering.

5. **B.** Someone who is sanctimonious is very smug, and someone who is lugubrious is very melancholy.

6. **B.** A dancer in one member of a whole ensemble. A student is one member of a whole class.

7. **D.** An anarchist promotes disorder, and a pacifist promotes peace.

8. **C.** A doctor's primary action is to heal patients. An author's primary action is to write books.

9. **E.** The police characteristically uphold the law in a community. The clergy characteristically uphold religion in a community.

10. **D.** Frigid is an extreme degree of something that is cool. To detest something is to dislike to an extreme degree.

11. **B.** A puddle is a small body of water, and an ocean is an enormous body of water. A crumb is a tiny portion of bread, and a loaf is a huge amount of bread.

12. **D.** A breeze is a soft wind. A gale is a strong and violent wind. A snowflake is one solitary piece of snow, and a blizzard is an abundance of large amounts of snow.

13. **C.** A croissant is a type of pastry, and a haiku is a type of poem.

14. **B.** There are many types of novels, including the romance novel. Likewise, there a many types of music, and rap music is one type.

15. **C.** A tanker is a type of ship, and a minivan is a type of automobile.

16. **E.** Whales live in the ocean and bees live in a hive.

17. **A.** If something is in pristine condition, then it is unspoiled. If something is tainted, then it is contaminated.

18. **E.** Birthing someone may result in life, and exposing someone may result in infection.

19. **D.** A state of meditation results in relaxation. A state of satiation results in satisfaction.

20. **C.** Placing a person in isolation will result in loneliness for that individual. Promoting a person will result in advancement for that individual.

21. **B.** The purpose of a place of sanctuary is refuge. Likewise, the purpose of a place of imprisonment is punishment.

22. **B.** The function of bathing is to achieve cleanliness, and the function of schooling is to achieve an education.

23. **D.** The function of smiling is to convey happiness. The function of scowling is to convey displeasure.

24. **C.** There are two hands that comprise a whole clock. There are two legs that comprise a whole body.

25. **B.** A quarter is part of a whole month, and a week is part of a month. Additionally, one quarter is one forth of a dollar, and one week is one forth of a month.

Arithmetic Reasoning

1. E. Let n represent the number of students in the band. Then $\frac{1}{3}n = 72$, so $n = 72 \times 3 = 216$.

2. A. Add the amount of money received and subtract the amount spent. $30 + $15 - $16 = $29.

3. D. If an item is discount 20%, the sale price is 80% of the original price. Let p represent the original price. Then $800 = 80\% \times p$ and $p = \frac{800}{80\%} = \frac{800}{.80} = $1,000$.

4. E. For a 30-hour week with $500 in sales, total earnings are $(30 \times $9.50) + (3\% \times $500) = $285 + $15 = 300.

5. D. The area of the circle with a radius of 3 is $\pi r^2 = \pi \times 3^2 = 9\pi$. The area of the larger circle is $4 \times 9\pi = 36\pi$. Therefore, $r^2 = 36$ so $r = \sqrt{36} = 6$. The radius of the larger circle is 6.

6. B. If 400 people fit in 8 subway cars, then $400 \div 8$, or 50, people fit in one subway car. Therefore, 50×5, or 250, people fit in 5 subway cars.

7. B. The earnings for 30 hours are $8.25 \times 30 = 247.50.

8. A. $3\frac{1}{4} - 2\frac{1}{8} = \frac{13}{4} - \frac{17}{8} = \frac{26}{8} - \frac{17}{8} = \frac{9}{8} = 1\frac{1}{8}$ more cups of flour.

9. D. There are 24 eggs in 2 dozen eggs. If 3 eggs are in an omelet, then $24 \div 3$, or 8 omelets can be made.

10. C. Since two runners finished in 80 seconds, the average of 80, 80, 72, and 68 must be found. This average is $\frac{80 + 80 + 72 + 68}{3} = \frac{300}{4} = 75$ seconds.

11. A. $20 - $3.95 = $16.05.

12. A. Using the ratio $\frac{\text{height}}{\text{shadow}}$, the proportion $\frac{3\frac{1}{2}}{6} = \frac{x}{24}$ models this situation, where x represents the height of the pole. Cross multiply. $3\frac{1}{2} \times 24 = 6x$ so $84 = 6x$ and $x = \frac{84}{6} = 14$ feet.

13. C. The overtime rate is $8.40 \times 1.5 = 12.60. Five hours of overtime were completed, so the total earnings are $($8.40 \times 40) + ($12.60 \times 5) = $336 + $63 = 399.

14. A. The amount of discount is $40 - $30 = 10. The percent of discount is the amount of discount divided by the original price. $\frac{10}{40} = \frac{1}{4} = 25\%$.

15. B. The volume of the original box is $3 \times 2\frac{1}{2} \times 2 = 15$. The volume of the box with the length and depth doubled is $6 \times 2\frac{1}{2} \times 4 = 60$. The amount of change in volume is $60 - 15 = 45$. The percent change is the amount of change in volume divided by the original volume. $\frac{45}{15} = 3 = 300\%$.

16. C. The amount of commission is $10\% \times $8,350 = 835. Total earnings are $300 + $835 commission $= $1,135$.

17. D. There are 3 feet in a yard, so a kitchen 4 yards by 5 yards is equivalent to (4×3) feet by (5×3) feet, or 12 feet by 15 feet. The area of the kitchen is $12 \times 15 = 180$ square feet. The cost to tile is $2.89 \times 180 = 520.20.

18. E. At the end of the first day, there are $1 - \frac{1}{8} = \frac{7}{8}$ of the magazines remaining. $\frac{7}{8} \times \frac{1}{4} = \frac{7}{32}$ sold the next day. So, at the end of the second day, there are $\frac{7}{8} - \frac{7}{32} = \frac{28}{32} - \frac{7}{32} = \frac{21}{32}$ of the magazines remaining.

19. D. Interest earned in one year is $300 \times 5\frac{1}{4}\% = 15.75. The total amount of the account after one year is $300 + $15.75 = 315.75.

20. D. Let m represent the minutes of the phone calls. The monthly charge for the first plan is $20 + 0.08m$. The monthly charge for the second plan is $12 + 0.12m$. When the monthly charges are the same, $20 + 0.08m = 12 + 0.12m$. Solve for m to find the number of minutes both plans have the same rate.

$$20 + 0.08m - 0.08m = 12 + 0.12m - 0.08m$$

$$20 = 12 + 0.04m$$

$$20 - 12 = 12 + 0.04m - 12$$

$$8 = 0.04m \text{ so } m = \frac{8}{0.04} = \frac{800}{4} = 200 \text{ minutes}$$

21. **C.** The perimeter of a rectangle is $l + w + l + w = 48$. Since $l = 3w$, the perimeter is $3w + w + 3w + w = 48$, so $8w = 48$ and $w = 6$. Therefore, the length is 3×6 or 18, and the area of the rectangle is $l \times w = 18 \times 3 = 54$.

22. **B.** The total number of stamps collected is $300 + 420 + 180 = 900$. The number of coins that can be collected is $\frac{900}{25} = 36$.

23. **C.** The proportion $\frac{1 \text{ cm}}{4 \text{ miles}} = \frac{x \text{ cm}}{10 \text{ miles}}$ models this situation. Cross multiply. $1 \times 10 = 4x$ so $10 = 4x$ and $x = \frac{10}{4} = 2\frac{1}{2}$ cm.

24. **C.** Let p represent the amount of the paycheck. $\frac{4}{13} p = \$26.80$ so $p = \$26.80 \frac{13}{4} = \$87.10$.

25. **A.** The proportion $\frac{\frac{1}{2} \text{ mile}}{4 \text{ minutes}} = \frac{x \text{ miles}}{15 \text{ minutes}}$ models this situation. Cross multiply. $\frac{1}{2} \times 15 = 4x$, so $\frac{15}{2} = 4x$ and $x = \frac{15}{2} \times \frac{1}{4} = \frac{15}{8} = 1\frac{7}{8}$ miles.

Reading Comprehension

1. **A.** A main idea is a general statement. The other choices are specific facts.

2. **A.** From the paragraph, you can infer that a *redundant* expression is one in which both words have the same meaning. *Cooperate* means *work together,* so it is an example of a redundant expression. Choice **C** may look appropriate because *review* means look at again. But, something can be reviewed more than one time.

3. **B.** Since both food products and beauty products are mentioned, this title best describes the paragraph as a whole.

4. **A.** The paragraph is written in the order of things to do, and this is the last action mentioned in the paragraph.

5. **D.** The paragraph explains why recycling is a good idea. The paragraph is not a story (choice **B**) and does not have a contrast (choice **C**). It does not tell what recycling is, so **A** is incorrect.

6. **C.** All of the other choices are discussed in the paragraph.

7. **C.** Because the car is more than three years old, the free replacement guarantee will not apply. **A** is not correct because it does not tell whether the customer will have to pay for the work. No information in the paragraph suggests that **B** would be what would happen. Although **D** may be a true statement, the situation in the paragraph does not describe any problem with the engine.

8. **D.** Choices **A** and **B** are statements that describe some, but not all, sonnets according to the paragraph. **C** is incorrect because the paragraph states that a sonnet has fourteen lines.

9. **A.** The paragraph states that Americans travel more in the summer. You can conclude that if they travel more, they will use more gasoline. And, the paragraph states that when people want to buy more of a product, the price goes up.

10. **B.** Answers **A** and **D** are examples of facsimiles; they do not define the word. **C** is incorrect because the paragraph indicates that ways of making facsimiles are ways of making copies.

11. **B.** The paragraph discusses Superman from the 1930s to the 1980s, so one can conclude he has been popular for a long time. Choices **C** and **D** are facts stated in the paragraph. Most people would agree with choice **A**, but it is not part of the information in the paragraph.

12. **A.** It is the only choice that states a fact about why pizza is a nutritious food.

13. **E.** The details in the paragraph about standing up, staring at the sky, the exclamation "there it is," and the applause and cheering show that the spectators are excited.

14. **C.** Since the paragraph gives reasons, it is explaining causes. Although the first sentence of the paragraph is a contrast, the paragraph does not explain the contrast, so **A** is an incorrect choice.

15. **D.** Since King's letter was a reply to the clergymen, he had to have written it after he read their letter.

16. **B.** This fact is stated in the second sentence of the paragraph.

17. A. The second sentence states that students in college classrooms are often yawning and sleepy. Thus, many college lectures might be described as dull.

18. C. The third sentence explains that snout structure is different in crocodiles and alligators.

19. A. This selection explains what a tsunami is. It does not focus on any other Japanese words, natural disasters, or the effects of a tsunami.

20. C. The first sentence discusses the fact that pyromaniacs rarely start fires. The last sentence explains what a pyromaniac is.

21. D. The first sentence of the selection states that carbon has varying forms, and the paragraph develops this topic sentence further.

22. B. The selection states that environmentalists believe natural gas to be a way to decrease pollution. The next paragraph states that natural gas vehicles emit up to 95% less pollution than their gasoline and diesel counterparts.

23. A. The first sentence of the second paragraph states that there is great emphasis on producing such vehicles.

24. D. Since vampire bats are thought to be ruthless blood suckers, many perceive them to be evil creatures.

25. C. The selection states that vampire bats' saliva might be useful in blood clotting, thus preventing heart attacks and strokes.

Data Interpretation

1. C. The first quarter of the year includes January through March. The three month totals add up to 22.

2. C. The total number of accidents is the sum of each month, which equals 79.

3. C. In September there were only 2 accidents, which was the least number to have occurred during the year.

4. E. There are 5,000 students at Smithfield High School, and 30% of them are sophomores.

30% of 5000 = .30 × 5000 = 1500.

5. C. There are 5,000 students at Smithfield High School, and 22% of them are seniors.

22% of 5000 = .22 × 5000 = 1100 seniors.

If 80% of the seniors are college bound, the 80% of 1100 = .80 × 1100 = 880 college bound seniors.

6. C. Read the explanation for Question 2 to see that there are 880 college bound seniors. If 30% of them plan to attend schools in the east, then 30% of 880 = .30 × 880 = 264.

7. B. If clothing represents 15% of the total budget, then 15% × (total budget) = .15 × (total budget) = $192. Therefore total budget is $192 ÷ .15 = $1280.

8. A. Whichever group encompasses the largest percent of the budget will be the group on which the most money is spent.

Housing and medical = 31% + 3% = 34%.	Choice **A** = 34%.
Food and Clothing = 18% + 15% = 33%.	Choice **B** = 33%.
Medical, entertainment, and savings = 3% + 9% + 10%.	Choice **C** = 22%.
Clothing and miscellaneous = 15% + 14% = 29%.	Choice **D** = 29%.
Food, medical, and entertainment = 18% + 3% + 9% = 30%.	Choice **E** = 30%.

Thus, the largest value is 34%, choice **A**.

9. B. Food represents 18% and savings represents 10%. The difference is 18 − 10 = 8. 8% of $1500 = .08 × $1500 = $120.

10. **E.** Entertainment represents 9%, and food represents 18%. Therefore, food is twice as much as entertainment. If $125 is spent on entertainment, then $2 \times \$125 = \$250$ is spent on food.

11. **E.** The monthly rental for apartment 2 is $600. If five people share apartment 2, they each pay $\$600 \div 5 = \$120$. The monthly rental for apartment 6 is $480. If four people share apartment 6, they each pay $\$480 \div \$120$. Each person pays the same amount.

12. **D.** There are 2 apartments that have 2 bathrooms. Apartment 2 rents for $600 a month and apartment 7 rents for $560 per month. The smallest fee for a 2 bathroom apartment would then be $560.

13. **B.** The total number of windows in the building is $7 + 7 + 4 + 5 + 3 + 5 + 7 = 38$. If the window cleaner charges $7.50 to clean each window, he will earn $\$7.50 \times 38 = \$285.00$.

14. **E.** Apartment 5 costs $400. 5% of $400 = $.05 \times \$400 = \$20$. A $20 increase would raise the cost to $400 + \$20 = \$420$.

    Apartment 4 costs $480. 5% of $480 = $.05 \times \$480 = \$24$. A $24 increase would raise the cost to $480 + \$24 = \$504$.

    Apartment 3 costs $460. 5% of $460 = $.05 \times \$460 = \$23$. A $23 increase would raise the cost to $460 + \$23 = \$483$.

    Apartment 2 costs $600. 5% of $600 = $.05 \times \$600 = \$30$. A $30 increase would raise the cost to $600 + \$30 = \$630$.

    Apartment 1 costs $520. 5% of $520 = $.05 \times \$520 = \$26$. A $26 increase would raise the cost to $520 + \$26 = \$546$. This is the answer for which we were looking.

15. **D.** The total number of male applicants is $25 + 50 + 70 + 75 + 60 + 35 = 315$. If 40% are accepted, then 60% will be rejected. 60% of $315 = .60 \times 315 = 189$.

16. **D.** At least 5'9" tall means 5'9" and above. This includes the 3 right-hand bars of the male applicant graph. $75 + 60 + 35 = 170$.

17. **A.** There are 60 women in the 5'5" to 5'6" range. There are 50 men in the 5'5" to 5'6" range. $60 - 50 = 10$.

18. **D.** If 7 females are added to the 5'1" to 5'2" range, there will be 37 females in that range. If 10 females are added to the 5'7" to 5'8" range, there will be 40 females in that range. Since 37 is not greater than 40, the answer is not choice **A**. Since 37 is not equal to 40, the answer is not choice **C**. No females are added to the 5'5" to 5'6" range, which has 60 females. Since 40 is not greater than 60, the answer is not choice **B**. If 8 females are added to the 5'3" to 5'4" range, there will be 63 females in that range. Since 63 is greater than 60 the answer is choice **D**.

19. **D.** The highest sale of burgers is $193, and the least is $44. The difference is $148.

20. **B.** The cold drinks were responsible for $803 in sales.

21. **D.** The lowest amount of sales were salads, with $272.

22. **E.** Club sandwiches during the 8–9 PM period sold $44. During the 1–2 AM period, the same amount of burgers was sold.

23. **E.** In week 2, the 40-year-old male consumed 1800 calories. In week 4, he consumed 1800. The increase was 0. Choice **A** = 0. In week 3, he consumed 1600 and 1800 in week 5. The increase was 200. Choice **B** = 200. In week 6, he consumed 2000 and 1800 in week 8. The increase was 200. Choice **D** = 200. In week 8, he consumed 1800 and 2200 in week 10. The increase was 400. Choice **E** = 400. This is the greatest increase.

24. **C.** In week 9, the 30-year-old male consumed 3000 calories. In week 9, the 40-year-old male consumed 2000 calories. $3000 = 1.5 \times 2000$.

25. **C.** To calculate the average daily calories over the 11-week period, we need to add up the values for all 11 weeks and then divide that total by 11.

    $1600 + 1600 + 1600 + 1600 + 1800 + 1600 + 1800 + 1800 + 1600 + 1800 + 2000 = 18,800$.

    $18,800 \div 11 = 1709$. 1709 is approximately 1700, and thus, choice **C** is correct.

Word Knowledge

1. **C.** **Extol** means to glorify.

2. **C.** A **talisman** is a charm.

3. **D.** **Trivial** means unimportant.

4. **E.** **Verbose** means wordy.

5. **B.** An **interloper** is an intruder. A thief may be an interloper, but an interloper is not necessarily a thief.

6. **A.** **Wan** means pale.

7. **A.** **Ruse** means trick.

8. **C.** **Prudence** means caution.

9. **B.** **Arraign** means accuse.

10. **E.** A **cubicle** is a small compartment.

11. **D.** **Feasible** means possible.

12. **B.** **Squelch** means silence.

13. **D.** To **quaver** is to tremble.

14. **A.** An **obstacle** is an impediment.

15. **C.** **Belligerent** means warlike.

16. **B.** **Recluse** means hermit.

17. **B.** **Caliber** means quality.

18. **C.** A **paradox** is something that seems contradictory.

19. **E.** **Inane** means silly.

20. **C.** **Pessimistic** means gloomy.

21. **A.** Something that is **grueling** is exhausting.

22. **D.** To be **deft** is to be skillful.

23. **A.** **Ideology** means philosophy.

24. **C.** **Lackadaisical** means lifeless.

25. **E.** **Advent** means arrival.

Mathematics Knowledge

1. **C.** Probability is $\frac{\text{number of expected outcomes}}{\text{number of possible outcomes}}$. Since one king was drawn and not replaced, three kings remain in the deck of 51 cards. So, the probability of drawing another king is $\frac{3}{51} = \frac{1}{17}$.

2. **A.** There are 60 minutes in an hour, 24 hours in one day, and 7 days in one week.

   So 1 week $= \frac{7\,\text{days}}{1\,\text{week}} \times \frac{24\,\text{hours}}{1\,\text{day}} \times \frac{60\,\text{minutes}}{1\,\text{hour}} = 7 \times 24 \times 60 = 10{,}080$ minutes.

3. **A.** $\frac{1}{8} = \frac{1}{2^3} = 2^{-3}$ so $2^{b+3} = 2^{-3}$ and $b + 3 = -3$. Therefore, $b + 3 - 3 = -3 - 3 = -6$.

4. **C.** Angles in a triangle add to $180°$. So $3x + 4x + 5x = 180°$ and $12x = 180°$. Dividing both sides by 12 results in $x = 15°$. The smallest angle is represented by $3x = 3(15°) = 45°$.

5. D. Following the correct order of operations produces:

$(3 - 1) \times 7 - 12 \div 2 = 2 \times 7 - (12 \div 2) = 14 - 6 = 8$.

6. B. Factors of 24 are $2 \times 2 \times 2 \times 3$. Factors of 36 are $2 \times 2 \times 3 \times 3$. The greatest common factor is $2 \times 2 \times 3 = 12$.

7. C. $3m - 12 + 12 = -6 + 12$

$3m = 6$

Dividing both sides by 3 results in $m = 2$.

8. C. Substitute $\frac{5}{2}$ for a. $\frac{1}{a} = \frac{1}{\frac{5}{2}} = 1 \div \frac{5}{2} = 1 \times \frac{2}{5} = \frac{2}{5}$.

9. C. The hypotenuse of the triangle is the diameter of the circle. By the Pythagorean Theorem, $d^2 = 6^2 + 8^2 = 36 + 64 = 100$. So, $d = \sqrt{100} = 10$, and the radius is $\frac{10}{2} = 5$.

10. E. Let n represent the number. If 12 is 15% of n, the $12 = 0.15n$. Divide both sides by 0.15. Therefore, $n = 80$.

11. A. Substitute -3 for x. Then $3(-3) + 7 = -9 + 7 = -2$.

12. C. Let p represent the unknown percent. Then $p \times \frac{3}{4} = \frac{1}{8}$. Solve for p by multiplying by the reciprocal of $\frac{3}{4} \times p \times \frac{3}{4} \times \frac{4}{3} = \frac{1}{8} \times \frac{4}{3} = \frac{4}{24} = \frac{1}{6}$. As a percent, $\frac{1}{6}$ is $16\frac{2}{3}\%$.

13. B. Divide the figure into a rectangle and triangle as shown.

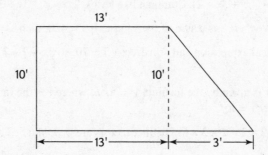

The area of the figure equals the area of the rectangle plus the area of the triangle. The rectangle = length × width or $10 \times 13 = 130$ ft^2; the triangle = $\frac{1}{2}$ base × height or $\frac{1}{2} \times 3 \times 10 = 15$ ft^2. Together, the area is $130 + 15 = 145$ ft^2.

14. A. Set the equation equal to 0 and factor. $x^2 + 6x - 16 = 0$ and $(x + 8)(x - 2) = 0$. Then, either $x + 8 = 0$ or $x - 2 = 0$ so $x = -8$ or $x = 2$. Since x is positive, $x = 2$ only.

15. B. The area of a square is s^2 where s is a side of the square. If $s^2 = 36$, then $s = 6$. The diagonal of a square forms two right triangles; d is the hypotenuse, and the two legs are 6 units long.

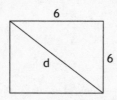

Using the Pythagorean Theorem, $d^2 = 6^2 + 6^2 = 36 + 36 = 72$. Therefore, $d = \sqrt{72} = 6\sqrt{2}$.

16. C. $3a + 3b = 3(a + b)$. Since $a + b = 6$, $3a + 3b = 3(6) = 18$.

17. B. Substitute 1 for p and solve for q. $7(1) + 5q = -3$ and $7 + 5q = -3$.

$7 + 5q - 7 = -3 - 7$ and $5q = -10$. Dividing both sides by 5 results in $q = -2$.

18. C. Slope is found by identifying two points on the line and finding the $\frac{\text{change in } y}{\text{change in } x}$. The points (0, 0) and (5, 2) form the slope $\frac{2-0}{5-0} = \frac{2}{5}$.

19. C. $\frac{9x^2y^3z - 12xy^2z^2}{3y^2} = \frac{9x^2y^3z}{3yz} - \frac{12xy^2z^2}{3yz}$ $3x^2y^2 - 4xyz$.

20. B.

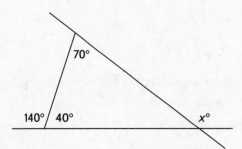

The angle adjacent to the 140° angle is 40° since supplementary angles add to 180°. The angles of a triangle add to 180° so the angle adjacent to angle x is $180° - 70° - 40° = 70°$. Angle x and 70° are supplementary, so $x = 180° - 70° = 110°$.

21. E. Subtraction can be changed to addition by changing the signs in the entire term being subtracted. $(2x^3 - 3x + 1) - (x^2 - 3x - 2) = (2x^3 - 3x + 1) + (-x^2 + 3x + 2)$. Combine like terms. $2x^3 - x^2 - 3x + 3x + 1 + 2 = 2x^3 - x^2 + 3$.

22. A. The area of a square is s^2, where s is a side of the square. If $s^2 = 400$, then $s = \sqrt{400} = 20$.

23. C. Translate to a mathematical expression and solve. $3x + 7 = 70$, so $3x + 7 - 7 = 70 - 7$ and $3x = 63$. Divide both sides by 3. Therefore, $x = 21$.

24. B. The volume of a cylinder is given by the formula $V = \pi r^2 h$, where r is the radius of the circular base and h is the height. Since $h = r$, $V = \pi r^2 r = \pi r^3$.

25. B. Prime factors of 120 are $2 \times 2 \times 2 \times 3 \times 5$. Distinct factors are 2, 3, and 5. Therefore, there are 3 distinct prime factors.

Answer Sheet for ASTB Practice Test 1

(Remove This Sheet and Use It to Mark Your Answers)

Math/Verbal Test

1 Ⓐ Ⓑ Ⓒ Ⓓ	11 Ⓐ Ⓑ Ⓒ Ⓓ	21 Ⓐ Ⓑ Ⓒ Ⓓ	31 Ⓐ Ⓑ Ⓒ Ⓓ
2 Ⓐ Ⓑ Ⓒ Ⓓ	12 Ⓐ Ⓑ Ⓒ Ⓓ	22 Ⓐ Ⓑ Ⓒ Ⓓ	32 Ⓐ Ⓑ Ⓒ Ⓓ
3 Ⓐ Ⓑ Ⓒ Ⓓ	13 Ⓐ Ⓑ Ⓒ Ⓓ	23 Ⓐ Ⓑ Ⓒ Ⓓ	33 Ⓐ Ⓑ Ⓒ Ⓓ
4 Ⓐ Ⓑ Ⓒ Ⓓ	14 Ⓐ Ⓑ Ⓒ Ⓓ	24 Ⓐ Ⓑ Ⓒ Ⓓ	34 Ⓐ Ⓑ Ⓒ Ⓓ
5 Ⓐ Ⓑ Ⓒ Ⓓ	15 Ⓐ Ⓑ Ⓒ Ⓓ	25 Ⓐ Ⓑ Ⓒ Ⓓ	35 Ⓐ Ⓑ Ⓒ Ⓓ
6 Ⓐ Ⓑ Ⓒ Ⓓ	16 Ⓐ Ⓑ Ⓒ Ⓓ	26 Ⓐ Ⓑ Ⓒ Ⓓ	36 Ⓐ Ⓑ Ⓒ Ⓓ
7 Ⓐ Ⓑ Ⓒ Ⓓ	17 Ⓐ Ⓑ Ⓒ Ⓓ	27 Ⓐ Ⓑ Ⓒ Ⓓ	37 Ⓐ Ⓑ Ⓒ Ⓓ
8 Ⓐ Ⓑ Ⓒ Ⓓ	18 Ⓐ Ⓑ Ⓒ Ⓓ	28 Ⓐ Ⓑ Ⓒ Ⓓ	
9 Ⓐ Ⓑ Ⓒ Ⓓ	19 Ⓐ Ⓑ Ⓒ Ⓓ	29 Ⓐ Ⓑ Ⓒ Ⓓ	
10 Ⓐ Ⓑ Ⓒ Ⓓ	20 Ⓐ Ⓑ Ⓒ Ⓓ	30 Ⓐ Ⓑ Ⓒ Ⓓ	

Mechanical Comprehension Test

1 Ⓐ Ⓑ Ⓒ	11 Ⓐ Ⓑ Ⓒ	21 Ⓐ Ⓑ Ⓒ
2 Ⓐ Ⓑ Ⓒ	12 Ⓐ Ⓑ Ⓒ	22 Ⓐ Ⓑ Ⓒ
3 Ⓐ Ⓑ Ⓒ	13 Ⓐ Ⓑ Ⓒ	23 Ⓐ Ⓑ Ⓒ
4 Ⓐ Ⓑ Ⓒ	14 Ⓐ Ⓑ Ⓒ	24 Ⓐ Ⓑ Ⓒ
5 Ⓐ Ⓑ Ⓒ	15 Ⓐ Ⓑ Ⓒ	25 Ⓐ Ⓑ Ⓒ
6 Ⓐ Ⓑ Ⓒ	16 Ⓐ Ⓑ Ⓒ	26 Ⓐ Ⓑ Ⓒ
7 Ⓐ Ⓑ Ⓒ	17 Ⓐ Ⓑ Ⓒ	27 Ⓐ Ⓑ Ⓒ
8 Ⓐ Ⓑ Ⓒ	18 Ⓐ Ⓑ Ⓒ	28 Ⓐ Ⓑ Ⓒ
9 Ⓐ Ⓑ Ⓒ	19 Ⓐ Ⓑ Ⓒ	29 Ⓐ Ⓑ Ⓒ
10 Ⓐ Ⓑ Ⓒ	20 Ⓐ Ⓑ Ⓒ	30 Ⓐ Ⓑ Ⓒ

CUT HERE

Math/Verbal Test

Time: 35 Minutes

37 Questions

Questions 1–5: Each of the following five questions, numbered 1–5, consists of an arithmetic problem followed by four possible answers. Select the one choice that is the correct answer.

1. Mr. Norwalk bought 24 gallons of gasoline, which enables him to drive 648 miles. On the average, how many miles did he get per gallon of gasoline?

   A. 25
   B. 26
   C. 27
   D. 28

2. How many blocks 6" × 4" × 4" can fit in a box 8' × 6' × 4'?

   A. 2
   B. 48
   C. 576
   D. 3456

3. Steve played in 14 basketball games. He scored a total of 53 field goals (2 points each) and 20 free throws (1 point each). What was his average score per game?

   A. 5
   B. 9
   C. 14
   D. 23

4. There are 800 employees at a company. If 60% drive to work and 30% take the train, how many employees arrive to work by car?

   A. 240
   B. 480
   C. 540
   D. 600

5. Min reads 3 hardcover mysteries and 4 soft cover mysteries. She reads 3 times as many nonfiction books as she did mysteries. How many nonfiction books did Min read?

   A. 9
   B. 12
   C. 18
   D. 21

Questions 6–10: The following questions consist of sentences in which one word is omitted. For each question, select the lettered choice that best complete the thought expressed in the sentence.

6. He felt that her participation was an _____ to the entire group.

   A. error
   B. asset
   C. agreement
   D. misunderstanding

7. He had a(n) ____ understanding of the problem.

   A. acute
   B. bitter
   C. miserable
   D. lazy

8. The report was ____ and to the point.

   A. ancient
   B. misunderstood
   C. boring
   D. concise

GO ON TO THE NEXT PAGE

9. She finally began to _____ to her illness.

A. overcome
B. succumb
C. welcome
D. achieve

10. The soldiers approached the bunker with _____.

A. stealth
B. disappointment
C. deception
D. limitation

Questions 11–15: Each of the following five questions, numbered 11–15, consists of an arithmetic problem followed by four possible answers. Select the one choice that is the correct answer.

11. In the election for Fairfield County Selectman, Mr. Williams got 33,172 votes, and Mr. Stevens got 25,752 votes. By how many votes did Mr. Williams win the election?

A. 4,377
B. 5,500
C. 6,257
D. 7,420

12. Sam buys 3 candy bars for 45 cents each and two packs of gum for 79 cents each. What is the total cost of this purchase?

A. $1.24
B. $2.93
C. $6.20
D. $6.24

13. Devin throws a football $7\frac{1}{3}$ yards. Carl throws it $2\frac{1}{2}$ times farther. How much farther did Carl's throw travel than Devin's?

A. $2\frac{1}{2}$ yards

B. $7\frac{1}{3}$ yards

C. 11 yards

D. $18\frac{1}{3}$ yards

14. This morning Wilson drove 13 miles to the store and then returned home. In the afternoon, he drove 9 miles to the movies and returned home. How much farther did Wilson travel in the morning?

A. 4 miles
B. 6 miles
C. 8 miles
D. 9 miles

15. Jared rents 3 videos for $8.00. What would the cost of 2 video rentals be?

A. $1.33
B. $5.00
C. $5.33
D. $6.00

The following questions consist of quotations containing one word that is incorrectly used because it is not in keeping with the meaning that each quotation is evidently intended to convey. Determine which word is incorrectly used. Then select from the lettered choices the word that, when substituted for the incorrectly used word, best helps to convey the intended meaning of the quotation.

16. "They had written to the authorities about the situation, but they were pleased by their response, especially since there seemed to be a total disregard for their welfare."

A. surprised
B. underprivileged
C. unhelpful
D. mistaken

17. "What the customers seem to require from a store and the products they purchase are honesty, culpability, and individuality."

A. disgust
B. status
C. feelings
D. reliability

18. "Families nourish us during childhood, and the values our families seek to maintain usually affect our identities in powerful ways, whether we adopt them wholly, modify them, or accept them completely."

    A. pretense
    B. reject
    C. behold
    D. deviate

19. "Some economists argue that as a result of large tax cuts, wealthy people invest their windfall, businesses thrive, jobs are created, and the new tax revenues created by these economic activities are smaller or equivalent to the amount of the original reduction."

    A. compensate
    B. regular
    C. thriftier
    D. larger

20. "After the disaster at the manufacturing plant, engineers stated that even if the safety systems had been activated, there were objections about whether they would have mitigated the damage done by the explosion."

    A. discuss
    B. observations
    C. doubts
    D. consideration

Questions 21–25: Each of the following five questions, numbered 21–25, consists of an arithmetic problem followed by four possible answers. Select the one choice that is the correct answer.

21. Wilma has a rope that is 27 inches long is cut into two pieces, such that one piece is twice as long as the other. What is the length of the shorter piece of rope?

    A. 10 inches
    B. 9 inches
    C. 8 inches
    D. 7 inches

22. Melodi eats $\frac{3}{8}$ of a pizza and divides the rest among her two friends. What percent of the pizza do her friends each receive?

    A. 62.50%
    B. 37.50%
    C. 31.25%
    D. 18.75%

23. Kim's favorite movie is 144 minutes long. Justin's favorite movie is 127 minutes long. How much longer is Kim's favorite movie?

    A. 17 minutes
    B. 23 minutes
    C. 36 minutes
    D. 44 minutes

24. Roger collects bottle caps. Each cap can be traded for 5 cents. If Roger receives $40.50, how many bottle caps did he trade?

    A. 810
    B. 405
    C. 200
    D. 8

25. A batch of cookies requires 2 cups of milk and 4 eggs. If you have 9 cups of milk and 9 eggs, how many batches of cookies can be made?

    A. 9
    B. 6
    C. 4
    D. 2

GO ON TO THE NEXT PAGE

Questions 26–30 are based on different reading passages. Answer each question on the basis of the information contained in the quotation.

26. "In January, 2002, a person buys a car that comes with a three year or 36,000 mile free replacement guarantee on the engine and transmission. In June 2005, the car has 34,300 miles on it. The transmission fails."

According to the situation described in the paragraph, the car dealer will

A. put in a new transmission.
B. give the person a new car.
C. not fix the transmission for free.
D. not replace the car's engine.

27. "A sonnet is a specific type of poem. It has fourteen lines. The lines must rhyme in a set pattern. Sometimes, the last six lines of a sonnet contrast with the first eight lines. Many sonnets are love poems."

To be a sonnet, a poem must

A. be a love poem.
B. present a contrast.
C. have fewer than fourteen lines.
D. rhyme in a specific way.

28. "When many people want to buy a product, the price will probably go up. In the summer, Americans travel more than they do at other times of the year. They may take planes or trains, and many families drive to their vacation spots."

From the information in the paragraph, you can conclude that

A. gasoline prices will rise in the summer.
B. gasoline prices will rise in the winter.
C. gasoline prices will go down in the summer.
D. gasoline prices will not change in any season.

29. "When you send a document to someone by electronic means, you are faxing it. The word "fax" comes from the word *facsimile*. Earlier ways of making facsimiles included photocopying and photographing. The oldest facsimiles were handwritten versions of original texts."

The word *facsimile* means

A. an electronic copy.
B. an exact copy.
C. any document.
D. a photocopy.

30. "The United States Supreme Court is the highest court in the nation. Its nine judges review cases from other courts. They decide if these courts have ruled in a way that agrees with the United States Constitution. But they cannot make new laws. Their decision is based on a majority vote of the nine judges."

The main idea of this paragraph is that

A. The Supreme Court has nine judges.
B. The Supreme Court is the highest court in the United States.
C. The Supreme Court cannot make new laws.
D. The Supreme Court's decisions are based on a majority vote.

Questions 31–35: Each of the following five questions, numbered 31–35, consists of an arithmetic problem followed by four possible answers. Select the one choice that is the correct answer.

31. A right triangle has an area of 24 feet. If one leg is 3 times as long as the other, what is the length of the longest side?

A. 12.6
B. 12
C. 8.4
D. 6.3

32. Interest earned on an account totals $100. If the interest rate is $7\frac{1}{4}$%, what is the principle amount?

    A. $725

    B. $1333

    C. $1379

    D. $1428

33. William can read 2 pages in 3 minutes. At this rate, how long will it take him to read a 360-page book?

    A. 30 minutes

    B. 2 hours

    C. 6 hours

    D. 9 hours

34. Tanya's bowling scores this week were 112, 156, 179, and 165. Last week, her average score was 140. How many points did her average improve?

    A. 18

    B. 13

    C. 11

    D. 8

35. Felix buys 3 books for $8.95 each. How much does he owe if he uses a $12.73 credit toward his purchase?

    A. $39.58

    B. $26.85

    C. $21.68

    D. $14.12

Questions 36 and 37 are based on reading passages. Answer each question on the basis of the information contained in the quotation.

36. "Early British colonists in Virginia typically came from England to plant tobacco, harvest it, and then return to their homeland to sell it; however, British colonists who came to New England did so to establish permanent colonies where they could practice their religious beliefs freely."

The preceding quotation best supports the statement: Motives for early colonists . . .

    A. sprang from a universal desire for freedom of religion.

    B. determined where they located their colonies.

    C. originated because of different kinds of terrain.

    D. evolved from a need for more income.

37. "Although many people consider Latin to be a dead language, studies have shown that a student's understanding of grammar and his vocabulary can be improved if he studies Latin and that his algebraic skills can be strengthened, especially in problem solving."

The preceding quotation best supports the statement that:

    A. Studying Latin can improve verbal and math skills.

    B. All students should study Latin.

    C. Basic arithmetic skills can be improved for students of all levels.

    D. Even if Latin is no longer a spoken language, everyone should be able to read it.

STOP. BEFORE MOVING ON TO THE NEXT SECTION, CHECK YOUR ANSWERS IF THERE IS STILL TIME LEFT.

Mechanical Comprehension Test

Time: 15 Minutes
30 Questions

Directions: This test is designed to measure your ability to learn and reason using mechanical terms. Each diagram is followed by a question or an incomplete statement. Select the choice that best answers the question or completes the statement.

1. A stone is tied to the end of a string and swings in a circular motion. If the speed of the stone is tripled, the centripetal force of the stone will become

   A. 3 times as great.
   B. 9 times as great.
   C. remains constant.

2. A skater is spinning with a constant angular momentum. If she pulls her arms in toward her body, her angular momentum will

   A. increase.
   B. decrease.
   C. remain constant.

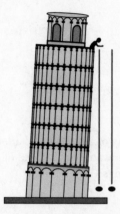

3. Two objects with different weights are dropped at the same moment from the top of the Leaning Tower of Pisa.

   A. Both objects hit the ground at the same time.

   B. The heavier object hits the ground first.

   C. The lighter object hits the ground first.

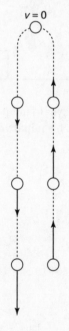

4. A ball thrown vertically upward has an initial potential energy of 100 J and an initial kinetic energy of 700 J. At the top of the trajectory, its energy in joules is

   A. 0

   B. 100

   C. 800

5. The input force required to lift a 200-N load W in the pulley arrangement shown in the figure is

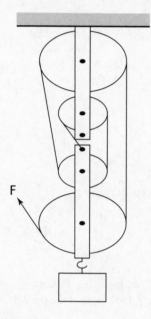

   A. 40 N

   B. 50 N

   C. 800 N

6. An object is thrown with a horizontal velocity of 10 m/s from the edge of a building that is 12.5 m above ground level. If the air resistance is negligible, the time t that it takes the object to reach the ground and the distance d from the building where it strikes the ground are most nearly

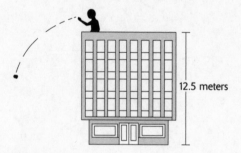

12.5 meters

   A. 3, 100

   B. 1.6, 16

   C. 3.2, 32

GO ON TO THE NEXT PAGE

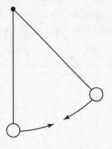

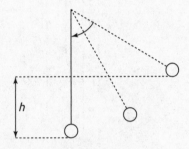

7. A simple pendulum has a frequency of oscillation f. To double f, the length of the pendulum should be

   A. increased by a factor of 2.
   B. increased by a factor of 4.
   C. decreased by a factor of 4.

8. Mr. James pushes against the wall with a force of 30 N for 30 s. If the wall does not move, then the work done on the wall is

   A. positive.
   B. negative.
   C. zero.

9. The velocity of a baseball 4 s after it is thrown vertically upward with a speed of 32.1 m/s is _____ m/s.

   A. 7.2
   B. 8.025
   C. 14.6

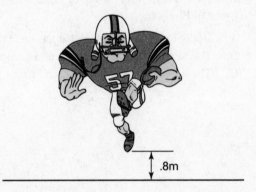

10. For a football player to jump vertically upward a distance of .8 m, his initial velocity must be _____ m/s.

   A. 3.92
   B. 4.27
   C. 4.62

11. For an object with simple harmonic motion, simultaneously its

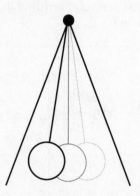

 A. displacement is maximum when its acceleration is maximum.

 B. velocity is maximum when its displacement is maximum.

 C. kinetic energy is maximum when its displacement is maximum.

12. A block of mass 3 kg slides along a horizontal tabletop. A horizontal force of 10 N and a downward vertical force of 17.4 N act on the block at the same time. If the coefficient of kinetic friction and table is 0.25, the net horizontal force exerted on the block is nearly

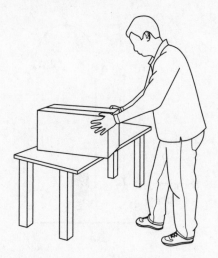

 A. 3 N

 B. 5 N

 C. 7 N

13. A man pulling a small box along the floor suddenly decides to raise his pulling hand. If the pulling force remains the same, the amount of work done to pull the box the same distance

 A. increases.

 B. decreases.

 C. remains the same.

14. An ice skater is touching her waist while spinning. Suddenly, the music changes, and she extends her hands out so that her fingers are twice as far from the axis of rotation. Her spin rate

 A. increases significantly.

 B. decreases significantly.

 C. remains the same.

GO ON TO THE NEXT PAGE

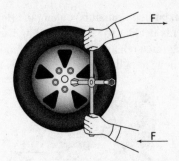

15. The torque required to loosen a nut that holds a wheel on a car has a magnitude of 56 N.m. If a .35 m lug wrench is used to loosen the nut when the angle of the wrench is 56 degrees, the force that must be exerted at the end of the wrench is

  A. 143 N
  B. 286 N
  C. 429 N

16. Two 5 kg blocks are linked by a slider rod assembly as shown in the figure. If the sliding surfaces are frictionless and if the speed of block A is 4 m/s, the speed of block B is

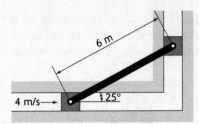

  A. 8.57 m/s
  B. 4.28 m/s
  C. 1.5 m/s

17. A 5 kg uniform rod 2 m long is suspended from the ceiling by a frictionless hinge. If the rod is free to pivot, the product of inertia of the rod about the pivotal point is

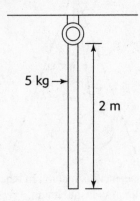

  A. 0 kg.m^2
  B. 20 kg.m^2
  C. 2.5 kg.m^2

Consider the diagram that follows where the mass m equals 10 kg and is guided by the frictionless rail shown. If the spring constant is $k = 1,000$ N/m and the spring is compressed sufficiently and released so that m barely reaches point B, answer the following four questions:

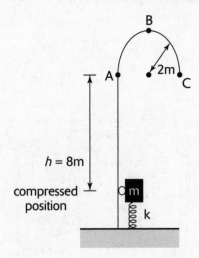

18. What is the initial compression x in the spring?

  A. 1.3 m
  B. 1.4 m
  C. 1.5 m

19. What is the kinetic energy of *m* at point A?

    A. 1.962 J

    B. 19.62 J

    C. 196.2 J

20. What is the velocity *v* of *m* at point A?

    A. 6.264 m/s

    B. 62.64 m/s

    C. 19.62 m/s

21. What is the energy stored in the spring if it is compressed 0.1 m?

    A. 100 J

    B. 50 J

    C. 5 J

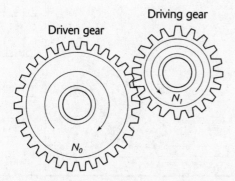

22. In the spur gear arrangement shown in the figure, the ratio of the number of teeth on the output gear (N_o) to the number of teeth on the input gear (N_i) is 2. The speed ratio of the input and output gears is

    A. $\frac{1}{4}$

    B. $\frac{1}{2}$

    C. 2

23. In the screw jack shown in the figure, if the ratio $R/p = 4$, the mechanical advantage (F_o/F_i) is most approximately

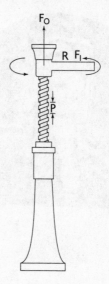

    A. 14

    B. 21

    C. 25

24. If the centers of a 800 kg mass and a 600 kg mass are separated by 0.25 m, then the magnitude of the gravitational force F between them is nearly_____ N.

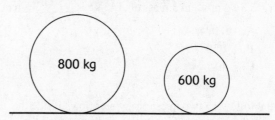

    A. 5.00×10^{-4}

    B. 5.00×10^{-5}

    C. 1.67×10^{-7}

GO ON TO THE NEXT PAGE

25. The weight of a 70 kg astronaut on the surface of a planet with a mass of 3×10^{24} kg and radius of 5×10^{6}m is nearly_____ N.

A. 686
B. 586
C. 560

26. The speed of a baseball with a momentum of 5.8 kg m/s and a mass of .145 kg is _____ m/s.

A. 0.084
B. 1.19
C. 40

In the following two questions, water flows inside the pipe with a circular cross section from A to B at the rate of 10 liters/second. The diameter of the pipe at A is 12 cm and 4 cm at B. Point B is 6 m higher than A and the pressure at B is 140 kilopascals.

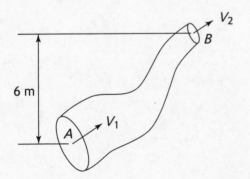

27. The velocity of the stream at point B is approximately

A. 4 m/s
B. 8 m/s
C. 12 m/s

28. The pressure at point B in kilopascals is approximately

A. 30
B. 40
C. 50

29. The 50 kg ball of the demolition equipment shown in the figure is pulled to the left until it is 1.8 m above its lowest point. Its velocity as it passes through its lowest point is approximately

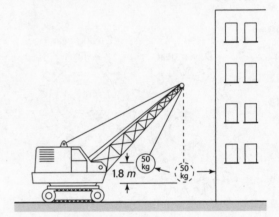

A. 32.25 m/s
B. 5.6 m/s
C. 5.9

30. A 24 kg skier moving with a velocity of .6 m/s collides with and sticks to a .26 kg skier moving with a velocity of .2 m/s. The final velocity v of the two skiers is _____ m/s.

A. .392
B. .184
C. 0.18

Answer Key for ASTB Practice Test 1

Math/Verbal

1. C	14. C	27. D
2. D	15. C	28. A
3. B	16. A	29. B
4. B	17. D	30. A
5. D	18. B	31. A
6. B	19. D	32. C
7. A	20. C	33. D
8. D	21. B	34. B
9. B	22. C	35. D
10. A	23. A	36. B
11. D	24. A	37. A
12. B	25. D	
13. C	26. C	

Mechanical Comprehension

1. B	11. A	21. C
2. C	12. C	22. B
3. A	13. C	23. C
4. B	14. B	24. A
5. A	15. B	25. C
6. B	16. A	26. B
7. B	17. A	27. B
8. C	18. B	28. A
9. A	19. C	29. C
10. A	20. A	30. A

ASTB Practice Test 1 Answers and Explanations

Math/Verbal Test

1. **C.** He got $\dfrac{648 \text{ miles}}{24 \text{ gallons}}$. Dividing 648 by 24 gives 27 miles per gallon.

2. **D.** Convert the dimensions of the box from feet to inches. 8' × 6' × 4' is equivalent to $(8 \times 12 \text{ in}) \times (6 \times 12 \text{ in}) \times (4 \times 12 \text{ in}) = 96 \text{ in} \times 72 \text{ in} \times 48 \text{ in}$. The volume = $96 \times 72 \times 48 = 331{,}776$. The volume of each block is $6 \times 4 \times 4 = 96$. The number of blocks that fit in the box is $\dfrac{331{,}776}{96} = 3456$.

3. **B.** This problem has several steps. To begin, you need to determine the number of points he scored. The 53 field goals give him $53 \times 2 = 106$ points. Adding on the 20 free throws gives him 126 points. The average per game is $126 \div 14 = 9$ points.

4. **B.** 60% arrive to work by car, so $800 \times 60\% = 480$.

5. **D.** Min read a total of 3 + 4 or 7 mysteries. Therefore, she read 3×7 or 21 nonfiction books.

6. **B.** An **asset** is a positive influence or help.

7. **A.** The word **acute** means sharp or keen.

8. **D.** **Concise** mean brief, of few words.

9. **B.** The word **succumb** means to give in to.

10. **A.** The word **stealth** means to move quietly.

11. **D.** You need to determine how many more votes Mr. Williams got than Mr. Stevens. Since $33{,}172 - 25{,}752 = 7{,}420$, Mr. Williams got 7,420 more votes.

12. **B.** The total cost of the purchase is $(3 \times \$0.45) + (2 + \$0.79) = \$1.35 + \$1.58 = \$2.93$.

13. **C.** Carl's throw went $7\frac{1}{3} \times 2\frac{1}{2} = \frac{22}{3} \times \frac{5}{2} = \frac{110}{6} = 18\frac{1}{3}$ yards. The difference between the two throws is $18\frac{1}{3} - 7\frac{1}{3} = 11$ yards.

14. **C.** The total distance traveled in the morning was $13 \times 2 = 26$ miles. The total distance traveled in the afternoon was $9 \times 2 = 18$ miles. The difference between the two distances is $26 - 18 = 8$ miles.

15. **C.** Using the ratio $\dfrac{\text{price}}{\text{video}}$, the proportion $\frac{8}{3} = \frac{x}{2}$ can be used to find the cost to rent two videos. Cross multiply. $8 \times 2 = 3x$ so $16 = 3x$ and $x = \frac{16}{3} = \$5.33$.

16. **A.** The word **pleased** is incorrect. Since the authorities seemed to disregard their welfare, they were surprised, which is a much more acceptable word.

17. **D.** The word **culpability** is incorrect here. Customers would want products, as well as the store, to be reliable.

18. **B.** The word **accept** is incorrect. To accept completely is the same as to adopt wholly. The word *or* indicates the sentence intends to provide an alternative. Changing **accept** to **reject** provides an alternative.

19. **D.** The word **smaller** is incorrect. The creation of economic activities would increase tax revenues rather than reducing them. **Larger** conveys the logic of the sentence.

20. **C.** The word **objections** is incorrect. The sentence means to convey the idea that damage might not have been lessened if the safety systems were working. Changing **objections** to **doubts** makes this meaning clear.

21. **B.** Let S = the length of the shorter piece of rope. Then, the longer piece is of length 2S, and $S + 2S = 27$, or $3S = 27$, so $S = 9$.

22. **C.** If $\frac{3}{8}$ of the pizza is eaten, then $1 - \frac{3}{8} = \frac{5}{8}$ remains. If that is divided by 2, then each receives $\frac{5}{8} \div 2 = \frac{5}{8} \times \frac{1}{2} = \frac{5}{16} = 0.3125 = 31.25\%$.

23. **A.** The difference in times is $144 - 127 = 17$ minutes.

24. **A.** Let c represent the number of caps traded in. Then $0.05c = 40.50$ and $c = \frac{40.50}{0.05} = 810$ caps.

25. **D.** With 9 cups of milk, $\frac{9}{2} = 4\frac{1}{2}$ or 4 full batches can be made. However, with 9 eggs, only $\frac{9}{4} = 2\frac{1}{4}$ or 2 full batches can be made. At most, only 2 batches can be made with the given ingredients.

26. **C.** Because the car is more than three years old, the free replacement guarantee will not apply. **A** is not correct because it does not tell whether the customer will have to pay for the work. No information in the paragraph suggests that **B** would be what would happen. Although **D** may be a true statement, the situation in the paragraph does not describe any problem with the engine.

27. **D.** Choices **A** and **B** are statements that describe some but not all sonnets according to the paragraph. **C** is incorrect because the paragraph states a sonnet has fourteen lines.

28. **A.** The paragraph states Americans travel more in the summer. You can conclude that if they travel more, they will use more gasoline. And, the paragraph states that when people want to buy more of a product, the price goes up.

29. **B.** Answers **A** and **D** are examples of facsimiles; they do not define the word. **C** is incorrect because the paragraph indicates that ways of making facsimiles are ways of making copies.

30. **A.** A main idea is a general statement. The other choices are specific facts.

31. **A.** The area of a triangle is $\frac{1}{2}bh$. Let b represent the length of one leg. Then $h = 3b$ so the area is $\frac{1}{2}bh = \frac{1}{2} \cdot b \cdot 3b = \frac{3}{2}b^2 = 24$ so $\frac{2}{3} \cdot \frac{3}{2}b^2 = \frac{2}{3} \cdot 24$ and $b^2 = 16$. $b = \sqrt{16} = 4$ and $h = 3 \times 4 = 12$. The longest side of a right triangle is the hypotenuse. Using the Pythagorean Theorem, $\text{leg}^2 + \text{leg}^2 = \text{hypotenuse}^2$ so $4^2 + 12^2 = c^2$ and $16 + 144 = c^2$. Therefore, $160 = c^2$ and $c = \sqrt{160} = 12.6$.

32. **C.** Interest = principle × rate. Let p represent the principle. Then $\$100 = p \times 7\frac{1}{4}\%$ so $p = \frac{\$100}{7\frac{1}{4}\%} = \frac{\$100}{0.0725} = \$1379$.

33. **D.** Using the ratio $\frac{\text{pages}}{\text{minutes}}$, the proportion $\frac{2}{3} = \frac{360}{x}$ can be used to find the time. Cross multiply. $2x = 3 \times 360$ so $2x = 1080$ and $x = \frac{1080}{2} = 540$ minutes. Convert minutes to hours. There are 60 minutes in one hour so $\frac{540}{60} = 9$ hours.

34. **B.** The average is found by adding up all the scores and dividing by the total number of scores. The average this week is $\frac{112 + 156 + 179 + 165}{4} = \frac{612}{4} = 153$. The amount of improvement is $153 - 140 = 13$.

35. **D.** The total cost of the purchase is $\$8.95 \times 3 = \$26.85$. With a \$12.73 credit, the amount owed is $\$26.85 - \$12.73 = \$14.12$.

36. **B.** Choice **A** is incorrect because it is too limited; it deals with only the New England colonists. Choice **C** is not correct because it focuses only on the Virginia colonists who chose to colonize fertile land to cultivate tobacco. Choice **D** also deals only with the Virginia colonists who sought to make money on their tobacco crop.

37. **A.** Choice **B** is incorrect because it is too broad; the quotation does not indicate that all students should study Latin. Choice **C** is incorrect because algebraic skills, not basic arithmetic skills, can be improved. Choice **D** is wrong because it is also too broad; everyone is not included in the quotation.

Mechanical Comprehension

1. **B.** The centripetal force of the stone is proportional to the square of the velocity.

2. **C.** The total angular momentum is equal to the product of the body's angular velocity and the moment of inertia. Pulling the arms toward the body increases the first by a certain ratio and decreases the second by the same ratio, thus keeping the angular momentum the same as the question states.

3. **A.** The travel time depends on the height above the ground and the acceleration of gravity; both of which are the same for both objects.

4. **B.** At the top of the trajectory, the ball stops and all the kinetic energy has already been converted to potential energy. Thus, the total energy is the sum of 100 and 700, or 800 J.

5. **A.** Since five strands support the movable load, the required force is 200/5 = 40 N.

6. **B.** $12.5 = \frac{1}{2} g t^2$, hence $t \approx 1.6$ s while $d = 1.6 (10) = 16$m.

7. **B.** Because the frequency of oscillation is inversely proportional to the square root of the length of the pendulum, the length has to be decreased by a factor of 4 for the frequency to be doubled.

8. **C.** Work is force times distance, which is zero in this example.

9. **A.** The final velocity is the initial velocity minus 4 times the acceleration of gravity (9.8 m/s) or 7.14 ($\approx$7.2) m/s.

10. **A.** Using the expressions $s = v_o t + \frac{1}{2} at^2$ and $v_f = v_o + at$, you obtain $t = .4$ and $v_o = 3.92$ m/s.

11. **A.** Since the direction of the vibrating body is reversed at the endpoint of its motion, its velocity must be zero when its displacement is a maximum. It then is accelerated toward the center by the restoring force until it reaches its maximum speed at the center of oscillation, that is, when its displacement is zero. Since the restoring force is maximum at the endpoint, its acceleration at that moment is also a maximum by Newton's second law of motion.

12. **C.** The net vertical force on the block = 3g (upward reaction force) – 17.4 (downward applied force) = 12 N. The resulting force of friction = 12 (0.25) = 3 N. Since friction acts against any motion, the net horizontal force on the block = 10 – 3 = 7 N.

13. **C.** Since work equals the travel distance times the component of the force along the direction of travel, the angle Θ between the pulling rope and the floor increases and, hence, both its cosine and the work done decrease.

14. **B.** The spin rate (or angular velocity) is inversely proportional to the distance from the axis of rotation, so that as the skater stretches her hands the distance from her hands to the axis of rotation increases, and the spin rate decreases slightly.

15. **B.** Because the torque $T = Fd \cos\Theta$ where F is the force, d is the arm and Θ is the angle between the force and the arm, you can solve for F to obtain 286 N.

16. **A.** If the velocity vectors of the two blocks are denoted by V_A and V_B, then the instantaneous center or rotation is at the intersection of the two vectors perpendicular to V_A and V_B. If the intersection point is denoted by C, then the distance BC is 6 cos 25° while the distance CA is 6 sin 25°. Furthermore, since the linear velocity equals the angular velocity ω times the arm of rotation, then $\omega = V_A/CA$ or V_B/BC. This leads to the result $V_B = (V_A)(BC)/CA = (4)(6 \cos 25°)/(6 \sin 25°) = 8.578$ m/s.

17. **A.** In this case, the product of inertia for the rod is zero since the pivotal point lies on an axis of symmetry.

18. **B.** If the compression of the spring is denoted by x, then $0.5 kx^2 = mgh$. Solving for x, you obtain $x = 1.4$ m.

19. **C.** The total energy of the system is constant and equals potential energy (PE) plus kinetic energy (KE), that is, $PE_A + KE_A = PE_B + KE_B$. Since $KE_B = 0$, you have $KE_A = PE_B – PE_A = mg(h+1) – mg = 196.2$ J.

20. **A.** Since $KE_A = 196.2 = 0.5 m v^2$, v = 6.624m/s.

21. **C.** The potential energy stored in the spring = $0.5 k x^2 = 5$ J.

22. **B.** The speed ratio of input to output gears equals the mechanical advantage, which is the ratio N_o/N_i, or 2.

23. **C.** The mechanical advantage equals 2π times the ratio R/p which is approximately 25.

24. **A.** $F = 6.67 \times 10^{-11} \times 800 \times 600/(0.25^2) = 5.12256 \times 10^{-4}$ N.

25. C. $F = 6.67 \times 3 \times 10^{24} \times 70/(5 \times 10^6)^2 = 560.28$N.

26. B. Because the momentum P equals the mass m multiplied by the velocity v, it follows that $v = P/m = 40$ m/s.

27. B. Velocity = rate of flow/cross sectional area = $10/[\pi(2)^2] = 7.96$.

28. A. Bernoulli's equation applied to this case yields a pressure of 30.3 kilopascals at point B.

29. C. Since the potential energy of the ball is converted to kinetic energy, the speed at the lowest point is $[2gh]^{1/2} = 5.9$ m/s where g = 9.8 m/s^2 and h = 1.8m.

30. A. Conservation of momentum requires that .24(.6) + .26(.2) = (.24 + .26)v. Hence, v = .392 m/s.

Answer Sheet for ASVAB Practice Test 1

(Remove This Sheet and Use It to Mark Your Answers)

Word Knowledge

1	Ⓐ Ⓑ Ⓒ Ⓓ	21	Ⓐ Ⓑ Ⓒ Ⓓ
2	Ⓐ Ⓑ Ⓒ Ⓓ	22	Ⓐ Ⓑ Ⓒ Ⓓ
3	Ⓐ Ⓑ Ⓒ Ⓓ	23	Ⓐ Ⓑ Ⓒ Ⓓ
4	Ⓐ Ⓑ Ⓒ Ⓓ	24	Ⓐ Ⓑ Ⓒ Ⓓ
5	Ⓐ Ⓑ Ⓒ Ⓓ	25	Ⓐ Ⓑ Ⓒ Ⓓ
6	Ⓐ Ⓑ Ⓒ Ⓓ	26	Ⓐ Ⓑ Ⓒ Ⓓ
7	Ⓐ Ⓑ Ⓒ Ⓓ	27	Ⓐ Ⓑ Ⓒ Ⓓ
8	Ⓐ Ⓑ Ⓒ Ⓓ	28	Ⓐ Ⓑ Ⓒ Ⓓ
9	Ⓐ Ⓑ Ⓒ Ⓓ	29	Ⓐ Ⓑ Ⓒ Ⓓ
10	Ⓐ Ⓑ Ⓒ Ⓓ	30	Ⓐ Ⓑ Ⓒ Ⓓ
11	Ⓐ Ⓑ Ⓒ Ⓓ	31	Ⓐ Ⓑ Ⓒ Ⓓ
12	Ⓐ Ⓑ Ⓒ Ⓓ	32	Ⓐ Ⓑ Ⓒ Ⓓ
13	Ⓐ Ⓑ Ⓒ Ⓓ	33	Ⓐ Ⓑ Ⓒ Ⓓ
14	Ⓐ Ⓑ Ⓒ Ⓓ	34	Ⓐ Ⓑ Ⓒ Ⓓ
15	Ⓐ Ⓑ Ⓒ Ⓓ	35	Ⓐ Ⓑ Ⓒ Ⓓ
16	Ⓐ Ⓑ Ⓒ Ⓓ		
17	Ⓐ Ⓑ Ⓒ Ⓓ		
18	Ⓐ Ⓑ Ⓒ Ⓓ		
19	Ⓐ Ⓑ Ⓒ Ⓓ		
20	Ⓐ Ⓑ Ⓒ Ⓓ		

Arithmetic Reasoning

1	Ⓐ Ⓑ Ⓒ Ⓓ	16	Ⓐ Ⓑ Ⓒ Ⓓ
2	Ⓐ Ⓑ Ⓒ Ⓓ	17	Ⓐ Ⓑ Ⓒ Ⓓ
3	Ⓐ Ⓑ Ⓒ Ⓓ	18	Ⓐ Ⓑ Ⓒ Ⓓ
4	Ⓐ Ⓑ Ⓒ Ⓓ	19	Ⓐ Ⓑ Ⓒ Ⓓ
5	Ⓐ Ⓑ Ⓒ Ⓓ	20	Ⓐ Ⓑ Ⓒ Ⓓ
6	Ⓐ Ⓑ Ⓒ Ⓓ	21	Ⓐ Ⓑ Ⓒ Ⓓ
7	Ⓐ Ⓑ Ⓒ Ⓓ	22	Ⓐ Ⓑ Ⓒ Ⓓ
8	Ⓐ Ⓑ Ⓒ Ⓓ	23	Ⓐ Ⓑ Ⓒ Ⓓ
9	Ⓐ Ⓑ Ⓒ Ⓓ	24	Ⓐ Ⓑ Ⓒ Ⓓ
10	Ⓐ Ⓑ Ⓒ Ⓓ	25	Ⓐ Ⓑ Ⓒ Ⓓ
11	Ⓐ Ⓑ Ⓒ Ⓓ	26	Ⓐ Ⓑ Ⓒ Ⓓ
12	Ⓐ Ⓑ Ⓒ Ⓓ	27	Ⓐ Ⓑ Ⓒ Ⓓ
13	Ⓐ Ⓑ Ⓒ Ⓓ	28	Ⓐ Ⓑ Ⓒ Ⓓ
14	Ⓐ Ⓑ Ⓒ Ⓓ	29	Ⓐ Ⓑ Ⓒ Ⓓ
15	Ⓐ Ⓑ Ⓒ Ⓓ	30	Ⓐ Ⓑ Ⓒ Ⓓ

Paragraph Comprehension

1	Ⓐ Ⓑ Ⓒ Ⓓ
2	Ⓐ Ⓑ Ⓒ Ⓓ
3	Ⓐ Ⓑ Ⓒ Ⓓ
4	Ⓐ Ⓑ Ⓒ Ⓓ
5	Ⓐ Ⓑ Ⓒ Ⓓ
6	Ⓐ Ⓑ Ⓒ Ⓓ
7	Ⓐ Ⓑ Ⓒ Ⓓ
8	Ⓐ Ⓑ Ⓒ Ⓓ
9	Ⓐ Ⓑ Ⓒ Ⓓ
10	Ⓐ Ⓑ Ⓒ Ⓓ
11	Ⓐ Ⓑ Ⓒ Ⓓ
12	Ⓐ Ⓑ Ⓒ Ⓓ
13	Ⓐ Ⓑ Ⓒ Ⓓ
14	Ⓐ Ⓑ Ⓒ Ⓓ
15	Ⓐ Ⓑ Ⓒ Ⓓ

Mathematics Knowledge

1	Ⓐ Ⓑ Ⓒ Ⓓ	16	Ⓐ Ⓑ Ⓒ Ⓓ
2	Ⓐ Ⓑ Ⓒ Ⓓ	17	Ⓐ Ⓑ Ⓒ Ⓓ
3	Ⓐ Ⓑ Ⓒ Ⓓ	18	Ⓐ Ⓑ Ⓒ Ⓓ
4	Ⓐ Ⓑ Ⓒ Ⓓ	19	Ⓐ Ⓑ Ⓒ Ⓓ
5	Ⓐ Ⓑ Ⓒ Ⓓ	20	Ⓐ Ⓑ Ⓒ Ⓓ
6	Ⓐ Ⓑ Ⓒ Ⓓ	21	Ⓐ Ⓑ Ⓒ Ⓓ
7	Ⓐ Ⓑ Ⓒ Ⓓ	22	Ⓐ Ⓑ Ⓒ Ⓓ
8	Ⓐ Ⓑ Ⓒ Ⓓ	23	Ⓐ Ⓑ Ⓒ Ⓓ
9	Ⓐ Ⓑ Ⓒ Ⓓ	24	Ⓐ Ⓑ Ⓒ Ⓓ
10	Ⓐ Ⓑ Ⓒ Ⓓ	25	Ⓐ Ⓑ Ⓒ Ⓓ
11	Ⓐ Ⓑ Ⓒ Ⓓ		
12	Ⓐ Ⓑ Ⓒ Ⓓ		
13	Ⓐ Ⓑ Ⓒ Ⓓ		
14	Ⓐ Ⓑ Ⓒ Ⓓ		
15	Ⓐ Ⓑ Ⓒ Ⓓ		

CUT HERE

CUT HERE

Word Knowledge

Time: 11 Minutes
35 Questions

Directions: Each question has an underlined and boldfaced word. You are to decide which of the four words in the choices most nearly means the same as the underlined boldface word and then mark the space on your answer form that has the same number and letter as your choice.

1. **Adversity** most nearly means

    A. helpful
    B. hardship
    C. loving
    D. ease

2. **Caustic** most nearly means

    A. smooth
    B. corrosive
    C. soft
    D. heavy

3. **Zest** most nearly means

    A. enjoyment
    B. sadness
    C. pilfer
    D. annoy

4. **Enigma** most nearly means

    A. pleasure
    B. discomfort
    C. haul
    D. mystery

5. **Punctual** most nearly means

    A. missing
    B. prompt
    C. late
    D. quick

6. **Loiter** most nearly means

    A. dawdle
    B. dirty
    C. enlarged
    D. faulty

7. **Meander** most nearly means

    A. skip
    B. overbearing
    C. wander
    D. wanting

8. **Parsimony** most nearly means

    A. generosity
    B. stinginess
    C. willingness
    D. payment

9. **Pithy** most nearly means

    A. full
    B. concise
    C. enlarged
    D. maximum

10. **Somber** most nearly means

    A. straiten
    B. tipsy
    C. elevated
    D. grave

GO ON TO THE NEXT PAGE

11. Docile most nearly means

    A. sweet

    B. easily led

    C. soft

    D. heavy

12. Hale most nearly means

    A. wet

    B. healthy

    C. snowy

    D. ill

13. Infinite most nearly means

    A. endless

    B. origin

    C. start

    D. find

14. Opulent most nearly means

    A. golden

    B. wealthy

    C. slim

    D. empty

15. Trite most nearly means

    A. pleasurable

    B. ordinary

    C. magnificent

    D. tawdry

16. Vital most nearly means

    A. healthy

    B. essential

    C. organs

    D. needless

17. Scurry most nearly means

    A. tumble

    B. stroll

    C. clean

    D. scamper

18. Prudent most nearly means

    A. toothy

    B. wise

    C. careless

    D. willing

19. Ardent most nearly means

    A. passionate

    B. swelter

    C. ignore

    D. filter

20. Bland most nearly means

    A. gourmet

    B. tasteless

    C. land-locked

    D. hoist

21. They tried not to **mar** the furniture.

    A. spoil

    B. move

    C. overturn

    D. sell

22. Several of the people in the audience began to **sway.**

    A. tumble head-over-heels

    B. move back and forth

    C. laugh

    D. jump around

23. Fortunately they had an **auxiliary** light.

    A. bright

    B. helping

    C. halogen

    D. welcome

24. You could tell that the carpenter was **deft** with his tools.

    A. angry

    B. foreign

    C. skillful

    D. careless

25. The crop was extremely **prolific** this year.

    A. wasted
    B. barren
    C. necessary
    D. fruitful

26. The movie seemed **bizarre** to the crowd.

    A. exciting
    B. slow
    C. scary
    D. strange

27. The gathering was a **tribute** to the policemen.

    A. show of respect
    B. protest
    C. dinner
    D. payment

28. The man was accused of **slandering** his opponent.

    A. hitting gently
    B. speaking untruth
    C. pleasing
    D. tricking

29. The mansions indicated the town's **affluence**.

    A. decline
    B. growth
    C. silence
    D. wealth

30. The old man became **reclusive**.

    A. annoyed
    B. solitary
    C. quiet
    D. obstinate

31. His work was of the highest **caliber**.

    A. price
    B. quality
    C. respect
    D. size

32. My mother gave me a present as an **incentive**.

    A. surprise
    B. motivator
    C. punishment
    D. accident

33. The workers began to **raze** the old building.

    A. burn
    B. sell
    C. repair
    D. demolish

34. **Solicit** as much advice as possible before your trip.

    A. worry about
    B. take
    C. ask for
    D. scorn

35. In the **interim,** I used my brother's car.

    A. winter
    B. meantime
    C. morning
    D. first stage

STOP. BEFORE MOVING ON TO THE NEXT SECTION, CHECK YOUR ANSWERS IF THERE IS STILL TIME LEFT.

ASVAB Practice Test 1

Paragraph Comprehension

Time: 13 Minutes
15 Questions

Read the following passages and select the choice that best answers the questions. Answers should be based only on what you read in the passage.

1. Health experts claim that an aspirin a day may cut the risk of developing polyps commonly found in colon cancer. However, a full-size aspirin does not cut the risk as much as the smaller baby aspirin does.

   The best title for this selection is

   A. Health Benefits of Aspirin
   B. Cancer and Aspirin Dosage
   C. Aspirin May Prevent Colon Cancer
   D. Colon Cancer Prevention

2. The debate continues among experts concerning whether organic foods are more healthy or just more expensive. Organic foods are those that are free of artificial pesticides and fertilizers and contain no herbicides.

   Organic foods are

   A. more healthy than regular foods.
   B. ones that do not contain any pesticides.
   C. inexpensive.
   D. ones that contain no herbicides.

3. Panthers refer to two different types of animals— the leopard and the concolour. Concolours are called by many other names: cougar, puma, mountain lion, and panther are just a few. In fact, the panther has more dictionary names than any other known predator.

   Which of the following is *not* mentioned as another name for the concolour?

   A. cougar
   B. mountain lion
   C. bobcat
   D. panther

Questions 4–5 relate to the following passage.

4. Thomas Alva Edison is one of the most well known inventors in history. He is most famous for inventions like the phonograph, the motion picture camera, and the light bulb. However, even Edison failed in a few attempts at invention, namely in trying to develop a better way to mine iron ore during the late 1880s and early 1890s. He was tenacious in his attempts to find a method that worked, but he eventually gave up after having lost all the money he had invested in iron ore mining projects.

   In this context, the word *tenacious* means

   A. angry.
   B. persistent.
   C. lazy.
   D. happy.

5. This passage is mainly about

   A. Edison's successful inventions.
   B. the light bulb.
   C. iron ore mining.
   D. Edison's invention attempt in iron ore mining.

6. In Alaska, there are long periods of darkness in certain regions since much of the state is located so far north of the Arctic Circle. Thus, those regions above the Arctic Circle experience unending daylight in the certain summer months and unending darkness in some winter months.

   It can be inferred from the preceding passage that

   A. all regions of Alaska experience unending dark in winter.
   B. all regions of Alaska experience unending daylight in summer.
   C. regions south of the Arctic Circle experience alternating dark and daylight in the winter and summer months.
   D. regions south of the Arctic Circle have unending daylight in summer.

7. In an age that stresses the importance of water conservation, there are many plants that require less water than other more traditionally grown plants. In order to optimize their water usage efficiency, experts recommend watering such plants during the cooler times of the day.

One may conclude from the preceding statements that water-efficient plants should be watered

A. at 12:00 noon, when the sun is at its hottest.
B. at 6:00 A.M., when the sun has just risen.
C. at 10:00 A.M., when the day is warming up.
D. at 3:00 P.M., before the sun goes down.

8. Water is needed to sustain us as human beings. In fact, the human body is comprised of ⅔ water. Since our bodies are so water dependent, we must drink water every day.

In this context, the word *comprised* means

A. consists of.
B. less than.
C. full of.
D. demands.

9. Obesity has become a national epidemic. Recent studies have shown that obesity is more serious than previously thought. In fact, obesity is harder on the health than cigarette smoking. Since 27% of Americans are currently obese, and 61% are overweight, this weight problem is exacting a huge cost from the medical community.

The percentage of Americans who are currently overweight is

A. 27%
B. 52%
C. 73%
D. 61%

10. Weight loss experts recommend lowered calorie intake and regular exercise to get rid of excess weight. However, lowering calories too much or exercising too strenuously can be detrimental to good health. Caloric intake should never go lower than 1200 calories per day, and exercise should consist of at least 30 minutes 4–5 times per week to achieve healthy weight loss.

The best title for this selection is

A. How to Achieve Healthy Weight Loss and Avoid Injury
B. Warning About Too Much Exercise
C. Weight Loss Woes
D. Caloric Recommendations for Weight Loss

Questions 11–12 are related to the following selection.

Recently, cellular phone use has become a nationwide epidemic. A new study confirms that this epidemic might not be such a positive one. The study found that drivers who talk on their cellular phones while driving perform 30% worse as drivers than drunk drivers do. Many have proposed using a hands-free cellular phone to solve this problem of dangerous driving. However, researchers discovered that even hands-free cellular phones distract drivers.

11. The author probably believes that

A. cellular phone use is not dangerous while driving.
B. hands-free cellular phones are safe for drivers to use.
C. cellular phones of any kind should never be used while driving.
D. cellular phones are a safe alternative to drunk driving.

12. This paragraph is mainly about

A. drunk driving.
B. hands-free cellular phones.
C. the dangers of driving with cellular phones.
D. the safe alternative that hands-free cellular phones provide.

GO ON TO THE NEXT PAGE

Questions 13–15 are related to the following passage.

Although carjacking has become more common in the past 10 years, there are several preventive measures that drivers can take. The first way to prevent carjacking is to never walk alone to your car at night. Another means of prevention is always driving with the windows rolled up and the doors locked.

Also, driving on well-lit and often traveled roads is another preventive measure that drivers can take to ensure their safety from carjacking.

13. The best title for this selection is

- **A.** Preventing Carjacking
- **B.** Carjacking Becoming More Common
- **C.** Driving Safety
- **D.** Night Driving Safety

14. Which of the following is not mentioned as a preventive measure against carjacking?

- **A.** driving on well-lit roads
- **B.** carrying pepper spray
- **C.** driving with windows rolled up
- **D.** never walking to your car alone at night

15. The author probably believes that

- **A.** it is almost impossible to avoid carjacking.
- **B.** carjacking cannot be avoided at night.
- **C.** carjacking never happens during the day.
- **D.** carjacking can often be avoided by employing simple preventive measures.

STOP. BEFORE MOVING ON TO THE NEXT SECTION, CHECK YOUR ANSWERS IF THERE IS STILL TIME LEFT.

Arithmetic Reasoning

Time: 36 Minutes

30 Questions

Select the choice that best answers the following questions.

1. Jack lives $6\frac{1}{2}$ miles from the library. If he walks $\frac{1}{3}$ of the way and takes a break, what is the remaining distance to the library?

- **A.** $5\frac{5}{6}$ miles
- **B.** 4 miles
- **C.** $4\frac{1}{3}$ miles
- **D.** $2\frac{1}{6}$ miles

2. Amelia casts a shadow 5 feet long. Her father, who is 6 feet tall, casts a shadow 8 feet long. How tall is Amelia?

- **A.** 6 feet 8 inches
- **B.** 4 feet 10 inches
- **C.** 4 feet 6 inches
- **D.** 3 feet 9 inches

3. John spent 30 minutes vacuuming, 12 minutes dusting, 37 minutes washing dishes, and 45 minutes resting. How many minutes did John spend cleaning?

- **A.** 34
- **B.** 79
- **C.** 100
- **D.** 124

4. A recipe calls for 3 cups of wheat and white flour combined. If $\frac{3}{8}$ of this is wheat flour, how many cups of white flour are needed?

- **A.** $1\frac{1}{8}$
- **B.** $1\frac{7}{8}$
- **C.** $2\frac{3}{8}$
- **D.** $2\frac{5}{8}$

5. Jared rents three videos for $8.00. What would the cost of two video rentals be?

    A. $1.33

    B. $5.00

    C. $5.33

    D. $6.00

6. Rockford is 439 miles from Springville and 638 miles from Davenport. How much closer is Rockford to Springville than Rockford to Davenport?

    A. 199 miles

    B. 201 miles

    C. 439 miles

    D. 1,077 miles

7. A winter coat is on sale for $150. If the original price was $200, what percent has the coat been discounted?

    A. 50%

    B. 40%

    C. 33%

    D. 25%

8. A square garden is to be built inside a circular area. Each corner of the square touches the circle. If the radius of the circle is 2, how much greater is the area of the circle than the square?

    A. $4 - 4\pi$

    B. $4 - 8\pi$

    C. $4\pi - 4$

    D. $4\pi - 8$

9. A blueprint has a scale of 3 feet per $\frac{1}{2}$ inch. If a bathroom is $1\frac{1}{2}$ inches $\times$ 2 inches, what are its actual dimensions?

    A. $4\frac{1}{2}$ feet $\times$ 6 feet

    B. 6 feet $\times -7\frac{1}{2}$ feet

    C. $7\frac{1}{2}$ feet $\times$ 9 feet

    D. 9 feet $\times$ 12 feet

10. A barrel holds 60 gallons of water. If a crack in the barrel causes $\frac{1}{2}$ a gallon to leak out each day, how many gallons of water remain after two weeks?

    A. 30

    B. 53

    C. $56\frac{1}{2}$

    D. 59

11. The basketball game starts at 8:00. If it is now 5:30, how much time is left before the game starts?

    A. 1 hour, 30 minutes

    B. 2 hours, 30 minutes

    C. 3 hours, 30 minutes

    D. 4 hours, 30 minutes

12. How many blocks $6" \times 4" \times 4"$ can fit in a box $8' \times 6' \times 4'$?

    A. 2

    B. 48

    C. 576

    D. 3,456

13. Janice buys a quart of milk and two dozen eggs. If milk costs $1.39 and eggs are $1.28 a dozen, how much change will Janice get back if she pays with a $10.00 bill?

    A. $3.95

    B. $5.94

    C. $6.05

    D. $7.33

14. There are 800 employees at a company. If 60% drive to work and 30% take the train, how many employees arrive to work by car?

    A. 240

    B. 480

    C. 540

    D. 600

GO ON TO THE NEXT PAGE

15. Min reads three hardcover mysteries and four soft cover mysteries. She reads three times as many nonfiction books as she did mysteries. How many nonfiction books did Min read?

A. 9
B. 12
C. 18
D. 21

16. The volume of a cube is 343 cm³. The surface area of the cube is

A. 7 cm²
B. 49 cm²
C. 294 cm²
D. 2401 cm²

17. Melodi eats $\frac{3}{8}$ of a pizza and divides the rest among her two friends. What percent of the pizza do her friends each receive?

A. 62.50%
B. 37.50%
C. 31.25%
D. 18.75%

18. Kim's favorite movie is 144 minutes long. Justin's favorite movie is 127 minutes long. How much longer is Kim's favorite movie?

A. 17 minutes
B. 23 minutes
C. 36 minutes
D. 44 minutes

19. Roger collects bottle caps. Each cap can be traded for 5 cents. If Roger receives $40.50, how many bottle caps did he trade?

A. 810
B. 405
C. 200
D. 8

20. A batch of cookies requires 2 cups of milk and 4 eggs. If you have 9 cups of milk and 9 eggs, how many batches of cookies can be made?

A. 9
B. 6
C. 4
D. 2

21. Find the value of *x* in the figure:

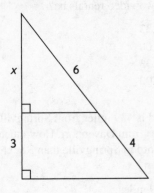

A. 4.5
B. 4.8
C. 5
D. 5.2

22. A piece of wood measuring 16.5 inches long is cut into 2.75 inch pieces. How many smaller pieces of wood are there?

A. 3
B. 5
C. 6
D. 8

23. Shanella has 17 quarters, 33 dimes, and 8 pennies. The total amount of money is

A. $7.63
B. $7.95
C. $5.80
D. $15.55

24. While dining out, Chad spent $25.00. If the bill totaled $21.00 before the tip was added, approximately what percent tip did Chad leave?

A. 16%
B. 19%
C. 21%
D. 25%

25. A right triangle has an area of 24 feet. If one leg is 3 times as long as the other, what is the length of the longest side?

A. 12.6
B. 12
C. 8.4
D. 6.3

26. Interest earned on an account totals $100. If the interest rate is $7\frac{1}{4}$%, what is the principle amount?

- **A.** $725
- **B.** $1333
- **C.** $1379
- **D.** $1428

27. Yan can read two pages in three minutes. At this rate, how long will it take him to read a 360-page book?

- **A.** 30 minutes
- **B.** 2 hours
- **C.** 6 hours
- **D.** 9 hours

28. Tanya's bowling scores this week were 112, 156, 179, and 165. Last week, her average score was 140. How many points did her average improve?

- **A.** 18
- **B.** 13
- **C.** 11
- **D.** 8

29. Felix buys 3 books for $8.95 each. How much does he owe if he uses a $12.73 credit toward his purchase?

- **A.** $39.58
- **B.** $26.85
- **C.** $21.68
- **D.** $14.12

30. The value of 18 quarters, 6 dimes, and 24 nickels is

- **A.** $5.34
- **B.** $6.30
- **C.** $18.84
- **D.** $24.24

STOP. BEFORE MOVING ON TO THE NEXT SECTION, CHECK YOUR ANSWERS IF THERE IS STILL TIME LEFT.

Mathematics Knowledge

Time: 24 Minutes
25 Questions

Select the choice that best answers the following questions.

1. Multiply $(2x + 1)(2x + 1)$.

- **A.** $2x^2 + 1$
- **B.** $4x^2 + 1$
- **C.** $4x^2 + 2x + 1$
- **D.** $4x^2 + 4x + 1$

2. $\frac{24}{96} - \frac{8}{12} =$

- **A.** $\frac{1}{4}$
- **B.** $\frac{5}{96}$
- **C.** $-\frac{5}{12}$
- **D.** $\frac{4}{21}$

3. The sum of $\sqrt{50} + 3\sqrt{72}$ is

- **A.** $4 + \sqrt{122}$
- **B.** $4\sqrt{122}$
- **C.** $7\sqrt{2}$
- **D.** $23\sqrt{2}$

4. The diagonal of a square is 10 inches. What is the area of the square?

- **A.** 40 in^2
- **B.** 50 in^2
- **C.** 100 in^2
- **D.** 150 in^2

GO ON TO THE NEXT PAGE

5. What is the diameter of a circle whose circumference is equivalent to its area?

    A. 2

    B. 3

    C. 4

    D. 6

6. Simplify $\dfrac{15\sqrt{3}}{\sqrt{5}}$.

    A. $3\sqrt{3}$

    B. $3\sqrt{15}$ H

    C. $15\sqrt{15}$

    D. $75\sqrt{3}$

7. Find the area of a triangle whose base is 3 inches less than its height.

    A. $\dfrac{1}{2}h^2 - 3h$

    B. $\dfrac{1}{2}h^2 - \dfrac{3}{2}h$

    C. $\dfrac{1}{2}h - \dfrac{3}{2}$

    D. $\dfrac{1}{2}h^2 - 3$

8. If $x = -3$ and $y = 2$, evaluate x^{2y}.

    A. -64

    B. -81

    C. 64

    D. 81

9. The product of two numbers is 117. If one of the numbers is 9, what is the other?

    A. 11

    B. 13

    C. 15

    D. 17

10. $\dfrac{3}{4} \div \dfrac{4}{3} =$

    A. 0

    B. 1

    C. $\dfrac{9}{16}$

    D. $\dfrac{16}{9}$

11. There are five more boys in the kindergarten class than girls. If there are 27 children all together, how many are boys?

    A. 10

    B. 11

    C. 16

    D. 22

12. Simplify $(3x^2 + 2x - 5) - (2x^2 - 5) + (4x - 7)$.

    A. $x^2 + 6x - 17$

    B. $x^2 + 4x - 7$

    C. $x^2 + 6x - 2$

    D. $x^2 + 6x - 7$

13. The product of the square of x and three less than x is

    A. $\sqrt{x}\,(x - 3)$

    B. $\sqrt{x}\,(3 - x)$

    C. $x^2(x - 3)$

    D. $x^2(3 - x)$

14. What is the measure of $\angle A$?

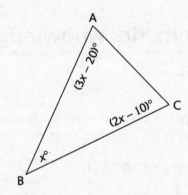

    A. $35°$

    B. $60°$

    C. $75°$

    D. $85°$

15. What is the probability of rolling a sum of 9 using two dice?

    A. $\dfrac{1}{4}$

    B. $\dfrac{1}{9}$

    C. $\dfrac{5}{12}$

    D. $\dfrac{7}{36}$

16. Round $(2.5)^4$ to the nearest tenth.

    A. 10.0

    B. 25.4

    C. 39.0

    D. 39.1

17. Which mathematical statement best represents the following?

    Six less a number is four.

    A. $6 = n - 4$

    B. $6 < n + 4$

    C. $6 - n = 4$

    D. $n - 6 = 4$

18. The least common multiple of 8, 12, and 20 is

    A. 4

    B. 24

    C. 60

    D. 120

19. If $\frac{m}{n} = \frac{3}{5}$, what is the value of $m + n$?

    A. 2

    B. 8

    C. $\frac{6}{5}$

    D. $\frac{9}{25}$

20. Simplify $\frac{x^2 - 25}{5 - x}$

    A. $x + 5$

    B. $x - 5$

    C. $-(x + 5)$

    D. $5 - x$

21. A rope is made by linking beads that are $\frac{1}{2}$" in diameter. How many feet long is a rope made from 60 beads?

    A. $2\frac{1}{2}$ ft

    B. 10 ft

    C. 30 ft

    D. 120 ft

22. What is the probability of flipping three heads in a row using a fair coin?

    A. $\frac{1}{2}$

    B. $\frac{2}{3}$

    C. $\frac{1}{8}$

    D. $\frac{3}{8}$

23. $-3(-4 - 5) - 2(-6) =$

    A. 0

    B. -5

    C. 15

    D. 39

24. Find the area of a regular hexagon whose sides measure 6 cm.

    A. 36

    B. $9\sqrt{2}$

    C. $54\sqrt{3}$

    D. 108

25. Squares ADEC, BCFG, and ABHI are shown. If the area of ADEC is 81 and the area of BCFG is 144, what is the perimeter of $\triangle ABC$?

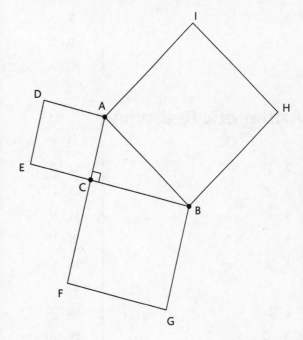

    A. 36

    B. 72

    C. 225

    D. 450

Answer Key for ASVAB Practice Test 1

Word Knowledge

1. B	13. A	25. D
2. B	14. B	26. D
3. A	15. B	27. A
4. D	16. B	28. B
5. B	17. D	29. D
6. A	18. B	30. B
7. C	19. A	31. B
8. B	20. B	32. B
9. B	21. A	33. D
10. D	22. B	34. C
11. B	23. B	35. B
12. B	24. C	

Paragraph Comprehension

1. C	6. C	11. C
2. D	7. B	12. C
3. C	8. A	13. A
4. B	9. D	14. B
5. D	10. A	15. D

Arithmetic Reasoning

1. C	11. B	21. A
2. D	12. D	22. C
3. B	13. C	23. A
4. B	14. B	24. B
5. C	15. D	25. A
6. A	16. C	26. C
7. D	17. C	27. D
8. D	18. A	28. B
9. D	19. A	29. D
10. B	20. D	30. B

Mathematics Knowledge

1. D	10. C	19. B
2. C	11. C	20. C
3. D	12. D	21. A
4. B	13. C	22. C
5. C	14. D	23. D
6. B	15. B	24. C
7. B	16. D	25. A
8. D	17. D	
9. B	18. D	

ASVAB Practice Test 1 Answers and Explanations

Word Knowledge

1. **B.** The correct answer is **hardship,** which means a difficult time or experience. The other choices are all positive words.

2. **B.** The correct answer is **corrosive,** which means harsh or stinging.

3. **A.** The correct answer is **enjoyment.** Zest means enthusiasm or delight.

4. **D.** The correct answer is **mystery.** Enigma refers to a puzzle or problem as mystery also suggests.

5. **B.** The correct answer is **prompt.** Prompt means precise or immediate.

6. **A.** The correct answer is **dawdle,** which means to loaf or waste time.

7. **C.** The correct answer is **wander,** which can mean to ramble or roam.

8. **B.** The correct answer is **stinginess.** Stingy means miserly, closefisted, or selfish.

9. **B.** The correct answer is **concise.** Concise means brief, to the point, or condensed.

10. **D.** The correct answer is **grave,** which can mean dismal or gloomy.

11. **B.** The correct answer is **easily led.** Docile can mean submissive, compliant, or tame.

12. **B.** The correct answer is **healthy.** Hale can mean hardy or fit as in good health.

13. **A.** The correct answer is **endless,** which can mean limitless or unbounded.

14. **B.** The correct answer is **wealthy,** which can mean rich or prosperous.

15. **B.** The correct answer is **ordinary.** Trite can mean commonplace, stale, or stereotyped.

16. **B.** The correct answer is **essential,** meaning important or necessary.

17. **D.** The correct answer is **scamper.** Scamper means to hasten or hustle.

18. **B.** The correct answer is **wise.** Prudent can mean sensible or cautious.

19. **A.** The correct answer is **passionate,** which can mean excitable or eager.

20. **B.** The correct answer is **tasteless,** which can mean dull or uninteresting.

21. **A.** The correct answer is **spoil,** which means to ruin or destroy.

22. **B.** The correct answer is **to move back and forth.** Sway in this sentence means to lean or incline.

23. B. The correct answer is **helping.** Auxiliary here means supplementary.

24. C. The correct answer is **skillful.** In this sentence deft means adept or proficient.

25. D. The correct answer is **fruitful.** Prolific in this sentence means abundant or plentiful.

26. D. The correct answer is **strange.** Bizarre can mean odd, weird, or unusual.

27. A. The correct answer is **a show of respect.** Tribute means acclaim or recognition.

28. B. The correct answer is **speaking untruth.** Slander can mean to vilify or to denigrate.

29. D. The correct answer is **wealth.** Affluence means riches or abundance.

30. B. The correct answer is **solitary.** Reclusive means reserved or aloof.

31. B. The correct answer is **quality.** Caliber means nature or essence.

32. B. The correct answer is **motivator.** Incentive means driving force or impetus.

33. D. The correct answer is **demolish,** which means to destroy, damage, or wreck.

34. C. The correct answer is **ask for.** Solicit means to beg or to implore.

35. B. The correct answer is **meantime.** Interim means time between events or interval.

Paragraph Comprehension

1. C. Aspirin is discussed as a possible preventive medication for colon cancer.

2. D. The last sentence states that organic foods do not contain herbicides.

3. C. The only name not listed in the paragraph as another name for the concolour is bobcat.

4. B. Since the selection states that Edison did not give up easily, one can assume that being tenacious is a synonym for being persistent.

5. D. The third sentence states that Edison had a few failed inventions, and the rest of the selection elaborates on the iron ore mining invention attempt.

6. C. The selection states that regions north of the Arctic Circle experience unending periods of daylight and dark. However, regions below the Arctic Circle are not included in this analysis of daylight and dark.

7. B. The selection states that such plants should be watered during the cooler parts of the day. 6:00 A.M. is the coolest time of day listed.

8. A. This choice is the only one that makes sense in the context of the first and last sentences. That is why our bodies are "water dependent" as the selection states.

9. D. The answer is stated in the fourth sentence of the selection.

10. A. The entire selection focuses on proper steps to ensure healthy weight loss and avoid injury by too much exercise or restricting calories too much.

11. C. The article discusses the dangers of driving with any type of cellular phone, thus, it can inferred that this is the best answer.

12. C. The article focuses on the dangerous nature of cellular phone usage while driving.

13. A. The first sentence of the paragraph states that there are many preventive measures drivers can take to avoid carjacking. The supporting sentences in the paragraph give specific ways to prevent carjacking.

14. B. Carrying pepper spray is not mentioned in the paragraph as a preventive measure against carjacking.

15. D. The author of the selection gives several practical ways to avoid carjacking. None of the other choices are statements that are made by the author. Thus, one may assume that carjacking can often be avoided by following the preventive measures given in the selection.

Arithmetic Reasoning

1. **C.** $\frac{1}{3}$ of $6\frac{1}{2}$ miles is $\frac{1}{3} \times 6\frac{1}{2} = \frac{1}{3} \times \frac{13}{2} = \frac{13}{6}$ miles walked. The remaining distance is

   $6\frac{1}{2} - \frac{13}{6} = \frac{13}{2} - \frac{13}{6} = \frac{39}{6} - \frac{13}{6} = \frac{26}{6} = 4\frac{1}{3}$ miles.

2. **D.** Using the ratio $\frac{\text{height}}{\text{shadow}}$, the proportion $\frac{x\,\text{feet}}{5\,\text{feet}} = \frac{6\,\text{feet}}{8\,\text{feet}}$ can be used to find the unknown height. Cross multiply.

   $8x = 5 \times 6$ so $8x = 30$ and $x = \frac{30}{8} = 3\frac{3}{4}$ feet. Convert $\frac{3}{4}$ feet to inches. $\frac{3}{4} \times 12 = 9$ inches. The height is therefore 3 feet 9 inches.

3. **B.** The time cleaning was 30 minutes + 12 minutes + 37 minutes = 79.

4. **B.** If $\frac{3}{8}$ is wheat flour, then $1 - \frac{3}{8}$ or $\frac{5}{8}$ is white flour. So $3 \times \frac{5}{8} = \frac{15}{8} = 1\frac{7}{8}$ cups of white flour is needed.

5. **C.** Using the ratio $\frac{\text{price}}{\text{video}}$, the proportion $\frac{8}{3} = \frac{x}{2}$ can be used to find the cost to rent two videos. Cross multiply.

   $8 \times 2 = 3x$ so $16 = 3x$ and $x = \frac{16}{3} = \$5.33$.

6. **A.** The difference in miles is $638 - 439 = 199$.

7. **D.** The percent discounted is the amount discounted divided by the original price. The amount discounted is $\$200 - \$150 = \$50$. The percent discounted is $\frac{50}{200} = 0.25 = 25\%$.

8. **D.**

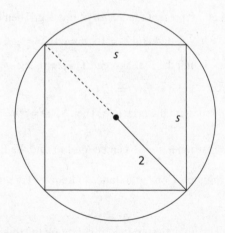

   Find the difference between the area of circle and the area of the square. The area of the circle is $\pi r^2 = \pi \cdot 2^2 = 4\pi$. The area of the square is s^2, where s represents the length of the square. The radius is half the length of the square's diagonal so the diagonal is 4. By the Pythagorean Theorem, $s^2 + s^2 = 4^2$. $2s^2 = 16$ so $s^2 = 8$. The difference in area is $4\pi - 8$.

9. **D.** If the blueprint shows $\frac{1}{2}$ inch for every 3 feet, then 1 inch represents 6 feet. The actual dimensions of a room $1\frac{1}{2}$ inches $\times$ 2 inches would be $\left(1\frac{1}{2} \times 6\right)$ by (2×6) or 9 feet by 12 feet.

10. **B.** In 2 weeks, or 14 days, $\frac{1}{2} \times 14 = 7$ gallons leak out, leaving $60 - 7 = 53$ gallons.

11. **B.** At 5:30, there are 30 minutes to 6:00 and two additional hours until 8:00 for a total of 2 hours and 30 minutes.

12. **D.** Convert the dimensions of the box from feet to inches. $8' \times 6' \times 4'$ is equivalent to $(8 \times 12\,\text{in}) \times (6 \times 12\,\text{in}) \times (4 \times 12\,\text{in}) = 96\,\text{in} \times 72\,\text{in} \times 48\,\text{in}$. The volume $= 96 \times 72 \times 48 = 331{,}776$. The volume of each block is $6 \times 4 \times 4 = 96$. The number of blocks that fit in the box is $\frac{331{,}776}{96} = 3{,}456$.

13. **C.** The cost for milk and two dozen eggs is $\$1.39 + (2 \times \$1.28) = \$3.95$. The change is $\$10.00 - \$3.95 = \$6.05$.

14. **B.** 60% arrive to work by car, so $800 \times 60\% = 480$.

15. D. Min read a total of 3 + 4 or 7 mysteries. Therefore, she read 3 × 7 or 21 nonfiction books.

16. C. The volume of a cube is s^3, where s represents the length of an edge. Surface area is $6s^2$. If the volume = 343 cm, then $s = \sqrt[3]{343} = \sqrt[3]{7 \times 7 \times 7} = 7$. So the surface area is $6 \times 7^2 = 6 \times 49 = 294$ cm^2.

17. C. If $\frac{3}{8}$ of the pizza is eaten, then $1 - \frac{3}{8} = \frac{5}{8}$ remains. If that is divided by 2, then each receives $\frac{5}{8} \div 2 = \frac{5}{8} \times \frac{1}{2} = \frac{5}{16} = 0.3125 = 31.25\%$.

18. A. The difference in times is 144 – 127 = 17 minutes.

19. A. Let c represent the number of caps traded in. Then $0.05c = 40.50$ and $c = \frac{40.50}{0.05} = 810$ caps.

20. D. With 9 cups of milk, $\frac{9}{2} = 4\frac{1}{2}$ or 4 full batches can be made. However, with 9 eggs, only $\frac{9}{4} = 2\frac{1}{4}$ or 2 full batches can be made. At most, only two batches can be made with the given ingredients.

21. A. The proportion $\frac{x}{6} = \frac{x+3}{10}$ can be used to find x. Cross multiply. $10x = 6(x + 3)$ and $10x = 6x + 18$. Bring all x terms to one side by subtracting $6x$ from each side. Then $4x = 18$ and $x = \frac{18}{4} = 4.5$.

22. C. The number of smaller pieces is $\frac{16.5}{2.75} = 6$.

23. A. The total amount is $(17 \times \$0.25) + (33 \times \$0.10) + (8 \times \$0.01) = \$4.25 + \$3.30 + \$0.08 = \$7.63$.

24. B. The percent tip is the amount of tip over the total before tip. The amount of the tip is $\$25.00 – \$21.00 = \$4.00$. The percent of the tip is $\frac{4}{21} = 0.19 = 19\%$.

25. A. The area of a triangle is $\frac{1}{2}bh$. Let b represent the length of one leg. Then $h = 3b$ so the area is $\frac{1}{2}bh = \frac{1}{2} \cdot b \cdot 3b = \frac{3}{2}b^2 = 24$ so $\frac{2}{3} \cdot \frac{3}{2}b^2 = \frac{2}{3} \cdot 24$ and $b^2 = 16$. $b = \sqrt{16} = 4$ and $h = 3 \times 4 = 12$. The longest side of a right triangle is the hypotenuse. Using the Pythagorean Theorem, $\text{leg}^2 + \text{leg}^2 = \text{hypotenuse}^2$ so $4^2 + 12^2 = c^2$ and $16 + 144 = c^2$. Therefore, $160 = c^2$ and $c = \sqrt{160} = 12.6$.

26. C. Interest = principle × rate. Let p represent the principle. Then $\$100 = p \times 7\frac{1}{4}\%$ so $p = \frac{\$100}{7\frac{1}{4}\%} = \frac{\$100}{0.0725} = \$1379$.

27. D. Using the ratio $\frac{\text{pages}}{\text{minutes}}$, the proportion $\frac{2}{3} = \frac{360}{x}$ can be used to find the time. Cross multiply. $2x = 3 \times 360$ so $2x = 1080$ and $x = \frac{1080}{2} = 540$ minutes. Convert minutes to hours. There are 60 minutes in one hour, so $\frac{540}{60} = 9$ hours.

28. B. The average is found by adding up all the scores and dividing by the total number of scores. The average this week is $\frac{112 + 156 + 179 + 165}{4} = \frac{612}{4} = 153$. The amount of improvement is $153 – 140 = 13$.

29. D. The total cost of the purchase is $\$8.95 \times 3 = \$26.85$. With a \$12.73 credit, the amount owed is $\$26.85 – \$12.73 = \$14.12$.

30. B. The total is $(18 \times \$0.25) + (6 \times \$0.10) + (24 \times \$0.05) = \$4.50 + \$0.60 + \$1.20 = \$6.30$.

Mathematics Knowledge

1. D. Using the distributive property, $(2x + 1)(2x + 1) = 4x^2 + 2x + 1 = 4x^2 + 4x + 1$.

2. C. The least common denominator of 96 and 12 is 96 so $\frac{24}{96} - \frac{8}{12} = \frac{24}{96} - \frac{64}{96} = \frac{-40}{96} = -\frac{5}{12}$.

3. D. Simplifying $\sqrt{50} + 3\sqrt{72}$ yields $\sqrt{25} \times 2 + 3\sqrt{36} \times 2 = 5\sqrt{2} + 18\sqrt{2} = 23\sqrt{2}$.

4. B.

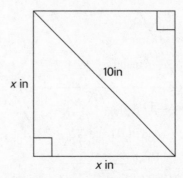

Let x represent a side of the square. The area of the square is x^2. To find the value of x^2, use the Pythagorean Theorem. $x^2 + x^2 = 10^2$ so $2x^2 = 100$ and $x^2 = \dfrac{100}{2}$ or 50.

5. C. The circumference of a circle is given by the formula $C = 2\pi r$ and the area of a circle is given by $A = \pi r^2$. If the circumference is equal to the area, then $2\pi r = \pi r^2$. Solving for r, $\dfrac{2\pi r}{\pi r} = \dfrac{\pi r^2}{\pi r}$ and $2 = r$. The diameter is $2r$, or 4.

6. B. $\dfrac{15\sqrt{3}}{\sqrt{5}} = \dfrac{15\sqrt{3}}{\sqrt{5}} \cdot \dfrac{\sqrt{5}}{\sqrt{5}} = \dfrac{15\sqrt{15}}{5} = 3\sqrt{15}$.

7. B. The area of a triangle is $\frac{1}{2}bh$. If the base is 3 inches less than the height, then $b = h - 3$. Substituting this value in for b gives $A = \frac{1}{2}(h-3)h = \frac{1}{2}h^2 - \frac{3}{2}h$.

8. D. If $x = -3$ and $y = 2$, then $x^2y = (-3)^{2(2)} = (-3)^4 = 81$.

9. B. Let x be the unknown number. Then $9x = 117$ and $x = \dfrac{117}{9} = 13$.

10. C. $\dfrac{3}{4} \div \dfrac{4}{3} = \dfrac{3}{4} \times \dfrac{3}{4} = \dfrac{9}{16}$

11. C. Let b represent the number of boys in the class and g represent the number of girls. Then $b + g = 27$. If $b = g + 5$, then $(g + 5) + g = 27$. $2g + 5 = 27$ and $2g = 22$ so $g = 11$. Therefore, the number of boys is $27 - 11$ or 16.

12. D. $(3x^2 + 2x - 5) - (2x^2 - 5) + (4x - 7) = 3x^2 + 2x - 5 - 2x^2 + 5 + 4x - 7 = 3x^2 - 2x^2 + 2x + 4x - 5 + 5 - 7 = x^2 + 6x - 7$.

13. C. The square of x is x^2. Three less than x is $x - 3$. Their product is $x^2(x-3)$.

14. D. The sum of all angles in a triangle equal $180°$. So $(3x - 20)° + x° + (2x - 10)° = 180°$. $3x + x + 2x - 20 - 10 = 180$ and $6x - 30 = 180$. Then $6x = 210$ and $x = \dfrac{210}{6} = 35$. Therefore, $\angle A$ is $3(35) - 20$ or $85°$.

15. B. There are 4 possible ways to roll a 9 using 2 dice: 3 and 6, 4 and 5, 5 and 4, 6 and 3. The total number of possible outcomes when rolling 2 dice is 6^2 or 36. Therefore, the probability of rolling a 9 is $\dfrac{4}{36} = \dfrac{1}{9}$.

16. D. $(2.5)^4 = 2.5 \times 2.5 \times 2.5 \times 2.5 = 39.0625$. Rounded to the nearest tenth is 39.1.

17. D. Six less a number is shown by $n - 6$. So six less a number is four is represented by $n - 6 = 4$.

18. D. Factors of 8 are $2 \times 2 \times 2$; factors of 12 are $2 \times 2 \times 3$; factors of 20 are $2 \times 2 \times 5$. The least common multiple of 8, 12, and 20 is $2 \times 2 \times 2 \times 3 \times 5$ or 120.

19. B. In the proportion $\dfrac{m}{n} = \dfrac{3}{5}$, let $m = 3$ and let $n = 5$. Therefore, $m + n = 3 + 5 = 8$.

20. C. $\dfrac{x^2 - 25}{5 - x} = \dfrac{(x+5)(x-5)}{5-x} = \dfrac{(x+5)(x-5)}{-(x-5)} = \dfrac{(x+5)}{-1} = -(x+5)$.

21. A. 60 beads $\times \frac{1}{2}$ inch = 30 inches. Converting this to feet gives 30 inches $\times \dfrac{1\,\text{foot}}{12\,\text{inches}} = \dfrac{30}{12} = 2\frac{1}{2}$ feet.

22. C. The probability of flipping one head is $\frac{1}{2}$. The probability of flipping three heads in a row is $\frac{1}{2} \times \frac{1}{2} \times \frac{1}{2}$ or $\frac{1}{8}$.

23. D. Using the correct order of operations, $-3(-4 - 5) - 2(-6) = -3(-9) - 2(-6) = 27 - (-12) = 27 + 12 = 39$.

24. C.

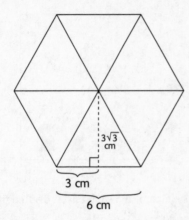

A regular hexagon is made up of six equilateral triangles. Find the area of one equilateral triangle and multiply that by 6 to find the area of the hexagon. The height, or altitude, of a triangle can be found by the Pythagorean Theorem. The right triangle formed by the altitude has a hypotenuse of 6 and a shorter leg of $\frac{6}{2}$, or 3. So $3^2 + h^2 = 6^2$, so $9 + h^2 = 36$ and $h^2 = 27$. Therefore, $h = \sqrt{27} = 3\sqrt{3}$. The area of one equilateral triangle is $\frac{1}{2}bh = \frac{1}{2} \cdot 6 \cdot 3\sqrt{3} = 9\sqrt{3}$ and the area of the hexagon is $6 \times 9\sqrt{3} = 54\sqrt{3}$.

25. A. Since the area of ADEC is 81, $AC = \sqrt{81} = 9$. Since the area of BCFG is 144, $BC = \sqrt{144} = 12$. Use the Pythagorean Theorem to find the length of the remaining side AB. $AB^2 = 9^2 + 12^2$ so $AB^2 = 81 + 144 = 225$ and $AB = \sqrt{225} = 15$. Therefore, the perimeter of the triangle = $9 + 12 + 15 = 36$.

PART III

FULL-LENGTH PRACTICE TESTS 2

Answer Sheet for AFOQT Practice Test 2

(Remove This Sheet and Use It to Mark Your Answers)

Part 1 Verbal Analogies

1	Ⓐ Ⓑ Ⓒ Ⓓ Ⓔ		16	Ⓐ Ⓑ Ⓒ Ⓓ Ⓔ
2	Ⓐ Ⓑ Ⓒ Ⓓ Ⓔ		17	Ⓐ Ⓑ Ⓒ Ⓓ Ⓔ
3	Ⓐ Ⓑ Ⓒ Ⓓ Ⓔ		18	Ⓐ Ⓑ Ⓒ Ⓓ Ⓔ
4	Ⓐ Ⓑ Ⓒ Ⓓ Ⓔ		19	Ⓐ Ⓑ Ⓒ Ⓓ Ⓔ
5	Ⓐ Ⓑ Ⓒ Ⓓ Ⓔ		20	Ⓐ Ⓑ Ⓒ Ⓓ Ⓔ
6	Ⓐ Ⓑ Ⓒ Ⓓ Ⓔ		21	Ⓐ Ⓑ Ⓒ Ⓓ Ⓔ
7	Ⓐ Ⓑ Ⓒ Ⓓ Ⓔ		22	Ⓐ Ⓑ Ⓒ Ⓓ Ⓔ
8	Ⓐ Ⓑ Ⓒ Ⓓ Ⓔ		23	Ⓐ Ⓑ Ⓒ Ⓓ Ⓔ
9	Ⓐ Ⓑ Ⓒ Ⓓ Ⓔ		24	Ⓐ Ⓑ Ⓒ Ⓓ Ⓔ
10	Ⓐ Ⓑ Ⓒ Ⓓ Ⓔ		25	Ⓐ Ⓑ Ⓒ Ⓓ Ⓔ
11	Ⓐ Ⓑ Ⓒ Ⓓ Ⓔ			
12	Ⓐ Ⓑ Ⓒ Ⓓ Ⓔ			
13	Ⓐ Ⓑ Ⓒ Ⓓ Ⓔ			
14	Ⓐ Ⓑ Ⓒ Ⓓ Ⓔ			
15	Ⓐ Ⓑ Ⓒ Ⓓ Ⓔ			

Part 2 Arithmetic Reasoning

1	Ⓐ Ⓑ Ⓒ Ⓓ Ⓔ		16	Ⓐ Ⓑ Ⓒ Ⓓ Ⓔ
2	Ⓐ Ⓑ Ⓒ Ⓓ Ⓔ		17	Ⓐ Ⓑ Ⓒ Ⓓ Ⓔ
3	Ⓐ Ⓑ Ⓒ Ⓓ Ⓔ		18	Ⓐ Ⓑ Ⓒ Ⓓ Ⓔ
4	Ⓐ Ⓑ Ⓒ Ⓓ Ⓔ		19	Ⓐ Ⓑ Ⓒ Ⓓ Ⓔ
5	Ⓐ Ⓑ Ⓒ Ⓓ Ⓔ		20	Ⓐ Ⓑ Ⓒ Ⓓ Ⓔ
6	Ⓐ Ⓑ Ⓒ Ⓓ Ⓔ		21	Ⓐ Ⓑ Ⓒ Ⓓ Ⓔ
7	Ⓐ Ⓑ Ⓒ Ⓓ Ⓔ		22	Ⓐ Ⓑ Ⓒ Ⓓ Ⓔ
8	Ⓐ Ⓑ Ⓒ Ⓓ Ⓔ		23	Ⓐ Ⓑ Ⓒ Ⓓ Ⓔ
9	Ⓐ Ⓑ Ⓒ Ⓓ Ⓔ		24	Ⓐ Ⓑ Ⓒ Ⓓ Ⓔ
10	Ⓐ Ⓑ Ⓒ Ⓓ Ⓔ		25	Ⓐ Ⓑ Ⓒ Ⓓ Ⓔ
11	Ⓐ Ⓑ Ⓒ Ⓓ Ⓔ			
12	Ⓐ Ⓑ Ⓒ Ⓓ Ⓔ			
13	Ⓐ Ⓑ Ⓒ Ⓓ Ⓔ			
14	Ⓐ Ⓑ Ⓒ Ⓓ Ⓔ			
15	Ⓐ Ⓑ Ⓒ Ⓓ Ⓔ			

Part 3 Reading Comprehension

1	Ⓐ Ⓑ Ⓒ Ⓓ Ⓔ		16	Ⓐ Ⓑ Ⓒ Ⓓ Ⓔ
2	Ⓐ Ⓑ Ⓒ Ⓓ Ⓔ		17	Ⓐ Ⓑ Ⓒ Ⓓ Ⓔ
3	Ⓐ Ⓑ Ⓒ Ⓓ Ⓔ		18	Ⓐ Ⓑ Ⓒ Ⓓ Ⓔ
4	Ⓐ Ⓑ Ⓒ Ⓓ Ⓔ		19	Ⓐ Ⓑ Ⓒ Ⓓ Ⓔ
5	Ⓐ Ⓑ Ⓒ Ⓓ Ⓔ		20	Ⓐ Ⓑ Ⓒ Ⓓ Ⓔ
6	Ⓐ Ⓑ Ⓒ Ⓓ Ⓔ		21	Ⓐ Ⓑ Ⓒ Ⓓ Ⓔ
7	Ⓐ Ⓑ Ⓒ Ⓓ Ⓔ		22	Ⓐ Ⓑ Ⓒ Ⓓ Ⓔ
8	Ⓐ Ⓑ Ⓒ Ⓓ Ⓔ		23	Ⓐ Ⓑ Ⓒ Ⓓ Ⓔ
9	Ⓐ Ⓑ Ⓒ Ⓓ Ⓔ		24	Ⓐ Ⓑ Ⓒ Ⓓ Ⓔ
10	Ⓐ Ⓑ Ⓒ Ⓓ Ⓔ		25	Ⓐ Ⓑ Ⓒ Ⓓ Ⓔ
11	Ⓐ Ⓑ Ⓒ Ⓓ Ⓔ			
12	Ⓐ Ⓑ Ⓒ Ⓓ Ⓔ			
13	Ⓐ Ⓑ Ⓒ Ⓓ Ⓔ			
14	Ⓐ Ⓑ Ⓒ Ⓓ Ⓔ			
15	Ⓐ Ⓑ Ⓒ Ⓓ Ⓔ			

Part 4 Data Interpretation

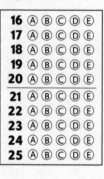

1	Ⓐ Ⓑ Ⓒ Ⓓ Ⓔ		16	Ⓐ Ⓑ Ⓒ Ⓓ Ⓔ
2	Ⓐ Ⓑ Ⓒ Ⓓ Ⓔ		17	Ⓐ Ⓑ Ⓒ Ⓓ Ⓔ
3	Ⓐ Ⓑ Ⓒ Ⓓ Ⓔ		18	Ⓐ Ⓑ Ⓒ Ⓓ Ⓔ
4	Ⓐ Ⓑ Ⓒ Ⓓ Ⓔ		19	Ⓐ Ⓑ Ⓒ Ⓓ Ⓔ
5	Ⓐ Ⓑ Ⓒ Ⓓ Ⓔ		20	Ⓐ Ⓑ Ⓒ Ⓓ Ⓔ
6	Ⓐ Ⓑ Ⓒ Ⓓ Ⓔ		21	Ⓐ Ⓑ Ⓒ Ⓓ Ⓔ
7	Ⓐ Ⓑ Ⓒ Ⓓ Ⓔ		22	Ⓐ Ⓑ Ⓒ Ⓓ Ⓔ
8	Ⓐ Ⓑ Ⓒ Ⓓ Ⓔ		23	Ⓐ Ⓑ Ⓒ Ⓓ Ⓔ
9	Ⓐ Ⓑ Ⓒ Ⓓ Ⓔ		24	Ⓐ Ⓑ Ⓒ Ⓓ Ⓔ
10	Ⓐ Ⓑ Ⓒ Ⓓ Ⓔ		25	Ⓐ Ⓑ Ⓒ Ⓓ Ⓔ
11	Ⓐ Ⓑ Ⓒ Ⓓ Ⓔ			
12	Ⓐ Ⓑ Ⓒ Ⓓ Ⓔ			
13	Ⓐ Ⓑ Ⓒ Ⓓ Ⓔ			
14	Ⓐ Ⓑ Ⓒ Ⓓ Ⓔ			
15	Ⓐ Ⓑ Ⓒ Ⓓ Ⓔ			

Part 5 Word Knowledge

1	Ⓐ Ⓑ Ⓒ Ⓓ Ⓔ		16	Ⓐ Ⓑ Ⓒ Ⓓ Ⓔ
2	Ⓐ Ⓑ Ⓒ Ⓓ Ⓔ		17	Ⓐ Ⓑ Ⓒ Ⓓ Ⓔ
3	Ⓐ Ⓑ Ⓒ Ⓓ Ⓔ		18	Ⓐ Ⓑ Ⓒ Ⓓ Ⓔ
4	Ⓐ Ⓑ Ⓒ Ⓓ Ⓔ		19	Ⓐ Ⓑ Ⓒ Ⓓ Ⓔ
5	Ⓐ Ⓑ Ⓒ Ⓓ Ⓔ		20	Ⓐ Ⓑ Ⓒ Ⓓ Ⓔ
6	Ⓐ Ⓑ Ⓒ Ⓓ Ⓔ		21	Ⓐ Ⓑ Ⓒ Ⓓ Ⓔ
7	Ⓐ Ⓑ Ⓒ Ⓓ Ⓔ		22	Ⓐ Ⓑ Ⓒ Ⓓ Ⓔ
8	Ⓐ Ⓑ Ⓒ Ⓓ Ⓔ		23	Ⓐ Ⓑ Ⓒ Ⓓ Ⓔ
9	Ⓐ Ⓑ Ⓒ Ⓓ Ⓔ		24	Ⓐ Ⓑ Ⓒ Ⓓ Ⓔ
10	Ⓐ Ⓑ Ⓒ Ⓓ Ⓔ		25	Ⓐ Ⓑ Ⓒ Ⓓ Ⓔ
11	Ⓐ Ⓑ Ⓒ Ⓓ Ⓔ			
12	Ⓐ Ⓑ Ⓒ Ⓓ Ⓔ			
13	Ⓐ Ⓑ Ⓒ Ⓓ Ⓔ			
14	Ⓐ Ⓑ Ⓒ Ⓓ Ⓔ			
15	Ⓐ Ⓑ Ⓒ Ⓓ Ⓔ			

Part 6 Mathematics Knowledge

1	Ⓐ Ⓑ Ⓒ Ⓓ Ⓔ		16	Ⓐ Ⓑ Ⓒ Ⓓ Ⓔ
2	Ⓐ Ⓑ Ⓒ Ⓓ Ⓔ		17	Ⓐ Ⓑ Ⓒ Ⓓ Ⓔ
3	Ⓐ Ⓑ Ⓒ Ⓓ Ⓔ		18	Ⓐ Ⓑ Ⓒ Ⓓ Ⓔ
4	Ⓐ Ⓑ Ⓒ Ⓓ Ⓔ		19	Ⓐ Ⓑ Ⓒ Ⓓ Ⓔ
5	Ⓐ Ⓑ Ⓒ Ⓓ Ⓔ		20	Ⓐ Ⓑ Ⓒ Ⓓ Ⓔ
6	Ⓐ Ⓑ Ⓒ Ⓓ Ⓔ		21	Ⓐ Ⓑ Ⓒ Ⓓ Ⓔ
7	Ⓐ Ⓑ Ⓒ Ⓓ Ⓔ		22	Ⓐ Ⓑ Ⓒ Ⓓ Ⓔ
8	Ⓐ Ⓑ Ⓒ Ⓓ Ⓔ		23	Ⓐ Ⓑ Ⓒ Ⓓ Ⓔ
9	Ⓐ Ⓑ Ⓒ Ⓓ Ⓔ		24	Ⓐ Ⓑ Ⓒ Ⓓ Ⓔ
10	Ⓐ Ⓑ Ⓒ Ⓓ Ⓔ		25	Ⓐ Ⓑ Ⓒ Ⓓ Ⓔ
11	Ⓐ Ⓑ Ⓒ Ⓓ Ⓔ			
12	Ⓐ Ⓑ Ⓒ Ⓓ Ⓔ			
13	Ⓐ Ⓑ Ⓒ Ⓓ Ⓔ			
14	Ⓐ Ⓑ Ⓒ Ⓓ Ⓔ			
15	Ⓐ Ⓑ Ⓒ Ⓓ Ⓔ			

CUT HERE

This second Practice Test will help you prepare for the actual AFOQT. The test contains those sections of the exam that are important for Officer Candidate School applicants. The six sections that will be tested are Verbal Analogies, Arithmetic Reasoning, Reading Comprehension, Data Interpretation, Word Knowledge, and Mathematics Knowledge. As you did with the first test, take these tests under simulated conditions—in a quiet room with a timer. After taking the tests, give yourself a day or so before you check your answers. Use the explanations to help you understand the material.

Part 1: Verbal Analogies

Time: 8 Minutes
25 Questions

Directions: This part of the test measures your ability to reason and see the relationships between words. Choose the answer that best completes the analogy developed at the beginning of each question.

1. COMPACT DISC is to AM RADIO as

    A. SUBMARINE is to TUGBOAT
    B. VICTROLA is to GRAMMAPHONE
    C. TELEGRAPH is to TELEPHONE
    D. RECORD PLAYER is to STEREO
    E. COMPUTER is to CALCULATOR

2. LIMP is to INJURY as

    A. LOSS is to SADNESS
    B. CATEGORY is to DETAIL
    C. HOLE is to PUNCTURE
    D. TEAR is to RUIN
    E. HOPE is to FEAR

3. PINE is to EVERGREEN as

    A. TALENT is to PRACTICE
    B. SEDAN is to AUTOMOBILE
    C. PEN is to PENCIL
    D. HUSKY is to POODLE
    E. BANK is to ECONOMY

4. RECONCILE is to QUARREL as

    A. GENTLE is to HARSH
    B. PRETEND is to FAKE
    C. START is to ACCELERATE
    D. UNITE is to DIVIDE
    E. ENVY is to GREED

5. MAP is to GEOGRAPHY as

    A. LABEL is to MARK
    B. LOCATION is to DISTANCE
    C. PROTRACTOR is to MATH
    D. DICTIONARY is to CROSSWORD
    E. CALENDAR is to MONTH

6. VERDICT is to JURY as

    A. FACT is to DETAIL
    B. CRIME is to OFFENDER
    C. JUDGE is to RULE
    D. TEACHER is to GRADE
    E. EVIDENCE is to WITNESS

7. SEARCH is to FIND as

    A. LOSE is to MISPLACE
    B. WATCH is to LOOK
    C. EXPLORE is to CREATE
    D. STUDY is to LEARN
    E. GRIN is to CONFUSE

8. WOLF is to WOODS as

    A. CAMEL is to DESERT
    B. MOUSE is to HOUSE
    C. GIRAFFE is to ZOO
    D. REPTILE is to WATER
    E. SKY is to ROBIN

GO ON TO THE NEXT PAGE

9. CHILD is to FATHER as

   A. MOTHER is to DAUGHTER
   B. KID is to BILLY GOAT
   C. GRANDFATHER is to NEPHEW
   D. COW is to CALF
   E. LAMB is to EWE

10. WATER is to CONCRETE as

   A. HEM is to SKIRT
   B. CHOCOLATE CHIP is to COOKIE
   C. COAL is to MINE
   D. MILK is to BATTER
   E. ENERGY is to JUMP

11. CLASSICAL is to RAP as

   A. PHOTOGRAPH is to DRAWING
   B. TALENT is to CREATIVE
   C. BLUES is to JAZZ
   D. BALLET is to CLOGGING
   E. LOUD is to BOISTEROUS

12. AMUSE is to ENTERTAIN as

   A. SCARE is to DETER
   B. TEACH is to EDUCATE
   C. CRY is to SCREAM
   D. RUN is to SCURRY
   E. LAUGH is to GIGGLE

13. HOSPITAL is to HEAL as

   A. COLLEGE is to CHALLENGE
   B. FINGER is to POINT
   C. STORE is to PURCHASE
   D. DINING ROOM is to CONVERSE
   E. VACATION is to SKYDIVE

14. CAMERA is to PHOTOGRAPHER as

   A. ROPE is to BOXER
   B. SAND is to BEACH
   C. BOTTLE is to WATER
   D. COW is to FARMER
   E. REGISTER is to SALESCLERK

15. HUE is to COLOR as

   A. SHADE is to LIGHT
   B. MAUVE is to RED
   C. TONE is to SOUND
   D. MASK is to HIDE
   E. PRIMARY is to SECONDARY

16. STREAM is to RIVER as

   A. PENINSULA is to OCEAN
   B. ATLANTIC is to PACIFIC
   C. MISSISSISSIPI is to NILE
   D. ISLAND is to CAPE
   E. POND is to LAKE

17. PILOT is to AIRCRAFT as

   A. DRIVER is to HIGHWAY
   B. NURSE is to NEEDLE
   C. CAPTAIN is to BOAT
   D. CARPENTER is to HAMMER
   E. AUTOMOBILE is to TRAVEL

18. WATERMELON is to VINE as

   A. SQUASH is to VEGETABLE
   B. STAPLE is to GUN
   C. CORN is to STALK
   D. BEAN is to LEGUME
   E. BLUEBERRY is to BUSH

19. MISER is to AVARICE as

   A. GIVER is to SURPRISE
   B. PHILANTHROPIST is to GENEROUS
   C. VEIL is to SHARE
   D. CONTRIBUTER is to HINDERANCE
   E. GREEDY is to SELFISH

20. PRUDENT is to CAUTIOUS as

   A. PIOUS is to SECULAR
   B. HEALTH is to VIGOR
   C. TRITE is to SPECIAL
   D. CAPRICIOUS is to IMPULSIVE
   E. SERENE is to ANTAGONIZE

21. INDELIBLE is to PERMANENT as

   A.   PERFECT is to PROFANE
   B.   REPAIR is to REPLACE
   C.   ADEQUATE is to PERMISSIBLE
   D.   EXTENSIVE is to BROAD
   E.   ETERNAL is to PERPETUAL

22. ILLICIT is to PERMITTED as

   A.   DECEITFUL is to FORTHRIGHT
   B.   BETRAYAL is to ADULTRY
   C.   BROKEN is to REPAIRED
   D.   CAPABLE is to PROFICIENT
   E.   ABUSE is to PUNISH

23. GERMANE is to RELEVANT as

   A.   ASKEW is to STRAIGHTEN
   B.   FLOUNDER is to STRUGGLE
   C.   DETAIL is to SUMMARIZE
   D.   EXAMINE is to TEST
   E.   ACRIMONIOUS is to BITTER

24. BOTANY is to PLANTS as

   A.   VOLCANOLOGY is to VOLCANOES
   B.   SEMANTICS is to WORDS
   C.   HISTOLOGY is to HISTORY
   D.   VIDEOGRAPHY is to MOVIES
   E.   PALEONTOLOGY is to ROCKS

25. RANDOM is to FAIR as

   A.   CAUTIOUS is to SAFE
   B.   AWAKEN is to MORNING
   C.   CREATIVE is to DECORATE
   D.   BELLIGERENT is to ANNOY
   E.   INTRODUCTION is to BEGIN

STOP. BEFORE MOVING ON TO THE NEXT SECTION, CHECK YOUR ANSWERS IF THERE IS STILL TIME LEFT.

Part 2: Arithmetic Reasoning

Time: 29 Minutes
25 Questions

Directions: This section of the test measures your mathematical reasoning or your ability to arrive at solutions to problems. Each problem is followed by five possible answers. Select the answer that is most nearly correct.

1. Ralph earns 15% commission on all sales over $5,000. Last month, his sales totaled $12,500. What were Ralph's earnings?

   A. $750
   B. $1,125
   C. $1,875
   D. $2,625
   E. $2,750

2. Boston is 439 miles from Hillsdale and 638 miles from Orion. How much closer is Boston to Hillsdale than Boston to Orion?

   A.   199 miles
   B.   201 miles
   C.   439 miles
   D.   1077 miles
   E.   1,439 miles

3. Willard weighs 209 pounds. If he loses 2 pounds per week, how much will he weigh in 7 weeks?

   A.   191 lbs.
   B.   195 lbs.
   C.   202 lbs.
   D.   207 lbs.
   E.   247 lbs.

4. Hamilton reads three hardcover mysteries and four soft cover mysteries. She reads three times as many nonfiction books as she did mysteries. How many nonfiction books did Hamilton read?

   A.   6
   B.   9
   C.   12
   D.   18
   E.   21

GO ON TO THE NEXT PAGE

5. In San Francisco, a taxi ride costs $3 for the first mile and $1 for each additional half mile. What is the cost of a 10-mile ride?

   A. $10
   B. $12
   C. $13
   D. $21
   E. $24

6. Erin collects bottle caps. Each cap can be traded for 5 cents. If Erin receives $40.50, how many bottle caps did he trade?

   A. 810
   B. 405
   C. 200
   D. 8
   E. 4

7. If you have 40 nickels and 12 dimes, what is the total amount of money that you have?

   A. $0.52
   B. $3.20
   C. $4.60
   D. $5.20
   E. $6.60

8. Louis spent 30 minutes vacuuming, 12 minutes dusting, 37 minutes washing dishes, and 45 minutes resting. How many minutes did Louis spend cleaning?

   A. 34
   B. 79
   C. 100
   D. 124
   E. 166

9. Helene can read one page in two minutes. If a book has 80 pages, how long will it take her to read?

   A. 160 minutes
   B. 120 minutes
   C. 80 minutes
   D. 40 minutes
   E. 20 minutes

10. A blueprint has a scale of 3 feet per $\frac{1}{2}$ inch. If a bathroom is $1\frac{1}{2}$ inches × 2 inches, what are its actual dimensions?

   A. $4\frac{1}{2}$ feet × 6 feet
   B. 6 feet × $7\frac{1}{2}$ feet
   C. $7\frac{1}{2}$ feet × 9 feet
   D. $8\frac{1}{2}$ feet × $8\frac{1}{2}$ feet
   E. 9 feet × 12 feet

11. The area of the following figure is

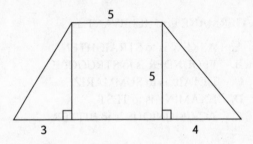

   A. 42.5
   B. 47
   C. 52.5
   D. 60
   E. 72

12. How many blocks 6" × 4" × 4" can fit in a box 8' × 6' × 4'?

   A. 2
   B. 48
   C. 576
   D. 3456
   E. 6912

13. A restaurant bill without tax and tip comes to $38.40. If a 15% tip is included after a 6% tax is added to the amount, how much is the tip?

   A. $6.11
   B. $5.76
   C. $5.15
   D. $2.30
   E. $1.15

14. Interest earned on an account totals $100. If the interest rate is $7\frac{1}{4}\%$, what is the principle amount?

    A. $725
    B. $1,333
    C. $1,379
    D. $1,428
    E. $1,522

15. The figure contains five equal squares. If the area is 405, what is the perimeter?

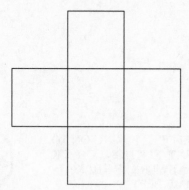

    A. 81
    B. 90
    C. 108
    D. 144
    E. 288

16. Ramon spent $25.00 at dinner. If the bill totaled $21.00 before the tip was added, approximately what percent tip did Ramon leave?

    A. 16%
    B. 19%
    C. 21%
    D. 25%
    E. 26%

17. Emily walked 45 yards north, 36 yards west, and 41 yards south. Daniel walked 16 yards north, 49 yards west, and 33 yards south. How much farther did Emily walk than Daniel?

    A. 20 yards
    B. 22 yards
    C. 24 yards
    D. 28 yards
    E. 30 yards

18. A 10-foot rope is to be cut into equal segments measuring 8 inches each. The total number of segments is

    A. 1
    B. 8
    C. 15
    D. 40
    E. 80

19. The value of 18 quarters, 6 dimes, and 24 nickels is

    A. $5.34
    B. $6.30
    C. $18.84
    D. $24.24
    E. $36.00

20. Jack agrees to pay back a $50,000 loan over a 10 year period. If the interest rate is 8%, what will his monthly payments be?

    A. $450
    B. $540
    C. $3,333
    D. $4,000
    E. $5,400

21. Taylor rents 3 videos for $8.00. What would the cost of 2 video rentals be?

    A. $1.33
    B. $5.00
    C. $5.33
    D. $6.00
    E. $6.75

22. Rachel can type 35 words per minute. If it takes her a half hour to type a document, about how many words are in the document?

    A. 900
    B. 1,050
    C. 1,500
    D. 2,100
    E. 2,440

GO ON TO THE NEXT PAGE

23. A square garden is to be built inside a circular area. Each corner of the square touches the circle. If the radius of the circle is 3, how much greater is the area of the circle than the square?

   A. $9 - \dfrac{9}{2}\pi$

   B. $9 - 9\pi$

   C. $9 - 18\pi$

   D. $9\pi - 9$

   E. $9\pi - 18$

24. Valerie ate $\dfrac{1}{4}$ of a peach pie and divides the remainder of the pie among her four friends. What fraction of the pie does each of her friends receive?

   A. $\dfrac{1}{3}$

   B. $\dfrac{7}{12}$

   C. $\dfrac{3}{16}$

   D. $\dfrac{1}{8}$

   E. $\dfrac{1}{16}$

25. Sophie casts a shadow 5 feet long. Her father, who is 6 feet tall, casts a shadow 8 feet long. How tall is Sophie?

   A. 6 feet 8 inches

   B. 4 feet 10 inches

   C. 4 feet 6 inches

   D. 3 feet 9 inches

   E. 2 feet 3 inches

STOP. BEFORE MOVING ON TO THE NEXT SECTION, CHECK YOUR ANSWERS IF THERE IS STILL TIME LEFT.

Part 3: Reading Comprehension

Time: 18 Minutes

25 Questions

Directions: This test is designed to measure your ability to read and understand paragraphs. For each paragraph and question, select the answers that best completes the statement or answers the question based on the passage. Do not bring in outside information.

1. Over the past few years, the speed limit in several states has been increased to 65 or more miles per hour on major highways. The number of serious accidents has also increased in that same time period. States with higher population density have reported the largest increase in accidents since the speed limits have increased.

From the information in the passage, you can conclude:

   A. All states have raised speed limits to 65 or more miles per hour on all highways.

   B. Serious accidents only happen when people are traveling at 65 or more miles per hour.

   C. States should lower the speed limits on major highways.

   D. States with higher population densities have more people who drive aggressively.

   E. The number of serious accidents in recent years can be attributed to higher rates of speed in locations with higher populations.

2. The Happiness Hotel has advertised a rate of $75.00, per couple, per night during the off-season. During peak season, which runs from October 12–March 31, the rates are $150.00 a night, and up. Susan and Derek would like to stay at the Happiness Hotel during their fall vacation. Which are the best dates for them to schedule their vacation for the lowest cost?

   A. November 3–7
   B. October 2–6
   C. October 15–21
   D. May 6–12
   E. October 9–12

3. President Lincoln gave the Gettysburg Address in November 1863, a few months after one of the bloodiest battles inside the United States. His speech, a brief two minutes in length, was a memorial for all those who had lost their lives, on both sides of the Civil War, and a call for honoring them by continuing the fight for freedom and democracy. Although Lincoln indicated in his speech that "the world will not long remember" what he said, the Gettysburg Address has become one of the most famous and important Presidential speeches in U.S. history.

   An appropriate title for this passage would be

   A. The Gettysburg Address
   B. Lincoln and the Civil War
   C. Death at Gettysburg
   D. Lincoln's Great Gettysburg Speech
   E. The Importance of the Civil War

4. Fauvism is a style of Modern Art that followed Impressionism. It is characterized by the use of vivid colors, bold brush strokes, and distorted forms. The name comes from the French, for "wild beast," partially because of how much the works contrasted with Impressionist pieces.

   You can infer from this passage that Impressionist art is

   A. not characterized by distorted forms.
   B. is full of distorted forms.
   C. is French art.
   D. never done with pastel colors.
   E. easier to create than Fauvist art.

5. The Civil Rights Era in the United States is one of the most important times in our history because it brought about greater equality for all citizens. Without the sacrifices of Rosa Parks, Martin Luther King, Jr., and numerous other individuals who gave up so much for their cause, our society would be more disparate than it is.

   The term "disparate" most likely means

   A. horrible.
   B. unhappy.
   C. unequal.
   D. frantic.
   E. outrageous.

6. Horses have distinctive vision qualities. They have difficulty seeing things as clearly as humans, and colors are not nearly as vivid for them. However, at night, when there is limited light, they have better vision than humans do.

   Based on this passage, if you had to travel a path at night, you

   A. should ride your horse because it can see better than you.
   B. should use a flashlight.
   C. should lead your horse so that neither of you trip.
   D. can ride your horse as fast as you want.
   E. get home as quickly as possible.

7. The factory received a 1% increase in orders for a period of 20 months. During that time, the number of employees was increased by 10% to handle the increased workload. The number of orders has been steadily decreasing over the last three weeks.

   The newer employees are most likely feeling

   A. contented.
   B. appeased.
   C. envious.
   D. sympathetic.
   E. concerned.

GO ON TO THE NEXT PAGE

8. *Animal Farm* by George Orwell is an allegory. Just as the citizens of Russia tried to create a communist society that provided equally for the needs of all of its citizens, the animals took over the farm in an attempt to ensure that each of the animals was treated fairly. Each character in the novel represents a real person or group that played a role in the Russian Revolution. In both the Russian Revolution and in *Animal Farm,* a dictator takes control of the government.

Based on this passage, allegory most likely means

   A. a novel about animals.

   B. a symbolic story.

   C. an essay.

   D. a fairy tale.

   E. a myth.

9. Lacrosse, a sport that is becoming more and more popular, requires speed and agility to play. A stick, or crosse, is used to catch and throw a hard ball across the field toward the goal without using your hands. The crosse is also used to scoop the ball up off the ground if it is not caught by a player.

Based on this passage, the sport that Lacrosse can best be uniquely compared to is

   A. basketball because a ball is used to score a goal.

   B. baseball because both use a stick.

   C. football because players must get the ball from one end of the field to the other.

   D. tennis because the racquet acts like the stick in lacrosse.

   E. soccer because neither allows the use of hands on the ball.

10. The number of subsistence farmers is steadily decreasing every year. Many of them have chosen to move to the cities where they can get work that is more profitable and less physically taxing. They want to do more than just get by on what they can produce for their own needs.

Based on this passage, a subsistence farmer is someone who

   A. produces primarily only what his family needs.

   B. works very hard to produce grains to sell.

   C. works very hard to save enough money to move to the city.

   D. raises only one type of product.

   E. does not have to work very hard to be successful.

11. The local furniture store is offering a special deal this month. If you purchase $1000 or more in furniture, you can defer payment for 13 months. Interest will not begin to accrue until the start of the 13th month, but after it does, it will be retroactive on the total amount of your purchase.

If you want to take best advantage of the deal, you should

   A. Pay for the furniture by the sixth month after your purchase.

   B. Defer your purchase until a year from now.

   C. Pay for the furniture within the next 12 months.

   D. Pay for your furniture 13 months from the date of your purchase.

   E. Pay 14 equal payments between the date of purchase until you have paid for the furniture.

12. A hurricane is a wind storm that forms over water. To be considered a hurricane, wind speeds must reach a minimum of 74 miles per hour. Hurricane season generally runs from May through October, when Atlantic islands and coasts are at most risk of being hit by one.

If you were planning a trip to Bermuda and wanted to eliminate your risk of ending up in a hurricane, you should plan your trip for

   A. May.

   B. June.

   C. September.

   D. October.

   E. November.

13. The Harlem Renaissance was a period of U.S. history in which African American musicians, artists, and writers produced a significant amount of work. The period, primarily from 1920 through the early 1930s, is seen as one of the first times when African Americans could produce works from their unique perspective with the chance to be recognized for their talents throughout American society.

You can infer from this passage that the Harlem Renaissance

A. provided many opportunities for African American writers to work for predominantly white companies.
B. gave African American youth an opportunity to develop role models and see a place for themselves in American culture.
C. was a time when African Americans could not find jobs.
D. enabled people living in Harlem to improve their physical surroundings.
E. allowed African Americans to become rich.

14. The child was very insolent. She continually questioned the authority of the babysitter and made it a point to prove him wrong.

The child could also be described as

A. haughty.
B. reverent.
C. respectful.
D. loyal.
E. naïve.

15. The sportsmanship of the players on the home team was incredible. With the way the other team was purposefully hitting hard, tripping people, and calling names, it is surprising that local kids did not try to retaliate. The credit is due to the coach, the community, and the team itself.

The author is most likely

A. proud to be part of the home team's community.
B. envious of the visiting team.
C. wishing he was playing for the home team.
D. trying to get invited to another game.
E. impressed by the home team's maturity.

16. A haiku is a Japanese poem. It is formed by using only three lines. The first and last lines are five syllables each, and the middle line is seven syllables.

The following could be the first line of a haiku:

A. One might find a local shark
B. Shark attacks small fish, guppies
C. Lonely shark smells food
D. Gentle shark wants to eat now
E. Sharks smoothly glide toward the scent

17. This orchard can produce a copious harvest, given the right growing conditions. If the weather cooperates and pests are kept under control, the fruit will grow very well.

Based on the information in this passage, copious most likely means

A. sufficient.
B. deficient.
C. suitable.
D. abundant.
E. meager.

18. It is important when starting a tropical fish aquarium to choose your fish carefully. Some tropical fish are predators of others. Many species have unique requirements for their environment that could be fatal to other species.

According to this passage,

A. You should conduct a lot of research before purchasing tropical fish.
B. You can put a variety of fish species together safely without having any concerns.
C. Your aquarium should be large enough for small fish to hide from predators.
D. Most fish enjoy the same levels of temperature and light.
E. A small aquarium is best.

GO ON TO THE NEXT PAGE

19. The Swiss Guard is a small, mostly ceremonial army whose duty it is to protect Vatican City and the Pope. The Guard members are trained to use modern weaponry, but also to use a sword and halberd. There are only approximately 100 Guards in service at any given time, with new recruits, who must be Roman Catholic and Swiss, being sworn in on May 6 of every year.

A fitting title for this passage would be

- **A.** Becoming a Swiss Guard
- **B.** The Pope's Protectors
- **C.** The Use of the Halberd
- **D.** Modern Soldiers
- **E.** Small Armies

20. Every April New Englanders and others around the world set their clocks forward in order to "save daylight." The purpose behind this is to use the sun for an hour longer during waking hours, instead of sleeping through it in the morning. In October, during the months with the shortest hours of daylight per day, we change our clocks back.

Daylight Savings Time is intended to

- **A.** create more hours of sunlight in a day.
- **B.** allow people to sleep in later during the spring and summer.
- **C.** get the best use of sunlight during waking hours.
- **D.** allow people to go to bed earlier in the summer.
- **E.** change working hours in the fall.

21. The platypus is a rare type of mammal. While it feeds the young from breast milk, it does not give birth to live babies. Their offspring are hatched from eggs.

From this passage, you can determine that most mammals

- **A.** hatch eggs.
- **B.** feed their young with eggs.
- **C.** give birth while feeding their young.
- **D.** give birth to live babies and feed them breast milk.
- **E.** have babies that produce milk.

Questions 22 and 23 are based on the following passage:

The Great Lakes are beautiful bodies of fresh water in North America that have suffered many problems throughout the twentieth century. Pollution from factories in the cities built on their shores has impacted the quality of the water and the ability of certain aquatic creatures to survive. Other problems have come about because of the introduction of alien organisms such as the sea lamprey and the zebra mollusk by shipping vessels that traveled from other parts of the world to the lakes through the seaway and canals.

22. From this passage, you can assume that the author is probably

- **A.** a politician wanting to improve economic conditions in cities around the Great Lakes.
- **B.** an environmentalist who has studied the changing patterns of the Great Lakes in the twentieth century.
- **C.** a storyteller who is comparing the way people used the Great Lakes in the seventeenth century to how they did in the twentieth century.
- **D.** an industrialist who wants to build new factories and ship goods across the Atlantic.
- **E.** a native of the Great Lakes region who is explaining why he is moving to the West Coast.

23. The seaway and the canals likely

- **A.** provide access to the Great Lakes from the ocean.
- **B.** create a pathway from the west coast to the east coast of the United States.
- **C.** were built before the twentieth century.
- **D.** are birthing grounds for sea lamprey.
- **E.** let pollution travel to the ocean.

24. Judaism, Christianity, and Islam, three of the five major world religions, are monotheistic. These religions all trace their roots back to Abraham, considered the patriarch of each of them. According to some scholars, Abraham was the first biblical figure who recognized one, and only one, deity.

According to this passage

A. Judaism, Christianity, and Islam have very little in common.

B. Judaism, Christianity, and Islam are the most important world religions.

C. Judaism, Christianity, and Islam have a core element of their religion, belief in only one deity, in common.

D. Judaism, Christianity, and Islam share the same followers.

E. Judaism, Christianity, and Islam share Abraham as their deity.

25. Red blood cells are vital to human survival. They transport oxygen from our lungs to the body's tissue cells and carry waste away from them. Red blood cells survive an average of 120 days, with new ones constantly being produced by our bone marrow.

According to this passage you can infer that

A. Red blood cells expire when we no longer need them.

B. Red blood cells carry oxygen to our lungs.

C. Red blood cells are needed only when our tissue cells have waste to be removed.

D. Red blood cells are important, but not necessary.

E. Red blood cells can be replaced, so the loss of small amounts of blood should generally not be a concern.

STOP. BEFORE MOVING ON TO THE NEXT SECTION, CHECK YOUR ANSWERS IF THERE IS STILL TIME LEFT.

Part 4: Data Interpretation

Time: 24 Minutes

25 Questions

Directions: Questions 1 through 3 are based on the following figure.

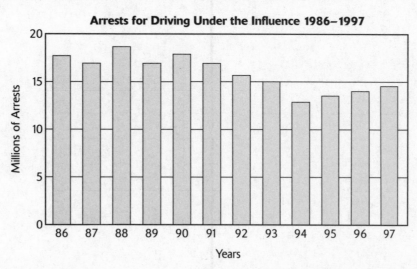

Arrests for Driving Under the Influence 1986–1997

1. In which years were the least amount of arrests made?

A. 1991–1993

B. 1992–1994

C. 1993–1995

D. 1994–1996

E. 1995–1997

2. Of the following, which years represent the highest number of arrests made?

A. 1988–1990

B. 1990–1992

C. 1991–1993

D. 1992–1994

E. 1993–1995

GO ON TO THE NEXT PAGE

3. What is the difference between the year of the highest number arrests and the lowest?

   A. 1.75 million
   B. 1.50 million
   C. 1.25 million
   D. 0.50 million
   E. 0.25 million

Questions 4–7 are based on the following pie charts that indicate the number of private schools (736) and students (42,000) in a particular region that are either religious or nonreligious.

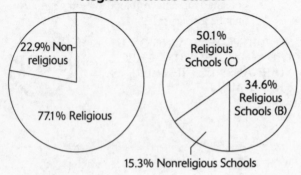

Regional Private Schools

22.9% Non-religious

77.1% Religious

50.1% Religious Schools (C)

34.6% Religious Schools (B)

15.3% Nonreligious Schools

4. How many students who practice Religion B attend private school?

   A. 145
   B. 11,390
   C. 14,532
   D. 17,508
   E. 21,237

5. How many nonreligious schools are there in this region?

   A. 149
   B. 168
   C. 567
   D. 1,685
   E. 2,744

6. Half of the nonreligious schools are co-ed; the others are either all male or all female. Approximately how many of the schools are co-educational?

   A. 66
   B. 73
   C. 85
   D. 93
   E. 171

7. How many students attend religious schools?

   A. 623
   B. 111,010
   C. 135,830
   D. 143,990
   E. 170,000

Questions 8–12 are based on the following table.

					Extras				
Automobile Comparison Table									
Model	**Weight (lbs)**	**Horse-power**	**# Cylinders**	**# Passengers**	**All Wheel Drive**	**CD Player**	**Sun-roof**	**Price**	**Mfg Rebate**
1	2500	220	6	5	No	Yes	No	$36,000	$1,500
2	2804	280	8	5	Yes	Yes	Yes	$42,000	$2,000
3	2200	360	6	4	No	No	No	$32,000	$3,500
4	3350	250	8	5	Yes	No	No	$37,400	$1,000
5	4095	390	4	4	Yes	No	Yes	$32,000	$4.000
6	2760	320	8	2	No	Yes	No	$36,000	$2,500
7	3100	295	4	4	No	Yes	No	$29,500	$1,000

8. Which two cars cost the same amount after the manufacturer's rebate?

- **A.** 2 and 6
- **B.** 1 and 4
- **C.** 5 and 7
- **D.** 4 and 6
- **E.** 3 and 7

9. What is the difference between the highest price car and the lowest price car before the manufacturer's rebate?

- **A.** $9,250
- **B.** $10,400
- **C.** $12,500
- **D.** $14,000
- **E.** $14,400

10. What is the difference between the lowest price car before rebate and the lowest price car after rebate?

- **A.** $1,000
- **B.** $1,500
- **C.** $2,000
- **D.** $2,500
- **E.** $3,000

11. Which car in the $30,000–$40,000 price range has the most number of extras?

- **A.** 1
- **B.** 3
- **C.** 4
- **D.** 5
- **E.** 6

12. What is the highest amount of horsepower in the car that carries the most passengers?

- **A.** 220
- **B.** 250
- **C.** 280
- **D.** 295
- **E.** 320

GO ON TO THE NEXT PAGE

Questions 13–16 are based on the following table.

Number of Trucker Trips by Month					
	January	*February*	*March*	*April*	*May*	*June*
John	4	7	3	6	6	6
Jim	3	2	5	4	8	1
Sue	4	6	2	4	5	7

13. In which month were the most trips taken?

   A. January

   B. February

   C. March

   D. April

   E. May

14. In which month were the least number of trips taken?

   A. January

   B. February

   C. March

   D. April

   E. May

15. What is the difference between the number of individual trips taken in a month and the least number of individual trips taken in a month?

   A. 4

   B. 5

   C. 6

   D. 7

   E. 8

16. What is the difference between the largest total of trips taken in a month and the least total number of trips taken in a month?

   A. 19

   B. 9

   C. 8

   D. 7

   E. 6

Questions 17–19 are based on the following chart.

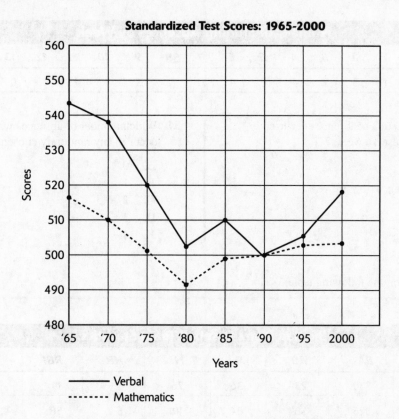

Standardized Test Scores: 1965-2000

— Verbal
------- Mathematics

17. In what year were the average Verbal and Math scores approximately the same?

    A. 1980

    B. 1985

    C. 1990

    D. 1995

    E. 2000

18. What is the approximate difference between the highest Verbal score and the lowest Math scores?

    A. 40

    B. 55

    C. 70

    D. 85

    E. 105

19. During what period of time was the least amount of improvement in Math scores?

    A. 1970–75

    B. 1975–80

    C. 1980–85

    D. 1985–90

    E. 1990–95

GO ON TO THE NEXT PAGE

Questions 20 and 21 are based on the following table.

Number of Student Absences by Week																
Week	**1**	**2**	**3**	**4**	**5**	**6**	**7**	**8**	**9**	**10**	**11**	**12**	**13**	**14**	**15**	**16**
Number of absences	1	3	2	4	0	4	0	2	5	1	1	1	0	2	2	1

20. How many total student absences occurred in school during these 16 weeks?

   A. 5
   B. 29
   C. 33
   D. 45
   E. 54

21. Which number of absences was most likely to occur in any randomly chosen week?

   A. 0
   B. 1
   C. 2
   D. 3
   E. 4

Question 22 is based on the following table.

Big Bad Bears Baseball Team Statistics								
	BA	**AB**	**R**	**H**	**HR**	**RBI**	**SO**	**SB**
A. Player	.330	230	36	76	3	19	18	7
R. Johnson	.325	587	84	191	6	58	40	8
M. Philbert	.392	305	49	89	20	57	61	0
C. Arcolo	.285	453	74	129	31	87	110	15
L. Browkaw	.270	174	20	47	6	19	53	6
P. Thompkins	.262	309	49	81	18	48	89	3
O. Silva	.256	558	58	143	9	62	74	5
W. Haroldsen	.248	311	37	77	4	35	53	9
S. Reboulet	.241	261	37	63	3	25	47	2
F. Williamson	.225	519	58	117	13	57	177	2

22. Of those players with 100 or more hits, who had the most home runs?

   A. Arcolo
   B. Philbert
   C. Johnson
   D. Silva
   E. Williamson

Questions 23–25 are based on the following table.

Federal Expenditures by Function (in Billions)			
	1998	*1999*	*2000*
National defense	$268.5	$276.7	$274.1
International affairs	13.1	15.5	16.1
General science	18.2	18.5	18.6
Energy	1.3	0.5	2.0
Natural resources	22.4	24.3	23.7
Agriculture	12.2	21.4	15.1
Commerce & housing	1.0	0.5	6.4
Transportation	40.3	42.6	46.4
Community development	9.7	10.4	10.2
Education & training	54.9	60.1	63.4
Health care services	131.4	143.1	152.3

23. Which government function shows the greatest increase in expenditures?

    A. National defense
    B. International affairs
    C. Transportation
    D. Community development
    E. Education & training

24. The greatest increase in expenditures between 1998 and 2000 was in which area of the government?

    A. National defense
    B. Natural resources
    C. Commerce
    D. Education & training
    E. Health care services

25. What is the difference between the least amount spent in 1998 versus the least amount spent in 2000?

    A. $1 billion
    B. $2 billion
    C. $3 billion
    D. $3.4 billion
    E. $4.3 billion

STOP. BEFORE MOVING ON TO THE NEXT SECTION, CHECK YOUR ANSWERS IF THERE IS STILL TIME LEFT.

Part 5: Word Knowledge Test

Time: 5 Minutes
25 Questions

Directions: This part of the test measures verbal comprehension involving your ability to understand written language. For each question choose the answer that means the same as the word in all capital letters.

1. DILEMMA

   A. punishment
   B. division in ranks
   C. ability to detect
   D. perplexing choice
   E. word with two meanings

2. CELESTIAL

   A. musical
   B. heavenly
   C. stately
   D. unmarried
   E. aged

3. MILITANT

   A. political
   B. mighty
   C. aggressive
   D. peaceable
   E. illegal

4. EMINENT

   A. noted
   B. moral
   C. future
   D. low
   E. unwise

5. OBSERVE

   A. resolve
   B. perceive
   C. organize
   D. stick in
   E. copy down

6. IDIOSYNCRASY

   A. stupidity
   B. virtue
   C. personal peculiarity
   D. foreign dialect
   E. similarity

7. SHABBY

   A. dishonest
   B. helpless
   C. vague
   D. nervous
   E. seedy

8. DESIST

   A. loiter
   B. stand
   C. hurry
   D. stumble
   E. stop

9. SUPPLANT

   A. spend
   B. unite
   C. recall
   D. replace
   E. purpose

10. EDIFICE

    A. tool
    B. large building
    C. garden
    D. mushroom
    E. set of books

11. COLLABORATE

    A. act jointly
    B. finish
    C. reprimand
    D. walk slowly
    E. arrange in order

12. USELESSNESS

    A. timelessness
    B. stinginess
    C. happiness
    D. futility
    E. worthless

13. UNINJURED

    A. blunt
    B. fashionable
    C. intact
    D. welcome
    E. attentive

14. ZEAL

    A. fervor
    B. sickly
    C. helpless
    D. impatience
    E. envious

15. DISPROVE

    A. unite
    B. collect
    C. slaughter
    D. tangle
    E. refute

16. CONSENSUS

    A. steadfastness of purpose
    B. general agreement
    C. lack of harmony
    D. informal vote
    E. impressive amount

17. SUBMISSIVE

    A. tangled
    B. grumbling
    C. self-satisfied
    D. treacherous
    E. compliant

18. GIRD

    A. stare
    B. thresh
    C. encircle
    D. complain
    E. perforate

19. DESERTION

    A. delay
    B. exemption
    C. slander
    D. defection
    E. respect

20. POACH

    A. squander
    B. trespass
    C. outwit
    D. bully
    E. borrow

21. IOTA

    A. first step
    B. sacred picture
    C. ornamental scroll
    D. very small quantity
    E. crystalline substance

22. SEVERE

    A. powerful
    B. austere
    C. helpless
    D. happy
    E. tortured

23. DECREASE

    A. joke
    B. reappear
    C. wane
    D. grieve
    E. rise

24. PILFER

    A. steal
    B. watchful
    C. quiet
    D. reserved
    E. held

25. CURT

    A. brief
    B. disconnected
    C. solid
    D. ruined
    E. divided

STOP. BEFORE MOVING ON TO THE NEXT SECTION, CHECK YOUR ANSWERS IF THERE IS STILL TIME LEFT.

Part 6: Mathematics Knowledge

Time: 22 Minutes
25 Questions

Directions: This section of the test measures your ability to use learned mathematical relationships. Each problem is followed by five possible answers. Select the answer that is most nearly correct.

1. If $w - 3 = 3 - w$, what is the value of w^2?

   A. 0
   B. 1
   C. 3
   D. 9
   E. 11

2. $\dfrac{5}{16} + \dfrac{9}{24} =$

   A. $\dfrac{11}{16}$
   B. $\dfrac{14}{40}$
   C. $\dfrac{7}{20}$
   D. $\dfrac{14}{48}$
   E. $\dfrac{16}{33}$

3. If $6m - 2$ is divided by 2, the result is -4. What is the value of m?

   A. -1
   B. 0
   C. 1
   D. 2
   E. 3

4. Simplify $5(a - 2) - (4a - 6)$.

   A. $a - 4$
   B. $a - 8$
   C. $a - 10$
   D. $a + 4$
   E. $5a + 8$

5. A car travels 20 miles in 30 minutes. At this rate, how far will the car travel in 2 hours?

   A. 40 miles
   B. 60 miles
   C. 80 miles
   D. 100 miles
   E. 120 miles

6. The cube of 8 is

   A. 2
   B. 24
   C. 512
   D. 600
   E. 8000

7. How many blocks with sides 4 inches in length can fit into a crate $3' \times 2' \times 2'$?

   A. 3
   B. 32
   C. 196
   D. 244
   E. 324

8. Evaluate $3r^3 - 2s^2 + t$ if $r = -1$, $s = -2$, and $t = -3$.

   A. 2
   B. 4
   C. -8
   D. -14
   E. -28

9. $0.00525 \div 0.01 =$

   A. 5.25
   B. 0.525
   C. 0.0525
   D. 0.000525
   E. 0.0000525

10. Simplify $\left(\dfrac{a^{-3} b^2}{2ab^{-1}} \right)^{-3}$

   A. $\dfrac{2a^6}{b}$
   B. $\dfrac{8a^{12}}{b^a}$
   C. $\dfrac{a^8}{8b^3}$
   D. $\dfrac{a^{12}}{8b^9}$
   E. $\dfrac{ab}{2}$

11. If the area of the circle is 169π, find the area of the square.

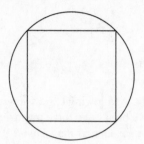

- **A.** 169
- **B.** 338
- **C.** 507
- **D.** 676
- **E.** 845

12. The area of the shaded region is

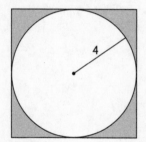

- **A.** $64 - 3\pi$
- **B.** $64 - 4\pi^2$
- **C.** $64 - 16\pi$
- **D.** $256 - 16\pi$
- **E.** $256 - 4\pi^2$

13. One-fourth of the cars purchased at a dealership are luxury models. If 360 luxury models were purchased last year, how many total cars were purchased?

- **A.** 90
- **B.** 250
- **C.** 1440
- **D.** 3600
- **E.** 4200

14. The cube root of 512 is

- **A.** 8
- **B.** 56
- **C.** $170\frac{2}{3}$
- **D.** 1536
- **E.** 3072

15. Find the product of $(3 - 4x)$ and $(3 + 4x)$.

- **A.** 9
- **B.** $9 + 12x - 16x^2$
- **C.** $9 - 16x^2$
- **D.** $9 + 16x^2$
- **E.** 25

16. If the diameter of a circle is increased by 100%, the area is increased by

- **A.** 50%
- **B.** 100%
- **C.** 200%
- **D.** 300%
- **E.** 400%

17. The radius of the smaller circle is $\frac{1}{3}$ as long as the larger. What percent of the figure shown is shaded?

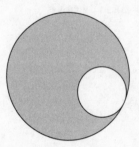

- **A.** 11%
- **B.** 25%
- **C.** 75%
- **D.** 89%
- **E.** 94%

18. Factor $2a^2 - 4ab + ab - 2b^2$

- **A.** $(a + 2b)(2a - b)$
- **B.** $(a - 2b)(2a + b)$
- **C.** $(2a - b)(a + 2b)$
- **D.** $(2a + b)(a - b)$
- **E.** $2(a + b)(a - b)$

19. Multiply $(5a^3bc^2)(-3a^2c)$.

- **A.** $-15a^5bc^3$
- **B.** $15a^5bc^3$
- **C.** $-15a^6bc^2$
- **D.** $2abc$
- **E.** $15abc^5$

GO ON TO THE NEXT PAGE

20. Floor tiling costs $13.50 per square yard. What would it cost to tile a room 15 feet long by 18 feet wide?

- **A.** $20
- **B.** $405
- **C.** $1350
- **D.** $3645
- **E.** $10,935

21. Given that the point $(x, 1)$ lies on a line with a slope of $-\frac{3}{2}$ and a y-intercept of -2, find the value of x.

- **A.** -2
- **B.** -1
- **C.** 1
- **D.** 2
- **E.** 3

22. If $2y + 6 = 3y - 2$, then $y =$

- **A.** -4
- **B.** -2
- **C.** 2
- **D.** 4
- **E.** 8

23. If $0.08z = 6.4$, then $z =$

- **A.** 0.8
- **B.** 8
- **C.** 80
- **D.** 800
- **E.** 1600

24. Which of the following expressions represents the cost of five books and three magazines if books cost twice as much as magazines?

- **A.** $8b$
- **B.** $8m$
- **C.** $11b$
- **D.** $13m$
- **E.** $30b$

25. The girl's basketball team won three times as many games as they lost. How many games were won if they played a total of 24 games?

- **A.** 6
- **B.** 8
- **C.** 12
- **D.** 18
- **E.** 24

CHECK YOUR ANSWERS IF
THERE IS STILL TIME LEFT.

STOP

Answer Key for AFOQT Practice Test 2

Verbal Analogies

1. E	10. D	19. B
2. C	11. D	20. D
3. B	12. B	21. E
4. D	13. C	22. A
5. C	14. E	23. E
6. E	15. A	24. B
7. D	16. E	25. A
8. A	17. C	
9. B	18. C	

Arithmetic Reasoning

1. B	10. E	19. B
2. A	11. A	20. A
3. B	12. D	21. C
4. E	13. A	22. B
5. D	14. C	23. E
6. A	15. C	24. C
7. B	16. B	25. D
8. B	17. C	
9. A	18. C	

Reading Comprehension

1. E	10. A	19. B
2. B	11. C	20. C
3. D	12. E	21. D
4. A	13. B	22. B
5. C	14. A	23. A
6. C	15. E	24. C
7. D	16. C	25. E
8. B	17. D	
9. E	18. A	

Data Interpretation

1. D	10. B	19. D
2. A	11. D	20. B
3. D	12. C	21. B
4. C	13. E	22. A
5. B	14. C	23. C
6. C	15. D	24. D
7. D	16. B	25. A
8. E	17. C	
9. C	18. B	

Word Knowledge

1. D	10. B	19. D
2. B	11. A	20. B
3. C	12. D	21. D
4. A	13. C	22. B
5. B	14. A	23. C
6. C	15. E	24. A
7. E	16. B	25. A
8. E	17. E	
9. E	18. C	

Mathematics Knowledge

1. D	10. B	19. A
2. A	11. B	20. B
3. A	12. C	21. A
4. A	13. C	22. E
5. C	14. A	23. C
6. C	15. C	24. D
7. E	16. E	25. D
8. A	17. D	
9. B	18. B	

AFOQT Practice Test 2 Answers and Explanations

Part 1: Verbal Analogies

1. **E.** A compact disc is more current technology than an AM radio. A computer is more current technology than a calculator.

2. **C.** An injury can cause a limp, and a puncture can cause a hole.

3. **B.** A pine is a type of evergreen, and a sedan is a type of automobile.

4. **D.** Reconcile means to bring together, and a quarrel separates. Similarly, to unite is to bring together, and to divide is to separate.

5. **C.** A map is a tool used in the study of geography, and a protractor is a tool used in the study of math.

6. **E.** A verdict is given by a jury that is serving the community by listening to a case, and evidence is given by an eyewitness, who offers testimony as a service to the community.

7. **D.** The purpose of a search is to find something, and the purpose of studying is to learn something.

8. **A.** One natural habitat of a wolf is the woods, and a camel's natural habitat would be the desert.

9. **B.** A child is the offspring of a male human, and a kid is the offspring of a male, or Billy, goat.

10. **D.** Water is a liquid required to make concrete, and milk is a liquid required for certain types of batters.

11. **D.** Classical and rap are two very different styles of music, as ballet and clogging are very different styles of dance.

12. **B.** We amuse people to entertain them and teach in order to educate.

13. **C.** A hospital is a specific place we go to primarily for healing, and a store is a place we primarily go to purchase things.

14. **E.** A camera (single lens, point and shoot, or digital) is a required tool for the photographer to do his job, as is a register (manual, electric, or computerized) for a salesclerk to do his job.

15. **A.** Hue is a quality of color, and tone is a quality of sound.

16. **E.** A stream is a small river; a pond is a small lake.

17. **C.** A pilot "drives" an aircraft, and a captain "drives" a boat.

18. **C.** A watermelon grows on a vine, and corn is a vegetable that grows on a stalk.

19. **B.** A miser tends to be avaricious (greedy), and a philanthropist tends to be generous.

20. **D.** A person who is prudent is cautious; a person who is capricious is impulsive.

21. **E.** Something that is indelible is permanent; something that is eternal is perpetual. All of the terms convey a sense of unending.

22. **A.** An act that is illicit is not permitted; a person who is deceitful is not forthright.

23. **E.** Germane is an adjective that means relevant. Acrimonious is an adjective that means bitter.

24. **B.** Botany is the scientific study of plants. Semantics is the scientific study of words.

25. **A.** The purpose of being random is to be fair. The purpose of being cautious is to be safe.

Part 2: Arithmetic Reasoning

1. **B.** The amount of commissions over \$5,000 is \$12,500 – \$5,000 = \$7,500. Earnings are \$7,500 × 15% = \$1,125.

2. **A.** The difference in miles is 638 – 439 = 199.

3. **B.** If 2 pounds are lost each week, then after 7 weeks, 7 × 2 = 14 pounds are lost. The weight after 7 weeks is 209 – 14 = 195 pounds.

4. **E.** Hamilton read a total of 3 + 4 or 7 mysteries. Therefore, she read 3 × 7 or 21 nonfiction books.

5. **D.** In a 10-mile trip, after the first mile, there are 9 additional miles. If each additional half mile is \$1, then an additional mile is \$2. The cost of the trip is \$3 for the first mile + (\$2 × 9) for the additional miles. \$3 + \$18 = \$21.

6. **A.** Let c represent the number of caps traded in. Then $0.05c = 40.50$ and $c = \dfrac{40.50}{0.05} = 810$ caps.

7. **B.** The total amount of money is (40 × \$0.05) + (12 × \$0.10) = \$2.00 + \$1.20 = \$3.20.

8. **B.** The time cleaning was 30 minutes + 12 minutes + 37 minutes = 79.

9. **A.** If 1 page can be read in 2 minutes, then 80 pages can be read in 80 × 2 or 160 minutes.

10. **E.** If the blueprint shows $\frac{1}{2}$ inch for every 3 feet, then 1 inch represents 6 feet. The actual dimensions of a room $1\frac{1}{2}$ inches × 2 inches would be $(1\frac{1}{2} \times 6)$ by (2 × 6) or 9 feet by 12 feet.

11. **A.** Add the areas of the two triangles and the square to find the total area. The area of the square is $5^2 = 25$. Both triangles have a height of 5. The area of one triangle is $\frac{1}{2}bh = \frac{1}{2} \cdot 3 \cdot 5 = \frac{15}{2} = 7.5$. The area of the other triangle is $\frac{1}{2}bh = \frac{1}{2} \cdot 4 \cdot 5 = \frac{20}{2} = 10$. The total area is 25 + 7.5 + 10 = 42.5.

12. **D.** Convert the dimensions of the box from feet to inches. 8' × 6' × 4' is equivalent to (8 × 12 in) × (6 × 12 in) × (4 × 12 in) = 96 in × 72 in × 48 in. The volume = 96 × 72 × 48 = 331,776. The volume of each block is 6 × 4 × 4 = 96. The number of blocks that fit in the box is $\dfrac{331,776}{96} = 3456$.

13. **A.** The tax on the bill is \$38.40 × 6% = \$2.30. The amount, including tax, is \$38.40 + \$2.30 = \$40.70. The tip is \$40.70 × 15% = \$6.11.

14. **C.** Interest = principle × rate. Let p represent the principle. Then $\$100 = p \times 7\frac{1}{4}\%$ so $p = \dfrac{\$100}{7\frac{1}{4}\%} = \dfrac{\$100}{0.0725} = \$1379$.

15. **C.** The area of one square is $\dfrac{405}{5} = 81$. So the length of each side is $\sqrt{81} = 9$. The total number of sides in the figure is 12, so the perimeter is 9 × 12 = 108.

16. **B.** The percent tip is the amount of tip over the total before tip. The amount of the tip is \$25.00 – \$21.00 = \$4.00. The percent of the tip is $\dfrac{4}{21} = 0.19 = 19\%$.

17. **C.** Emily walked 45 + 36 + 41 = 122 yards. Daniel walked 16 + 49 + 33 = 98 yards. The difference between these two distances is 122 – 98 = 24 yards.

18. **C.** The total number of inches in a 10 foot rope is 10 × 12 = 120 inches. The number of 8 inch segments that can be cut is $\dfrac{120}{8} = 15$.

19. **B.** The total is (18 × \$0.25) + (6 × \$0.10) + (24 × \$0.05) = \$4.50 + \$0.60 + \$1.20 = \$6.30.

20. **A.** The interest on a \$50,000 loan is \$50,000 × 8% = \$4,000. The amount that must be paid back is \$50,000 + \$4,000 = \$54,000. There are 120 months in 10 years. If this is to be paid over a 10-year period, each monthly payment will be $\dfrac{\$54,000}{120} = \$450$.

21. **C.** Using the ratio $\dfrac{\text{price}}{\text{video}}$, the proportion $\dfrac{8}{3} = \dfrac{x}{2}$ can be used to find the cost to rent two videos. Cross multiply. $8 \times 2 = 3x$ so $16 = 3x$ and $x = \dfrac{16}{3} = \$5.33$.

22. **B.** There are 30 minutes in a half hour. 30 × 35 = 1,050 words.

23. **E.** Find the difference between the area of the circle and the area of the square. The area of the circle is $\pi r^2 = \pi \cdot 3^2 = 9\pi$. The area of the square is s^2, where s represents the length of the square. The radius is half the length of the square's diagonal so the diagonal is 6. By the Pythagorean Theorem $s^2 + s^2 = 6^2$. $2s^2 = 36$ so $s^2 = 18$. The difference in area is $9\pi - 18$.

24. **C.** After eating $\frac{1}{4}$ of a pie, what remains is $1 - \frac{1}{4} = \frac{3}{4}$. If 4 friends share the remainder, then each received $\frac{3}{4} \div 4 = \frac{3}{4} \times \frac{1}{4} = \frac{3}{16}$.

25. **D.** Using the ratio $\frac{\text{height}}{\text{shadow}}$, the proportion $\frac{x \text{ feet}}{5 \text{ feet}} = \frac{6 \text{ feet}}{8 \text{ feet}}$ can be used to find the unknown height. Cross multiply. $8x = 5 \times 6$ so $8x = 30$ and $x = \frac{30}{8} = 3\frac{3}{4}$ feet. Convert $\frac{3}{4}$ feet to inches. $\frac{3}{4} \times 12 = 9$ inches. The height is therefore 3 feet 9 inches.

Part 3: Reading Comprehension

1. **E.** Serious accidents can be linked to higher speeds in areas where there are more people. Choice **A** is incorrect because the passage states that several, not all, states have raised speed limits. Choice **B** is incorrect because the passage does not address all conditions related to serious accidents. Choice **C** is incorrect because the passage does not indicate that the problem applies to all states that have raised the speed limit. Choice **D** is incorrect because the article does not address driver aggressiveness.

2. **B.** Their vacation will be in the fall, but prior to the nights the rates increase. Choice **E** is incorrect because one night will be at the higher rate.

3. **D.** The passage is about the greatness of Lincoln's speech at Gettysburg. Choice **A** is incorrect because the passage is not itself the Gettysburg Address—Lincoln's actual speech is known as that. Choice **B** and Choice **E** are incorrect because the passage is about Lincoln's speech, not about the Civil War in general. Choice **C** can be eliminated because the passage is about Lincoln's speech, not the deaths at Gettysburg.

4. **A.** The passage notes that Fauvism is in contrast to Impressionism. Since Fauvism uses distorted forms, you can infer that Impressionism does not.

5. **C.** One meaning of disparate is unequal. A clue in the question is the idea that the civil rights movement brought about greater equality, and the passage points out the actions of the leaders helped bring that about.

6. **C.** The passage is about how horses can see better than humans at night, so if you are out at night with your horse, you can assume that you are safer by riding your horse and relying on its vision over yours.

7. **D.** The newer workers are probably not contented, appeased, or sympathetic because there is a chance they could lose their job. Although they might be jealous of the workers who have been there longer, they are most likely to be concerned about whether their job is truly in danger or not.

8. **B.** The characters in *Animal Farm* symbolize the real people or groups that played roles in the Russian Revolution. The plot of the novel symbolizes the Russian Revolution itself. Choice **A** is incorrect because the emphasis in the passage is on how the novel represents the Russian Revolution, not on the animals. Choice **C** can be eliminated because the passage identifies *Animal Farm* as a novel, not an essay, and Choice **D** and Choice **E** can be eliminated because both of those styles of storytelling contain references to magical or spiritual worlds.

9. **E.** Soccer and lacrosse are most similar because neither allow the use of the hands. The other responses can be eliminated primarily because the similarities noted are not unique to lacrosse and the sport noted.

10. **A.** A subsistence farmer produces what the family needs in order to survive. The passage does not address what type of products are raised, so Choice **B** and Choice **D** can be eliminated. Choice **C** can be eliminated because the passage does not address saving money, and Choice **E** is incorrect because the passage indicates that farming is physically hard work.

11. **C.** If you pay within the 12 months, you will ensure that the interest is not calculated and applied to your purchase. Paying earlier does not give you full advantage of the deal, and payments that start after the 13th month begins will trigger the interest accrual.

12. E. Since hurricane season is over in October, November (Choice **E**) would be the best month of the options given to plan a trip to Bermuda in the hopes of avoiding one.

13. B. The Harlem Renaissance produced a lot of music, literature, and art that was admired by all communities, thus giving young African Americans a hope that they could be similarly respected if they followed their heroes. Choice **A**, Choice **D**, and Choice **E** can be eliminated because the passage does not address where African Americans worked, what their living conditions were like, or whether fame also brought fortune. Choice **C** can be eliminated because the passage does not address whether African Americans could find jobs during that time period.

14. A. Insolent means to be rude in a haughty manner.

15. E. Choice **A** can be eliminated because there is no evidence the author is part of that community. Choice **B** is wrong because the passage does not indicate she has reason to be jealous of the other team. Choice **C** and Choice **D** can be eliminated because there is no reason to believe the author needed to be invited to the game or that she is of the age to play for the team.

16. C. It is the only option with five syllables.

17. D. If weather conditions and pests are beneficial, then the orchard will produce abundant, or large amounts of, fruit. Choice **A** and Choice **C** should be eliminated because they mean basically the same thing, and Choice **B** and Choice **E** should be eliminated because good growing conditions would not result in a disappointing (meager or deficient) result.

18. A. Because there are so many aspects to the longevity of a fish species, it is best to research the needs of the various fish you might want to choose before you select your aquarium and what to put in it.

19. B. The passage gives general information about the Swiss Guard but does not tell how to become a member, Choice **A,** or how to use a halberd, Choice **C.** Answers **D** and **E** can be eliminated because the article does not cover modern soldiers or small armies in general, but only to the extent that the Swiss Guard can be described in those ways.

20. C. Daylight savings time is intended to make best use of daylight hours while people are usually awake. Since most people sleep during early morning hours, the daylight is shifted forward an hour giving them more daylight than if they slept through that hour in the morning.

21. D. The passage indicates that the platypus is unlike most mammals because it does not give birth to live babies, but that it is like them because it provides milk for its young.

22. B. An environmentalist who is studying the problems of the Great Lakes region would be most apt to discuss the issues presented in the passage. You can rule out Choice **A** and Choice **D** because a politician would not focus on the negative and an industrialist would not point out problems created already by industry if planning to bring in new factories. Choice **C** can be eliminated because the passage does not discuss the condition of the Great Lakes in the seventeenth century. Finally, a person moving out west would probably not focus solely on the problems of the Great Lakes as the reason for the move.

23. A. There is no evidence in the article to support the other options.

24. C. The passage identifies all three religions as monotheistic, or believing in only one deity.

25. E. Red blood cells are continually being made by our bone marrow so they can be replaced.

Part 4: Data Interpretation

1. D. All three years in this range are less than 1.5 million. Although Choice **E**, 1995–1997, is also less than 1.5 million, 1994 is the lowest and helps bring down the total of the three years in Choice **D**.

2. A. This requires some careful calculations, because the bars of the graph don't, at first, provide a clear answer.

1988 = 1.9 million	1999 = 1.7 million
1989 = 1.7	1990 = 1.75
1990 = <u>1.75</u>	1991 = <u>2.75</u>
5.25	5.20

3. **D.** To find the answer, subtract the lowest (1995 = 1.4 millions) from the highest (1998 = 1.9 million).

4. **C.** If there are 42,000 students and Religion B represents 34.6% of the students, then

$$.346 \times 42,000 = 14,532$$

5. **B.** There are 736 schools in this region, and 22.9% are nonreligious. Thus,

$$.229 \times 736 = 168$$

6. **C.** The nonreligious schools represent almost 23%. Half of that is 11.5%. Therefore,

$$.115 \times 736 = 84.64 \text{ or } 85 \text{ schools.}$$

7. **D.** There are a total of 84.7% who attend religious schools (34.6% Religion B and 50.1% Religion C).

$$.847 \times 736 = 143,990$$

8. **E.** After rebate both cost $28,500.

$$\text{Car 3: } \$32,000 - \$3,500 = \$28,500$$

$$\text{Car 7: } \$29,500 - \$1,000 = \$28,500$$

9. **C.** The highest price car before rebate is car #2 ($42,000). The lowest price car is #7 ($29,500)

$$\$42,000 - \$29,500 = \$12,500.$$

10. **B.** Car #5 is the lowest price car after rebate ($28,000) and car #7 is the lowest price car before rebate ($29,500).

$$\$29,500 - \$28,000 = \$1,500$$

11. **D.** Car #5 has both all-wheel drive and a sunroof. Cars 1, 3, 4, and 6 each have only one extra.

12. **C.** Car #2 carries 5 passengers and has 280 horsepower. Cars 1 and 4 also carry 6 passengers but have lower horsepower. Car #7 (295 hsp) and #6 (320 hsp) carry fewer passengers.

13. **E.** In the month of May, there were a total of 19 trips.

14. **C.** In March, there were only 10 trips taken.

15. **D.** Jim had the most number of trips taken (8) and also had the least number of trips taken (1). The difference is $8 - 1 = 7$.

16. **B.** The total number of trips taken in any month was in May (19) and the least was in March (10). The difference is $19 - 10 = 9$.

17. **C.** The average score of 500 for both math and verbal tests was in 1990.

18. **B.** The highest Verbal score was approximately 545 in 1965 and the lowest Math score was about 490 in 1980. There difference is, therefore, $545 - 490 = 55$.

19. **D.** Between 1985–1990 there appears to be almost level (no) growth in Math scores.

20. **B.** The total number of absences is $1 + 3 + 2 + 4 + 0 + 4 + 0 + 2 + 5 + 1 + 1 + 1 + 0 + 2 + 2 + 1 = 29$.

21. **B.** The number 0 appears three times in the table. The number 1 appears five times in the table. The number 2 appears four times in the table. The number 3 appears one time in the table. The number 4 appears two times in the table. The number that appears most often is the number that is most likely to occur in any randomly chosen week. The correct answer is 1, choice **B**.

22. **A.** Arcolo had 129 hits and 31 home runs. Philbert had only 89 hits, so he's not in the running. Johnson had 191 hits but only 6 home runs. Silva had 143 hits but only 9 home runs, and Williamson had 117 hits and only 13 home runs. Thus, Arcolo had the most home runs of hitters with more than 100 hits.

23. **C.** You can eliminate **A** and **D** since their expenditures went down. If you find the difference between the two columns, you'll see that choice **C** = $3.8 billion. Education, Choice **E**, is close, at $3.3 billion, and International affairs is only $0.6 billion.

24. **D.** The difference between 1998 and 2000 was an increase of $85 billion in Education. Because time is limited on these exams, you have to estimate. You should be able to eliminate the lowest numbers like Choices **B**, **C**, and **E** and then calculate the correct numbers for **A** and **D**.

25. **A.** The least amount spent in 1998 is $1 billion in Commerce. The least amount spent in 2000 is $2 billion in Energy. The difference is $1 billion.

Part 5: Word Knowledge

1. **D.** A dilemma is a perplexing choice.

2. **B.** The word celestial means heavenly.

3. **C.** The word militant means aggressive.

4. **A.** One who is eminent is a noted person.

5. **B.** To observe is to perceive.

6. **C.** Idiosyncrasy is a personal peculiarity.

7. **E.** Something that is shabby is seedy.

8. **E.** To desist is to stop.

9. **E.** The word supplant means to replace.

10. **B.** An edifice is a large building.

11. **A.** To collaborate is to act jointly.

12. **D.** Uselessness means futility.

13. **C.** Uninjured means intact. It also means together.

14. **A.** The word zeal means fervor.

15. **E.** To disapprove means to refute.

16. **B.** A consensus is a general agreement.

17. **E.** Submissive means compliant.

18. **C.** To gird means to encircle.

19. **D.** Desertion means defection.

20. **B.** To poach means to trespass.

21. **D.** An iota is a very small quantity.

22. **B.** A person who is severe is austere.

23. **C.** The word decrease means to wane.

24. **A.** To pilfer means to steal.

25. **A.** To be curt is to be brief.

Part 6: Mathematics Knowledge

1. **D.** Solve for w by adding w to both sides. $w - 3 + w = 3 - w + w$ so $2w - 3 = 3$. Adding 3 to both sides gives $2w = 6$. So $\frac{2w}{2} = \frac{6}{2}$ and $w = 3$. Therefore, $w^2 = 3^2 = 9$.

2. **A.** The least common multiple of the divisors 16 and 24 is 48. $\frac{5}{16} + \frac{9}{24} = \frac{15}{48} + \frac{18}{48} = \frac{33}{48} = \frac{11}{6}$.

3. **A.** $\frac{6m - 2}{2} = -4$ so $3m - 1 = -4$. Solve for m by adding 1 to both sides. $3m - 1 + 1 = -4 + 1$ and $3m = -3$. Dividing both sides by 3 gives $m = -1$.

4. A. $5(a-2) - (4a-6) = 5a - 10 - 4a + 6 = a - 4.$

5. C. There are 120 minutes in 2 hours. Setting up a proportion yields $\frac{20\ miles}{30\ minutes} = \frac{x\ miles}{120\ minutes}$. Cross multiplying results in $30x = 20 \times 120$ or $30x = 2400$. Dividing both sides by 30 gives $x = \frac{2400}{30} = 80$ miles.

6. C. The cube of 8 is $8^3 = 8 \times 8 \times 8 = 512.$

7. E. The volume of each cube is $4 \times 4 \times 4 = 64$ in^3. The volume of the crate, in inches, is $(3 \times 12) \times (2 \times 12) \times (2 \times 12) = 20{,}736$ in^3. The number of blocks that can fit in the crate is $\frac{20736}{64} = 324.$

8. A. Substituting the given values for r, s, and t into $3r^3 - 2s^2 + t$ gives $3(-1)^3 - 2(-2)^2 + (-3) = 3(-1) - 2(4) - 3 = -3 + 8 - 3 = 2.$

9. B. $0.00525 \div 0.01 = \frac{0.00525}{0.01} = 0.525.$

10. B. $\left(\frac{a^{-3}b^2}{2ab^{-1}}\right)^{-3} = \frac{a^9 b^{-6}}{2^{-3} a^{-3} b^3} = 2^3 a^{9-(-3)} b^{-6-3} = 8a^{12}b^{-9} = \frac{8a^{12}}{b^9}.$

11. B. The area of the circle is $\pi r^2 = 169\pi$. So $r^2 = 169$ and $r = 13$. The radius represents half the diagonal of the square, so the diagonal is 26 units long. If x represents the length of a side of the square, then x^2 is the area of the square. Using the Pythagorean Theorem, $x^2 + x^2 = 26^2$ and $2x^2 = 676$. Therefore $x^2 = \frac{676}{2} = 242.$

12. C. The area of the shaded region equals the area of the square minus the area of the circle. Since the radius of the circle is 4, the square has a side length of 8. The area of the square is 8^2 or 64. The area of the circle is $\pi r^2 = \pi(4)^2 = 16\pi$. The shaded region, therefore, is $64 - 16\pi.$

13. C. $\frac{1}{4}$ of the total cars, t, sold are luxury. Luxury cars sold = 360, so $\frac{1}{4}t = 360$ and $t = 360 \times 4 = 1{,}440$ total cars sold.

14. A. The cube root of 512 is $\sqrt[3]{512} = \sqrt[3]{8 \times 8 \times 8} = 8.$

15. C. $(3 - 4x)(3 + 4x) = 9 + 12x - 12x - 16x^2 = 9 - 16x^2.$

16. E. The radius $r = \frac{d}{2}$. The area of the circle is $(\pi r^2) = \pi\left(\frac{d}{2}\right)^2 = \frac{\pi d^2}{4}$. If the diameter is increased 100%, the diameter is $2d$ and $r = 2d/2 = d$. The area of the enlarged circle is $\pi r^2 = \pi d^2$. The enlarged circle is $\frac{\pi d^2}{\frac{\pi d^2}{4}} = \pi d^2 \div \frac{\pi d^2}{4} = \pi d^2 \cdot \frac{4}{\pi d^2} = 4$ or 400% bigger.

17. D. Let the radius of the smaller circle = 1. Then the radius of the larger circle is 3. The shaded region is found by subtracting the area of the smaller circle from the area of the larger circle. The area of the smaller circle is $\pi(1)^2$ or π. The area of the larger circle is $\pi(3)^2$ or 9π. The shaded region is $9\pi - \pi$ or 8π. The percent of the whole figure that is shaded is $\frac{8\pi}{9\pi} = 0.8888 = 89\%.$

18. B. Group the first two terms and the last two terms together: $(2a^2 - 4ab) + (ab - 2b^2)$. Factoring out common terms from each group gives $2a(a - 2b) + b(a - 2b)$. Common to both terms is $(a - 2b)$. Factoring this out results in $(a - 2b)(2a + b).$

19. A. $(5a^3bc^2)(-3a^2c) = 5 \times -3 \times a^{3+2} bc^{2+1} = -15\ a^5 bc^3.$

20. B. The area of a room 15 feet wide by 18 feet long is $15 \times 18 = 270$ square feet. Since there are 3 feet in a yard, there are 3×3 or 9 feet in a square yard. Convert 270 square feet to square yards. $\frac{270}{9} = 30$ square yards. Since the cost is \$13.50 per square yard, the total cost is $\$13.50 \times 30$ or \$405.

21. A. The equation of a line with a slope of $-\frac{3}{2}$ and a y-intercept of -2 is $y = -\frac{3}{2}x - 2$. To find the value of x in the point $(x, 1)$, substitute 1 for y and solve the equation for x. Then $1 = -\frac{3}{2}x - 2$ and $3 = -\frac{3}{2}x$. So $(3)\left(-\frac{2}{3}\right) = \left(-\frac{2}{3}\right)\left(-\frac{3}{2}\right)x$ and $x = -\frac{6}{3}$ or $-2.$

22. E. Subtract $2y$ from both sides. $2y + 6 - 2y = 3y - 2 - 2y$ so $6 = y - 2$. Adding 2 to both sides gives $y = 8.$

23. **C.** If $0.08z = 6.4$ then $\frac{0.08z}{0.08} = \frac{6.4}{0.08}$. Moving the decimal two places to the right in both the numerator and denominator gives $z = \frac{640}{8} = 80$.

24. **D.** If books are twice as much as magazines, then $b = 2m$. 5 books + 3 magazines $= 5b + 3m$. Substituting $2m$ for b gives $5(2m) + 3m = 10m + 3m = 13m$.

25. **D.** Let w represent the games won and l represent the games lost. Then $w = 3 \times l = 3l$. The total number of games played is $w + l = 24$. Substituting $3l$ in for w yields $3l + l = 24$ or $4l = 24$. The number of losses is $\frac{24}{4} = 6$ and the number of wins is $24 - 6 = 18$.

Answer Sheet for ASTB Practice Test 2

(Remove This Sheet and Use It to Mark Your Answers)

Math/Verbal Test

1 Ⓐ Ⓑ Ⓒ Ⓓ	11 Ⓐ Ⓑ Ⓒ Ⓓ	21 Ⓐ Ⓑ Ⓒ Ⓓ	31 Ⓐ Ⓑ Ⓒ Ⓓ
2 Ⓐ Ⓑ Ⓒ Ⓓ	12 Ⓐ Ⓑ Ⓒ Ⓓ	22 Ⓐ Ⓑ Ⓒ Ⓓ	32 Ⓐ Ⓑ Ⓒ Ⓓ
3 Ⓐ Ⓑ Ⓒ Ⓓ	13 Ⓐ Ⓑ Ⓒ Ⓓ	23 Ⓐ Ⓑ Ⓒ Ⓓ	33 Ⓐ Ⓑ Ⓒ Ⓓ
4 Ⓐ Ⓑ Ⓒ Ⓓ	14 Ⓐ Ⓑ Ⓒ Ⓓ	24 Ⓐ Ⓑ Ⓒ Ⓓ	34 Ⓐ Ⓑ Ⓒ Ⓓ
5 Ⓐ Ⓑ Ⓒ Ⓓ	15 Ⓐ Ⓑ Ⓒ Ⓓ	25 Ⓐ Ⓑ Ⓒ Ⓓ	35 Ⓐ Ⓑ Ⓒ Ⓓ
6 Ⓐ Ⓑ Ⓒ Ⓓ	16 Ⓐ Ⓑ Ⓒ Ⓓ	26 Ⓐ Ⓑ Ⓒ Ⓓ	36 Ⓐ Ⓑ Ⓒ Ⓓ
7 Ⓐ Ⓑ Ⓒ Ⓓ	17 Ⓐ Ⓑ Ⓒ Ⓓ	27 Ⓐ Ⓑ Ⓒ Ⓓ	37 Ⓐ Ⓑ Ⓒ Ⓓ
8 Ⓐ Ⓑ Ⓒ Ⓓ	18 Ⓐ Ⓑ Ⓒ Ⓓ	28 Ⓐ Ⓑ Ⓒ Ⓓ	
9 Ⓐ Ⓑ Ⓒ Ⓓ	19 Ⓐ Ⓑ Ⓒ Ⓓ	29 Ⓐ Ⓑ Ⓒ Ⓓ	
10 Ⓐ Ⓑ Ⓒ Ⓓ	20 Ⓐ Ⓑ Ⓒ Ⓓ	30 Ⓐ Ⓑ Ⓒ Ⓓ	

Mechanical Comprehension Test

1 Ⓐ Ⓑ Ⓒ	11 Ⓐ Ⓑ Ⓒ	21 Ⓐ Ⓑ Ⓒ
2 Ⓐ Ⓑ Ⓒ	12 Ⓐ Ⓑ Ⓒ	22 Ⓐ Ⓑ Ⓒ
3 Ⓐ Ⓑ Ⓒ	13 Ⓐ Ⓑ Ⓒ	23 Ⓐ Ⓑ Ⓒ
4 Ⓐ Ⓑ Ⓒ	14 Ⓐ Ⓑ Ⓒ	24 Ⓐ Ⓑ Ⓒ
5 Ⓐ Ⓑ Ⓒ	15 Ⓐ Ⓑ Ⓒ	25 Ⓐ Ⓑ Ⓒ
6 Ⓐ Ⓑ Ⓒ	16 Ⓐ Ⓑ Ⓒ	26 Ⓐ Ⓑ Ⓒ
7 Ⓐ Ⓑ Ⓒ	17 Ⓐ Ⓑ Ⓒ	27 Ⓐ Ⓑ Ⓒ
8 Ⓐ Ⓑ Ⓒ	18 Ⓐ Ⓑ Ⓒ	28 Ⓐ Ⓑ Ⓒ
9 Ⓐ Ⓑ Ⓒ	19 Ⓐ Ⓑ Ⓒ	29 Ⓐ Ⓑ Ⓒ
10 Ⓐ Ⓑ Ⓒ	20 Ⓐ Ⓑ Ⓒ	30 Ⓐ Ⓑ Ⓒ

Math/Verbal Test

Time: 35 Minutes

37 Questions

Directions: Select the answer choice that best satisfies the question.

Questions 1–5: Each of the following five questions consists of an arithmetic problem followed by four possible answers. Select the one choice that is the correct answer.

1. Which mathematical statement best represents the following?

   Six less a number is four.

   A. $6 = n \, (\, 4$
   B. $6 < n + 4$
   C. $6 - n = 4$
   D. $n - 6 = 4$

2. A cylinder whose height is 8 inches has a volume of 128π cm^3. If the radius is doubled and its height is cut in half, the volume of the resulting cylinder is

   A. 64π cm^3
   B. 128π cm^3
   C. 256π cm^3
   D. 512π cm^3

3. Fencing costs $4.75 per foot. Posts cost $12.50 each. How much will it cost to fence a garden if 10 posts and 34 feet of fencing are needed?

   A. $472.50
   B. $336.50
   C. $315.50
   D. $286.50

4. Multiply $(2x + 1)(2x + 1)$.

   A. $2x^2 + 1$
   B. $4x^2 + 1$
   C. $4x^2 + 2x + 1$
   D. $4x^2 + 4x + 1$

5. How much change would you get back from a $20 bill if you purchased 8 CD covers costing $1.59 each?

   A. $7.28
   B. $10.41
   C. $12.00
   D. $18.41

Questions 6–10: The following five questions consist of sentences in which one word is omitted. For each question, select the lettered choice that best completes the thought expressed in the sentence.

6. The students arrived home late since they tended to _____ on the way home.

   A. splash
   B. run
   C. dawdle
   D. jump

7. In an effort to _____ the impending riot, negotiators worked through the night to reach a settlement.

   A. hasten
   B. ignore
   C. resent
   D. forestall

GO ON TO THE NEXT PAGE

8. Mediators need to be _____ in order to treat both sides fairly.

    A. prejudiced
    B. impartial
    C. unlawful
    D. pleasant

9. Their meal was _____, and their enjoyment of it was not put off by the size of the bill that was presented to them.

    A. sumptuous
    B. radiant
    C. luxurious
    D. filling

10. He never got to the _____ of the plan, because he was interrupted by his boss when she entered the conference room.

    A. beginning
    B. fault
    C. date
    D. crux

Questions 11–15: Each of the following five questions consists of an arithmetic problem followed by four possible answers. Select the one choice that is the correct answer.

11. The sum of 2 feet $2\frac{1}{2}$ inches, 4 feet $3\frac{3}{8}$ inches, and 3 feet $9\frac{3}{4}$ inches is

    A. 9 feet $\frac{7}{8}$ inches
    B. 9 feet $9\frac{5}{8}$ inches
    C. 10 feet $\frac{5}{8}$ inches
    D. 10 feet $3\frac{5}{8}$ inches

12. The scale on a map shows 500 feet for every $\frac{1}{4}$ inch. If two cities are 6 inches apart on the map, what is the actual distance they are apart?

    A. 125 feet
    B. 750 feet
    C. 2,000 feet
    D. 12,000 feet

13. What is the probability of rolling a sum of 9 using two dice?

    A. $\frac{1}{4}$
    B. $\frac{1}{9}$
    C. $\frac{5}{12}$
    D. $\frac{7}{36}$

14. Three boxes are needed to hold 18 reams of paper. How many boxes are needed for 90 reams?

    A. 5
    B. 6
    C. 9
    D. 15

15. One gallon of paint covers 400 square feet. How many gallons are needed to cover 2,225 square feet?

    A. 5 gallons
    B. 6 gallons
    C. 7 gallons
    D. 8 gallons

The following five questions consist of quotations containing one word that is incorrectly used and not in keeping with the meaning that each quotation is evidently intended to convey. Determine which word is incorrectly used. Then, select from the lettered choices the word that, when substituted for the incorrectly used word, would best help to convey the intended meaning of the quotation.

16. "One of the many chicken-and-egg questions stalking the cancer researchers is what came first, the cancer epidemic or the discovery of the nucleotides. Were they able to define the disease in terms of genetic research?"

    A. welcoming
    B. perplexing
    C. helping
    D. stalling

17. "I've often wondered how authors develop their characters and stories. Is it by traversing themselves in the source of the material? Do they relocate and live the part? Do they spend their days interviewing people at the local coffee house?"

    A. showing
    B. excluding
    C. immersing
    D. failing

18. "As the convoy rolled into the station, two vehicles sped directly to the gas pump, and three jeeps formed a traverse roadblock around the area. They had cordoned off the perimeter to any onlookers, while slowly circling around us."

    A. mobile
    B. sullen
    C. flagrant
    D. stalled

19. "He was a thrilling loner and moved to the Alaskan territories, enduring long, cold months of hunger, illness, and the 24-hour a day darkness. The word 'complaint' was not part of his vocabulary."

    A. helpless
    B. fallen
    C. weary
    D. stoic

20. "Although the quality of the products from abroad is often high quality, a stellar shipment of the material was extremely disappointing to its end users, and has caused some fundamental problems with the arrangement."

    A. sad
    B. ersatz
    C. gigantic
    D. late

Questions 21–25: Each of the following five questions consists of an arithmetic problem followed by four possible answers. Select the one choice that is the correct answer.

21. The sum of $\sqrt{50} + 3\sqrt{72}$ is

    A. $4 + \sqrt{122}$
    B. $4\sqrt{122}$
    C. $7\sqrt{2}$
    D. $23\sqrt{2}$

22. An appliance originally costing $1,000 goes on sale one week for 25% off. The following week, it is discounted an additional 10%. What is the new sale price of the appliance?

    A. $650
    B. $675
    C. $750
    D. $900

23. Dennis ran a race in 2.2 minutes. Kayla ran the same race in 124 seconds. What is the difference between these two times?

    A. 2 seconds
    B. 8 seconds
    C. 14 seconds
    D. 22 seconds

24. What is the diameter of a circle whose circumference is equivalent to its area?

    A. 2
    B. 3
    C. 4
    D. 6

25. If 3 cans of soup cost $5.00, how much do 10 cans cost?

    A. $15.00
    B. $16.45
    C. $16.67
    D. $17.33

GO ON TO THE NEXT PAGE

Questions 26–30 are based on different reading passages. Answer each question on the basis of the information contained in the quotation.

26. "In election times, those people who volunteer or donate money for a political campaign may eventually become committeemen, if they are elected in a primary election. Their main responsibility is to secure a good turnout of his or her party's voters in an election."

Based on the preceding quotation, committeemen are

A. elected in a primary.
B. chosen by the amount of money donated.
C. picked by the political party if they have a good turnout.
D. appointed by the candidates.

27. "A map can show the natural features of the earth, such as rivers, lakes, and mountains. This type of map is called a topographic map. A relief map is used to show the height of the land surfaces of the earth, as well as altitudes of plains, plateaus, hills, and mountains."

According to the preceding quotation, a topographic map would be best used in order to

A. buy farming land.
B. plan a car trip.
C. trace the route of an airplane.
D. find out how tall Mt. Everest is.

28. "I have spent years sending out stories and poetry to magazines. For every one acceptance I've received, I've probably garnered about 30–40 rejections. Oh, the responses are polite, but they hurt, nonetheless. However, you develop perseverance and fortitude. Otherwise, I'd be doing something else."

According to the passage, the author

A. doesn't mind rejection.
B. is used to being rejected.
C. is driven to be a writer.
D. wants to be doing something else.

29. "When out on the golf links, you should be planning strategy—thinking two or three shots ahead. It's the secret of success. What if I miss the fairway; what's the easiest place to make a shot? You'd want to avoid having to pitch out of a sand trap or losing the ball in the pond. How's the wind blowing? It can affect both the direction and distance of your ball."

According to the passage

A. golfers have to use many different clubs.
B. the wind and weather will hurt your game.
C. pitching out of a sand trap is always difficult.
D. your game can improve if you plan ahead.

30. "More than 75 people from eight different nations were involved in the design of the new airplane. Each country had its own agenda, and its representatives were insistent on expressing them and pushing the point. Through the superb leadership of General Harvey, all points were considered, some rejected, others morphed into an amalgam of positive plans for each part of the plane, its weapons package, and its final, successful development."

According to the passage

A. "Too many cooks spoil the broth."
B. many countries had their feelings hurt.
C. the airplane was a result of many diverse concepts.
D. General Harvey offended some of the participants.

Questions 31–35: Each of the following five questions consists of an arithmetic problem followed by four possible answers. Select the one choice that is the correct answer.

31. A savings account earns $2\frac{1}{4}\%$ interest each year. How much interest is earned on a $1,000 deposit after a 5-year period?

A. $22.50
B. $100.00
C. $112.50
D. $150.00

32. The product of two numbers is 117. If one of the numbers is 9, what is the other?

    A. 11
    B. 13
    C. 15
    D. 17

33. Vanda put some water in the freezer. When she removed it, the water's temperature was 0° C. Leaving it out will raise the temperature 4° F each hour. At this rate, when will the water's temperature be 52° F?

    A. 4 hours
    B. 5 hours
    C. 13 hours
    D. 52 hours

34. Sandy bought $4\frac{1}{2}$ lbs of apples and 6 kiwi fruits. Brandon bought $3\frac{1}{4}$ lbs of apples and 9 kiwi fruits. If apples cost \$1.39 per lb and kiwis are 2 for \$1.00, how much more money did Sandy spend than Brandon?

    A. \$0.24
    B. \$0.94
    C. \$1.54
    D. \$2.32

35. $-3(-4 - 5) - 2(-6) =$

    A. 0
    B. −5
    C. 15
    D. 39

Questions 36 and 37 are based on reading passages. Answer each question on the basis of the information contained in the quotation.

36. "Since 1750, about the beginning of the Age of Steam, the earth's population has more than quadrupled. This increase has not been an evolutionary phenomenon with biological causes. Yet there was an evolution. It took place in the world's economic organization."

The preceding quotation best supports the theory that the population's increase was the result of

    A. the steam engine.
    B. evolution.
    C. biology.
    D. economy.

37. "The six-year-old child is about the best example that can be found of that type of inquisitiveness that causes irritated adults to exclaim, 'curiosity killed the cat.' To this child, the world is a fascinating place to be explored and investigated quite thoroughly, but such a world is bounded by the environment in which he or the people he knows live, but constantly expanding through new experiences."

Based on the preceding quotation, the author's attitude toward children appears to be

    A. despair.
    B. indifference.
    C. optimism.
    D. exasperation.

STOP. BEFORE MOVING ON TO THE NEXT SECTION, CHECK YOUR ANSWERS IF THERE IS STILL TIME LEFT.

Mechanical Comprehension Test

Time: 15 Minutes
30 Questions

Directions: This test is designed to measure your ability to learn and reason using mechanical terms. Each diagram is followed by a question or an incomplete statement. Select the choice that best answers the question or completes the statement.

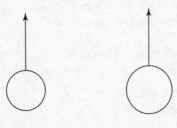

1. Two balls of different masses are thrown vertically up from the same point and at the same time. The two balls will experience the same change in

   A. velocity.
   B. kinetic energy.
   C. distance.

2. People driving up a mountain would find that their mass would _____, and their weight would _____.

   A. increase, decrease
   B. decrease, increase
   C. decrease, remain the same

3. The angular velocity of the second hand of a clock is _____ rad/s.

  A. 105
  B. 9.53
  C. 6.28

4. A ball is thrown horizontally from the top of a building. At the same time, another ball is dropped from the same height. Which ball will hit the ground first?

  A. The ball thrown horizontally.
  B. The ball dropped from rest.
  C. Both will hit the ground at the same time.

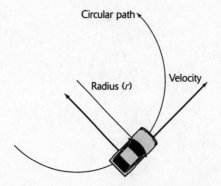

5. For a car moving around a circular track at a constant speed, the acceleration is

  A. away from the center of the circle.
  B. toward the center of the circle.
  C. level.

6. Which of the following best describes the path in the air of a ball after it is thrown by one player to another?

  A. straight line
  B. parabola
  C. circle

GO ON TO THE NEXT PAGE

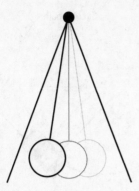

7. If a mass at the end of a simple pendulum with a small amplitude of motion is increased by a factor of 2, other things remaining constant,

    A. its period will double.

    B. it will have the same frequency.

    C. the frequency remains the same.

8. An 80 kg man jumps with a velocity of 3 m/s off the bow of a 120 kg boat initially at rest. Ignoring the friction of the water on the boat, the velocity v of the boat after the man jumps will be _____ m/s.

    A. −1

    B. −1.5

    C. −2

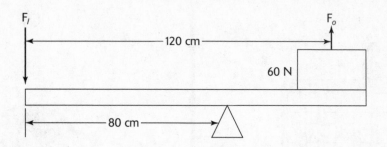

9. A 60 N weight is lifted by the lever arrangement shown in the figure. If the weight of the lever is negligible, the ideal mechanical advantage (F_o/F_i) and the input force (F_i) required to achieve equilibrium are

   A. 3, 30 N
   B. 2, 30 N
   C. 2, 120 N

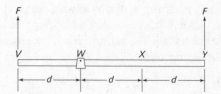

11. A massless horizontal rigid rod of length 3d is pivoted at a fixed point W, and two forces each of magnitude F are applied vertically upward as shown in the figure. To achieve rod equilibrium, a third vertical force of magnitude F is to be applied at which of the labeled points?

   A. V or X only
   B. X or Y only
   C. V or W only

10. An arrow is shot vertically upward. As the arrow approaches its maximum altitude, the amount of work done against gravity

   A. increases and then decreases.
   B. remains the same.
   C. decreases only.

GO ON TO THE NEXT PAGE

12. A ball is thrown vertically upward with a speed of 14.5 m/s from the top of a building that is 50 meters tall. The ball will reach the ground after a time of _____ s.

    A. 1.48

    B. 2.96

    C. 5

13. A 4kg ball moving at a speed of 2 m/s collides head-on with another ball of 2kg mass and 4 m/s speed. If the two balls stick together, their joint speed after the elastic collision is _____ m/s.

    A. 0

    B. 1

    C. 2

14. The gain in kinetic energy if a 400 kg satellite moves from a distance of 3×10^6 m above the surface of the Earth to a point 1.5×10^6 m above the surface is _____ J. The mass of the Earth is 5.98×10^{24} kg, and the radius of the Earth is 6.37×10^6 m.

    A. 0.39×10^9

    B. 1.7×10^9

    C. 3.25×10^9

15. In order for Jean to drive her station wagon at constant speed around a curve, she must

   A. accelerate.
   B. decelerate.
   C. neither accelerate or decelerate.

GO ON TO THE NEXT PAGE

B.

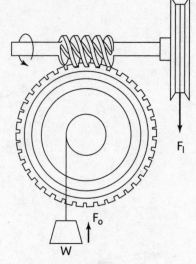

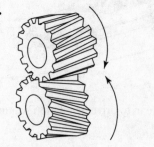

C.

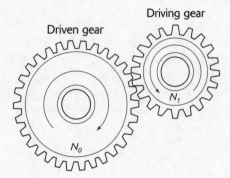

16. A foul ball hit vertically upward with an initial speed of 46.8 m/s will take _____ s to reach the top of its trajectory.

   A.   9.56
   B.   5.82
   C.   4.78

17. The most common gear drive system is shown in the figure in part

   A.

Driven gear   Driving gear

18. A bicycle collides head on with a large car moving at the same speed. Following the collision, the bicycle and the car stick together. Which of the two had the larger change in momentum?

A. The bicycle.
B. The car.
C. The changes were equal.

19. An astronaut lands on Jupiter. Which of the following is true?

A. Mass increases, but weight decreases.
B. Mass remains the same, but weight increases.
C. Mass decreases and weight decreases.

20. A wheel is rotating with a constant frequency. A point on the outside of the wheel compared to a point near the center has _____ linear speed and _____ angular speed.

A. the same, a smaller
B. a greater, the same
C. a smaller, the same

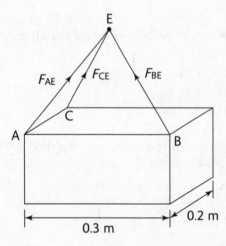

21. The box shown in the figure has uniform density and a total weight of 120 N. If the box is suspended by three cables of identical length and if point E is 40 cm above the top surface of the box, then the tension T in cable CE is nearly

A. 16 N
B. 20 N
C. 27 N

GO ON TO THE NEXT PAGE

Consider the following diagram where a uniform steel rod of length L = 3 m and mass m = 12 kg is pivoted at the frictionless point A. The rod is released from a position of 60° above the horizontal plane and strikes point B at the top of the spring when the rod reaches the horizontal position AB. The spring constant is k = 100 kN/m, and the mass moment of inertia of the rod is I = $mL^2/3$. Study the diagram carefully and select from the choices in the next two questions.

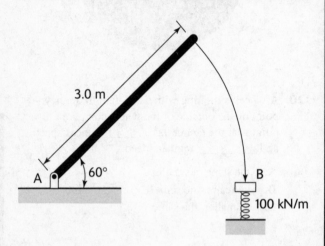

22. What is the velocity of the rod when it strikes the spring?

    A. 8.74 m/s

    B. 6.95 m/s

    C. 5.97 m/s

23. How far will the rod bounce after striking the spring at point B?

    A. 1.06 m

    B. 1.56 m

    C. 2.56 m

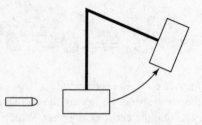

24. A 15 g bullet is fired into a 3 kg block of plastic suspended from the ceiling by a string. As a result of the impact, the block with the bullet swings 12 cm above its original level. The velocity of the bullet as it strikes the block is nearly

    A. 3.08 m/s

    B. 308 m/s

    C. 3,080 m/s

25. Ignoring air resistance, the acceleration of a person sliding down an inclined plane with a constant coefficient of kinetic friction

    A. is constant.

    B. increases with time.

    C. decreases with time.

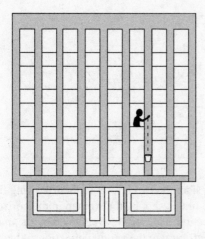

26. An object is dropped from a building. If the speed of impact is to be tripled, how much higher should the object be?

    A. 3 times

    B. 6 times

    C. 9 times

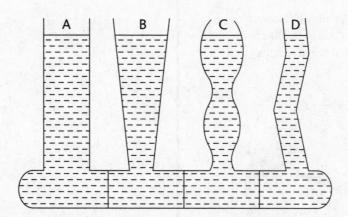

27. The four partitioned compartments A, B, C, and D shown in the figure are filled to the same height. After the partition walls are suddenly removed, the liquid level adjusts itself so that

    A. the liquid rises in A and drops in B, C, and D.

    B. the liquid rises in C and drops in A, B, and D.

    C. the liquid level stays the same.

GO ON TO THE NEXT PAGE

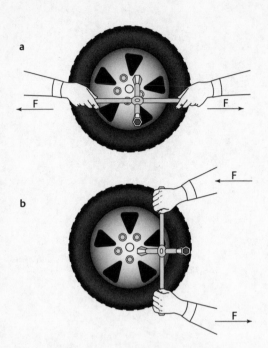

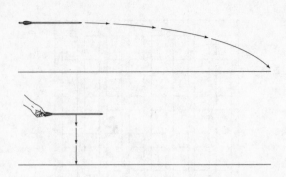

28. The forces exerted on the lug wrench are to the right and left as shown in figures a and b.

- **A.** The nut in figure a may be loosened.
- **B.** The nut in figure b may be loosened.
- **C.** The nut in either figure a or b may be loosened.

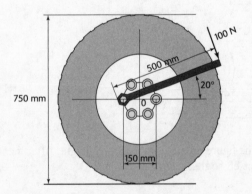

29. A force of 100 N is applied to the far end of the wrench to tighten a bolt that holds the wheel to the axle. For the position of the wrench shown in the figure, the moment produced by this force about the center point O is approximately

- **A.** 4. 32 N. m
- **B.** 43. 2 N. m
- **C.** 432 N. m

30. Consider the two arrows in the following figure. The first is shot by the woman in the horizontal direction. The second is dropped by the man and travels only in the vertical direction. Which arrow arrives at the ground first?

- **A.** The arrow shot by the woman.
- **B.** The arrow dropped by the man.
- **C.** The two arrows arrive at the ground at the same time.

IF THERE IS STILL TIME LEFT, CHECK YOUR ANSWERS.

Answer Key for ASTB Practice Test 2

Math/Verbal

1. D	14. D	27. A
2. C	15. B	28. C
3. D	16. B	29. D
4. D	17. C	30. C
5. A	18. A	31. C
6. C	19. D	32. B
7. D	20. B	33. B
8. B	21. D	34. A
9. A	22. B	35. D
10. D	23. B	36. D
11. D	24. C	37. C
12. D	25. C	
13. B	26. A	

Mechanical Comprehension

1. A	11. A	21. C
2. C	12. C	22. A
3. A	13. A	23. C
4. C	14. C	24. B
5. B	15. A	25. A
6. B	16. C	26. C
7. C	17. A	27. E
8. C	18. C	28. B
9. B	19. B	29. B
10. B	20. C	30. C

ASTB Practice Test 2 Answers and Explanations

Math/Verbal

1. **D.** Six less a number is shown by $n - 6$. So six less a number is four is represented by $n - 6 = 4$.

2. **C.** The volume of a cylinder is $\pi r^2 h$. In the original cylinder, $\pi r^2 8 = 128\pi$ so $r^2 = \frac{128\pi}{8\pi} = 16$ and the radius, r, equals $\sqrt{16} = 4$. In the new cylinder, the radius is doubled to 8, and the height is cut in half to 4. The resulting volume is $\pi \cdot 8^2 \cdot 4 = 256\pi$ cm^3.

3. **D.** The total cost for the posts and fencing is $(10 \times \$12.50) + (34 \times \$4.75) = \$125.00 + \$161.50 = \$286.50$.

4. **D.** Using the distributive property, $(2x + 1)(2x + 1) = 4x^2 + 2x + 2x + 1 = 4x^2 + 4x + 1$.

5. **A.** The cost of the 8 CD covers is $8 \times \$1.59 = \$12.72$. The change received back is $\$20.00 - \$12.72 = \$7.28$.

6. **C.** The word **dawdle** means to go slowly.

7. **D.** The word **forestall** means to delay.

8. **B.** The word **impartial** means without prejudice.

9. **A.** **Sumptuous** means luxurious or magnificent.

10. **D.** The word **crux** means the essential idea, usually on that requires a solution.

11. **D.** First add the number of feet together and then add the number of inches.

$$2 \text{ ft} + 4 \text{ ft} + 3 \text{ ft} = 9 \text{ ft}.$$

$$2\frac{1}{2} in + 3\frac{3}{8} in + 9\frac{3}{4} in = \frac{5}{2} + \frac{27}{8} + \frac{39}{4} = \frac{20}{8} + \frac{78}{8} = \frac{125}{8} = 15\frac{5}{8} in.$$

$$15\frac{5}{8} in = 1 ft \ 3\frac{5}{8} \text{ in. so all together } 9 \text{ ft} + 1 \text{ ft} \ 3\frac{5}{8} in = 10 ft \ 3\frac{5}{8} \text{ in.}$$

12. **D.** The proportion $\frac{500 \ ft}{\frac{1}{4} in} = \frac{x \ ft}{6 \ in}$ can be used to find the number of actual distance. Cross multiply. $500 \times 6 = \frac{1}{4}x$ so $3,000 = \frac{1}{4}x$ and $x = 3,000 \times 4 = 12,000$ ft.

13. **B.** There are 4 possible ways to roll a 9 using 2 dice: 3 and 6, 4 and 5, 5 and 4, 6 and 3. The total number of possible outcomes when rolling 2 dice is 6^2 or 36. Therefore, the probability of rolling a 9 is $\frac{4}{36} = \frac{1}{9}$.

14. **D.** The proportion $\frac{3 \text{ boxes}}{18 \text{ reams}} = \frac{x \text{ boxes}}{90 \text{ reams}}$ can be used to find the number of boxes. Cross multiply. $3 \times 90 = 18x$ so $270 = 18x$ and $x = \frac{270}{18} = 15$ boxes.

15. **B.** If one gallon covers 400 square feet, then $\frac{2225}{400} = 5.5625$ or 6 whole gallons are needed to cover 2,225 square feet.

16. **B.** The word **perplexing** means confusing.

17. **C.** The word **immersing** means to dip into, in this case, the author would dip themselves into the sources.

18. **A.** The word **mobile** means movable. In this case, the jeeps continued to move around the area.

19. **D.** The word **stoic** means not showing passion, pain, or distress. He was not a complainer, according to the passage.

20. **B.** The word **ersatz** means artificial, usually an inferior substitution.

21. **D.** Simplifying $\sqrt{50} + 3\sqrt{72}$ yields $\sqrt{25} \times 2 + 3\sqrt{36} \times 2 = 5\sqrt{2} + 18\sqrt{2} = 23\sqrt{2}$.

22. **B.** The discounted amount after the first week is $\$1,000 \times 25\% = \$250$ so the sale price is $\$1,000 - \$250 = \$750$. The discounted amount after the second week is $\$750 \times 10\% = \$75$ so the sale price is $\$750 - \$75 = \$675$.

23. **B.** Convert 2.2 minutes to seconds. $2.2 \times 60 = 132$ seconds. The difference in the two times is $132 - 124 = 8$ seconds.

24. C. The circumference of a circle is given by the formula $C = 2\pi r$ and the area of a circle is given by $A = \pi r^2$. If the circumference is equal to the area, then $2\pi r = \pi r^2$. Solving for r, $\frac{2\pi r}{\pi r} = \frac{\pi r^2}{\pi r}$ and $2 = r$. The diameter is $2r$, or 4.

25. C. The proportion $\frac{\$5.00}{3\,cans} = \frac{\$x}{10\,cans}$ can be used to find the cost of 10 cans. Cross multiply. $5 \times 10 = 3x$ so $50 = 3x$ and $x = \frac{50}{3} = \$16.67$.

26. A. The question clearly states that in order to become a committeeman, one must be elected in a primary election. None of the other choices are stated in the passage.

27. A. Because a topographic map shows the natural resources, it would be of great use when purchasing farmland. Choice **D** would require a relief map.

28. C. From what you can infer, the author is driven to be a writer. How else could he withstand the rejections, despite the fact that they hurt his feelings.

29. D. The passage is about considering various things that can affect a golf game and strategizing, so that you're not adversely affected. By planning ahead, your game will improve.

30. C. Choices **B** and **D** are similar, and although they may be true, these ideas are not stated in the passage. Choice **A** is incorrect, since the passage says there was a successful development of the airplane.

31. C. Interest = principle × rate × time. Interest = $\$1,000 \times 2\frac{1}{4}\% \times 5 = \$1,000 \times 0.0225 \times 5 = \$112.50$.

32. B. Let x be the unknown number. Then $9x = 117$ and $x = \frac{117}{9} = 13$.

33. B. 0° C is equivalent to a Fahrenheit temperature of $0°(\frac{9}{5}) + 32 = 32°$ F. To become 52° F, it must rise 20° F. If it rises 4° F every hour, then $\frac{20}{4}$ or 5 hours later, it will be at 52° F.

34. A. The cost of Sandy's purchase is $(4\frac{1}{2} \times \$1.39) + (6 \times \$0.50) = \$9.26$. The cost of Brandon's purchase is $(3\frac{1}{4} \times \$1.39) + (9 \times \$0.50) = \$9.02$. Sandy spent $\$9.26 - \$9.02 = \$0.24$ more.

35. D. Using the correct order of operations, $-3(-4-5) - 2(-6) = -3(-9) - 2(-6) = 27 - (-12) = 27 + 12 = 39$.

36. D. Although the passage says that there was an evolution, it continues to say that this evolution "took place in the world's economic organization."

37. C. The author of this quotation describes the 6-year-old child in a positive, optimistic manner, using words like "inquisitiveness," "fascinating," and "new experiences." The other choices in the question are negative aspects (despair, indifference, and exasperation).

Mechanical Comprehension

1. A. Acceleration will be the same for both arrows. Momentum and energy are dependent on mass and will, therefore, be different. Only the change in velocity will be the same for both arrows.

2. C. Mass is independent of gravity, and weight is proportional to the acceleration of gravity, which decreases with height or distance away from the center of the Earth.

3. A. Each rotation of the second hand amounts to 2π radians over 60 seconds. Hence, the angular velocity $\frac{2\pi}{60}$ or .105.

4. C. The horizontal component of the velocity of the first ball has no effect on the vertical travel and initially both balls have zero vertical velocity.

5. B. From Newton's second law of motion, the centripetal force, or the inward force necessary to maintain uniform circular motion, is the product of mass and centripetal acceleration.

6. B. Neglecting friction with air, the velocity vector of the ball has a horizontal component that remains constant and a vertical component that suffers deceleration due to the force of gravity. Because distance is speed multiplied by time, the path gradually curves downward due to gravity.

7. C. If the acceleration of gravity is constant, the period (and hence the frequency) is determined solely by the length of the connecting cord or rod.

8. **C.** The law of conservation of momentum requires that $80(3) + 0 = -120 \, v$, and hence $v = -2$ m/s.

9. **B.** For equilibrium the clockwise and counterclockwise movements must be the same, that is, $F_i \times 80 = F_o \times 40$, or $F_i = 30$ N and $F_o/F_i = 60/30 = 2$.

10. **B.** The work done does not depend on time or path of travel because the deceleration of the arrow is constant.

11. **A.** For rod equilibrium, the clockwise and counterclockwise torques must be equal, that is, $(F \text{ at } V + F \text{ at } V)(d) = (F \text{ at } Y)(2d)$ or $(F \text{ at } V)D = (F \text{ at } Y)(2d) - (F \text{ at } X)D$, which means that the third force can only be applied upward at V or downward at X.

12. **C.** Using the expressions $s = v_o t + 1/2at^2$ and $v_f = v_o + at$, you set the time of travel as the sum of t_1 to travel the distance s_1 from the top of the building to the maximum height and t_2, s_2 as the corresponding values from the maximum height to the ground. Substituting numbers, you obtain $t_1 = 1.48$ s, $s_1 = 10.72$ m and $t_2 = 3.52$, $s_2 = 50$ m so that the total time $= 1.48 + 3.52 = 5$ s

13. **A.** Because this is an elastic collision, momentum is conserved. Hence $4(2) - 2(4) = (4 + 2)v$, that is, $v = 0$ m/s.

14. **C.** $K + \dfrac{\left(6.67 \times 10^{-11}\right)\left(400\right)\left(5.98 \times 10^{24}\right)}{\left(6.37 \times 10^{6} + 3 \times 10^{6}\right)} = \dfrac{\left(6.67 \times 10^{-11}\right)\left(400\right)\left(5.98 \times 10^{24}\right)}{\left(6.37 \times 10^{6} + 1.5 \times 10^{6}\right)}$, or $K = \times 3.25 \times 10^{9}$ J.

15. **A.** Because only a component of the original velocity is available while turning, she must accelerate to maintain her original speed.

16. **C.** The time required is $\dfrac{46.9}{9.8} \approx 4.785$.

17. **A.** The most common is the spur gear drive system shown in Figure A.

18. **C.** Because the momentum is conserved, there is no change in speed due to the collision, and the momentum of both remains the same.

19. **B.** Mass cannot change because of changes in gravitational acceleration, but weight changes, and in this case increases because the gravitational acceleration is higher.

20. **C.** The farther the particle is from the axis of rotation of a rigid body, the greater its linear speed because the linear speed is 2π times the product of the frequency of rotation and the radius of rotation. On the other hand, the angular speed is the linear speed divided by the radius of rotation, thus, resulting in both points having the same angular speed.

21. **C.** From the given dimensions, BC and BE are 0.721 m and 0.616 m, respectively. Examination of the force in cable AE shows that it must be 0 since its component along the top surface of the box toward the unsuspended corner is not balanced. The remaining cables BE and CE share the weight equally so that each has a vertical component of force equal to 60N. Hence $T = (60)(.616/.5) = 27.035$ N.

22. **A.** If the mass of the rod is assumed to be at the centroid, then the average drop height $h = 0.5 \, L \sin 60°$. Also the kinetic energy of the rod is $0.5 \, I \, \omega^2$, which equals the average potential energy of the rod on impact or mgh, where ω is the angular velocity in rad/s. Solving for ω we obtain 2.9146 rad/s, which corresponds to a linear velocity $v = L\omega = 8.744$ m/s.

23. **C.** Because the system is frictionless and ideal, energy is conserved and the tip of the rod returns to its original position at $L \sin 60° = 2.598$ m.

24. **B.** Letting the masses of the bullet and block be m and M, their initial velocities be u and U, and their combined velocity be V, the conversion from kinetic to potential energy requires that $\frac{1}{2}(m + M)V^2 = (m + M)gh$, where h is the increment in height (12 cm). This leads to $V = 1.533$ m/s. The conservation of momentum requires that $mu + MU = (m + M)V$, where $U = 0$. Hence, solving for u, you obtain $308.258 = 308$ m/s.

25. **A.** The acceleration is the ratio of the force and the mass. The mass remains the same, while the net force is set by the mass, acceleration of gravity, slope of the inclined plane and the coefficient of kinetic friction (which are all constant). Thus, the acceleration remains the same.

26. C. The new height should be nine times greater since the speed of impact is proportional to the square root of the height.

27. E. The liquid pressure (and hence liquid level) is independent of the cross-sectional area or shape of the container.

28. B. The forces in figure b are not in equilibrium and the nut therefore may be loosened.

29. B. Taking moments about O, you obtain net moment M = 100(.50 – .0725 cos 20°) = 43.187 N.m.

30. C. The horizontal component of the velocity of the arrow shot by the woman has no effect on the travel time, assuming that the air resistance is negligible.

Answer Sheet for ASVAB Practice Test 2

(Remove This Sheet and Use It to Mark Your Answers)

CUT HERE

Word Knowledge

1 Ⓐ Ⓑ Ⓒ Ⓓ
2 Ⓐ Ⓑ Ⓒ Ⓓ
3 Ⓐ Ⓑ Ⓒ Ⓓ
4 Ⓐ Ⓑ Ⓒ Ⓓ
5 Ⓐ Ⓑ Ⓒ Ⓓ
6 Ⓐ Ⓑ Ⓒ Ⓓ
7 Ⓐ Ⓑ Ⓒ Ⓓ
8 Ⓐ Ⓑ Ⓒ Ⓓ
9 Ⓐ Ⓑ Ⓒ Ⓓ
10 Ⓐ Ⓑ Ⓒ Ⓓ
11 Ⓐ Ⓑ Ⓒ Ⓓ
12 Ⓐ Ⓑ Ⓒ Ⓓ
13 Ⓐ Ⓑ Ⓒ Ⓓ
14 Ⓐ Ⓑ Ⓒ Ⓓ
15 Ⓐ Ⓑ Ⓒ Ⓓ
16 Ⓐ Ⓑ Ⓒ Ⓓ
17 Ⓐ Ⓑ Ⓒ Ⓓ
18 Ⓐ Ⓑ Ⓒ Ⓓ
19 Ⓐ Ⓑ Ⓒ Ⓓ
20 Ⓐ Ⓑ Ⓒ Ⓓ

21 Ⓐ Ⓑ Ⓒ Ⓓ
22 Ⓐ Ⓑ Ⓒ Ⓓ
23 Ⓐ Ⓑ Ⓒ Ⓓ
24 Ⓐ Ⓑ Ⓒ Ⓓ
25 Ⓐ Ⓑ Ⓒ Ⓓ
26 Ⓐ Ⓑ Ⓒ Ⓓ
27 Ⓐ Ⓑ Ⓒ Ⓓ
28 Ⓐ Ⓑ Ⓒ Ⓓ
29 Ⓐ Ⓑ Ⓒ Ⓓ
30 Ⓐ Ⓑ Ⓒ Ⓓ
31 Ⓐ Ⓑ Ⓒ Ⓓ
32 Ⓐ Ⓑ Ⓒ Ⓓ
33 Ⓐ Ⓑ Ⓒ Ⓓ
34 Ⓐ Ⓑ Ⓒ Ⓓ
35 Ⓐ Ⓑ Ⓒ Ⓓ

Arithmetic Reasoning

1 Ⓐ Ⓑ Ⓒ Ⓓ
2 Ⓐ Ⓑ Ⓒ Ⓓ
3 Ⓐ Ⓑ Ⓒ Ⓓ
4 Ⓐ Ⓑ Ⓒ Ⓓ
5 Ⓐ Ⓑ Ⓒ Ⓓ
6 Ⓐ Ⓑ Ⓒ Ⓓ
7 Ⓐ Ⓑ Ⓒ Ⓓ
8 Ⓐ Ⓑ Ⓒ Ⓓ
9 Ⓐ Ⓑ Ⓒ Ⓓ
10 Ⓐ Ⓑ Ⓒ Ⓓ
11 Ⓐ Ⓑ Ⓒ Ⓓ
12 Ⓐ Ⓑ Ⓒ Ⓓ
13 Ⓐ Ⓑ Ⓒ Ⓓ
14 Ⓐ Ⓑ Ⓒ Ⓓ
15 Ⓐ Ⓑ Ⓒ Ⓓ

16 Ⓐ Ⓑ Ⓒ Ⓓ
17 Ⓐ Ⓑ Ⓒ Ⓓ
18 Ⓐ Ⓑ Ⓒ Ⓓ
19 Ⓐ Ⓑ Ⓒ Ⓓ
20 Ⓐ Ⓑ Ⓒ Ⓓ
21 Ⓐ Ⓑ Ⓒ Ⓓ
22 Ⓐ Ⓑ Ⓒ Ⓓ
23 Ⓐ Ⓑ Ⓒ Ⓓ
24 Ⓐ Ⓑ Ⓒ Ⓓ
25 Ⓐ Ⓑ Ⓒ Ⓓ
26 Ⓐ Ⓑ Ⓒ Ⓓ
27 Ⓐ Ⓑ Ⓒ Ⓓ
28 Ⓐ Ⓑ Ⓒ Ⓓ
29 Ⓐ Ⓑ Ⓒ Ⓓ
30 Ⓐ Ⓑ Ⓒ Ⓓ

Paragraph Comprehension

1 Ⓐ Ⓑ Ⓒ Ⓓ
2 Ⓐ Ⓑ Ⓒ Ⓓ
3 Ⓐ Ⓑ Ⓒ Ⓓ
4 Ⓐ Ⓑ Ⓒ Ⓓ
5 Ⓐ Ⓑ Ⓒ Ⓓ
6 Ⓐ Ⓑ Ⓒ Ⓓ
7 Ⓐ Ⓑ Ⓒ Ⓓ
8 Ⓐ Ⓑ Ⓒ Ⓓ
9 Ⓐ Ⓑ Ⓒ Ⓓ
10 Ⓐ Ⓑ Ⓒ Ⓓ
11 Ⓐ Ⓑ Ⓒ Ⓓ
12 Ⓐ Ⓑ Ⓒ Ⓓ
13 Ⓐ Ⓑ Ⓒ Ⓓ
14 Ⓐ Ⓑ Ⓒ Ⓓ
15 Ⓐ Ⓑ Ⓒ Ⓓ

Mathematics Knowledge

1 Ⓐ Ⓑ Ⓒ Ⓓ
2 Ⓐ Ⓑ Ⓒ Ⓓ
3 Ⓐ Ⓑ Ⓒ Ⓓ
4 Ⓐ Ⓑ Ⓒ Ⓓ
5 Ⓐ Ⓑ Ⓒ Ⓓ
6 Ⓐ Ⓑ Ⓒ Ⓓ
7 Ⓐ Ⓑ Ⓒ Ⓓ
8 Ⓐ Ⓑ Ⓒ Ⓓ
9 Ⓐ Ⓑ Ⓒ Ⓓ
10 Ⓐ Ⓑ Ⓒ Ⓓ
11 Ⓐ Ⓑ Ⓒ Ⓓ
12 Ⓐ Ⓑ Ⓒ Ⓓ
13 Ⓐ Ⓑ Ⓒ Ⓓ
14 Ⓐ Ⓑ Ⓒ Ⓓ
15 Ⓐ Ⓑ Ⓒ Ⓓ

16 Ⓐ Ⓑ Ⓒ Ⓓ
17 Ⓐ Ⓑ Ⓒ Ⓓ
18 Ⓐ Ⓑ Ⓒ Ⓓ
19 Ⓐ Ⓑ Ⓒ Ⓓ
20 Ⓐ Ⓑ Ⓒ Ⓓ
21 Ⓐ Ⓑ Ⓒ Ⓓ
22 Ⓐ Ⓑ Ⓒ Ⓓ
23 Ⓐ Ⓑ Ⓒ Ⓓ
24 Ⓐ Ⓑ Ⓒ Ⓓ
25 Ⓐ Ⓑ Ⓒ Ⓓ

CUT HERE

Word Knowledge

Time: 11 Minutes

35 Questions

Directions: Each question has an underlined and boldfaced word. You are to decide which of the four words in the choices most nearly means the same as the underlined boldface word and then mark the space on your answer form that has the same number and letter as your choice.

1. **Obscure** most nearly means

   A. bright
   B. hidden
   C. wicked
   D. outmoded

2. **Comprise** most nearly means

   A. value
   B. interrupt
   C. include
   D. understand

3. **Parley** most nearly means

   A. danger
   B. anniversary
   C. conference
   D. promise

4. **Implore** most nearly means

   A. recall
   B. settle
   C. beg
   D. bomb

5. **Upright** most nearly means

   A. scholarly
   B. usual
   C. finished
   D. honorable

6. **Furor** most nearly means

   A. disturbance
   B. agreement
   C. information
   D. suggestion

7. **Brunt** most nearly means

   A. sly scheme
   B. illegal act
   C. principal force
   D. information

8. **Quirk** most nearly means

   A. plot of a novel
   B. happy poem
   C. useless gesture
   D. peculiar twist

9. **Revamp** most nearly means

   A. rescue
   B. join
   C. revise
   D. reply

10. **Teem** most nearly means

    A. abound
    B. dry up
    C. make legal
    D. notice

GO ON TO THE NEXT PAGE

11. Naive most nearly means

   A. drowsy

   B. innocent

   C. sensitive

   D. delicate

12. Menial most nearly means

   A. spiritual

   B. lowly

   C. untruthful

   D. clever

13. Goad most nearly means

   A. set

   B. protect

   C. carry

   D. spur

14. Aversion most nearly means

   A. greed

   B. rivalry

   C. intense dislike

   D. declaration of protest

15. Plaintive most nearly means

   A. mournful

   B. musical

   C. awkward

   D. smooth

16. Residue most nearly means

   A. dwelling

   B. remainder

   C. debt

   D. sample

17. Bungle most nearly means

   A. complain

   B. handle badly

   C. talk boastfully

   D. approach

18. Advocate most nearly means

   A. flatter

   B. caution

   C. recommend

   D. charge

19. Calamitous most nearly means

   A. disastrous

   B. inexperienced

   C. scheming

   D. slanderous

20. Jilt most nearly means

   A. fill in

   B. move about

   C. pick up

   D. cast aside

21. Futile most nearly means

   A. violent

   B. one-sided

   C. weary

   D. useless

22. Incessant most nearly means

   A. even

   B. dirty

   C. loud

   D. continuous

23. Prattle most nearly means

   A. sell

   B. babble

   C. storm

   D. explain

24. Quarry most nearly means

   A. caliber

   B. prey

   C. initial

   D. request

25. Effigy most nearly means

   A. representation

   B. shadow

   C. parade

   D. ancestor

In the following questions, select the word or phrase that best completes the sentence.

26. He showed a lot of _____ for the new project.

- **A.** operation
- **B.** mood
- **C.** zest
- **D.** false alarm

27. There was too much _____ between them to resolve the problem.

- **A.** happiness
- **B.** pleasure
- **C.** willingness
- **D.** acrimony

28. The accountant noticed a _____ between the two accounts.

- **A.** disbelief
- **B.** wariness
- **C.** system
- **D.** discrepancy

29. The student often took _____ notes in class.

- **A.** copyrighted
- **B.** copious
- **C.** tricky
- **D.** sincere

30. His teacher adopted a _____ attitude toward the boy.

- **A.** paternal
- **B.** thrifty
- **C.** narrow-minded
- **D.** old fashioned

31. They were disappointed that their new car was not the same _____ as their old one.

- **A.** similarity
- **B.** length
- **C.** caliber
- **D.** hope

32. It was a _____ exercise that left them exhausted.

- **A.** surprising
- **B.** insulting
- **C.** embarrassing
- **D.** grueling

33. Although the surgery was _____, they decided to take a trip anyway.

- **A.** welcome
- **B.** unplanned
- **C.** imminent
- **D.** frightening

34. She found that his comments _____ her, and therefore, she avoided him.

- **A.** rankled
- **B.** pleased
- **C.** enjoined
- **D.** soothed

35. The magician was extremely _____ when he did close-up magic.

- **A.** silly
- **B.** deft
- **C.** fleeting
- **D.** wary

STOP. BEFORE MOVING ON TO THE NEXT SECTION, CHECK YOUR ANSWERS IF THERE IS STILL TIME LEFT.

Paragraph Comprehension

Time: 13 Minutes
15 Questions

Read the following passages and select the choice that best answers the questions. Answers should be based only on the passage.

1. Jennifer uses hyperbole a lot. She told me yesterday that she was so tired she could sleep for four days straight.

   Based on this passage, hyperbole probably means

   A. lying.
   B. being funny.
   C. exaggerating.
   D. confusing.

2. The Greeks used the agora as a meeting place. While they were buying their food and supplies, they would catch up with one another on the news and gossip, as well as make plans for entertainment and political activities.

   The agora is probably most like

   A. a farmer's market or flea market.
   B. a school or college.
   C. a movie theater.
   D. city hall.

Questions 3–5 are based on the following passage:

Every year the Pulitzer Prize is awarded to a very few authors, playwrights, journalists, and musicians. It was established on the death of Joseph Pulitzer, a Hungarian-born American journalist and philanthropist who encouraged excellence. Pulitzer used his wealth by establishing in his will a journalism school at Columbia University, as well as the Pulitzer Prizes. His will created an advisory board for the prizes and specified the first categories of awards: journalism, drama, history, and literature. Over time, additional awards have been added, including poetry, photography, and, most recently, online journalism. The Pulitzer is one of the most respected awards given to American writers and artists.

3. Joseph Pulitzer probably earned his wealth

   A. by inheriting it.
   B. by being a professor.
   C. in the newspaper business.
   D. by authoring a best selling novel.

4. Based on the information in this passage, you could predict that philanthropists are people who

   A. give prizes to people for hard work.
   B. leave money to universities in their wills.
   C. use their wealth to help and reward others.
   D. believe that it is the responsibility of the government to recognize excellence in its citizens.

5. To win the Pulitzer Prize would be

   A. an honor.
   B. only the result of very hard work.
   C. an embarrassment.
   D. an indignity.

6. Abraham Lincoln is known for his assiduousness and determination. Even though he attempted many different careers and ran for several different political offices in his life, he failed on most occasions. His first true success was winning the presidency and leading the United States through the Civil War.

   Assiduousness most likely means

   A. consistency.
   B. persistence.
   C. efficiency.
   D. stability.

7. There are many types of plants that require different levels of care. For instance, annual plants must be replanted on a yearly basis, while perennials do not. Perennials can renew themselves for several years, unless they are not hardy enough to survive the winter.

Based on this passage, you can grow perennials

- **A.** with minimum care.
- **B.** without any care.
- **C.** without having to replant them every year.
- **D.** without weeding them.

8. Property taxes are due on or before September 15 every year. The Town Tax Collector must have your payment by the end of the day on September 15th, or you will have to pay the penalty. The penalty is 2% on your total bill per month that it is late.

It is September 14th. To avoid a penalty on your property tax, you should

- **A.** drop the bill off at Town Hall on your way home from work.
- **B.** put the bill in the mail after work that day.
- **C.** mail the bill overnight from your office.
- **D.** call the Tax Collector and ask for an extension.

9. Jade carving is a craft that is believed to have been invented in China about 3000 B.C.E. The Aztecs in Mexico also treasured the mineral, using it and the craft to create jewelry and artwork. The Aztecs prized the stone so much that at one time it was accepted as payment for taxes.

One possible result of using jade to pay for taxes could be

- **A.** more wealth for the government.
- **B.** Aztecs with mixed origin (particularly Chinese) having better ability to pay taxes.
- **C.** more deaths of people mining for jade.
- **D.** loss of art in the form of sculptures and jewelry from recycling the jade.

10. Predicting volcanic eruptions is possible given thorough knowledge of the volcano's history and whether or not tools to take certain measurements can be placed where needed. However, similar to earthquakes, the predications are based on probabilities and do not mean that we can control whether and when they happen.

Based on this passage, predicting volcanic activity

- **A.** is too difficult to bother doing.
- **B.** is helpful only to the extent that we can warn people.
- **C.** is a waste of time because it does not make a difference.
- **D.** can cause the volcano to explode.

11. The invention of the radio changed the world in several ways. In addition to speeding up the time it takes to get the news, it exposed people to many different types of entertainment. For instance, country music has been around for more than 100 years, but before the radio was common, it was confined to the Appalachian Mountain region. After the radio was commonplace, many people across the United States began to enjoy the "new" style of music.

An appropriate title for this piece would be

- **A.** The History of Country Music
- **B.** Radio Expanded Our World
- **C.** Appalachian Melodies
- **D.** Radio News

12. There is a legend that Noah did not take any cats on the Ark with him. However, he discovered that the mice and rats created quite a nuisance. He asked the lion for help, and the lion sneezed, producing the cats.

Based on this passage, you can infer that a legend

- **A.** is a story passed down through generations.
- **B.** has a plot of good versus evil.
- **C.** provides a supernatural explanation for a natural occurrence.
- **D.** has a moral.

GO ON TO THE NEXT PAGE

ASVAB Practice Test 2

13. SCUBA diving is a very dangerous activity if you are not properly trained. The biggest problem is if you stay under water for a long time, where your lungs are compressed by the weight of the water, and rise to the surface too quickly. Doing so will cause what is known as decompression sickness, or "the bends." This is because the water pressure causes nitrogen gas to build up in the body, creating air bubbles as the pressure is released. The size and location of the bubbles can impair blood flow or tissue or nerve processes.

You can infer from this paragraph that

A. the human body does not need a lot of nitrogen.
B. oxygen bubbles can cause "the bends."
C. carbon dioxide builds up when you cannot exhale under water.
D. you should never dive very deep for very long.

14. The child's fever was beginning to abate. Her mother started to worry less and decided not to take her to the emergency room.

Based on this passage, the word abate most likely means

A. increase.
B. deviate.
C. fluctuate.
D. subside.

15. This year I have seen seven amazing movies. The best one, however, is the new one about the civil war that is based on a novel. After I saw the movie, I read the book and was even more entertained. The characters were much more real because of the details and insights I did not get from the movie.

This person will probably

A. stop seeing so many movies.
B. read more novels in the future.
C. watch only those movies that are based on novels.
D. write a book based on a movie.

STOP. BEFORE MOVING ON TO THE NEXT SECTION, CHECK YOUR ANSWERS IF THERE IS STILL TIME LEFT.

Arithmetic Reasoning

Time: 36 Minutes
30 Questions

Select the choice that best answers the following questions.

Questions 1–5: A passing average on quizzes recruits take is 70%. The table below gives the number of questions that each of five recruits answered correctly on each of three quizzes.

RECRUIT	QUIZ ONE (10 questions)	QUIZ TWO (20 questions)	QUIZ THREE (10 questions)
Abner	8	8	8
Frank	10	15	9
Gigi	8	18	5
William	9	18	10

1. What percent did Gigi earn on the second quiz?

   A. 18

   B. 36

   C. 50

   D. 90

2. What was the total number of questions on the three quizzes?

   A. 30

   B. 37

   C. 40

   D. 118

3. What average did Abner get on the three quizzes?

   A. 8

   B. 24

   C. 60

   D. 80

4. Whose average was the best?

   A. Abner

   B. Frank

   C. Gigi

   D. William

5. How many of the recruits earned a passing average for the quizzes?

   A. 0

   B. 2

   C. 3

   D. Not enough information to tell

Questions 6–7 are based on the following information. OCS Candidate Shim completed the mile and a half run in 30 minutes.

6. What is her speed in miles per hour?

   A. 2.6

   B. 3

   C. 26

   D. 30

7. How far would Candidate Shim run at that rate in 2 hours?

   A. 5.2 miles

   B. 6 miles

   C. 52 miles

   D. 60 miles

8. A cookie recipe calls for $1\frac{1}{2}$ cups of flour. If the batch is split in half, how much flour should be used?

   A. 3 cups

   B. $1\frac{1}{4}$ cup

   C. 1 cup

   D. $\frac{3}{4}$ cup

9. Tina buys five notebooks for $3.88. How much will she pay for 15 notebooks?

   A. $19.40

   B. $11.64

   C. $2.52

   D. About $2.33

10. Clem spent $1\frac{1}{2}$ hours raking the lawn, 30 minutes planting seeds, 45 minutes sweeping the sidewalk, and 20 minutes cleaning up after the dog. How many minutes longer did it take for Clem to rake than to plant the seeds?

   A. 1

   B. $28\frac{1}{2}$

   C. 30

   D. 60

11. Roberto walks five miles each day. Yesterday, he walked $1\frac{3}{4}$ miles in the morning and $\frac{2}{5}$ of a mile right after lunch. How many miles did he need to walk later in the day to accomplish his goal of five miles?

   A. $2\frac{17}{20}$

   B. 3

   C. $4\frac{4}{9}$

   D. $2\frac{3}{20}$

GO ON TO THE NEXT PAGE

12. Elle jogs 3 miles each day during the week and 4 miles each day on the week-end. How many miles does she jog in three weeks?

    A. 21
    B. 23
    C. 63
    D. 69

Questions 13–15: A mixture contains the following: $1\frac{1}{2}$ cups of sugar, 3 cups of flour, $\frac{1}{2}$ cup of raisins, and $\frac{2}{3}$ cup of chocolate chips.

13. What is the total number of cups in the mixture?

    A. $5\frac{2}{3}$
    B. $4\frac{4}{7}$
    C. $4\frac{3}{5}$
    D. $4\frac{2}{7}$

14. How many more cups of chocolate chips than raisins are used?

    A. $1\frac{1}{2}$
    B. 1
    C. $\frac{3}{5}$
    D. $\frac{1}{6}$

15. If the recipe were tripled, how many cups of chocolate chips would be required?

    A. $4\frac{1}{2}$
    B. $3\frac{1}{2}$
    C. 2
    D. $\frac{2}{3}$

16. Rhoda drives $5\frac{3}{4}$ miles to get to work. Her route home is $7\frac{1}{3}$ miles. How much farther does she drive to get home?

    A. 4 miles
    B. $2\frac{4}{7}$ miles
    C. $2\frac{2}{7}$ miles
    D. $1\frac{7}{12}$ miles

17. The ratio of tulips to roses to daffodils in the garden is 5:8:3. If the garden contains 32 flowers, then how many daffodils are in the garden?

    A. 20
    B. 11
    C. 28
    D. 6

Questions 18 and 19 are based on the following information: Desi makes a down payment of $250 on a television. He then makes four payments of $325 each.

18. How much does Desi pay for the television?

    A. $575
    B. $1475
    C. $1550
    D. $2300

19. If Desi had paid cash for the television, he would have saved 10%. How much would the cash price of the television have been?

    A. $425
    B. $1395
    C. $1400
    D. $2150

20. If Ali can buy four blouses for $26, then how many could she buy for $39?

    A. 2
    B. almost 3
    C. 5
    D. 6

Questions 21 and 22 are based on the following: Karl wants to have an item costing $110 delivered to Jasmine for her birthday. Deluxe delivery of the item would cost an additional $22. Special delivery of the item would cost an additional $30.

21. What would the total charge be to Karl if he opted for special delivery?

    A. $52
    B. $118
    C. $140
    D. $162

22. How much more would Karl pay to have the item delivered special delivery as opposed to deluxe delivery?

- **A.** $140
- **B.** $132
- **C.** $118
- **D.** $8

23. Alicia has earned 85%, 90%, and 62% on the first of her three tests. If she wants to have at least an 84% average in her class, what is the minimum score she must earn on the fourth test?

- **A.** 27%
- **B.** 54%
- **C.** 89%
- **D.** 99%

24. Bart's shadow is 1 foot long. Molly, his big sister, casts a shadow that is $2\frac{1}{2}$ feet long. If Molly is 5 feet tall, then how tall is Bart?

- **A.** $1\frac{1}{2}$ feet
- **B.** 2 feet
- **C.** $3\frac{1}{2}$ feet
- **D.** 8 feet

25. A piece of rope measure 1 yard, 2 feet, and 3 inches. How long is the rope in inches?

- **A.** 133
- **B.** 63
- **C.** 51
- **D.** 39

Questions 26–28 are based on the following information: Della took $\frac{1}{2}$ hour to clean the bathroom. She cleaned the kitchen in $\frac{3}{4}$ of an hour. Jill's room took $\frac{5}{6}$ of an hour to clean. She finished her cleaning in the den. That took her $\frac{2}{3}$ of an hour.

26. Which room took the longest to clean?

- **A.** bathroom
- **B.** den
- **C.** Jill's room
- **D.** kitchen

27. How much longer did it take to clean Jill's room than to clean the bathroom?

- **A.** $\frac{1}{4}$ of an hour
- **B.** $\frac{1}{3}$ of an hour
- **C.** $\frac{1}{6}$ of an hour
- **D.** $\frac{1}{8}$ of an hour

28. How long did it take Della to clean all three rooms?

- **A.** $\frac{11}{24}$ of an hour
- **B.** $\frac{11}{17}$
- **C.** $1\frac{8}{15}$ hours
- **D.** $2\frac{3}{4}$ hours

29. Arthur spent 5 minutes reading history, 20 minutes studying biology, 15 minutes working on geography, and 30 minutes doing his economics. How many hours did Arthur spend studying for his four courses?

- **A.** 70
- **B.** 1
- **C.** $1\frac{1}{10}$
- **D.** $1\frac{1}{6}$

30. Jill Swanson logged the following hours last week.

	MON	TUES	WED	THURS	SAT
HOURS	8.5	8	10.1	9	8.25

How many minutes overtime did she put in if a regular work week for her is 42 hours?

- **A.** 231
- **B.** 111
- **C.** 3.85
- **D.** 1.85

STOP. BEFORE MOVING ON TO THE NEXT SECTION, CHECK YOUR ANSWERS IF THERE IS STILL TIME LEFT.

Mathematics Knowledge

Time: 24 Minutes
25 Questions

Directions: Select the choice that best answers the following questions.

1. How many degrees are in the interior angles of a ten-sided polygon, (a decagon)?

   A. 180
   B. 360
   C. 1440
   D. 1800

Questions 2 and 3 are based on the following.

Police Officer Reginald Dole confiscated 25 items, as indicated in the table.

QUANTITY	ITEM
11	Television
5	CD Player
3	Watch
2	Diamond Ring
2	Can Opener
1	Garden Hose
1	Computer

2. How many more televisions than garden hoses did he confiscate?

   A. 1
   B. 6
   C. 9
   D. 10

3. If the value of each of the CD players that he confiscated is $199, then how much are all of the CD players in his possession worth?

   A. $199
   B. $400
   C. $995
   D. $1,000

4. The height of a rectangle is 5 cm, and the base is 12 cm. How long is its diagonal?

   A. 7 cm
   B. 13 cm
   C. 17 cm
   D. 34 cm

5. $\frac{35}{49} - \frac{10}{15} =$

   A. $\frac{1}{21}$
   B. $\frac{8}{11}$
   C. $\frac{25}{34}$
   D. $\frac{45}{64}$

6. Solve $(3x - 1)^2$.

   A. $9x^2 - 1$
   B. $9x^2 - 6x + 1$
   C. $6x^2 - 6x + 1$
   D. $9x^2 + 1$

7. The following table shows the number of traffic violations recorded for two weeks in Delamar County.

VIOLATION	QUANTITY WEEK ONE	QUANTITY WEEK TWO
Speeding	11	3
Not wearing seat belt	5	5
Not stopping for stopped school bus	3	7
Running red light	9	0
Parking in restricted spot	2	4

What expression provides an accurate representation of the total number of violations for the second week?

A. $11 + 3$
B. $11 + 5 + 3 + 9 + 2$
C. $11 + 3 + 5 + 5 + 3 + 7 + 9 + 4$
D. $3 + 5 + 7 + 0 + 4$

8. The difference between $5\sqrt{98}$ and $\sqrt{32}$ is

A. $4\sqrt{122}$
B. $5\sqrt{130}$
C. $31\sqrt{2}$
D. 40

9. How many degrees are in the three interior angles of a scalene triangle?

A. 100
B. 180
C. 360
D. cannot be determined from the information given

10. What is the circumference of a circle that has an area of 100π?

A. 10π
B. 20
C. 20π
D. 100π

11. Simplify $\dfrac{-6\sqrt{8}}{\sqrt{2}}$.

A. -12
B. $-6\sqrt{2}$
C. -24
D. 24

12. The area of a square is 25 m²; what is the length of the perimeter?

A. $5\sqrt{2}$ m
B. 10 m
C. 20 m
D. 100 m

13. $36(15 + 85)$ is equivalent to which of the following?

A. $36(15) + (36 + 85)$
B. $85 + 15(36)$
C. $36(85) + 15(36)$
D. $(85 + 15)(36)$

14. Officer McCarthy arrested Claudia Vagabonder. Claudia had in her pockets the following bills: four $20s, eighteen $10s, and eleven $5s. Which of the following expressions could Officer McCarthy use to calculate the total value of the bills?

A. $4(20) \cdot 18(10) \cdot 11(5)$
B. $(4 + 18 + 11)(20 + 10 + 5)$
C. $4(20) + 8(10) + 11(5)$
D. $4(20) + 18(10) + 11(5)$

15. $\dfrac{35}{16} \div \dfrac{5}{8} =$

A. $1\dfrac{1}{2}$
B. $\dfrac{2}{3}$
C. $1\dfrac{1}{3}$
D. $\dfrac{5}{4}$

16. Officer Mallard arrested a group of students from the high school. Six of them were sophomores, eight of them were juniors, and the rest of them were seniors. If there were twenty-four students in the group, how would Officer Mallard figure out how many were seniors?

A. $6 + 8 + 24$
B. $(24 - 6) + (24 - 8)$
C. $(24 - 6) - (24 - 8)$
D. $24 - (6 + 8)$

GO ON TO THE NEXT PAGE

ASVAB Practice Test 2

Questions 17–19 are based on the following.

Denver Johnson stopped the drivers of the following vehicles during the first hour of each of his shifts over the weekend.

FRIDAY PM SHIFT			SATURDAY AM SHIFT			SUNDAY AM SHIFT		
#	Color	Make	#	Color	Make	#	Color	Make
2	Blue	Pontiac	1	Red	Saturn	1	Green	Subaru
3	Yellow	Saturn	2	Blue	Dodge	1	Blue	Dodge
1	Red	Saturn	2	Black	Jeep	1	Blue	Subaru
2	Blue	Jeep	5	Blue	Jeep	1	Black	Subaru
2	Red	Pontiac	6	Black	Chevrolet	1	Green	Dodge
4	Green	Honda				1	Silver	Subaru
						5	Yellow	Subaru

17. What is the total number of green cars stopped by Denver over the weekend?

A. 1 + 0 + 2
B. 1 + 0 + 1
C. 4 + 0 + 1
D. 4 + 0 + (1 + 1)

18. How many Saturn automobiles were stopped?

A. 1 + 1 + 1
B. 2 + 1 + 0
C. 4 + 1 + 0
D. 4 + 1 + 9

19. What is the ratio of black cars to red cars to blue cars that Denver stopped on Saturday?

A. 1:1:5
B. 5:1:0
C. 0:1:7
D. 8:1:7

20. A triangle has sides of length 4 dm, 6 dm, and 10 dm. What is the perimeter of the triangle?

A. 10 dm
B. 20 dm
C. 120 dm
D. 240 dm

21. What is the sum of the acute angles of any right triangle?

A. More information is necessary to answer this question.
B. 90
C. 180
D. 270

22. The circumference of a circle is 10π inches. What is the radius of the circle?

A. 5
B. 10
C. 5π
D. 10π

23. A regular pentagon, a five-sided polygon with equal sides, has a perimeter of 16.5 feet. What is the length of each side?

A. 3.1 feet
B. 3.3 feet
C. 31 feet
D. 33 feet

24. The perimeter of a polygon can always be determined by:

    A.   multiplying the base times the height
    B.   multiplying π times the diameter
    C.   adding the sides and then doubling that value
    D.   adding all of the sides

25. A cubic container measuring four inches on each edge holds how many cubic inches of water?

    A.   12 cubic inches
    B.   16 cubic inches
    C.   48 cubic inches
    D.   64 cubic inches

STOP. IF THERE IS STILL TIME LEFT, CHECK YOUR ANSWERS.

Answer Key for ASVAB Practice Test 2

Word Knowledge

1. B	13. D	25. A
2. C	14. C	26. C
3. C	15. A	27. D
4. C	16. B	28. D
5. D	17. B	29. B
6. A	18. C	30. A
7. C	19. A	31. C
8. D	20. D	32. D
9. C	21. D	33. C
10. A	22. D	34. A
11. B	23. B	35. B
12. B	24. B	

Paragraph Comprehension

1. C	6. B	11. B
2. A	7. C	12. C
3. D	8. A	13. A
4. C	9. D	14. D
5. A	10. B	15. B

Arithmetic Reasoning

1. D	11. A	21. C
2. C	12. D	22. D
3. C	13. A	23. D
4. D	14. D	24. B
5. C	15. C	25. B
6. B	16. D	26. C
7. B	17. D	27. B
8. D	18. C	28. D
9. B	19. B	29. D
10. D	20. D	30. B

Mathematics Knowledge

1. C	**10.** C	**19.** D
2. D	**11.** A	**20.** B
3. C	**12.** C	**21.** B
4. B	**13.** C	**22.** A
5. A	**14.** D	**23.** B
6. B	**15.** A	**24.** D
7. D	**16.** D	**25.** D
8. C	**17.** D	
9. B	**18.** C	

ASVAB Practice Test 2 Answers and Explanations

Word Knowledge

1. B. Obscure means **hidden.**

2. C. To comprise means **include.**

3. C. To parley is a **conference.**

4. C. To implore means to **beg.**

5. D. In terms of the choices, the word upright means **honorable.** It's important to select the meaning of the word based on the choices given.

6. A. A furor is a **disturbance.**

7. C. The brunt of something is its **principal force.**

8. D. A quirk is a **peculiar twist.**

9. C. To revamp is to **revise.**

10. A. Teem means **abound.** It might be used in a sentence such as "The forest was teeming with wildlife."

11. B. Naïve means **innocent.**

12. B. Menial means **lowly,** often used as a "menial task."

13. D. To goad means to **spur** on.

14. C. Aversion means an **intense dislike.**

15. A. The word plaintive means **mournful.**

16. B. The word residue means the **remainder,** such as "He left the residue of the coffee grounds on the bottom of the cup."

17. B. To bungle is to **handle badly.**

18. C. The verb advocate means to **recommend.**

19. A. The word calamitous means **disastrous.**

20. D. To jilt means to **cast aside.**

21. D. An effort that is futile is **useless.**

22. D. The word incessant means **continuous,** such as "The noise of the drill was incessant."

23. B. To prattle means to **babble.**

24. B. A quarry means **prey.** This is not to be confused with a quarry where they dig stone, marble, and so on. One hunts a quarry.

25. A. An effigy is a **representation.** Dissatisfied sports fans often burn an effigy of the losing coach.

26. C. Zest means **excitement.**

27. D. Acrimony means **bitterness.** None of the other choices is logical, since there's an expression of negativity in the sentence.

28. D. Discrepancy means a **difference,** which would be logical in terms of the sentence and the phrase "two accounts."

29. B. Copious means **voluminous.**

30. A. The word paternal means **fatherly.**

31. C. Caliber means **quality.** The other choices aren't logical in the sentence.

32. D. Grueling means **exhausting.**

33. C. Imminent means **immediate.** If you don't know the meaning of the word when you encounter it, try the other words to see whether they fit logically. There are certain key words in a sentence that should give you clues to the answer.

34. A. Rankled means **annoyed,** which is a logical reason to avoid someone.

35. B. Deft means **skillful,** a necessary ability for a magician.

Paragraph Comprehension

1. C. The correct answer is exaggerating. Jennifer might have felt like she could sleep for four days straight, but she most likely would not.

2. A. The agora is most like a farmer's market or flea market where different people bring their goods to sell and use the time to catch up on other events.

3. D. The passage states that Pulitzer was a journalist, so he most probably earned his wealth in the newspaper business. There is no evidence for the other responses in the passage.

4. C. While **A** and **B** could be answers, they are more narrow in scope than **C** is.

5. A. It is considered an honor to receive the Pulitzer Prize. The passage states that it is one of the most respected awards for American writers and artists.

6. B. Assiduous means persistent. Even though President Lincoln faced a lot of failures, he was persistent in his efforts to succeed at something. He was not consistent **A** because he tried different careers, nor stable **D** because he had failures that caused him to seek changes. The passage does not address the idea of efficiency **C**.

7. C. The passage states that while annuals have to be replanted yearly, perennials do not.

8. A. To ensure that you do not have to pay a penalty, you should personally deliver your tax payment on the 14th. Although mailing it through an overnight service would likely get it there on time, you are still making a rather significant payment just to get the bill paid on time.

9. D. Many pieces of art were lost through the use of jade as a payment form. **A** can be eliminated because the government would get the same amount of wealth no matter how the taxes were paid. **B** is incorrect because you do not have to be of Chinese origin to work with jade. **C** is not a likely result.

10. B. Since volcanoes cannot be controlled, the best we can do is warn people so that they can take appropriate precautions with their lives and belongings.

11. B. The main idea of the sentence is that the radio brought new things to people. **A**, **C**, and **D** can all be eliminated because those are examples of how radio provided new ways to get information and entertainment.

12. C. Since the story explains the creation of cats (a natural occurrence) through a supernatural means (sneeze of a lion), and it is identified as a legend, **C** has to be the answer.

13. A. The passage notes that there is a "nitrogen build-up," which indicates that there is too much nitrogen in the system. This indicates that the body does not need a great amount of nitrogen to survive because it is not processing it.

14. D. The mother was no longer as worried, so the fever must have been decreasing. Subside means to decrease, as does abate.

15. B. The person discovered that a novel can bring a deeper understanding to characters than a movie sometimes can, so she/he may choose to read more novels in the future because of this.

Arithmetic Reasoning

1. D. $\frac{18}{20} = \frac{9}{10} = .9 = 90\%$.

2. C. $10 + 20 + 10 = 40$.

3. C. Abner answered a total of 24 questions correctly. $\frac{24}{40} = \frac{3}{5} = .6 = 60\%$.

4. D. This table has one additional column that shows the total number of questions each recruit answered correctly. William did the best. (You need not actually calculate the average of each recruit. The person with the most correct answers has the best average. You would divide each total by the total number of questions in order to calculate each recruit's average.)

RECRUIT	QUIZ ONE, (10 ?'s)	QUIZ TWO, (20 ?'s)	QUIZ THREE, (10 ?'s)	TOTAL CORRECT
Abner	8	8	8	24
Frank	10	15	9	34
Gigi	8	18	5	31
William	9	18	10	37

5. C. In the following table, another column has been added at the end that indicates the average of each recruit.

RECRUIT	QUIZ ONE, (10 questions)	QUIZ TWO, (20 questions)	QUIZ THREE, (10 questions)	TOTAL CORRECT	AVERAGE
Abner	8	8	8	24	$^{24}/_{40} = 3/5 = .6 = 60\%$
Frank	10	15	9	34	$^{34}/_{40} = 17/20 = .85 = 85\%$
Gigi	8	18	5	31	$^{31}/_{40} = .775 = 77.5\%$
William	9	18	10	37	$^{37}/_{40} = .925 = 92.5\%$

Passing is 70%. So, Frank, Gigi, and William all pass. That makes 3!

6. B. You begin with miles per minute. Then, by multiplying by a form of 1, you eliminate the minutes, (60 minutes = 1 hour).

$$\frac{1\frac{1}{2}\ miles}{30\ minutes} = \frac{\frac{3}{2}\ miles}{30\ minutes} \times \frac{60\ minutes}{1\ hour} = \frac{\frac{3}{2}\ miles}{1} \times \frac{3\ miles}{1\ hour} = 3\ mph$$

Another approach would be to recognize that 30 minutes is one-half hour. So, doubling that to get one hour would require doubling the distance run.

7. B. At the rate of 3 miles per hour, Officer Shim would run 6 miles, calculated by taking her rate times her time, 3 times 2.

8. D. $\frac{1}{2} \cdot 1\frac{1}{2} = \frac{1}{2} \cdot \frac{3}{2} = \frac{3}{4}$.

9. B.

$$\frac{5\ notebooks}{\$3.88} = \frac{15\ notebooks}{x}$$

$$5x = 15(3.88)$$

$$5x = 58.2$$

$$\frac{5x}{5} = \frac{58.2}{5}$$

$$x = 11.64$$

10. D. It took Clem $1\frac{1}{2}$ hours to rake the lawn and 30 minutes to plant seeds. The raking took him 90 minutes, $(1\frac{1}{2} \cdot 60)$. So, 90 minutes – 30 minutes = 60 minutes. (Of course, you could also take $1\frac{1}{2}$ hour – $\frac{1}{2}$ hour because 30 minutes is $\frac{1}{2}$ hour. That would give 1 hour, which is 60 minutes.)

11. A. First, find the number of miles Roberto walked in the morning and right after lunch:

$1\frac{3}{4} + \frac{2}{5} = 1\frac{15}{20} + \frac{8}{20} = 1\frac{23}{20} = 1 + 1\frac{3}{20} = 2\frac{3}{0}$. Then, subtract this from his goal of 5 miles:

$5 - 2\frac{3}{20} = (4+1) - 2\frac{3}{20} = \left(4 + \frac{20}{20}\right) - 2\frac{3}{20} = 4\frac{20}{20} - 2\frac{3}{20} = 2\frac{17}{20}$.

12. D. Elle jogs $3 \cdot 5 = 15$ miles during the week and $2 \cdot 4 = 8$ miles during the weekend. This is a total of 23 miles each week. Multiply this by 3 weeks to get a total of 69 miles.

13. A. $1\frac{1}{2} + 3 + \frac{1}{2} + \frac{2}{3} = 3 + \left(1\frac{1}{2} + \frac{1}{2}\right) + \frac{2}{3} = 3 + 2 + \frac{2}{3} = 5\frac{2}{3}$.

14. D. $\frac{2}{3} - \frac{1}{2} = \frac{4}{6} - \frac{3}{6} = \frac{1}{6}$.

15. C. $3 \cdot \frac{2}{3} = \frac{3}{1} \cdot \frac{2}{3} = \frac{2}{1} = 2$: Tripling requires multiplication by 3. Since 3 is a whole number, you turn it into a fraction by dividing by 1. Next, cancel the 3s. Finally 2 divided by $1 = 2$.

16. D. $7\frac{1}{3} - 5\frac{3}{4} = 7\frac{4}{12} - 5\frac{9}{12} = \left(6 + 1 + \frac{4}{12}\right) - 5\frac{9}{12} = \left(6 + \frac{12}{12} + \frac{4}{12}\right) - 5\frac{9}{12} = 6\frac{16}{12} - 5\frac{9}{12} = 1\frac{7}{12}$.

17. D. A table could be used to organize the information.

	TULIPS	ROSES	DAFFODILS	TOTAL
RATIO	5	8	3	16
MUTLIPLY BY				
ACTUAL NUMBER				32

So, if there are really 32 flowers, you should multiply each value of the ratio by 2. The updated table follows.

	TULIPS	ROSES	DAFFODILS	TOTAL
RATIO	5	8	3	16
MUTLIPLY BY	2	2	2	2
ACTUAL NUMBER	10	16	6	32

18. C. $-250 + 4(\$325) = \$250 + \$1300 = \$1550$.

19. B. 10% of $1550 = .1($1550) = $155

$1550 − $155 = $1395

20. D.

$$\frac{4 \text{ blouses}}{\$26} = \frac{x \text{ blouses}}{\$39}$$

$$26x = 4(39)$$

$$26x = 156$$

$$\frac{26x}{26} = \frac{156}{26}$$

$$x = 6$$

21. C. $110 + $30 = $140.

22. D. $30 − $22 = $8.

23. D. Let x be the lowest possible score Alicia could earn to have her 84% average.

$$\frac{85 + 90 + 62 + x}{4} = 84$$

$$\frac{237 + x}{4} = 84$$

$$237 + x = 336$$

$$x = 99$$

Add up the scores of the four tests and divide by the number of tests in order to get the average. Adding the scores she earned on the first three tests gives the accumulated points she has earned. Then, multiply both sides of the equation by 4. Finally, subtract 237 on each side of the equation to get x. Therefore, Alicia would have to earn at least a 99% on the fourth test in order to achieve her 84% average.

24. B. Set up a proportion with length of shadow in the numerator of each fraction and height of individual in the denominator.

$$\frac{1}{B} = \frac{2\frac{1}{2}}{5}$$

$$\frac{1}{B} = \frac{\frac{5}{2}}{5}$$

$$\frac{5}{2}B = 1(5)$$

$$\frac{5}{2}B = 5$$

$$B = 5\left(\frac{2}{5}\right) = \frac{5}{1} \cdot \frac{2}{5} = \frac{1}{1} \cdot \frac{2}{1} = \frac{2}{1} = 2$$

The final step is to multiply a whole number by a fraction. The whole number is made to look like a fraction by showing division by 1. Then, the 5s cancel. Bart's height, then, is 2 feet.

25. B. The rope measures 36 inches + 24 inches + 3 inches. There are 36 inches in a yard and 12 inches in a foot. The total number of inches in the rope is 36 + 24 + 3 = 63.

26. C. The bathroom took 30 minutes; the kitchen took 45 minutes; Jill's room took 50 minutes; and the den took 40 minutes to clean. (Multiply each fraction by 60, the number of minutes in 1 hour.) So, Jill's room took Della the longest to clean.

27. B. $\frac{5}{6} - \frac{1}{2} = \frac{5}{6} - \frac{3}{6} = \frac{2}{6} = \frac{1}{3}$.

28. **D.** $\frac{1}{2} + \frac{3}{4} + \frac{5}{6} + \frac{2}{3} = \frac{6}{12} + \frac{9}{12} + \frac{10}{12} + \frac{8}{12} = \frac{6+9+10+8}{12} = \frac{33}{12} = \frac{11}{4} = 2\frac{3}{4}$.

The least common denominator for the four fractions is 12. After all of the fractions have been converted to 12th's, add the numerators. The resulting fraction can be reduced by dividing the numerator and the denominator by 3. That results in another improper fraction, so divide the denominator into the numerator. The remainder goes over the denominator. Hence, the final answer is $2\frac{3}{4}$.

29. **D.** Arthur spent (5 + 20 + 15 + 30) minutes studying. This is a total of 70 minutes. One hour is 60 minutes. So, Arthur studied for 1 hour and 10 minutes. This is $1\frac{10}{60}$ or $1\frac{1}{6}$ hours.

30. **B.** Jill logged (8.5 + 8 + 10.1 + 9 + 8.25) hours. That is 43.85 hours. A regular work week for the officer is 42 hours. The difference, then, is 43.85 − 42 = 1.85 hours. Convert this to minutes by multiplying by 60, 1.85(60) = 111.

Mathematics Knowledge

1. **C.** The number of degrees in the interior angles of any polygon is found by taking the number of sides minus two, then multiplying by 180°. Subtracting two from the number of sides gives you the number of nonoverlapping triangles formed. The 180° is the number of degrees in each triangle.

2. **D.** The table indicates 11 televisions and 1 garden hose. So, subtract 11 − 1 = 10.

3. **C.** Each of the 5 CD players is worth $199. The total amount they are worth is 5($199) = $995.

4. **B.** The diagonal of the rectangle is the hypotenuse of the right triangle with legs of length 5 and 12. Using the Pythagorean Theorem, $a^2 + b^2 = c^2$, you get $5^2 + 12^2 = c^2$. Hence, $25 + 144 = 169 = c^2$. Then, $c = 13$.

5. **A.** If you reduce these fractions first, the result is $\frac{5}{7} - \frac{2}{3}$. The first fraction was reduced by dividing the numerator and the denominator by 7, and the second was reduced by dividing numerator and denominator by 5. The least common denominator for this exercise is now 21. So, $\frac{5}{7} - \frac{2}{3} = \frac{15}{21} - \frac{14}{21} = \frac{1}{21}$.

6. **B.** FOIL is the process for this exercise. Firsts, outsides, insides, lasts should be multiplied. Then, those products are all added. The result is

$$(3x-1)^2 = (3x-1)(3x-1) = 3x \cdot 3x + 3x \cdot -1 + -1 \cdot 3x + (-1)(-1) = 9x^2 - 3x - 3x + 1 = 9x^2 - 6x + 1$$

7. **D.** Just be sure to look at the correct column of the table. Total indicates addition.

8. **C.** Difference indicates subtraction. First, the radicals need to be simplified.

$$5\sqrt{98} - \sqrt{32} = 5\sqrt{49 \cdot 2} - \sqrt{16 \cdot 2} = 5\sqrt{49}\sqrt{2} - \sqrt{16}\sqrt{2} = 5 * 7\sqrt{2} - 4\sqrt{2} =$$
$$35\sqrt{2} - 4\sqrt{2} = (35 - 4)\sqrt{2} = 31\sqrt{2}$$

9. **B.** The sum of the interior angles of any triangle is 180.

10. **C.** The formula for the area of a circle is $A = pr^2$. The radius of this circle, then, is 10. The circumference of a circle is $C = p = 2pr$. If the radius is 10, then the diameter is double that, 20. The circumference is 20π.

11. **A.** You can divide the radicals first, since they are both square roots. So doing, you get

$$\frac{-6\sqrt{8}}{\sqrt{2}} = -6\sqrt{\frac{8}{2}} = -6\sqrt{4} = -6 \cdot 2 = -12.$$

12. **C.** The area of a square is $A = s^2$. A square with an area of $25m^2$ has a side of length $5m$. The perimeter is the distance all the way around the square, which would be $4 \cdot 5m = 20m$.

13. **C.** Use the distributive property to get 36(15 + 85) = 36(15) + 36(85). Commuting the two terms results in 36(85) + 36(15). Commuting the second term, the final answer is 36(85) + 15(36).

14. **D.** Multiply the number of bills by the denomination of each bill to get the value of all of one type of bill. Then, add those products to get the grand total.

15. **A.** $\frac{35}{16} \div \frac{5}{8} = \frac{35}{16} \cdot \frac{8}{5}$ Now, 35 and 5 are each divided by 5, and 16 and 8 are each divided by 8: $\frac{7}{2} \cdot \frac{1}{1} = \frac{7}{2} = 3\frac{1}{2}$. The product is calculated by multiplying the numerators together and the denominators together. The final step is changing the improper fraction into a mixed number by dividing the denominator into the numerator. The remainder is put over the denominator.

16. **D.** Officer Mallard knew the number of sophomores and juniors. That total is subtracted from the total number of students to calculate the number of seniors.

17. **D.** Add the number of green cars stopped each day. There were 4 on Friday, none on Saturday, and 2 on Sunday.

18. **C.** Add the 4 that were stopped on Friday to the 1 that was stopped on Saturday to the 0 that were stopped on Sunday.

19. **D.** A ratio is a comparison of numbers. The ratio of black to red to blue cars stopped on Saturday, (second column), is 8 to 1 to 7.

20. **B.** The perimeter of a triangle is found by adding all the sides: $4 + 6 + 10 = 20$. The unit of measure is decimeter.

21. **B.** Any triangle had a total of $180°$. A right angle measures $90°$. Subtracting 90 from 180 gives 90.

22. **A.** The circumference of a circle is $C = 2\pi r = \pi d$. This circle, with a circumference 10π, has a diameter of 10. The radius is one-half of that, 5.

23. **B.** The perimeter of a regular pentagon would be found by multiplying the length of one side by 5: $P = s(5)$, $16.5 = s(5)$. Dividing each side of the equation by 5 results in $3.3 = s$.

24. **D.** That is all there is to it!

25. **D.** A cubic container's volume would be calculated with the formula $V = e^3$. This container measures 4 inches on each edge. So, $V = 4^3 = 64$.

Military Career Opportunities

For almost 45 years, the military's personnel requirements and overall strategies had been shaped by the need to be prepared to deal with a short-notice, global war with the former Soviet Union. Given the dramatic developments in Eastern Europe, the former Soviet Union, and Africa, the military services are refocusing their strategy on a peacetime mission and on readiness for regional conflicts and contingencies. Despite the recent conflicts in Afghanistan and Iraq that have required a strong presence of the United States military, it is anticipated that over the next few decades, there will be a reduction in the number of active-duty officers.

Although the active-duty military services will decline in size, they will still need substantial numbers of new officers to replace those who are retiring, as well as those needed to meet personnel requirements in new technical areas as such areas are developed. New officers are usually college graduates with bachelor's degrees. They must meet the physical, academic, and moral standards set by their service to be accepted into programs for becoming an officer (commissioning programs).

Officers usually begin their careers gaining experience in their chosen occupational field. Working closely with more senior officers, they also begin supervising small groups of enlisted people. As officers become more experienced and advance in responsibility and rank, they direct more enlisted personnel, begin to lead other officers, and may eventually become the senior leaders and managers of the military. Commanding officers are responsible for every detail of U.S. ground and naval forces, ships, flying squadrons, and amphibious assault forces.

Military Officer Occupations

Officers lead and manage activities in every occupational specialty in the military. They must be able to learn detailed information quickly to be effective in the changing assignments and environments they will experience during their careers.

One of the characteristics of a successful leader is willingness to serve. Officers serve their country daily, sometimes placing themselves in danger. They are responsible for the well-being, training, and readiness of the people they lead.

Officers are also trained in specific occupational skills. They manage the military supply system and care for the health of combat and support personnel and their dependents. They analyze military intelligence and lead technicians on land or aboard ships.

Some officers, such as infantry and submarine officers, work in jobs directly related to combat. These occupations are open only to men. In other occupations, certain combat-related duty assignments are closed to women. According to federal law and policy, women may not be assigned to duty where there is a high probability of direct exposure to combat.

A large number of men and women in the military work in occupations that support the combat forces. They are essential to the readiness and strength of the combat forces.

Together, the five services offer employment opportunities in over 1,500 officer job specialties. To help you explore military officer careers, these specialties are grouped into 61 occupations. The 61 occupations are organized into nine broad groups:

- Executive, Administrative, and Managerial
- Human Services
- Media and Public Affairs
- Health Diagnosing and Treating Practitioner
- Health Care
- Engineering, Science, and Technical
- Service
- Transportation
- Combat Specialty

Over two-thirds of all military officer occupations have counterparts in the civilian world of work. For example, there are personnel managers, optometrists, electrical engineers, lawyers, and management analysts in both the military and civilian work forces.

The services offer training and advancement opportunities in each occupation. No matter which occupation newly commissioned officers enter, they find a well defined career path leading to increased responsibility and higher pay.

How to Use This Careers Section

Because of the organization of this section, it should be easy to find a career or occupation in which you can find satisfaction. You can start by skimming this chapter, reading through the different jobs that are available. There are probably dozens that you never even thought of before.

When reading any of these officer occupational descriptions, remember that it is a summary of similar job specialties across all of the military services. Individual job specialties may differ somewhat from those described in this section, but you can get more information through your recruiter. We've also indicated the different branches of service in which you would find these occupations. This can help you when you decide to leave the service.

Officer Occupational Descriptions

Executive, Administrative, and Managerial Occupations

Communications Managers

Army

Navy

Marine Corps

Coast Guard

Instant worldwide communication among air, sea, and land forces is vital to military operations. The services operate some of the largest and most complex communication networks in the world. Communications managers plan and direct the operation of military communication systems. They also manage personnel in communications centers and relay stations.

What They Do

Communications managers in the military perform some or all of the following duties:

Develop rules or procedures for sending and receiving communications

Direct personnel who operate computer systems and electronic telecommunications and satellite communications equipment

Develop ways to track and ensure security of communications

Direct personnel who maintain and repair communications equipment

Develop budgets for communications centers

Special Requirements

A 4-year college degree, preferably in engineering, mathematics, computer science, or related fields, is required to enter this occupation.

Helpful Attributes

Helpful attributes include:

Interest in working with computers, radios, and electronic equipment

Interest in technical work

Work Environment

Communications managers usually work in communications centers on land or aboard ships.

Training Provided

Job training consists of 12 to 32 weeks of classroom instruction. Training length varies depending on specialty. Course content typically includes:

Communications theory and security

Communications-electronics management

Satellite communications, including tactical ground terminals

Electronic principles, technologies, and systems

Tactical combat communications systems

Further training occurs on the job and through advanced courses.

Civilian Counterparts

Civilian communications managers work for private firms involved with telephone and telegraph communications, radio and TV broadcasting, and satellite communications. They perform duties similar to those performed by military communications managers. Depending on their specialty, they may also be called station managers, operations managers, or communications superintendents.

Opportunities

The services have about 4,200 communications managers. On average, they need 100 new communications managers each year. After job training, communications managers are assigned to manage or assist in managing a communications center. With experience, they may advance to senior management or command positions.

Emergency Management Officers

Army
Navy
Marine Corps
Coast Guard

The military must be prepared for all types of emergencies, from natural disasters, such as floods, earthquakes, and hurricanes, to enemy attacks. Emergency management officers prepare warning, control, and evacuation plans. They also coordinate emergency response teams during natural disasters.

What They Do

Emergency management officers in the military perform some or all of the following duties:

Organize emergency teams for quick responses to disaster situations

Research ways to respond to possible disaster situations

Conduct training programs for specialized disaster response teams

Develop joint disaster response plans with local, state, and federal agencies

Obtain supplies, equipment, and protection equipment

Develop warning systems and safe shelters

Direct disaster control centers

Special Requirements

A 4-year college degree is normally required to enter this occupation.

Helpful Attributes

Helpful fields of study include physical and environmental sciences, engineering, law enforcement, and business or public administration.

Helpful attributes include:

Interest in developing detailed plans

Ability to remain calm in stressful situations

Ability to express ideas clearly and concisely

Work Environment

Emergency management officers usually work in offices while developing disaster response plans. They work outdoors while inspecting shelters or directing emergency response teams.

Training Provided

Job training consists of 2 to 9 weeks of classroom instruction. Training length varies depending on specialty. Course content typically includes:

Disaster planning

Procedures for nuclear, biological, and chemical decontamination

Effects of radiation

Procedures for nuclear accident teams

Civilian Counterparts

Civilian emergency management officers work for federal, state, and local governments, including law enforcement and civil defense agencies. They perform duties similar to those performed by military emergency management officers.

Opportunities

The services have about 500 emergency management officers. On average, they need 20 new emergency management officers each year. After job training, emergency management officers are assigned to command centers or planning sections, where they develop emergency plans and training programs. In time, they may advance to senior management positions.

Finance and Accounting Managers

Army
Air Force
Navy
Marine Corps
Coast Guard

Each year, the services spend billions of dollars on personnel, equipment, and supplies. Only through careful management can military funds be put to their best use. Finance and accounting managers direct and manage the financial affairs of the military. They also advise commanders on financial and accounting matters.

What They Do

Finance and accounting managers in the military perform some or all of the following duties:

Set policies for the use of military funds

Direct the preparation of budgets and financial forecasts

Advise management personnel on accounting, budgeting, and fiscal matters

Develop ways to track financial transactions

Prepare and examine financial records and reports

Direct the activities of finance and accounting staff

Training Provided

Job training consists of 2 to 16 weeks of classroom instruction. Training length varies depending on specialty. Course content typically includes:

Financial management techniques, including budget preparation and review

Financial management techniques

Military accounting

Duties of finance and accounting managers

Personnel management and payroll procedures

Statistical analysis and fiscal planning

Special Requirements

A 4-year college degree in accounting, finance, or a related field is required to enter this occupation. Some specialties require a master's degree in business administration or recognition as a Certified Public Accountant (CPA).

Helpful Attributes

Helpful attributes include:

Preference for working with numbers and statistics

Interest in work requiring accuracy and attention to detail

Interest in planning and directing the work of others

Work Environment

Finance and accounting managers work in large finance or accounting offices.

Civilian Counterparts

Civilian finance and accounting managers work for businesses, accounting firms, universities, hospitals, or government agencies. They perform duties similar to those performed by military finance and accounting managers. They usually specialize in certain areas of finance and accounting, such as budgets, internal auditing, or cost accounting. In large business firms, they may be called executive controllers or company treasurers.

Opportunities

The services have about 2,100 finance and accounting managers. On average, they need 70 new finance and accounting managers each year. After job training, managers are assigned to finance and accounting offices. Initially, they perform work in accounting, auditing, or finance management operations. With experience, they may advance to senior management and command positions.

Food Service Managers

Army
Navy
Air Force
Marine Corps
Coast Guard

The military serves food to hundreds of thousands of service members each day. Meals must be carefully planned and prepared to ensure good nutrition and variety. Food service managers direct the facilities that prepare and serve food.

What They Do

Food service managers in the military perform some or all of the following duties:

Manage the cooking and serving of food at mess halls

Direct the operation of officers' dining halls

Determine staff and equipment needed for dining halls, kitchens, and meat-cutting plants

Set standards for food storage and preparation

Estimate food budgets

Maintain nutritional and sanitary standards at food service facilities

Special Requirements

A 4-year college degree is normally required to enter this occupation.

Helpful Attributes

Helpful fields of study include food service management, nutrition, and business administration.

Helpful attributes include:

Interest in nutrition and food preparation

Interest in planning and directing the work of others

Work Environment

Food service managers usually work in food service facilities. They may manage facilities in field camps or aboard ships.

Training Provided

Job training consists of 12 to 16 weeks of classroom instruction. Course content typically includes:

Food service operations and management

Resource management

Nutritional meal planning

Hotel management

Civilian Counterparts

Civilian food service managers work for hotels, restaurants, and cafeterias. They perform duties similar to those performed by military food service managers.

Opportunities

The services have about 1,500 food service managers. On average, they need 150 new food service managers each year. After job training, food service managers may work independently or under the supervision of other officers. With experience, they may manage one or more large facilities. In time, they may advance to senior management positions.

Health Services Administrators

Army

Navy

Air Force

Coast Guard

In hospitals and clinics, all of the departments—emergency, X-ray, nursing, maintenance, administration, and food service—must work together to provide quality health care. Health services administrators manage hospitals, clinics, and other health care facilities. They also manage individual departments or specific health care programs within a hospital.

What They Do

Health services administrators in the military perform some or all of the following duties:

Develop and manage budgets for health care facilities or programs

Meet with hospital department heads to plan services and keep the health care facility running smoothly

Direct personnel activities, such as hiring, employee evaluation, staff development, and recordkeeping

Plan for delivering health services during emergencies and test these plans during exercises

Direct the day-to-day operations of the nursing department

Direct the operations of support departments, such as maintenance, food services, or administration

Special Requirements

A 4-year college degree in health care, public health, business, nursing administration, or a related field is required to enter most of the specialties in this occupation. Some specialties require further education or prior experience in the health services field.

Helpful Attributes

Helpful attributes include:

Interest in planning and directing the work of others

Interest in working closely with people

Ability to express ideas clearly and concisely

Interest in health care

Work Environment

Health services administrators work in hospitals, clinics, and other health care facilities. Most work at facilities on land, but some work aboard hospital ships and ships with large sick bays.

Training Provided

Job training is provided for some specialties in this occupation. This training consists of 10 to 12 weeks of classroom instruction and practical exercises. Course content typically includes:

Planning and directing health services

Patient unit management

Nursing service administration

Civilian Counterparts

Civilian health services administrators usually work for hospitals, clinics, nursing homes, health maintenance organizations (HMOs), or other health care facilities. They may also work for colleges and universities, public health agencies, insurance companies, or health management firms. Civilian health services administrators perform duties similar to those performed in the military. Depending on the programs or facilities they manage, civilian health services administrators may also be called hospital administrators, nursing services directors, emergency medical services coordinators, and outpatient services directors.

Opportunities

The services have about 3,100 health services administrators. On average, they need 200 new health services administrators each year. After job training, health services administrators may be assigned to a variety of positions depending on their specialty. Usually, they work under the direction of experienced officers. With experience, they may manage one or more departments in a facility. In time, they may direct a health services facility. Eventually, they may advance to senior management positions responsible for planning health services at many facilities.

International Relations Officers

Army

Navy

Air Force

Marine Corps

Information about the military capabilities of foreign countries is vital to our national defense. Our leaders need to know the strengths and weaknesses of both friendly and unfriendly countries. International relations officers collect, analyze, and report information about foreign countries to be used for military planning.

What They Do

International relations officers in the military perform some or all of the following duties:

Collect and report information about the military forces of foreign countries

Hold meetings with foreign military and government officials

Analyze political, social, and economic matters in foreign countries

Project foreign political trends

Advise commanders about situations in foreign countries

Special Requirements

A 4-year college degree is normally required to enter this occupation. Some specialties require an advanced degree. Knowledge of the people and language of one or more foreign countries may be required.

Helpful Attributes

Helpful fields of study include political science, history, and international affairs.

Helpful attributes include:

Ability to express ideas clearly and concisely

Interest in collecting and analyzing data

Interest in living and working in a foreign country

Interest in working closely with people

Work Environment

International relations officers work mainly in offices of U.S. embassies and missions located overseas.

Training Provided

Job training is provided in some specialties. Training length varies by entry requirements and specialty area. Course content typically includes:

Political and cultural awareness

Development of foreign area expertise

Organization and functions of diplomatic missions

Further training occurs on the job.

Civilian Counterparts

Civilians who perform work similar to the work of international relations officers are employed mainly by government agencies, such as the Department of State. Called foreign service officers, they work in U.S. embassies and missions overseas. Other civilian counterparts include political scientists, university instructors, and advisors to corporations doing business overseas.

Opportunities

The services have about 200 international relations officers. On average, they need 10 new international relations officers each year. Normally, international relations officers are selected from among officers who have several years of military experience. They are selected from a variety of military career fields. These officers usually return to their main career field after several years of duty as international relations officers.

Law Enforcement and Security Officers

Army
Navy
Air Force
Marine Corps
Coast Guard

The military services have their own police forces to protect lives and property on military bases and to patrol our coastal waters. Law enforcement and security officers command military police units that enforce laws and investigate crimes. They also plan and direct programs to protect property, communications, and classified information.

What They Do

Law enforcement and security officers in the military perform some or all of the following duties:

Direct the enforcement of military law

Develop policies and programs to prevent crime and reduce traffic accidents

Supervise the arrest, custody, transfer, and release of offenders

Plan and direct criminal investigations and investigations of suspected treason, sabotage, or espionage

Plan for the security of military bases and office buildings and direct security procedures

Manage military correctional facilities

Help in ballistics, forgery, fingerprinting, and polygraph (lie detector) examinations

Special Requirements

A 4-year college degree is normally required to enter this occupation. Some specialties require further education or prior experience in law enforcement and security.

Helpful Attributes

Helpful fields of study include business administration, criminal justice, psychology, sociology, and public administration.

Helpful attributes include:

Interest in law enforcement and crime prevention

Interest in planning and directing the work of others

Work Environment

Law enforcement and security officers in the military usually work in offices while planning and directing law enforcement and security activities. They may work outdoors while directing investigations, observing prisoners, and inspecting security systems.

293

Training Provided

Job training consists of 7 to 28 weeks of classroom instruction. Training length varies depending on specialty. Course content typically includes:

Law enforcement administration

Management of security problems

Investigation procedures and reporting

Military law

Civilian Counterparts

Civilian law enforcement and security officers work in federal, state, and local prisons, intelligence and law enforcement agencies, and private security companies. Some also operate their own security firms or become private detectives. They perform duties similar to those performed in the military. They may also be called police chiefs, chief inspectors, prison wardens, security managers, or chief deputy sheriffs.

Opportunities

The services have about 2,400 law enforcement and security officers. On average, they need 125 new law enforcement and security officers each year. After job training, officers are assigned to command police, security, or investigative units. Depending on ability and experience, law enforcement and security officers may be assigned to direct one or more large law enforcement units.

Management Analysts

Army

Navy

Air Force

Marine Corps

Coast Guard

Good management minimizes waste and inefficiency. By improving its management techniques, the military makes the best use of its human and material resources. Management analysts study and suggest better ways to organize, staff, and manage military activities.

What They Do

Management analysts in the military perform some or all of the following duties:

Measure work load and calculate how many persons are needed to perform the work

Study the information needs of managers and design manual or computerized systems to satisfy them

Design organizations for new or existing offices

Analyze work to be performed and develop an efficient implementation plan

Design rules or procedures for work activities or information flow

Gather data for studies by conducting interviews and reviewing records

Write reports and give briefings on findings

Special Requirements

A 4-year college degree is normally required to enter this occupation.

Helpful Attributes

Helpful fields of study include management, operations research, and business or public administration. Helpful attributes include:

Interest in solving problems

Interest in collecting and analyzing data

Ability to express ideas clearly and concisely

Work Environment

Management analysts normally work in offices, although they sometimes study work that occurs outdoors.

Training Provided

Job training consists of 6 to 10 weeks of classroom instruction. Training length varies depending on specialty. Course content typically includes:

Management engineering techniques

Methods of statistical analysis

Internal review and analysis techniques

Systems analysis procedures

Civilian Counterparts

Civilian management analysts often work in private management consulting firms. Many others work in hospitals, universities, government agencies, or manufacturing firms. Civilian management analysts perform duties similar to those performed in the military. They may specialize in areas such as records management analysis or systems management analysis.

Opportunities

The services have about 200 management analysts. On average, they need 10 new management analysts each year. After job training, management analysts are assigned to analysis teams. With experience, they may advance to senior management or command positions.

Personnel Managers

Navy
Army
Air Force
Marine Corps
Coast Guard

As with civilian employers, the military tries to find the best person for each job and encourages each individual to realize his or her full potential. Personnel managers direct programs to attract and select new personnel for the services, assign them to jobs, provide career counseling, and maintain personnel records.

What They Do

Personnel managers in the military perform some or all of the following duties:

Plan recruiting activities to interest qualified young people in the military

Direct testing and career counseling for military personnel

Classify personnel according to job aptitude, interest, and service need

Direct the assignment of personnel to jobs and training

Direct personnel recordkeeping operations

Establish standards to determine the number of people to assign to activities

Study military jobs to see how they can be improved and kept up-to-date with technology

Plan for hiring, training, and assigning personnel for the future

Develop programs to prevent and resolve equal opportunity problems

Special Requirements

A 4-year college degree is normally required to enter this occupation.

Work Environment

Personnel managers work in offices.

Helpful Attributes

Helpful fields of study include personnel management, organizational development, industrial psychology, and labor relations.

Helpful attributes include:

Interest in working closely with people

Interest in planning and directing the work of others

Interest in working with computers

Training Provided

Job training consists of 5 to 16 weeks of classroom instruction. Course content typically includes:

Military personnel policies and objectives

Automated personnel systems

Career development programs

Equal opportunity problems

Management and organizational concepts

Further training occurs in advanced courses.

Civilian Counterparts

Civilian personnel managers work for all types of businesses and industries, as well as for government agencies. They perform duties similar to those performed by military personnel managers. Depending on their specialty, they may also be called employment relations directors, employment managers, occupational analysts, industrial relations directors, equal employment opportunity representatives, or affirmative action coordinators.

295

Opportunities

The services have about 3,500 personnel managers. On average, they need 100 new personnel managers each year. After job training, personnel managers may be assigned to many different types of work, depending on their specialties. Usually, they begin by working under experienced personnel managers. In time, they may advance to senior management and command positions.

Postal Directors

Navy
Marine Corps

The military operates its own postal system, which is an extension of the U.S. Postal Service. This system handles mail sent between the services and civilians. Postal directors manage the postal operations for military bases and naval fleets.

What They Do

Postal directors in the military perform some or all of the following duties:

Direct the operation of post offices and mail rooms on military bases and ships

Work with the U.S. Postal Service to forward service mail

Keep information on the location and mailing addresses of military personnel

Prepare reports on postal operations

Inspect post office activities and records

Investigate postal irregularities

Special Requirements

A 4-year college degree is normally required to enter this occupation.

Helpful Attributes

Helpful fields of study include business or public administration and transportation management.

Helpful attributes include:

Ability to plan and organize

Interest in administrative work

Ability to express ideas clearly and concisely

Interest in working closely with others

Work Environment

Postal directors usually work in offices and postal facilities.

Training Provided

Job training consists of 4 weeks of classroom instruction. Course content typically includes:

Organization of postal operations

Post office services, such as money orders and certified mail

Procedures for handling international mail

Civilian Counterparts

Civilian postal directors work for the U.S. Postal Service. Also called postmasters, they perform duties similar to those performed by military postal directors.

Opportunities

The services have about 100 officers working as postal directors. On average, they need 10 new postal directors each year. Postal directors are usually selected from among officers who make their career in the various administration or management fields. Postal operations is only one of many administrative specialties they may work in at some time during their military careers. Officers normally do not have a career exclusively in postal operations.

Purchasing and Contracting Managers

Army
Navy
Air Force
Marine Corps
Coast Guard

The military buys billions of dollars worth of equipment, supplies, and services from private industry each year. The services must make sure their purchases meet military specifications and are made at a fair price. Purchasing and contracting managers negotiate, write, and monitor contracts for purchasing equipment, materials, and services.

What They Do

Purchasing and contracting managers in the military perform some or all of the following duties:

Review requests for supplies and services to make sure they are complete and accurate

Prepare bid invitations or requests for proposals for contracts with civilian firms, which specify the type, amount, price, and delivery date for supplies or services

Review bids or proposals and award contracts

Prepare formal contracts, specifying all terms and conditions

Review work to make sure that it meets the requirements of contracts

Special Requirements

A 4-year college degree is normally required to enter this occupation.

Helpful Attributes

Helpful fields of study include management and business or public administration.

Helpful attributes include:

Ability to develop detailed plans

Interest in work requiring accuracy and attention to detail

Interest in negotiating

Work Environment

Purchasing and contracting managers work in offices.

Training Provided

Job training consists of 3 to 10 weeks of classroom instruction. Training length varies depending on specialty. Course content typically includes:

Purchasing and accounting procedures

Use of computers in contract administration

Supply and financial management

Further training occurs through advanced courses.

Civilian Counterparts

Civilian purchasing and contracting managers work for a wide variety of employers, including engineering, manufacturing, and construction firms. They perform duties similar to those performed by military purchasing and contract managers. They may also be called procurement services managers, purchasing directors, contracts administrators, or material control managers.

Opportunities

The services have about 7,700 purchasing and contracting managers. On average, they need 200 new purchasing and contracting managers each year. After training, purchasing and contracting managers work with and advise commanders on contract proposals. With experience, they may advance to senior management and command positions.

Recruiting Managers

Navy

Air Force

Marine Corps

Coast Guard

Each year, over 300,000 young men and women enlist in the military, making it the country's largest employer of youth. The services recruit young people with the kinds of talent needed to succeed in today's military. Recruiting managers plan and direct the activities of recruiting specialists who provide information to young people about military careers.

What They Do

Recruiting managers in the military perform some or all of the following duties:

Plan programs to inform young people about military careers

Direct staff in local recruiting offices who carry out programs to inform the public about military careers

Speak with local civic groups, schools, parents, and young people about military careers

Prepare reports and brief commanders on recruiting goals and results

Special Requirements

A 4-year college degree is normally required to enter this occupation.

Helpful Attributes

Helpful fields of study include personnel management, communications, and public relations.

Helpful attributes include:

Interest in working closely with people

Ability to speak effectively to large and small groups of people

Work Environment

Recruiting managers usually work in offices.

Training Provided

No initial job training is provided to officers in this occupation.

Civilian Counterparts

Civilian recruiting managers work for personnel departments in business and government, searching for employment candidates. They also work for colleges, directing the activities of recruiters in their effort to attract talented high school students.

Opportunities

The services have about 100 recruiting managers. On average, they need 10 new managers each year. Normally, officers must be in the military for a few years before they are eligible to become recruiting managers. They do not always make a career in the recruiting field. Some spend only a few years in recruiting and then change to another occupation, often in the field of personnel or administration. Officers remaining in recruiting may advance to senior management or command positions in this field.

Store Managers

Army
Navy
Marine Corps
Coast Guard

The military operates retail stores for the convenience of service men and women. In some areas, particularly overseas, the goods and services offered at military stores, laundries, and barbershops are not otherwise available. Store managers direct the operation of retail service, food, and merchandise outlets. They also manage personnel who store food, supplies, and equipment.

What They Do

Store managers in the military perform some or all of the following duties:

Direct personnel in purchasing, pricing, and selling food, supplies, and equipment

Direct personnel in receiving, storing, and issuing supplies and equipment

Supervise the inspection, care, and testing of products before their use or sale

Plan training programs for new workers

Direct inventory, accounting, and other record keeping activities

Plan and prepare store budgets

Special Requirements

A 4-year college degree is normally required to enter this occupation.

Helpful Attributes

Helpful fields of study include management, accounting, marketing, business administration, and industrial management.

Helpful attributes include:

Interest in planning work schedules

Interest in managing a business

Interest in planning and directing the work of others

Work Environment

Store managers work in retail stores or warehouses on land and aboard ships.

Training Provided

Job training consists of 5 to 10 weeks of classroom instruction. Training length varies depending on specialty. Course content typically includes:

Accounting and record keeping

Inventory control

Retail store and warehouse management

Personnel and office administration

Budget management

Civilian Counterparts

Civilian store managers may work in many kinds of retail businesses. Some manage grocery, department, discount, and other large stores. Others manage warehouses that receive, store, and issue merchandise and supplies for retail outlets. Civilian store managers perform duties similar to those performed in the military. They may also be called retail store managers and distribution warehouse managers.

Opportunities

The services have about 1,000 store managers. On average, they need 70 new store managers each year. After job training, store managers are assigned to supply, exchange, or food service units. With experience, they may advance to senior management and command positions.

Supply and Warehousing Managers

Army

Navy

Air Force

Marine Corps

Coast Guard

The military needs vast amounts of supplies to feed and supply their personnel. Tons of materials such as food, fuel, medicine, and ammunition must be ordered, stored, and distributed each day. Supply and warehousing managers plan and direct personnel who order, receive, store, and issue equipment and supplies.

What They Do

Supply and warehousing managers in the military perform some or all of the following duties:

Analyze the demand for supplies and forecast future needs

Direct personnel who receive, inventory, store, and issue supplies and equipment

Manage the inspection, shipping, handling, and packaging of supplies and equipment

Direct the preparation of reports and records

Evaluate bids and proposals submitted by potential suppliers

Study ways to use space and distribute supplies efficiently

Special Requirements

A 4-year college degree is normally required to enter this occupation.

Helpful Attributes

Helpful fields of study include business administration, inventory management, and operations research. Helpful attributes include:

Interest in planning and directing the work of others

Ability to express ideas clearly and concisely

Work Environment

Supply and warehousing managers usually work in offices and warehouses. At times, they may be exposed to loud noise from machines and equipment.

Training Provided

Job training consists of 2 to 16 weeks of classroom instruction. Training length varies depending on specialty. Course content typically includes:

Warehousing and storage procedures

Handling and packaging procedures

Administrative procedures

Field supply management

Planning for future supply needs

Civilian Counterparts

Civilian supply and warehousing managers work for storage companies, manufacturers, hospitals, schools, and government agencies. They perform duties similar to those performed by military supply and warehousing managers. They may also be called warehouse managers or operations managers.

Opportunities

The services have about 8,300 supply and warehousing managers. On average, they need 400 new managers each year. After job training, supply and warehousing managers are assigned to positions in supply or munitions management. With experience, they may advance to senior management or command positions.

Teachers and Instructors

Army

Navy

Air Force

Marine Corps

Coast Guard

The military provides training and educational opportunities for all personnel. Teachers and instructors conduct classes in such academic subjects as engineering, physical science, social science, and nursing. Teachers and instructors teach military personnel subjects that are related to their military occupations.

What They Do

Teachers and instructors in the military perform some or all of the following duties:

Develop course content, training outlines, and lesson plans

Prepare training aids, assignments, and demonstrations

Deliver lectures

Conduct laboratory exercises and seminars

Give tests and evaluate student progress

Diagnose individual learning difficulties and offer help

Special Requirements

A 4-year college degree is normally required to enter this occupation. Some specialties require a master's degree.

Helpful Attributes

Helpful attributes include:

Ability to express ideas clearly and concisely

Interest in teaching

Preference for working closely with people

Work Environment

Teachers and instructors usually work in classrooms and lecture halls.

Training Provided

No initial job training is provided to officers in this occupation.

Civilian Counterparts

Civilian teachers and instructors work in junior colleges, colleges, and universities. They perform duties similar to those performed in the military. They may teach several different courses within the same field of study.

Opportunities

The services have about 1,800 officers working as teachers or instructors. On average, 100 officers become

military teachers and instructors each year. They are usually selected from officers trained and working in a military occupation. Many officers return to their regular occupations after teaching, but some remain as fulltime teachers. Eventually, teachers may become tenured professors at the service academies or other military colleges or managers of education programs.

Training and Education Directors

Army
Navy
Air Force
Marine Corps
Coast Guard

The military places great importance on training to prepare service men and women for their military careers. Programs include training in technical skills, physical fitness, and leadership development. Training and education directors plan, develop, and manage education and training programs for military personnel.

What They Do

Training and education directors in the military perform some or all of the following duties:

Develop new training courses

Review and approve course material and training outlines prepared by instructors

Plan and evaluate new teaching methods

Assign duties to instructors, curriculum planners, and training aids specialists

Evaluate the progress of students and instructors

Train instructors in course subject matter

Develop training and educational policies and objectives

Coordinate training for military personnel at civilian schools or through correspondence courses

Special Requirements

A 4-year college degree is normally required to enter this occupation. Some specialties require a master's degree.

Training Provided

No initial job training is provided to officers in this occupation.

Helpful Attributes

Helpful fields of study include education, physical education, organizational development, personnel management, and industrial psychology.

Helpful attributes include:

Interest in developing educational programs

Preference for working with people

Interest in work involving many subject areas

Work Environment

Education and training directors work in offices and classroom training facilities. Those directing physical training work in gyms or outdoor settings.

Civilian Counterparts

Civilian training and education directors work in schools, colleges, universities, vocational and technical schools, and training departments in business and industry. They perform duties similar to those performed by military training and education directors. They may also be called educational program directors, vocational training directors, and education supervisors.

Opportunities

The services have about 2,500 officers working as training and education directors. On average, they need 150 officers to become training directors each year. Training and education directors are usually selected from officers in many different occupational fields. They may direct training in their own or another occupational field. This occupation is normally available to officers who have had experience in an occupation besides education.

Transportation Maintenance Managers

Army
Navy
Air Force
Marine Corps
Coast Guard

The military's transportation system is made up of many different kinds of carriers, including ships, aircraft, trucks, and buses. Repair and maintenance schedules for each type of vehicle must be carefully planned and managed.

Transportation maintenance managers direct personnel who repair and maintain the military's transportation equipment.

What They Do

Transportation maintenance managers in the military perform some or all of the following duties:

Direct repair shop and garage operations

Set work schedules for repair shop staff

Oversee the ordering and use of repair parts, equipment, and supplies

Check repairs to make sure they are complete and finished on schedule

Oversee the preparation of maintenance records and reports

Develop maintenance standards and policies

Plan and develop training programs for staff

Special Requirements

A 4-year college degree is normally required to enter this occupation.

Helpful Attributes

Helpful fields of study include business administration, transportation management, vehicle and maintenance operations, and mechanical engineering. Helpful attributes include:

Interest in planning and directing the work of others

Interest in developing detailed plans

Work Environment

Transportation maintenance managers work in offices located in maintenance yards, shops, and garages.

Training Provided

Job training consists of 16 to 22 weeks of classroom instruction. Course content typically includes:

Management of aircraft or aircraft electronics (avionics) maintenance

Management of vehicle, railroad, and other equipment maintenance

Use of management information systems

Civilian Counterparts

Civilian transportation maintenance managers work in auto, bus, truck, and heavy construction equipment repair garages. They also work for aircraft service companies, aircraft builders, and commercial airline companies. They perform duties similar to those performed by military transportation maintenance managers.

Opportunities

The services have about 4,000 transportation maintenance managers. On average, they need 100 new transportation maintenance managers each year. After job training, transportation maintenance managers gain experience managing maintenance personnel. In time, they may become managers of larger maintenance facilities and advance to command positions.

Transportation Managers

Army

Navy

Air Force

Marine Corps

Coast Guard

Each year, the military transports thousands of service men and women and tons of material to bases across the U.S. and overseas. Ships, aircraft, trucks, buses, and trains are all part of the military's transportation system. Transportation managers direct the transport of military personnel and material by air, road, rail, and water.

What They Do

Transportation managers in the military perform some or all of the following duties:

Determine the fastest and most economical way to transport cargo or personnel

Direct the packing and crating of cargo

Direct the loading of freight and passengers

Schedule shipments to ensure fast and timely deliveries

Schedule pick-up and delivery of shipments

Oversee the handling of special items, such as medicine and explosives

See that transport forms, records, and reports are prepared correctly

Special Requirements

A 4-year college degree is normally required to enter this occupation.

Helpful Attributes

Helpful fields of study include transportation management, supply management, operations research, logistics, and business or public administration.

Helpful attributes include:

Interest in planning and directing the work of others

Ability to work under tight schedules

Work Environment

Transportation managers work in cargo and passenger terminals and depots.

Training Provided

Job training consists of between 8 and 12 weeks of classroom instruction. Training length varies depending on specialty. Course content typically includes:

Transportation management

Ways to work with civilian and other military service carriers

Freight classifications

Handling of special items, such as medicine and explosives

Civilian Counterparts

Civilian transportation managers work for airlines, railroads, bus lines, trucking companies, and shipping firms. They perform duties similar to those performed by military transportation managers. However, civilian transportation managers normally specialize in one area of transportation, such as air, water, truck, or railroad transportation.

Opportunities

The services have about 8,000 transportation managers. On average, they need 140 new transportation managers each year. After job training, transportation managers gain experience on the job. In time, they may advance to senior management or command positions in cargo transportation operations.

Human Service Occupations

Chaplains

Army

Navy

Air Force

The military provides for the spiritual needs of its personnel by offering religious services, moral guidance, and counseling. Chaplains conduct military worship services for military personnel and perform other spiritual duties covering beliefs and practices of all religious faiths.

What They Do

Chaplains in the military perform some or all of the following duties:

Conduct worship services in a variety of religious faiths

Perform religious rites and ceremonies, such as weddings and funeral services

Visit and provide spiritual guidance to personnel in hospitals and to their families

Counsel individuals who seek guidance

Promote attendance at religious services, retreats, and conferences

Oversee religious education programs, such as Sunday school and youth groups

Train lay leaders who conduct religious education programs

Prepare religious speeches and publications

Helpful Attributes

Helpful attributes include:

Ability to express ideas clearly and concisely

Interest in planning and directing the work of others

Sensitivity to the needs of others

Special Requirements

A master's degree in theology is required to enter this occupation. Ordination and ecclesiastical endorsement from a recognized religious denomination are also required.

Training Provided

Job training consists of 3 to 7 weeks of classroom instruction. Course content typically includes:

Role and responsibility of military chaplains

Administration and leadership techniques

Training and education methods

Procedures for planning programs

Pastoral counseling methods

Further training occurs on the job and through advanced courses.

Work Environment

Chaplains in the military usually work in offices, hospitals, and places of worship. Those assigned to sea duty work aboard ships. Those assigned to land combat units sometimes work outdoors.

Civilian Counterparts

Civilian chaplains work in places of worship, hospitals, universities, and correctional institutions. They perform duties similar to those performed in the military. However, they are almost always affiliated with a particular religious faith. Chaplains are also called clergy, ministers, preachers, priests, or rabbis.

Opportunities

The services have about 1,500 chaplains of various faiths. On average, they need 50 new chaplains each year. Military chaplains may advance to become directors of religious programs in their services.

Social Workers

Army

Navy

Air Force

The military needs close cooperation and a spirit of teamwork among its men and women. Social workers focus on improving conditions that cause social problems, such as drug and alcohol abuse, racism, and sexism.

What They Do

Social workers in the military perform some or all of the following duties:

Counsel military personnel and their family members

Supervise counselors and caseworkers

Survey military personnel to identify problems and plan solutions

Plan social action programs to rehabilitate personnel with problems

Plan and monitor equal opportunity programs

Conduct research on social problems and programs

Organize community activities on military bases

Physical Demands

Social workers need to be able to speak clearly and distinctly to work with clients.

Special Requirements

A 4-year college degree in social work or related social sciences is required to enter this occupation. Some specialties require a master's degree.

Work Environment

Social workers in the military usually work in offices or clinics.

Helpful Attributes

Helpful attributes include:

Desire to help others

Sensitivity to the needs of others

Ability to express ideas clearly and concisely

Interest in research and teaching

Training Provided

Job training consists of 16 to 24 weeks of instruction. Course content typically includes:

Ways of controlling drug and alcohol abuse among military personnel

Management of equal opportunity programs

Civilian Counterparts

Civilian social workers work for hospitals, human service agencies, and federal, state, county, and city governments. They perform duties similar to those performed by military social workers. However, civilian social workers usually specialize in a particular field, such as family services, child welfare, or medical services. They may also be called social group workers, medical social workers, psychiatric social workers, and social welfare administrators.

Opportunities

The services have about 100 social workers. On average, they need 10 new social workers each year. After job training, social workers are assigned to counseling or assistance centers. With experience, they may advance to senior management positions.

Media and Public Affairs Occupations

Audiovisual and Broadcast Directors

Army
Navy
Air Force
Marine Corps

The services produce many motion pictures, videotapes, and TV and radio broadcasts. These productions are used for training, news, and entertainment. Audiovisual and broadcast directors manage audiovisual projects. They may direct day-to-day filming or broadcasting or manage other directors.

What They Do

Audiovisual and broadcast directors in the military perform some or all of the following duties:

Plan and organize audiovisual projects, including films, videotapes, TV and radio broadcasts, and artwork displays

Determine the staff and equipment needed for productions

Set production controls and performance standards for audiovisual projects

Direct the preparation of scripts and determine camera-shooting schedules

Direct actors and technical staff during performances

Special Requirements

A 4-year college degree is normally required to enter this occupation.

Helpful Attributes

Helpful fields of study include audiovisual production, cinematography, communications, and graphic arts.

Helpful attributes include:

Interest in organizing and planning activities

Interest in planning and directing the work of others

Ability to transform ideas into visual images

Work Environment

Audiovisual and broadcast directors usually work in studios or offices. They may direct film crews on location in military camps or combat zones.

Training Provided

Job training consists of 15 to 19 weeks of classroom instruction. Training length varies depending on specialty. Course content typically includes:

Public information management principles

Management of military broadcasting facilities

Motion picture and television production management

Civilian Counterparts

Civilian audiovisual and broadcast directors work for television networks and stations, motion picture companies, public relations and advertising firms, and government agencies. They perform duties similar to those performed by military audiovisual and broadcast directors.

Opportunities

The services have about 100 audiovisual and broadcast directors. On average, they need 10 new audiovisual and broadcast directors each year. After job training, audiovisual and broadcast directors work in production units directing the work of audiovisual technicians and specialists. In time, they may advance to management positions in the broadcasting and public affairs fields.

Music Directors

Army

Navy

Air Force

Marine Corps

Bands have a long tradition in the armed services. Military bands all over the world provide music for marching and parade activities, concerts, and stage presentations. Music directors plan, develop, and direct the activities of military bands. They also conduct band performances during concerts and parades.

What They Do

Music directors in the military perform some or all of the following duties:

Plan musical programs

Lead bands and choirs in performances

Supervise training and rehearsal of musicians and choirs

Determine funding needs for bands and choirs

Plan purchases of instruments, equipment, and facilities

Provide commanders with ideas for musical programs and ceremonies

Physical Demands

A "good ear" for musical notes is required.

Special Requirements

A 4-year college degree in music or music education is required to enter this occupation.

Helpful Attributes

Helpful attributes include:

Interest in music theory

Appreciation for many types of music, including marches, classics, pop, and jazz

Interest in planning and organizing the work of others

Work Environment

Music directors usually work in offices and band halls. They may work outdoors when conducting or practicing for parades.

305

Training Provided

Job training consists of 20 to 40 weeks of classroom instruction. Training length varies depending on specialty. Course content typically includes:

Band arranging and conducting

Concert and marching band styles and techniques

Band administration and management

Civilian Counterparts

Many civilian music directors work for college and high school music departments and civic and community orchestras. Others work in the motion picture, television, and studio recording industries. Civilian music directors perform duties similar to those performed in the military. They may also be called band directors, band leaders, orchestra leaders, or conductors.

Opportunities

The services have about 70 music directors. On average, they need 10 new music directors each year. After job training, music directors are assigned to military band units, where they plan and direct musical programs. With experience, they may assume command of larger military bands or direct the activities of several bands.

Public Information Officers

Army

Navy

Air Force

Marine Corps

Coast Guard

The services have public information officers to keep the public informed about the military. These officers answer questions from the news media, members of Congress, private citizens, and service personnel. They also prepare reports and news releases about activities on military bases and service policies and operations.

What They Do

Public information officers in the military perform some or all of the following duties:

Supervise the preparation of reports and other releases to the public and the military

Brief military personnel before they meet with the public and the news media

Provide information to newspapers, TV and radio stations, and civic organizations

Schedule and conduct interviews and news conferences

Plan activities to improve public relations

Special Requirements

A 4-year college degree is normally required to enter this occupation.

Helpful Attributes

Helpful fields of study include journalism, communications, public relations, and advertising.

Helpful attributes include:

Ability to write clearly and simply

Ability to speak effectively in public

Interest in news and current events

Training Provided

Job training consists of 8 weeks of classroom instruction. Course content typically includes:

Department of Defense policies

Principles of public information and community relations

Civilian Counterparts

Civilian public information officers work for large corporations, government agencies, colleges and universities, and community groups. They perform duties similar to those performed by military public information officers. They may also be called public relations representatives and corporate communications specialists.

Work Environment

Public information officers usually work in offices.

Opportunities

The services have about 200 public information officers. On average, they need 10 new public information officers each year. After job training, public information officers normally direct specialists who gather information for reports, respond to requests for information, and write news releases. With experience, public information officers prepare and give briefings, speeches, and interviews. Eventually, they may advance to senior public affairs positions.

Health Diagnosing and Treating Practitioner Occupations

Dentists

Army

Navy

Air Force

Coast Guard

Dental care is a basic health service provided to men and women in the military. Military dentists examine, diagnose, and treat diseases and disorders of the mouth. They may practice general dentistry or work in one of several specialties.

What They Do

Dentists in the military perform some or all of the following duties:

Examine patients' teeth and gums to detect signs of disease or tooth decay

Examine X-rays to determine the soundness of teeth and the alignment of teeth and jaws

Locate and fill tooth cavities

Perform oral (mouth) surgery to treat problems with teeth, gums, or jaws

Develop and fit dentures (artificial teeth) to replace missing teeth

Construct and fit dental devices, such as braces and retainers, for straightening teeth

Plan dental health programs for patients to help prevent dental problems

Special Requirements

A doctor of dentistry degree and additional training in a dental specialty are required to enter this occupation.

Helpful Attributes

Helpful attributes include:

Desire to help others

Good eye-hand coordination

Work Environment

Dentists work in hospitals and dental clinics on land and aboard ships.

Civilian Counterparts

Civilian dentists work in private practice, public health facilities, and dental research organizations. They perform duties similar to those performed in the military and specialize in similar areas. Depending on their specialty, dentists may also be called oral pathologists, endodontists, oral surgeons, orthodontists, pedodontists, prosthodontists, periodontists, or public health dentists.

Training Provided

No initial job training is provided to officers in this occupation.

Opportunities

The military has about 1,900 dentists. On average, the services need 100 new dentists each year. Newly commissioned dentists are assigned to dental clinics to practice general dentistry or a dental specialty. Positions for dentists in the Coast Guard are filled by U.S. Public Health Service Officers. Dentists who demonstrate leadership and managerial qualities may advance to administer dental facilities and programs.

Optometrists

Army

Navy

Air Force

Eye care is part of the full health coverage provided to military personnel. The most common eye problem is the need for corrective lenses. Optometrists examine eyes and treat vision problems by prescribing glasses or contact lenses. They refer patients with eye diseases to ophthalmologists (eye medical doctors).

What They Do

Optometrists in the military perform some or all of the following duties:

Check patient vision using eye charts

Examine eyes for glaucoma and other diseases

Measure patient nearsightedness, farsightedness, depth perception, and other vision problems using optical instruments

Prescribe corrective lenses

Prescribe training exercises to strengthen weak eye muscles

Instruct patients on how to wear and care for contact lenses

Special Requirements

A doctor of optometry degree and a state license to practice optometry are required to enter this occupation.

Helpful Attributes

Helpful attributes include:

Preference for working closely with people

Desire to help others

Interest in work requiring accuracy and attention to detail

Work Environment

Optometrists work in clinics and hospitals.

Training Provided

No initial job training is provided to officers in this occupation. The Army has a program to provide financial support to optometry students in return for a period of obligated service.

Civilian Counterparts

Most civilian optometrists work in private practice. Some work for hospitals, clinics, public health agencies, or optical laboratories. Civilian optometrists perform duties similar to those performed in the military.

Opportunities

The services have about 250 optometrists. On average, they need 20 new optometrists each year. Newly commissioned optometrists are assigned to clinics or hospitals. In time, they may advance to senior management positions in the health service field.

Physicians and Surgeons

Army

Navy

Air Force

Coast Guard

Military physicians and surgeons represent all of the major fields of medical specialization. Physicians and surgeons are the chief providers of medical services to military personnel and their dependents. They examine patients, diagnose their injuries or illnesses, and provide medical treatment.

What They Do

Physicians and surgeons in the military perform some or all of the following duties:

Examine patients to detect abnormalities in pulse, breathing, or other body functions

Determine presence and extent of illness or injury by reviewing medical histories, X-rays, laboratory reports, and examination reports

Develop treatment plans that may include medication, therapy, or surgery

Perform surgery to treat injuries or illnesses

Advise patients on their health problems and personal habits

Coordinate the activities of nurses, physician assistants, medical specialists, therapists, and other medical personnel

Conduct medical research

Special Requirements

A doctor of medicine or osteopathy degree and advanced training in a medical specialty are required to enter this occupation.

Helpful Attributes

Helpful attributes include:

Desire to help others

Ability to express ideas clearly and concisely

Work Environment

Physicians and surgeons work in hospitals and clinics on land and aboard ships.

Training Provided

No initial job training is provided to officers in this occupation. However, advanced courses and programs in medical specialties are available. In addition, scholarships for advanced medical training are available in return for an obligated period of military service.

Civilian Counterparts

Civilian physicians work for hospitals or clinics or in private practice. They perform the same duties and work in the same areas of specialization as military physicians.

Opportunities

The services have a total of about 7,070 physicians and surgeons, including all general practitioners and specialists. On average, they need 760 new physicians and surgeons each year. The services give several hundred scholarships yearly to attend civilian medical schools or the Uniformed Services University of the Health Sciences in Bethesda, Maryland, in return for an obligated period of military service after graduation. The services normally hire physicians who have completed medical school and their internships. However, some services have programs to grant early officer commissions to civilians who are in medical school, internship, or residency status in return for an obligated period of service. Positions for physicians and surgeons in the Coast Guard are filled by U.S. Public Health Service Officers. After gaining experience in the military, physicians and surgeons may advance to senior management or command positions in the services' medical corps.

Psychologists

Army
Navy
Air Force
Coast Guard

Psychological research and treatment are important to national defense. Research can show how to improve military training, job assignment, and equipment design. Treatment can help personnel cope with stress. Psychologists conduct research on human behavior and treat patients with mental problems.

What They Do

Psychologists in the military perform some or all of the following duties:

Conduct research on human and animal behavior, emotions, and thinking processes

Conduct research on aptitude and job performance

Give psychological tests and interpret results to diagnose patients' problems

Treat patients individually and in groups

Conduct experiments to determine the best equipment design, work procedures, and training course content

Write research reports

Direct research projects performed by outside contractors

Special Requirements

A 4-year college degree in psychology is required to enter this occupation. Some specialties require a master's degree.

Helpful Attributes

Helpful attributes include:

Desire to help others

Interest in scientific research

Interest in mathematics and statistics

Work Environment

Psychologists usually work in offices, hospitals, clinics, and other medical facilities on land and aboard ships.

Civilian Counterparts

Some civilian psychologists treat patients in private practice, hospitals, school systems, and mental health centers. They are called clinical psychologists, counseling psychologists, or educational psychologists. Other civilian psychologists conduct research work for universities, research firms, and government agencies. They are called experimental psychologists, social psychologists, and psychometricians.

Training Provided

No initial job training is provided for officers in this occupation. Advanced courses are available in some specialties.

Opportunities

The services have about 300 psychologists. On average, they need 30 new psychologists each year. Positions for psychologists in the Coast Guard are filled by U.S. Public Health Service Officers. With experience, they may lead projects of their own. New clinical psychologists may treat patients in military clinics. Eventually, both research and clinical psychologists may become directors of offices or laboratories.

Health Care Occupations

Dietitians

Army

Navy

Air Force

Coast Guard

Dietitians are part of the military's health care staff. They are experts in the nutritional needs of hospital patients and outpatients. Dietitians manage medical food service facilities and plan meals for hospital patients and outpatients who need special diets.

What They Do

Dietitians in the military perform some or all of the following duties:

Set policies for hospital food service operations

Inspect hospital food service and preparation areas to be sure they meet sanitation and safety standards

Plan and organize training programs for medical food service personnel

Develop special diets for patients based on instructions from doctors

Plan menus for hospital meals

Interview patients to determine whether they are satisfied with their diet

Develop hospital food service budgets

Provide information on nutrition to the military community

Special Requirements

A 4-year college degree in food and nutrition or institutional management is required to enter this occupation. Some specialties require completion of a general dietetic internship.

Helpful Attributes

Helpful attributes include:

Desire to help others

Interest in nutrition and food preparation

Interest in interpreting scientific and medical data

Work Environment

Dietitians work in hospitals, clinics, and aboard ships.

Civilian Counterparts

Civilian dietitians work in hospitals, clinics, and other health care facilities. They perform duties similar to those performed by military dietitians. Dietitians also work for college food services, restaurants, industrial food services, and research institutions. Civilian dietitians may specialize in specific areas of dietetics, such as consultation, clinical dietetics, and community health.

Training Provided

No initial job training is provided to officers in this occupation. However, the Air Force and Army offer internship programs in dietetics that are approved by the American Dietetic Association.

Opportunities

The services have about 200 dietitians. On average, 20 new dietitians are needed each year. Newly commissioned dietitians are assigned to military hospitals, clinics, or ships, where they plan and direct the work of food service personnel. Positions for dietitians in the Coast Guard are filled by U.S. Public Health Service Officers. They may advance to senior management positions in hospital food service programs.

Physical and Occupational Therapists

Army

Navy

Air Force

Coast Guard

Physical and occupational therapies are programs of treatment and exercise for patients disabled from illness or injury. Physical and occupational therapists plan and administer therapy to help patients adjust to disabilities, regain independence, and prepare to return to work.

What They Do

Physical and occupational therapists in the military perform some or all of the following duties:

Test and interview patients to determine the extent of their disabilities

Plan and manage individual physical or occupational therapy programs

Consult with doctors and other therapists to discuss appropriate therapy and evaluate patients' progress

Administer exercise programs and heat and massage treatments

Counsel patients and their families to help create a positive attitude for recovery

Special Requirements

A 4-year college degree in physical or occupational therapy and completion of a clinical program in physical or occupational therapy are required to enter this occupation. Depending on specialty, a state physical therapy license or eligibility for registration with the American Occupational Therapy Association may also be required.

Helpful Attributes

Helpful attributes include:

Desire to help others

Interest in developing detailed plans and treatments

Patience to work with people whose injuries heal slowly

Ability to communicate effectively

Physical Demands

Physical and occupational therapists may have to lift and support patients during exercises and treatments.

Work Environment

Physical and occupational therapists work in hospitals, clinics, rehabilitation centers, and other medical facilities.

Training Provided

No initial job training is provided to officers in this occupation.

Civilian Counterparts

Civilian physical and occupational therapists work in hospitals, rehabilitation centers, nursing homes, schools, and community mental health centers. They perform duties similar to those performed by military therapists. Civilian physical and occupational therapists often specialize in treating a particular type of patient, such as children, the elderly, the severely disabled, or those who have lost arms or legs (amputees).

Opportunities

The services have about 300 physical and occupational therapists. On average, they need 30 new therapists each year. Positions for physical and occupational therapists in the Coast Guard are filled by U.S. Public Health Service Officers. Physical and occupational therapists have the opportunity to advance to senior management or command positions in medical administration.

Physician Assistants

Army

Navy

Air Force

Coast Guard

Physician assistants provide routine health care for patients, freeing physicians to concentrate on more serious health problems. Physician assistants examine, diagnose, and treat patients under the supervision of medical doctors.

What They Do

Physician assistants in the military perform some or all of the following duties:

Record medical histories, examine patients, and make initial diagnoses

Treat common illnesses or injuries, calling in supervising physicians for serious health problems

Perform routine physical examinations and collect specimens for laboratory tests

Order laboratory studies, such as blood tests, urinalysis, and X-rays

Provide information to patients about diet, family planning, use of drugs, and the effect of treatments

Provide emergency care in situations where doctors are not available

Special Requirements

Graduation from an accredited training program for physician assistants that is recognized by the services is normally required to enter this occupation. Depending upon the service, however, military job training may be available.

Work Environment

Physician assistants work in hospitals and clinics on land and aboard ships.

Training Provided

Job training, when available from the services, consists of about 40 weeks of classroom instruction, including practice in providing patient health care. Course content typically includes:

Fundamental medical care procedures

Principles of behavioral and dental science

Health care administration techniques

Civilian Counterparts

Civilian physician assistants work in hospitals, clinics, doctor's offices, and nursing homes. They perform duties similar to those performed by military physician assistants.

Helpful Attributes

Helpful attributes include:

Self-confidence and the ability to remain calm in stressful situations

Patience with others, especially those in pain or stress

Desire to help others

Ability to express ideas clearly and concisely

Opportunities

The services have about 400 physician assistants. On average, they need 20 new physician assistants each year. After job training, physician assistants provide health care under close supervision. With experience, they work more independently, although they remain under the supervision of a doctor. In time, they may advance to management positions in the military health care field.

Registered Nurses

Army

Navy

Air Force

Coast Guard

Nurses are a key part of the staff at military hospitals and clinics. Registered nurses direct nursing teams and give patients individual care to help them recover from illness or injury.

What They Do

Registered nurses in the military perform some or all of the following duties:

Help physicians treat patients

Give injections of pain killers, antibiotics, and other medicines as prescribed by physicians

Change bandages and dressings

Assist physicians during surgery

Provide life support treatment for patients needing emergency care

Provide care for mental health patients

Keep records of patients' condition

Supervise practical nurses, nurse aides, and other support personnel

Helpful Attributes

Helpful attributes include:

Desire to help others

Ability to express ideas clearly and concisely

Self-confidence and the ability to remain calm under pressure

Civilian Counterparts

Civilian registered nurses work in hospitals, clinics, and private medical facilities. They also work for public health agencies, nursing homes, and rehabilitation centers. Civilian registered nurses perform duties similar to those performed in the military. They often specialize and may be known as public health nurses, nurse practitioners, or general duty nurses.

Special Requirements

Graduation from an accredited school of nursing and a license to practice nursing are required to enter this occupation.

Training Provided

Job training consists of 14 to 27 weeks of classroom instruction. Training length varies depending on specialty. Course content typically includes:

Practices and principles of military nursing

Care of emotionally disturbed patients

Health care for children

Nursing techniques

Anesthesia, respiratory therapy, and cardiopulmonary resuscitation

Work Environment

Registered nurses work in hospitals and clinics. Some work in sick bays aboard ships or in mobile field hospitals. Others work in airplanes that transfer patients to medical centers.

Opportunities

The services have about 5,000 registered nurses. On average, they need 700 new registered nurses each year. Positions for registered nurses in the Coast Guard are filled by U.S. Public Health Service Officers. Depending on the prior experience that nurses bring with them to the military, their job assignments may vary. After job training, inexperienced nurses work under close supervision. Experienced nurses normally work under less supervision. In time, nurses may become nurse supervisors. Eventually, they may become directors of nursing in hospitals or advance to senior health service management positions.

Speech Therapists

Army
Navy
Air Force
Coast Guard

Speech therapists work as part of military medical teams. Speech therapists evaluate and treat patients with hearing and speech problems.

What They Do

Speech therapists in the military perform some or all of the following duties:

Talk with patients to discuss hearing and speaking problems and possible causes and treatment

Identify speaking and language problems

Examine the ears, including the entire auditory (hearing) system

Evaluate examination and test data to determine the type and amount of hearing loss

Treat hearing problems using hearing aids and other treatments

Assist patients in selecting and using hearing aids

Conduct programs to help patients improve their speaking skills

Research new techniques for treating hearing and speaking problems

Special Requirements

A master's degree in either audiology or speech therapy is required to enter this occupation depending on the occupational specialty.

Training Provided

No initial job training is provided to officers in this occupational group.

Helpful Attributes

Helpful attributes include:

Desire to help others

Interest in scientific work

Patience to work with people whose injuries heal slowly

Work Environment

Speech therapists work in therapy labs, clinics, and medical centers.

Civilian Counterparts

Civilian speech therapists work in hospitals, clinics, schools, and research centers. They perform duties similar to those performed by military speech therapists. Depending on their specialty, civilian speech therapists may also be called audiologists or speech pathologists.

Opportunities

The services have about 70 speech therapists. On average, they need 10 new therapists each year. Positions for speech therapists in the Coast Guard are filled by U.S. Public Health Service Officers. After displaying leadership abilities, speech therapists may advance to senior management and command positions in the medical field.

Engineering, Science, and Technical Occupations

Aerospace Engineers

Navy
Air Force
Marine Corps
Coast Guard

Although private companies build the military's aerospace equipment, military engineers are responsible for seeing that all equipment meets service needs. Aerospace engineers design and direct the development of military aircraft, missiles, and spacecraft:

What They Do

Aerospace engineers in the military perform some or all of the following duties:

Plan and conduct research on aircraft guidance, propulsion, and weapons systems

Study new designs for aircraft, missiles, and spacecraft

Help select private companies to build military aircraft, missiles, and spacecraft

Monitor production of aircraft, missiles, and spacecraft

Decide what tests should be conducted of prototypes (full-scale test models)

Conduct stress analysis and wind tunnel tests with aircraft and missile prototypes

Special Requirements

A 4-year college degree in aeronautical, astronautical, or mechanical engineering is required to enter this occupation.

Helpful Attributes

Helpful attributes include:

Interest in concepts and principles of engineering

Interest in working with mathematical formulas

Interest in planning and directing research projects

Work Environment

Aerospace engineers work in offices or laboratories.

Civilian Counterparts

Civilian aerospace engineers usually work in the aircraft manufacturing industry. Some work for the Department of Defense, the National Aeronautics and Space Administration (NASA), and other government agencies. As in the military, civilian aerospace engineers may specialize in one type of aerospace product, such as aircraft, missiles, or space vehicles. They may also specialize in engineering specialties such as product design, testing, or production research. Depending on their specialty, they may be called aeronautical engineers, aeronautical test engineers, or stress analysts.

Training Provided

No initial job training is provided to officers in this occupation.

Opportunities

The services have about 2,900 aerospace engineers. On average, they need 350 aerospace engineers each year. Newly commissioned aerospace engineers are usually assigned to engineering research and development units or laboratories. They work under the direction of experienced officers conducting research. With experience, they may serve as research and development managers or laboratory managers.

Air Traffic Control Managers

Army
Navy
Air Force
Marine Corps

Air traffic control centers often have several sections giving instructions to military aircraft. One section gives take-off and landing instructions. Another gives ground instructions. A third section tracks planes in flight. Air traffic control managers direct the operations of air traffic control centers.

What They Do

Air traffic control managers in the military perform some or all of the following duties:

Plan work schedules for air traffic controllers

Evaluate job performance of controllers

Manage air traffic control center operations to ensure safe and efficient flights

Inspect control center facilities and equipment

Direct tests of radar equipment and controller procedures

Investigate and find solutions to problems in control center operations

Control air traffic using radar and radios

Direct training for air traffic controllers

Physical Demands
Air traffic control personnel must pass a demanding physical exam as required by the Federal Aviation Administration (FAA).

Work Environment
Air traffic control managers work in air traffic control towers and centers at airfields and aboard ships.

Helpful Attributes
Helpful fields of study include aeronautical engineering, computer science, and liberal arts.

Helpful attributes include:

Interest in work requiring accuracy and attention to detail

Ability to remain calm in stressful situations

Decisiveness

Ability to manage in accordance with strict standards

Special Requirements
A 4-year college degree is normally required to enter this occupation. Certification by the FAA must usually be obtained during military training.

Training Provided
Job training consists of 6 to 11 weeks of classroom instruction. Training length varies depending on specialty. Course content typically includes:

Air traffic control management

Operational procedures for air traffic control

Communications and radar procedures

Aircraft recognition

Take-off, landing, and ground control procedures

Civilian Counterparts
Civilian air traffic control managers work at commercial airports. They perform duties similar to those performed by military air traffic control managers.

Opportunities
The services have about 300 air traffic control managers. On average, they need 10 new air traffic control managers each year. After job training, managers are assigned to air traffic control centers at airfields or aboard ships, where they gain experience in air traffic control management. They may advance to senior management and command positions in the aviation field.

Chemists

Army

Navy

Air Force

Marine Corps

The military conducts research in chemistry and biochemistry to develop new materials for military equipment, better medicines, and defenses against biological and chemical agents. Chemists conduct and manage research in chemistry, chemical engineering, and biology.

What They Do
Chemists in the military perform some or all of the following duties:

Conduct experiments in chemical synthesis, structure, and interactions

Establish strength and durability standards for materials used to build aircraft, ships, and other equipment

Test materials to identify defects and determine if they meet minimum military standards

Conduct chemical research for military and medical uses, such as protecting people from radiation, chemicals, and biological agents

Oversee research projects under contract to universities and industrial firms

Prepare technical reports and make research recommendations

Training Provided
No initial job training is provided to officers in this occupation.

Helpful Attributes

Helpful attributes include:

Interest in working with mathematical formulas

Interest in scientific study and research

Work Environment

Chemists work in laboratories and offices. Although they observe strict safety precautions, chemists may be exposed to hazardous substances.

Civilian Counterparts

Civilian chemists usually work in research and development for private industry, primarily in new product development. They also work for government agencies, colleges, and universities. Civilian chemists perform duties similar to those performed by chemists in the military. They sometimes specialize in areas such as organic chemistry, inorganic chemistry, physical chemistry, or biochemistry.

Special Requirements

A 4-year degree in chemistry, chemical engineering, or biology is required to enter this occupation.

Opportunities

The services have about 1,700 chemists. On average, they need 150 new chemists each year. Newly commissioned chemists are usually assigned to military laboratory facilities, where they perform duties in a chemistry specialty area. With experience, they may manage research and development units and advance to command positions.

Civil Engineers

Army

Navy

Air Force

Coast Guard

Marine Corps

Airfields, roads, bridges, buildings, power plants, docks, and water treatment plants on military bases around the world are continually being built, repaired, and improved. Civil engineers plan, design, and direct the construction of military facilities.

What They Do

Civil engineers in the military perform some or all of the following duties:

Study the need for roads, airfields, buildings, and other facilities

Direct surveys of construction areas

Design construction projects

Help select contractors to build facilities

Check construction progress to see that it meets plans

Plan and direct facility maintenance and modernization

Plan temporary facilities for use in emergencies

Keep master plans for military bases up to date

Special Requirements

A 4-year college degree in civil, architectural, sanitary, or environmental engineering, or another closely related field, is required to enter this occupation.

Helpful Attributes

Helpful attributes include:

Interest in engineering principles and concepts

Interest in working with mathematical formulas

Training Provided

No initial job training is provided to officers in this occupation. However, advanced courses are offered to support medical service and environmental control building programs.

Civilian Counterparts

Civilian civil engineers work for engineering firms, construction companies, and government agencies. Some may work for public utilities, railroads, and manufacturing firms. Civilian civil engineers perform duties similar to those performed in the military; however, they often specialize in certain types of projects.

Work Environment

Civil engineers work in offices when designing projects or reviewing reports. They work outdoors when overseeing survey or construction activities.

Opportunities

The services have about 4,700 civil engineers. On average, they need 450 new civil engineers each year. Newly commissioned civil engineers usually assist senior engineering officers in planning and design. With experience, they may manage construction projects and, eventually, engineering offices. In time, they may advance to senior management or command positions in the engineering field.

Computer Systems Officers

Army

Navy

Air Force

Marine Corps

Coast Guard

The military uses computers in almost every aspect of its operations. Military computers are used to process payroll and personnel information, control the targeting and firing of weapons systems, account for money, and make it easier to communicate around the world. Computer systems officers direct the operations of computer centers and are involved in the planning and development of computer systems.

What They Do

Computer systems officers in the military perform some or all of the following duties:

Prepare data processing plans and budgets

Develop and monitor contracts for data processing equipment and services

Translate military objectives and needs into computer systems requirements

Design and maintain computer software and data bases

Plan and oversee the installation of new equipment

Direct teams of computer systems specialists and computer programmers

Special Requirements

A 4-year college degree in computer science, computer or industrial engineering, business administration, or a related field is required to enter this occupation. Some specialties require a master's degree.

Helpful Attributes

Helpful attributes include:

Interest in working with computers

Interest in working with mathematical models and formulas

Interest in technical work

Work Environment

Computer systems officers in the military work in offices or at computer sites on military bases or aboard ships.

Training Provided

Job training consists of 5 to 18 weeks of classroom instruction. Training length varies depending on specialty. Course content typically includes:

Fiscal and contract management

Assessment of computer equipment needs

Computer systems development and project management

Civilian Counterparts

Civilian computer systems officers work for a wide variety of employers, such as banks, hospitals, manufacturers, financial firms, government agencies and firms that design and test computer systems. They perform duties similar to those performed by military computer systems officers. They may also be called information systems directors, ADP or EDP managers, computer systems engineers, software engineers, or systems analysts.

Opportunities

The services have about 3,500 computer systems officers. On average, they need 150 new computer systems officers each year. After job training, computer systems officers are assigned to units where they work in teams of engineers, systems analysts, and computer programmers. With experience and demonstrated leadership, they may advance to senior management or command positions in the computer systems field.

Electrical and Electronics Engineers

Army

Navy

Air Force

Marine Corps

Coast Guard

Equipment such as radar, missile guidance systems, and communication equipment depends on advanced electronics. Electrical and electronics engineers design, develop, and test electrical and electronic equipment. They also direct equipment installation and repair.

What They Do

Electrical and electronics engineers in the military perform some or all of the following duties:

Direct research to improve and develop computer, navigation, and other electronic systems

Direct equipment installation and repair

Develop test standards and operating instructions for electrical and electronic systems

Design and develop test instruments

Test new or modified equipment to check its performance and reliability

Review test data, report results, and recommend actions

Special Requirements

A 4-year college degree in electrical, electronic, or communications engineering is required to enter this occupation.

Helpful Attributes

Helpful attributes include:

Interest in engineering concepts and principles

Interest in planning and directing research projects

Interest in working with mathematical formulas

Work Environment

Electrical and electronics engineers usually work in offices while planning research studies and designing electronic systems. They may work outdoors when overseeing the installation of new equipment.

Civilian Counterparts

Civilian electrical and electronics engineers work for manufacturers of electrical and electronic equipment. Many work for government agencies, public utilities, and engineering firms. Civilian electrical and electronics engineers perform duties similar to those performed in the military. However, they usually specialize in product areas, such as computers, communications, or aerospace

systems. They may also be called electronics design engineers and electronics test engineers.

Training Provided

Initial job training is usually provided on the job. Classroom training is provided for some specialties in this occupation. Course content typically includes:

Combat and tactical communications systems

Telecommunications center systems

Signal center site defense systems

Opportunities

The services have about 1,000 electrical and electronics engineers. On average, they need 50 new engineers each year. After job training, electrical and electronics engineers are usually assigned to engineering research and development units or to communications centers. Initially, they conduct studies and supervise research and development staff. With experience, they may advance to senior management positions, such as engineering staff officer, research and development manager, or communications center director.

Environmental Health and Safety Officers

Army
Navy
Air Force
Marine Corps
Coast Guard

The services take great care to ensure safe working conditions and a clean environment. A clean, safe, and healthy environment results in happier employees and better work. Environmental health and safety officers study the air, ground, and water to identify and analyze sources of pollution and its effects. They also direct programs to control safety and health hazards in the work place.

What They Do

Environmental health and safety officers in the military perform some or all of the following duties:

Determine methods to collect environmental data for research projects and surveys

Analyze data to identify pollution problem areas

Inspect food samples to detect any spoilage or disease

Develop pollution control plans and policies

Conduct health education programs

Work with civilian public health officials in performing studies and analyzing results

Special Requirements

A 4-year college degree is normally required to enter this occupation. A degree in biomedical or biological science is required to enter some specialties in this occupation.

Training Provided

No initial job training is provided to officers in this occupation.

Helpful Attributes

Helpful fields of study include chemistry, biology, environmental sciences, soil science, civil engineering, and veterinary science.

Helpful attributes include:

Interest in protecting the environment

Interest in conducting research or analytical studies

Interest in work requiring accuracy and attention to detail

Work Environment

Environmental health and safety officers normally work in offices or research laboratories. They work outdoors while conducting environmental studies and surveys or inspecting facilities.

Civilian Counterparts

Civilian environmental health and safety officers work for engineering firms, manufacturing firms, and government agencies. They perform duties similar to those performed by military environmental health and safety officers. Depending on their specialty, they may be called environmental scientists, air pollution analysts, soil analysts, industrial hygienists, or water quality analysts.

Opportunities

The services have about 350 environmental health and safety officers. On average, they need 20 new environmental health and safety officers each year. Positions for environmental health and safety officers in the Coast Guard are filled by U.S. Public Health Service Officers.

New environmental health and safety officers are assigned to environmental health teams. After demonstrating leadership qualities, they may advance to senior management or command positions.

Industrial Engineers

Army

Navy

Air Force

Marine Corps

Coast Guard

Because the military is so large, small savings in personnel or equipment costs can result in savings of millions of dollars. Industrial engineers design ways to improve how the military uses its people and equipment.

What They Do

Industrial engineers in the military perform some or all of the following duties:

Study how workers and tasks are organized

Measure work load and calculate how many people are needed to perform work tasks

Study and improve the way work is done and equipment is used

Plan and oversee the purchase of equipment and services

Plan and direct quality control and production control programs

Special Requirements

A 4-year college degree in industrial engineering, industrial management, or a related field is required to enter this occupation.

Helpful Attributes

Helpful attributes include:

Interest in technical work

Ability to plan and organize studies

Interest in working with mathematical models and formulas

Interest in working closely with people

319

Work Environment

Industrial engineers usually work in offices. They may work outdoors while performing field studies or overseeing the installation of equipment and systems.

Training Provided

Job training is offered for some specialties. Training length varies from 8 to 16 weeks of classroom instruction, depending on the specialty. Course content typically includes:

Management standards, principles, and policies

Problem analysis and decision making

Production and purchasing methods

Civilian Counterparts

Civilian industrial engineers work primarily in manufacturing and consulting firms. They also work in other industries and businesses, including insurance companies, retail stores, banks, public utilities, and hospitals. Civilian industrial engineers perform duties similar to those performed in the military. Depending on the specialty, they may also be called production engineers, safety engineers, production planners, or quality control engineers.

Opportunities

The services have about 200 industrial engineers. On average, they need 10 new industrial engineers each year. After job training, industrial engineers are usually assigned to an engineering, management evaluation, or procurement unit. With experience, they may advance to command or policy-making positions in engineering, administration, or other fields.

Intelligence Officers

Army

Navy

Air Force

Marine Corps

Coast Guard

Information about the size, strength, location, and capabilities of enemy forces is essential to military operations and national defense. To gather information, the services rely on aerial photographs, human observation, and electronic monitoring using radar and supersensitive radios. Intelligence officers gather technical intelligence needed for military planning.

What They Do

Intelligence officers in the military perform some or all of the following duties:

Direct sea, ground, and aerial surveillance

Prepare plans to intercept foreign communications transmissions

Direct the analysis of aerial photos and other intelligence data

Oversee the writing of intelligence reports

Brief commanders on intelligence findings

Help plan military missions

Direct the use of computer systems to store and process intelligence data

Gather and analyze technical intelligence

Helpful Attributes

Helpful fields of study include cryptology, computer science, mathematics, and engineering.

Helpful attributes include:

Interest in solving problems

Interest in collecting and analyzing data

Ability to organize and manage activities

Ability to work with abstract problems

Training Provided

Job training consists of 23 to 26 weeks of classroom instruction. Course content typically includes:

Air, ground, and sea intelligence operations

Photograph interpretation and evaluation

Use of radar and electronic surveillance equipment

Reconnaissance equipment and weapons systems

Further training occurs on the job and through advanced courses.

Special Requirements

A 4-year college degree is normally required to enter this occupation.

Physical Demands

Normal color vision is required to work with map over-lays and color photos.

Work Environment

Intelligence officers work in offices on land and aboard ships. They may work in the field on maneuvers and military exercises.

Civilian Counterparts

Civilian intelligence officers generally work in federal agencies, such as the Central Intelligence Agency (CIA) and Federal Bureau of Investigations (FBI). They perform duties similar to those performed by military intelligence officers.

Opportunities

The services have about 6,550 intelligence officers. On average, they need 305 new intelligence officers each year. After job training, intelligence officers are assigned to intelligence units, military operations sections, or command posts. With experience, they may become com-manders of intelligence units or directors of information gathering sections.

Lawyers

Army

Navy

Air Force

Marine Corps

Coast Guard

The military has its own system of laws and courts. Lawyers administer activities within the military judicial system. They also perform legal research, prosecute and defend court cases, and preside over military courts. They provide legal services for military personnel and represent the services in civil and international legal matters.

What They Do

Lawyers in the military perform some or all of the following duties:

Give legal advice about government real estate, commercial contracts, patents, and trademarks

Prepare pretrial advice for clients in court-martial cases

Act as prosecuting attorney, defense attorney, or judge in court cases

Prepare legal documents, such as wills and powers of attorney

Interpret laws, directives, regulations, and court decisions

Preside over court cases and make judgments based on the Uniform Code of Military Justice

Help train new lawyers

Special Requirements

A degree in law is required to enter this occupation. In addition, most specialties require a membership to the bar in either federal court or the highest court of a state.

Helpful Attributes

Helpful attributes include:

Interest in working with and researching legal concepts

Ability to write clearly and concisely

Ability to speak effectively in public

Sensitivity to the needs of others

Work Environment

Lawyers work in legal offices and courtrooms on land and aboard ships.

Training Provided

Job training consists of 8 to 12 weeks of classroom in-struction. Training length varies depending on specialty. Course content typically includes:

Military trial procedures

Application of the Uniform Code of Military Justice

Methods of obtaining evidence

Court-martial advocacy techniques

Further training occurs on the job and through advanced courses.

Civilian Counterparts

Civilian lawyers work in private practice and for law firms, government, corporations, and nonprofit groups. They perform duties similar to those performed by military lawyers. Civilian lawyers, however, usually specialize in a particular field. There are several fields of civilian law, such as divorce, trade, and antitrust that military lawyers do not practice.

Opportunities

The services have about 2,500 lawyers. On average, they need 200 new lawyers each year. With experience, lawyers may be appointed military judges. In time, lawyers may advance to senior management positions in the legal field.

Life Scientists

Army

Navy

Air Force

The military conducts studies of human and animal diseases to understand their causes and to find treatments. Harmful pests and bacteria are studied to find ways to protect people and food against illness or infection. Life scientists study the biology and chemistry of living organisms.

What They Do

Life scientists in the military perform some or all of the following duties:

Study bacteria and parasites to determine how they invade and affect humans or animals

Study the effects of diseases, poisons, and radiation on laboratory animals

Study the effects of drugs, chemicals, and gases on living organisms

Study ways of protecting humans through immunization from disease

Direct blood banks and study blood chemistry

Study the effects of aerospace flight, temperature, and movement on human physiology

Study food storage and handling methods

Study ways of keeping bases and ships free from pests and contagious diseases

Conduct experiments and write technical reports

Special Requirements

A 4-year college degree is normally required to enter this occupation. Some specialties require a master's degree or medical degree.

Training Provided

No initial job training is provided to officers in this occupation. However, advanced courses are available in some specialties.

Helpful Attributes

Helpful fields of study include biochemistry, biology, microbiology, and pharmacology.

Helpful attributes include:

Interest in scientific work

Ability to express ideas clearly and concisely

Interest in mathematics, chemistry, biology, medicine, and medical research

Interest in collecting and analyzing scientific data

Work Environment

Life scientists work in medical, clinical, and research laboratories and, at times, in food processing or storage plants. They may work outdoors while conducting field work on land or aboard ships.

Civilian Counterparts

Civilian life scientists work for universities, government agencies, medical laboratories, blood banks, pharmaceutical firms, chemical companies, or in private practice. They perform duties similar to those performed by military life scientists. Depending on their specialty, civilian life scientists may be called biochemists, biologists, entomologists, immunologists, medical technologists, pharmacologists, physiologists, toxicologists, or veterinarians.

Opportunities

The services have about 500 life scientists. On average, they need 30 new life scientists each year. Newly commissioned life scientists are normally assigned to a laboratory, where they conduct research under the direction of more experienced scientists. In time, life scientists may manage their own research projects and direct other officers. Eventually, they may become directors of research laboratories or hold other senior management positions in the health research field.

Marine Engineers

Navy

Coast Guard

Ships and submarines must be designed for speed, strength, stability, and safety. Improvements in ship equipment, hull design, and deck layout can improve operations. Marine engineers design ships, submarines, and other watercraft for military use. They also oversee the construction and repair of ships and marine equipment.

What They Do

Marine engineers in the military perform some or all of the following duties:

Study new ways of designing and building ship hulls

Develop and test shipboard combat and salvage equipment

Oversee the construction, maintenance, and repair of ship hulls and equipment

Manage research programs to solve naval engineering problems

Oversee the installation, operation, and repair of marine equipment and systems

Evaluate marine research data and prepare technical reports

Special Requirements

A 4-year college degree in marine engineering is required to enter this occupation.

Helpful Attributes

Helpful attributes include:

Interest in technical work

Ability to plan and organize research projects

Interest in ships and shipbuilding

Training Provided

No initial job training is provided to officers in this occupation.

Civilian Counterparts

Civilian marine engineers work in the shipbuilding industry. They also work for government agencies and ship machinery manufacturers. Civilian marine engineers perform duties similar to those performed in the military. They may also be called marine equipment research engineers, marine architects, marine equipment design engineers, marine surveyors, and port engineers.

Work Environment

Marine engineers do much of their work outdoors at shipyards while overseeing shipbuilding and repair activities. They work in offices while directing vessel design and development activities.

Opportunities

The services have about 100 marine engineers. On average, they need 10 new marine engineers each year. Newly commissioned marine engineers may be assigned to engineering or marine research and development laboratories. They may also be assigned to work in shipyards with vessel maintenance and repair units. With experience, marine engineers may advance to senior engineering management and command positions.

Meteorologists

Navy
Air Force
Marine Corps

Meteorology is the study of the weather and weather forecasting. Military operations such as troop movements, airplane flights, missile launches, and ship movements rely on accurate weather information. Meteorologists study weather conditions and prepare current and long-range weather forecasts.

What They Do

Meteorologists in the military perform some or all of the following duties:

Direct personnel who collect weather data

Observe weather conditions from airplanes

Interpret weather data received from satellites and weather balloons

Prepare short-range and long-range weather forecasts

Relay forecast updates and violent weather warnings to military and civilian authorities

Train staff in data collection and interpretation

Physical Demands

Meteorology specialties involving air observation require applicants to pass a demanding flight physical exam.

Helpful Attributes

Helpful attributes include:

Interest in scientific work

Interest in collecting and analyzing data

Interest in working with mathematical formulas

Interest in planning and directing the work of others

Special Requirements

A 4-year college degree, with course work in meteorology, is usually required to enter this occupation.

Training Provided

Job training consists of 6 to 15 weeks of classroom instruction. Course content typically includes:

Identification of common weather patterns

Methods of analyzing weather conditions

Use of radar and satellite systems for weather data collection

Use of computers for compiling, analyzing, and plotting weather data

Techniques and procedures of forecasting

Work Environment

Meteorologists usually work in weather stations or operations centers where weather information can be collected, analyzed, and plotted using computers. Sometimes they work outdoors while making weather observations.

Civilian Counterparts

Civilian meteorologists work for government agencies, radio and television stations, and airlines. They perform duties similar to those performed by military meteorologists.

Opportunities

The services have about 800 meteorologists. On average, they need 40 new meteorologists each year. After job training, meteorologists are assigned to land-based or ship-board weather stations. With experience, they may advance to senior management and command positions.

Nuclear Engineers

Army

Navy

Marine Corps

The military has been a pioneer in the use of nuclear energy. The military uses nuclear energy for power plants, strategic weapons, and defense systems. Nuclear engineers direct research and development projects to improve military uses of nuclear energy. They also direct nuclear power plant operations.

What They Do

Nuclear engineers in the military perform some or all of the following duties:

Direct projects to improve nuclear power plants in ships and submarines

Direct research on the uses and effects of nuclear weapons

Develop safety procedures for handling nuclear weapons

Assist high-level officials in creating policies for developing and using nuclear technology

Direct operations and maintenance of nuclear power plants

Special Requirements

A 4-year college degree in physics, chemistry, or nuclear engineering is required to enter this occupation. Some specialties in this occupation require a master's degree.

Work Environment

Nuclear engineers work in offices, research laboratories, and power plant control centers, either on land or aboard nuclear-powered ships and submarines.

Helpful Attributes

Helpful attributes include:

Interest in scientific and technical work

Interest in planning and directing complex research projects

Interest in working with mathematical formulas

Interest in concepts and principles of engineering

Training Provided

No initial job training is provided to officers in this occupation. However, advanced training is available.

Civilian Counterparts

Civilian nuclear engineers work for firms that build and operate nuclear power plants and that develop and manufacture nuclear weapons. Many also work for public utilities, government agencies, and colleges and universities. Civilian nuclear engineers perform duties similar to those performed in the military.

Opportunities

The services have about 100 nuclear engineers. On average, they need 10 new nuclear engineers each year. Newly commissioned nuclear engineers are usually assigned to nuclear research laboratories, nuclear power plants (on shore or aboard ships), or other defense facilities. With experience, they may advance to senior management or command positions.

Oceanographers

Navy
Coast Guard

The military needs navigational charts and maps to safely travel the oceans. Accurate oceanographic and weather forecasts are also needed to plan military operations. Oceanographers study ocean tides, currents, weather, and the physical features of the ocean floor.

What They Do

Oceanographers in the military perform some or all of the following duties:

Direct personnel who collect oceanographic data

Conduct research on the effects of water and atmosphere on military warning and weapon systems

Direct the preparation of ocean, sea, and waterway charts, maps, and publications

Oversee the preparation of oceanographic and weather forecasts

Collect information on ice conditions in ocean shipping lanes

Collect information about ocean currents for support of military operational planning

Advise commanders about ocean and sea conditions to assist in search and rescue missions

Special Requirements

A 4-year college degree is normally required to enter this occupation.

Helpful Attributes

Helpful fields of study include oceanography, geology, marine engineering, and hydrology.

Helpful attributes include:

Preference for doing scientific work

Interest in sailing and being at sea

Interest in conducting research or analytical studies

Training Provided

No initial job training is provided to officers in this occupation.

Civilian Counterparts

Civilian oceanographers usually work for colleges and universities, where they are primarily involved in research. Some work for federal government agencies, such as the National Oceanic and Atmospheric Administration (NOAA) and for state and local governments that border on the ocean. Civilian oceanographers perform duties similar to those performed in the military.

Work Environment

Oceanographers work outdoors in all climates while collecting oceanographic information. They work in offices while preparing oceanographic publications and charts.

Opportunities

The services have about 100 oceanographers. On average, they need 10 new oceanographers each year. Newly commissioned oceanographers work in their specialty areas, usually with a senior officer. With experience, they work more independently. In time, they may advance to senior management or command positions.

Physicists

Army
Navy
Air Force
Coast Guard

The goal of military research is to improve the technologies used for national defense. Through physics research, new materials for building ships, aircraft, and weapons are discovered. Physicists direct research and development projects on physical matter and energy.

What They Do

Physicists in the military perform some or all of the following duties:

Plan and conduct experiments in aerodynamics, optics, geophysics, biophysics, and astrophysics

Conduct research to improve methods of radiation detection and protection

Analyze strength, flexibility, weight, and other properties of metals, plastics, and other materials

Conduct studies regarding the use of nuclear-powered engines

Write technical reports on experiments performed

Assist in research and development projects to improve radio and other communications equipment

Oversee research projects under contract to universities and industrial firms

Manage laboratories or field staff to conduct experiments

Special Requirements

A 4-year college degree in physics, chemistry, or nuclear engineering is required to enter this occupation. Some specialties require a master's degree.

Helpful Attributes

Helpful attributes include:

Interest in scientific and technical work

Interest in mathematics and physics

Interest in conducting research and analytical studies

Work Environment

Physicists usually work in research and development laboratories.

Training Provided

No initial job training is provided to officers in this occupation.

Civilian Counterparts

Civilian physicists work primarily in research and development for private industry, colleges and universities, and government agencies. They perform duties similar to those performed by military physicists. Civilian physicists usually specialize in one area of physics, such as nuclear, astronomical, health, or medical physics.

Opportunities

The services have about 100 physicists. On average, they need 10 new physicists each year. Newly commissioned physicists work as part of research teams. With experience, they may lead research projects of their own. After demonstrating leadership abilities, they may advance to senior management positions in a variety of scientific fields.

Space Operations Officers

Navy
Air Force
Marine Corps

Orbiting satellites and other space vehicles are used for national security, communications, weather forecasting, and space exploration. Space operations officers manage space flight planning, training, mission control, and other activities involved in launching and recovering spacecraft. They may also be astronauts who command space flights or who serve as crew members.

What They Do

Space operations officers in the military perform some or all of the following duties:

Manage activities of the flight control facility, including mission planning and training

Manage operation of guidance, navigation, and propulsion systems for ground and space vehicles

Develop space flight simulation exercises to train astronauts

Plan space stations

Direct space center launch and recovery activities

Command and pilot space shuttles

Perform in-orbit tasks and experiments aboard spacecraft

Monitor foreign space flights and missile launches

Physical Demands

Astronaut testing and training are very physically demanding. Officers must be in top physical shape to qualify for the astronaut shuttle program. Space operations officers must have normal color vision to read charts, graphics, and control panels.

Special Requirements

A 4-year college degree in science or engineering is required to enter the space operations field. A bachelor of science degree in engineering, mathematics, physical science, or life science is required to qualify as an astronaut.

Helpful Attributes

Helpful attributes include:

Interest in scientific research

Decisiveness

Ability to work well as a member of a team

Interest in space travel and desire to explore new frontiers

Civilian Counterparts

Most civilian space operations officers work for the National Aeronautics and Space Administration (NASA) in launch and mission control. They perform duties similar to those performed by military space operations officers. Some civilian space operations officers work for private corporations and firms that operate space satellites.

Work Environment

Launch and mission control space operations officers work in offices. Astronauts are required at times to work in a zero gravity environment in training as well as in space flight.

Training Provided

Job training for mission control officers consists of about 1 year of classroom instruction and practical experience. Course content typically includes:

Evaluation of space transport systems

Development of space mission plans

Methods for conducting space flight training programs

Development of space flight simulation exercises

Further training occurs on the job and through academic courses. Astronauts must complete the NASA astronaut candidate training school. They also receive 1 year of practical training in space transport systems.

Opportunities

The services have about 800 space operations officers. On average, they need 50 new space operations officers each year. After job training, new space operations officers are assigned to space operations, launch and mission control centers, or research facilities. With experience and special training, they have the opportunity to work in various areas such as astronautics or space flight control. Eventually, they may manage a space and ballistic missile warning facility, a satellite command center, a space launch system, a space systems analysis facility, or a manned space flight. Although Marine Corps officers may become astronauts and hold other positions in space operations, at present only the Navy and Air Force have defined career programs in this area.

Surveying and Mapping Managers

Army
Navy
Marine Corps

The military conducts land surveys to construct roads, airfields, and bridges. Land measurements are also needed to make maps and charts of unknown areas. Surveying and mapping managers plan and direct surveying and mapmaking operations.

What They Do

Surveying and mapping managers in the military perform some or all of the following duties:

Plan surveys and aerial photography missions

Direct the activities of survey teams

Direct the calculation of latitude and longitude, slope, elevation, and other features of the land

Direct mapmaking and drafting activities

Advise commanders about distance and location during military operations

Special Requirements
A 4-year college degree in photographic science, cartography, photogrammetry, or a related field is required to enter this occupation.

Helpful Attributes
Helpful attributes include:

Interest in planning and directing the work of others

Ability to visualize land features from maps and charts

Interest in construction and engineering

Physical Demands
Normal color vision is required to read color maps and aerial photographs.

Work Environment
Surveying and mapping managers usually work in engineering offices. They may work outdoors when assisting survey teams or during military operations.

Training Provided
Job training consists of 10 to 13 weeks of classroom instruction. Course content typically includes:

Mapmaking and charting techniques

Survey methods

Management of mapmaking programs

Civilian Counterparts
Civilian surveying and mapping managers usually work for engineering firms, where they manage construction project planning. They perform duties similar to those performed by military surveying and mapping managers. They may also be called land surveyors, cartographic supervisors, or photogrammetric engineers.

Opportunities
The services have about 400 surveying and mapping managers. On average, they need 10 new managers each year. After job training, surveying and mapping managers are usually assigned to engineering, surveying, or intelligence units or to mapmaking laboratories. Eventually, they may advance to senior management or command positions in the engineering field.

Transportation Occupations

Airplane Navigators

Navy
Air Force
Marine Corps
Coast Guard

Pilots rely on the precision and skill of the navigator to keep the aircraft on course. Airplane navigators use radar, radio and other navigation equipment to determine position, direction of travel, intended course, and other information about their flights.

What They Do
Airplane navigators in the military perform some or all of the following duties:

Direct aircraft course using radar, sight, and other navigation methods

Operate radios and other communication equipment to send and receive messages

Locate other aircraft using radar equipment

Operate bombardier systems during bombing runs

Inspect and test navigation and weapons systems before flights

Guide tankers and other airplanes during in-flight refueling operations

Provide pilots with instrument readings, fuel usage, and other flight information

Physical Demands

Airplane navigators, like pilots, have a physically and mentally demanding job. Navigators are required to have excellent vision and must be in top physical shape.

Special Requirements

A 4-year college degree is required to enter this occupation. Although there are women airplane navigators, some specialties are open only to men.

Work Environment

Airplane navigators perform their work in aircraft. They may be stationed at airbases or aboard aircraft carriers anywhere around the world.

Training Provided

Job training consists of 6 to 12 months of classroom instruction. Course content typically includes:

Principles and methods of navigation

Operation of communication, weapon, and radar systems

Inspection and testing of navigation equipment and systems

Combat and bombing navigation procedures and tactics

Practical experience in navigation is gained through training in aircraft simulators and through about 100 hours of actual flying time. Further training occurs on the job and through advanced courses.

Helpful Attributes

Helpful fields of study include cartography, geography, and surveying.

Helpful attributes include:

Ability to read maps and charts

Interest in work requiring accuracy and attention to detail

Ability to respond quickly to emergencies

Strong desire to fly

Civilian Counterparts

Civilian airplane navigators work for passenger and cargo airlines. With the exception of duties that are combat-related, their duties are similar to those performed by military navigators.

Opportunities

The services have about 4,000 airplane navigators. On average, they need 50 new navigators each year. After job training, airplane navigators are assigned to flying sections for duty. They work as officer crewmembers on bombers, tankers, fighters, or other airplanes. In time, they may advance to senior management or command positions.

Airplane Pilots

Army

Navy

Air Force

Marine Corps

Coast Guard

The military operates one of the largest fleets of specialized airplanes in the world. Supersonic fighters and bombers fly combat missions. Large transports carry troops and equipment. Intelligence gathering airplanes take photographs from high altitudes. Military airplane pilots fly the thousands of jet and propeller airplanes operated by the services.

What They Do

Airplane pilots in the military perform some or all of the following duties:

Check weather reports to learn about flying conditions

Develop flight plans showing air routes and schedules

Contact air traffic controllers to obtain take-off and landing instructions

Fly airplanes by controlling engines, rudders, elevators, and other controls

Monitor gauges and dials located on cockpit control panels

Perform combat maneuvers, take photographs, transport equipment, and patrol areas to carry out flight missions

Physical Demands

Airplane pilots must pass the most demanding physical test of any job in the military. To be accepted for pilot training, applicants must have 20/20 vision and be in top physical condition. They must have very good eye-hand coordination and have extremely quick reaction times to maneuver at high speeds.

Special Requirements

A 4-year college degree is normally required to enter this occupation. Although the military has many women pilots, specialties involving duty in combat airplanes are open only to men. Because all Marine Corps planes are combat planes, there are no women pilots in the Marines.

Work Environment

Airplane pilots may be stationed at airbases or aboard aircraft carriers anywhere in the world. They fly in all types of weather conditions. Military pilots take off and land on airport runways and aircraft carrier landing decks.

Training Provided

Pilot training is a 2-year program covering 1 year each in initial and advanced training. Initial training includes time spent in flight simulators, classroom training, officer training, and basic flight training. Course content typically includes:

Aircraft aerodynamics

Jet and propeller engine operation

Operation of aircraft navigation systems

Foul weather flying

Federal Aviation Administration (FAA) regulations

This is among the most challenging training given by the services; not everyone who attempts this training can meet the strict requirements for completion. Advanced training begins when pilots successfully complete initial training and are awarded their "wings." Advanced training consists of instruction in flying a particular type of aircraft.

Helpful Attributes

Helpful fields of study include physics and aerospace, electrical, or mechanical engineering.

Helpful attributes include:

Strong desire to fly airplanes

Self-confidence and ability to remain calm in stressful situations

Determination to complete a very demanding training program

Civilian Counterparts

Civilian airplane pilots who work for passenger airlines and air cargo businesses are called commercial pilots. Other civilian pilots work as flight instructors at local airports, as crop dusters, or as pilots transporting business executives in company planes. Many commercial pilots began their career in the military.

Opportunities

The services have about 18,000 airplane pilots. On average, they need 150 new pilots each year. After initial and advanced training, most pilots are assigned to flying squadrons to fly the types of aircraft for which they were trained. In time, pilots train for different aircraft and missions. Eventually, they may advance to senior management or command positions.

Helicopter Pilots

Army
Navy
Air Force
Marine Corps
Coast Guard

Helicopters can take off from and land on small areas. They can also hover in one spot in the air. The military uses these versatile aircraft to transport troops and cargo, perform search and rescue missions, and provide close combat support for ground troops. Helicopter pilots fly the many helicopters operated by the services.

What They Do

Helicopter pilots in the military perform some or all of the following duties:

Prepare flight plans showing air routes and schedules

Fly helicopters by controlling engines, flight controls, and other systems

Monitor gauges and dials located on cockpit control panels

Perform combat maneuvers, spot and observe enemy positions, transport troops and equipment, and evacuate wounded troops

Check weather reports to learn about flying conditions

Physical Demands

Helicopter pilots must pass some of the most demanding physical tests of any job in the military. To be accepted for pilot training, applicants must have excellent vision and be in top physical condition. They must have very good eye-hand-foot coordination and have quick reflexes.

Special Requirements

A 4-year college degree is normally required to enter this occupation. Some specialties in the Army do not require a 4-year college degree, but are only open to personnel who have been in the service for several years and who are selected for a special pilot training program. Although there are women helicopter pilots, some specialties are open only to men. The Marine Corps has no women helicopter pilots because all specialties involve duty in combat aircraft.

Helpful Attributes

Helpful fields of study include physics and aerospace, electrical, or mechanical engineering.

Helpful attributes include:

Strong desire to fly aircraft

Determination to complete a very demanding training program

Self-confidence and ability to remain calm under stress

Training Provided

Job training consists of 1 to 2 years of academic and flight instruction. Flight training consists of at least 80 hours of flying time. Training length varies depending on specialty. Course content typically includes:

Principles of helicopter operation

Principles of helicopter inspection

Flying techniques and emergency procedures

Combat skills and tactics

Work Environment

Helicopter pilots are stationed at military bases or aboard aircraft carriers around the world. They fly in all types of weather conditions. Helicopter pilots take off and land from airports, forward landing areas, and ship landing decks.

Civilian Counterparts

Civilian helicopter pilots work for police forces, local commuter services, and private businesses. They also work as crop dusters, fire fighters, traffic spotters, and helicopter flight instructors.

Opportunities

The military has about 3,300 helicopter pilots. On average, the services need 80 new pilots each year. After receiving their pilot rating, helicopter pilots are assigned to flying units. With experience, they may become group leaders or flight instructors. Helicopter pilots may advance to senior management and command positions.

Ship and Submarine Officers

Army

Navy

Coast Guard

Ships and submarines are organized by departments, such as engineering, communications, weapons, and supply. Ship and submarine officers work as team members to manage the various departments aboard their vessels.

What They Do

Ship and submarine officers in the military perform some or all of the following duties:

Command vessels of all sizes at sea or in coastal waters

Plan and manage the operating departments, under the captain's direction

Plan and manage training exercises, such as target practice, aircraft operations, damage control drills, and searches for enemy submarines

Evaluate subordinate personnel and recommend awards and promotions

Direct search and rescue missions

Physical Demands

Good vision and normal color vision are required for reading color-coded charts and maps and, for submarine duty, for adjusting to red-light vision prior to surfacing at night.

Special Requirements

A 4-year college degree is normally required to enter this occupation. Although there are women ship officers, some assignments, such as submarine duty, are open only to men.

Work Environment

Ship and submarine officers work aboard their vessels. Engineering officers are subjected to hot, humid, and noisy environments. Submarine officers work in confined spaces for extended periods.

Training Provided

Job training consists of classroom instruction and practical experience in one of the following departments: air, weapons, operations, communications, engineering, deck, administration, or supply. Training length varies depending on specialty. Course content typically includes:

Management and organization of ship or submarine operations

Responsibilities of the individual departments

Piloting and navigation of ships

Interpretation of maritime laws and policies

Further training occurs on the job and through advanced courses.

Civilian Counterparts

Civilian ship officers work for private maritime passenger, freight, and tanker firms. With the exception of duties that are combat related, their duties are similar to those performed by military ship officers.

Helpful Attributes

Helpful fields of study include engineering, oceanography, mathematics, and computer science.

Helpful attributes include:

Ability to organize and direct the work of others

Interest in sailing and being at sea

Ability to motivate and lead others

Opportunities

The services have about 3,000 ship and submarine officers. On average, they need 50 new ship and submarine officers each year. After job training, officers are assigned

to management positions in one of the ship's departments working under more experienced officers. With experience and demonstrated ability to lead, they assume greater responsibility. Depending on their specialty, ship and submarine officers gain experience in more than one department. Also, they are regularly reassigned to different ships or submarines where they meet and work with new people. Between sea tours, they work and attend training at shore bases. Eventually, ship and submarine officers may be selected to command a vessel.

Ship Engineers

Army
Navy
Coast Guard

Engines are a ship's main source of power for propulsion, heat, and electricity. Ship engines are massive; some are as large as the power plants that generate electricity for small cities. Ship engineers direct the engineering departments aboard ships and submarines. They are responsible for engine operations, maintenance, and repair. They are also responsible for shipboard heating and power generation.

What They Do

Ship engineers in the military perform some or all of the following duties:

Direct engine room operations in nuclear or diesel-powered vessels

Direct crews that inspect and maintain the electrical generators that supply power for lights, weapons, and equipment

Direct crews that inspect and maintain the heating plants and air conditioning systems

Direct crews that inspect and maintain ship transmission and propulsion systems

Direct engine room repairs

Special Requirements

A 4-year college degree is normally required to enter this occupation. Nuclear specialties require a 4-year college degree in nuclear engineering.

Helpful Attributes

Helpful fields of study include civil, mechanical, and electrical engineering.

Helpful attributes include:

Interest in planning and directing the work of others

Interest in engines and machines

Work Environment

Ship engineers work in engine rooms, where the noise levels and temperatures may be high.

Training Provided

Job training consists of 3 to 12 months of instruction. Training length varies depending on specialty; the time required for nuclear specialties is the longest. Course content typically includes:

Inspection and maintenance of marine engines, electrical systems, and fuel systems

Operation and maintenance of steam plants and related machinery

Further training occurs on the job and through advanced courses. Nuclear specialties involve extensive training in reactor operations.

Civilian Counterparts

Civilian ship engineers work for shipping lines, transport companies, and some government agencies. They perform duties similar to those performed by military ship engineers. Civilian ship engineers may also be called engineers or marine engineers.

Opportunities

The services have about 600 ship engineers. On average, they need 10 new ship engineers each year. After job training, ship engineers work as assistant engineers under the direction of a chief engineer. With experience, they may advance to become chief engineer in charge of an engineering department. Eventually, they may advance to senior management and command positions.

Combat Specialty Occupations

Artillery Officers

Army
Navy
Marine Corps
Coast Guard

The military uses artillery to support infantry and tank units in combat and to protect land and sea forces from air attack. Artillery officers direct artillery crew members as they position, maintain, and fire guns, cannons, howitzers, and rockets at enemy positions and aircraft. They normally specialize by type of artillery.

What They Do

Artillery officers in the military perform some or all of the following duties:

Direct training activities of artillery and gun crew members

Direct fire control operations and firing procedures

Direct naval gunnery operations

Select location of artillery and coordinate their use with infantry and tank units

Direct air defense missile system operations

Direct maintenance of artillery fire control equipment

Physical Demands

Physical requirements vary depending upon the type of artillery unit to which the officer is assigned. In most instances, artillery officers must meet very demanding physical requirements. They must be able to perform for long periods of time without rest and to work under stress.

Special Requirements

A 4-year college degree is normally required to enter this occupation. Although there are women artillery officers, some specialties in this occupation are open only to men.

Helpful Attributes

Helpful fields of study include engineering, physics, and chemistry.

Helpful attributes include:

Ability to motivate and lead others

Decisiveness

Willingness to accept a challenge and face danger

Training Provided

Job training consists of 3 to 19 weeks of classroom instruction and field training under simulated combat

333

conditions. Training length varies depending on specialty. Course content typically includes:

Artillery tactics

Ammunition handling procedures

Fire direction control procedures

Air defense artillery duties

Further training occurs on the job and through advanced courses.

Work Environment

Artillery officers live and work under the same conditions as the personnel they lead. Some artillery officers spend a lot of time in field training exercises, where they work, eat, and sleep outdoors and in tents. Others work and live aboard ships.

Civilian Counterparts

Although the job of artillery officer has no equivalent in civilian life, the leadership and administrative experiences it provides are similar to those used in many civilian management occupations.

Opportunities

The services have about 11,200 artillery officers. On average, they need 700 new artillery officers each year. After training, new artillery officers usually assist commanders in directing artillery units. After demonstrating leadership ability, they may advance to command positions.

Infantry Officers

Army
Marine Corps

In peacetime, the infantry stays ready to defend the country anywhere in the world. In combat, the infantry is deployed to capture or destroy enemy forces on the ground and to repel enemy invasions. Infantry officers direct, train, and lead infantry units.

What They Do

Infantry officers in the military perform some or all of the following duties:

Gather and evaluate intelligence on enemy strength and positions

Develop offensive and defensive battle plans

Coordinate plans with armor, artillery, and air support units

Direct construction of bunkers, fortifications, and obstacles to support and camouflage infantry positions

Direct the use of infantry weapons and equipment, such as machine guns, mortars, rocket launchers, and armored personnel carriers

Develop and supervise infantry unit training

Direct administrative activities

Physical Demands

Infantry officers must meet the same demanding physical requirements as the infantrymen they command. They must be in excellent physical condition to perform strenuous activities over long periods of time, sometimes without sleep or rest.

Special Requirements

A 4-year college degree is normally required to enter this occupation. This occupation is open only to men.

Work Environment

Because infantry officers must be prepared to lead their troops anywhere in the world that the infantry is needed, they work and train in all climates and weather conditions. During training exercises, as in real combat situations, infantry officers work, eat, and sleep outdoors and in tents. When not in the field, infantry officers perform administrative and management duties in offices.

Training Provided

Job training consists of 8 to 14 weeks of classroom instruction and field training under simulated combat conditions. Training length varies depending on specialty. Course content typically includes:

Infantry leadership roles

Infantry squad and platoon tactics

Modern offensive and defensive combat techniques

Helpful Attributes

Helpful fields of study include engineering, history, physical education, and business or public administration.

Helpful attributes include:

Ability to motivate and lead others

Willingness to accept a challenge and face danger

Interest in land battle history and strategy

Civilian Counterparts

Although the job of infantry officer has no equivalent in civilian life, the leadership and administrative skills it provides are similar to those used in many civilian managerial occupations.

Opportunities

The services have about 11,000 infantry officers. On average, they need 700 new infantry officers each year. After job training, infantry officers are assigned to infantry units as platoon leaders. They direct training and tactical exercises for war games. Advancement in the infantry is based on ability to lead. Infantry officers with proven ability to lead may assume command positions.

Missile System Officers

Army

Navy

Air Force

Marine Corps

Ballistic missiles are powerful weapons that travel thousands of miles to their targets. They are fired from underground silos, submarines, and land-based launchers. Missile system officers direct missile crews as they target, launch, test, and maintain ballistic missiles.

What They Do

Missile system officers in the military perform some or all of the following duties:

Stand watch as members of missile launch crews

Direct testing and inspection of missile systems

Direct missile maintenance operations

Direct early-warning launch training exercises

Direct security operations at missile sites

Direct the storage and handling of nuclear warheads

Direct operation of fail-safe and code verification systems

Special Requirements

A 4-year college degree is normally required to enter this occupation. For some specialties, a master's degree in management is preferred.

Helpful Attributes

Helpful fields of study include engineering, physics, computer science, and business or public administration.

Helpful attributes include:

Ability to motivate and lead others

Ability to remain calm in stressful situations

Ability to learn and precisely follow complex procedures

Work Environment

Missile system officers work in underground launch command centers, in submarines, and in ground-level missile sites.

Training Provided

Job training consists of 12 to 19 weeks of classroom instruction and training on missile system simulations. Training length varies depending on specialty. Course content typically includes:

Missile targeting

Security and code authentication

Launch operations

Maintenance programs

Further training occurs on the job and through advanced courses.

Civilian Counterparts

Although the job of missile system officer has no equivalent in civilian life, the leadership skills it provides are similar to those used in many civilian occupations.

Opportunities

The services have about 1,000 missile system officers. On average, they need 100 new officers each year. After job training, new missile system officers normally learn the details of missile operations by focusing on one aspect at a time under the direction of experienced officers. In time, they manage one or more divisions at a missile site, assuming more responsibility. Eventually they may advance to senior management and command positions in missile operations or other areas in their service.

Special Operations Officers

Army
Navy
Air Force
Marine Corps

Each service has specially trained forces to perform rapid strike missions. These elite forces stay in a constant state of readiness to strike anywhere in the world on a moment's notice. Special operations officers lead special operations forces in offensive raids, demolitions, intelligence gathering, and search and rescue missions. Due to the wide variety of missions, special operations officers are trained swimmers, parachutists, and survival experts.

What They Do

Special operations officers in the military perform some or all of the following duties:

Train personnel in parachute, scuba diving, and special combat techniques

Plan missions and coordinate plans with other forces as needed

Train personnel for special missions using simulated mission conditions

Lead special forces teams in accomplishing mission objectives

Direct and supervise administrative activities of special forces units

Physical Demands

Special operations officers must meet very demanding physical requirements. Good eyesight, night vision, and physical conditioning are required to reach mission objectives by parachute, over land, or underwater. Good eye-hand coordination is required to detonate or deactivate explosives. In most instances, special operations officers are required to be qualified swimmers, parachutists, and endurance runners.

Special Requirements

A 4-year college degree is normally required to enter this occupation. Selection as a special operations officer is very competitive. This occupation is open only to men.

Helpful Attributes

Helpful fields of study include physical education, engineering, physical sciences, history, and business or public administration.

Helpful attributes include:

Ability to remain calm and decisive under stress

Willingness to accept a challenge and face danger

Willingness to stay in top physical condition

Determination to complete a very demanding training program

Work Environment

Because special operations officers must be prepared to go anywhere in the world they are needed, they train and work in all climates, weather conditions, and settings. They may work in cold water and dive from submarines or small underwater craft. They may also be exposed to harsh temperatures, often without protection, during missions into enemy-controlled areas.

Training Provided

Job training consists of up to 20 weeks of formal classroom training and practical experience. Training length varies depending on specialty. Course content typically includes:

Physical conditioning, scuba diving, swimming, and parachuting

Mission planning techniques

Handling and using explosives

Reconnaissance techniques

Additional training occurs on the job. Basic skills are kept sharp through planning and conducting exercises under simulated mission conditions.

Civilian Counterparts

Although the job of special operations officer has no equivalent in civilian life, the leadership and administrative skills it provides are similar to those used in many civilian management occupations, particularly law enforcement.

Opportunities

The services have about 1,900 special operations officers. On average they need 20 new special operations

Military Career Opportunities

officers each year. After training, special operations officers usually assist commanders in directing special operations forces. After demonstrating leadership ability, they may assume command positions.

Tank Officers

Army
Marine Corps

In peacetime, tank and armor units stay ready to defend the country anywhere in the world. In combat, they operate tanks, armored vehicles, and amphibious assault vehicles to engage and destroy the enemy. Tank officers lead tank and armor units. They normally specialize by type of tank unit, such as armor, cavalry, or amphibious assault.

What They Do

Tank officers in the military perform some or all of the following duties:

Gather and evaluate intelligence or enemy strength and positions

Formulate battle plans

Coordinate actions with infantry, artillery, and air support units

Plan and direct communications

Direct operations of tanks, amphibious assault vehicles, and support equipment

Plan and supervise tactical and technical training of a tank unit

Direct unit administrative activities

Physical Demands

Tank officers must meet the same demanding physical requirements as the troops they command. They must be physically fit and able to hold up under the stress of combat conditions.

Special Requirements

A 4-year college degree is normally required to enter this occupation. This occupation is open only to men.

Work Environment

Tank officers work and train in all climates and weather conditions. To remain ready for combat, tank units must

regularly train under simulated combat conditions. During these exercises, tank officers are on the move, working, eating, and sleeping outdoors and in tents. When not in training, tank officers perform administrative duties in offices.

Training Provided

Job training consists of 4 to 20 weeks of classroom and field training. Training length varies depending on specialty. Course content typically includes:

Weapons and equipment maintenance

Tank and armor operations, principles, and tactics

Night maneuvers

Role of the platoon leader

Further training occurs on the job and through specialized courses.

Helpful Attributes

Helpful fields of study include engineering, geography, physical sciences, history, and business or public administration.

Helpful attributes include:

Ability to motivate and lead others

Willingness to accept a challenge and face danger

Decisiveness

Interest in tanks and battlefield strategy

Civilian Counterparts

Although the job of tank officer has no equivalent in civilian life, the leadership and administrative skills it provides are similar to those used in many civilian managerial occupations.

Opportunities

The services have about 5,200 tank officers. On average, they need 350 new tank officers each year. New tank officers are assigned to tank and armor units as platoon leaders. Advancement in armor is based on ability to lead. Tank officers with proven ability to lead may assume command positions.

Officer Career Paths

The following are general descriptions of the military career development process. These 13 Military Career Paths are based on the occupations found in the previous section.

Airplane Navigators

Navy

Air Force

Marine Corps

Coast Guard

Airplane navigators are vital flight crew members of some of the world's most sophisticated airplanes. As a navigator, you will operate complex electronic navigation systems to bring your airplane safely through its missions. You may also operate weapons systems. You begin your career in a squadron, flying on missions such as air combat, ground attack, submarine hunting, paratroop, or cargo delivery. As you become more experienced and skilled, you will serve in positions of increasing responsibility. There are opportunities to become a squadron commander.

Duty Assignment

Airplane navigators fly in airplanes to and from military bases in the U.S. and overseas. Some fly in airplanes that take off and land on aircraft carriers at sea. Navigators are usually assigned to flying squadrons made up of 10 to 25 airplanes and the crews needed to fly and maintain them. Navigators who fly on long-range airplanes such as bombers, tankers, and transports are usually assigned to bases in the U.S. These navigators have good opportunities for overseas flights. Navigators of fighter, fighter-bomber, or ground attack airplanes have excellent opportunities for overseas duty, particularly in Europe and the Pacific Islands. At some point in their careers, navigators are usually assigned to jobs that do not require them to fly. These assignments may be with headquarters staff or in a different occupation entirely.

Related Military Occupations

If you are interested in a career as an airplane navigator, you may also want to consider a career as a helicopter pilot or airplane pilot. See the Transportation Occupations cluster in the Military Officer Occupations section of this book for descriptions of these occupations. The career of airplane pilot is also described in the next military officer career description.

Advancement

Airplane navigators must have excellent concentration to operate sophisticated electronic navigation, communications, computer, and radar equipment for long periods of time. They must be able to keep their concentration during strenuous flight maneuvers. They need to know manual navigation techniques as a backup for automated equipment. They may also have to locate and track aerial, submarine, or surface targets and to operate weapons systems. The ability to work as a team with their pilot and other air crew is essential.

To advance in rank, navigators must have superior records of performance throughout their careers and be proven leaders. They must use their initiative to develop their skills, complete advanced education, and seek leadership positions within their squadrons. Their performance in non-flying duty assignments will also be critical for advancement.

Navigators compete with their peers for promotions and career-enhancing assignments. Only the best-qualified personnel are selected for advancement, and competition intensifies with each increase in rank.

Specialization

Airplane navigators usually specialize in one type of airplane throughout their career. The basic airplane types include:

High-performance jet fighters, fighter-bombers, or ground attack planes

Long-range, strategic bombers

Large tanker airplanes that provide in-flight refueling

Special high-altitude reconnaissance planes

Medium- or long-range antisubmarine patrol planes

Long-range, multi-engine heavy transport planes

When assigned to non-flying duty tours, airplane navigators often specialize in areas that will help them in senior staff positions later in their careers. These "second careers" may be in areas such as engineering, computer science, or personnel management.

Training

Initial training for airplane navigators includes about 12 months of demanding classroom and in-flight training. Training covers navigation, communications, principles of flight, major airplane systems, meteorology, and flight operations. Student navigators are given experience in day, night, aerobatic, and basic military airplane missions. After initial training, navigators are given advanced training in one type of airplane, such as a fighter, ground attack, bomber, reconnaissance, or transport plane. Navigators must continue on-the-job flight training throughout their careers.

Advanced training is available in areas such as ground attack tactics, dog-fighting (air-to-air combat tactics), and air battle management. Navigators receive transition training whenever their airplane is modified or replaced by a new airplane. There are opportunities to attend graduate school for advanced technical or management degrees.

Navigators are also given opportunities for professional military education to prepare them for senior officer positions. These programs include study of military subjects such as strategy, tactics, and planning large-scale operations. They may be completed either by correspondence or full-time study.

Typical Career Path (with time line)

Navigator (4 years)

Navigators who earn their wings are assigned to a flying squadron. Depending on the type of airplane and mission, they:

Locate and track land targets, aircraft, ships, or submarines

Monitor automated navigational systems using manual navigation techniques

Operate communications equipment

Plan missions and tactics with their pilots, considering weather, fuel, and aircraft loading

Practice normal and emergency operating procedures

Senior Navigator (9–11 years)

After mastering the requirements of their assigned mission area and gaining experience as leaders, navigators may advance to become senior navigators. At this level, they:

Plan and accompany their pilots on operational missions

Instruct new navigators in their squadron duties and responsibilities

Guide strategic bombers to their targets

Teach student navigators how to use weapons systems and navigate

Explain mission plans and assignments to flight crews

Flight Operations Director (15–18 years)

Senior navigators who are experts in navigation and their flying missions and who are outstanding leaders may advance to become flight operations directors. At this level, they:

Plan squadron flight missions

Teach flight crews advanced mission operations and tactics

Manage a squadron department, such as maintenance, training, or safety

Advise squadron commanders on readiness of aircraft and crews

Evaluate officers' flying, leadership, and management skills

Squadron Commander

Flight operations directors who have excellent navigation experience and who are outstanding leaders may advance to senior positions. At this level, they:

Command a squadron, flight operations group, or air facility

Advise headquarters commanders on squadron operations matters

Fly missions to maintain their skills

Direct flight operations of a major command

Airplane Pilots

Army

Navy

Air Force

Marine Corps

Coast Guard

Military pilots fly the most sophisticated combat and transport airplanes in the world. As a pilot, you will plan flying missions, brief your air crews, and fly frequently to keep your performance at its peak. You begin your career in a squadron, flying the airplane you were trained to fly—a supersonic jet fighter, high-altitude reconnaissance plane, or huge cargo transport. As you gain experience and skill, you will serve in positions of increasing responsibility. There are opportunities to become a squadron commander.

Duty Assignment

Airplane pilots fly their airplanes to and from military bases in the U.S. and overseas. Some fly airplanes that take off and land on aircraft carriers at sea. Pilots are usually assigned to flying squadrons made up of 10 to 25 airplanes and the crews needed to fly and maintain them. Pilots of long-range airplanes, such as bombers, tankers, and transports are usually assigned to bases in the U.S. These pilots have good opportunities for overseas flights. Pilots of fighter, fighter-bomber, or ground attack airplanes have excellent opportunities for overseas duty, particularly in Europe and the Pacific. At some point in their careers, pilots are usually assigned to jobs that do not require them to fly. These assignments may be with headquarters staff or in a different occupation entirely.

Related Military Occupations

If you are interested in a flying career, you may also want to consider a career as a helicopter pilot or an airplane navigator. See the Transportation Occupations cluster in the Military Officer Occupations section of this book for descriptions of these occupations. The career of airplane navigators is also described in the previous military officer career description.

Advancement

Airplane pilots must be outstanding fliers. They must be able to fly their airplanes safely through the maneuvers required by their missions. They must be experts in their plane's fuel, flight control, electrical, and weapons systems. All pilots are regularly tested on their knowledge of airplane systems in written examinations, "check flights," and in-flight simulators.

To advance, pilots must be superb aviators and maintain their skills throughout their careers. They must have consistently excellent flying records and be proven leaders. Pilots are expected to use their initiative to develop their skills, complete advanced education, and seek leadership positions in their squadron. Their performance in non-flying duty assignments will also be critical for advancement.

Pilots compete with their peers for promotion and career enhancing assignments. Only the best-qualified personnel are selected for advancement, and competition intensifies with each increase in rank.

Specialization

Airplane pilots usually specialize in one type of airplane throughout their careers. The basic airplane types include:

High-performance jet fighters, fighter-bombers, or ground attack planes

Long-range, strategic bombers

Large tanker airplanes that provide in-flight refueling

Special high-altitude reconnaissance planes

Medium- or long-range anti-submarine patrol planes

Long-range multi-engine heavy transport planes

Lightweight utility planes

When assigned to non-flying duty tours, airplane pilots often specialize in areas that will help them in senior staff positions later in their careers. These "second careers" may be in areas such as engineering, computer science, or personnel management.

Training

Initial training for pilots includes up to 18 months of demanding classroom and in-flight training. Student pilots learn principles of aerodynamics, major airplane systems, meteorology, navigation, communications, and federal and service flight rules and regulations. They practice flying in all types of weather, day and night. They also practice flying in formation and basic aerobatics. After initial training, pilots are given advanced training in one type of airplane, such as a fighter, ground attack, bomber, reconnaissance, or transport plane. Pilots must continue on-the-job flight training throughout their careers.

Advanced training is available in areas such as ground attack tactics, dogfighting (air-to-air combat tactics), and directing air strikes. Pilots receive transition training whenever their airplanes are modified or replaced by new generation airplanes. There are opportunities to attend graduate school for advanced technical and management degrees.

Pilots are also given opportunities for professional military education to prepare them for senior officer positions. These programs include study of military subjects such as strategy, tactics, and planning large-scale operations. They may be completed either by correspondence or full-time study.

Typcial Career Path (with time line)

Pilot (4 years)

Pilots who earn their wings are assigned to a flying squadron. Depending on the type of aircraft and mission, they:

Plan flights, considering weather, fuel, and aircraft loading

Fly missions alone, as part of a group of airplanes, or as copilot in a large airplane

Plan missions and tactics

Practice emergency and normal operating procedures

Senior Pilot (9–11 years)

After mastering the requirements of their assigned mission area and gaining experience as leaders, pilots may advance to become senior pilots. Senior pilots:

Plan and fly operational missions

Fly as first pilot in a large airplane

Lead flights of two or more aircraft on missions

Instruct new pilots in their squadron duties and responsibilities

Teach student pilots to fly

Explain mission plans and assignments to flight crews

Flight Leader (15–18 years)

Pilots who are expert in their flying mission and demonstrate outstanding leadership qualities may advance to become flight leaders. At this level, they:

Lead several airplanes on flying missions, such as air-strikes, patrols, or transporting cargo

Instruct pilots in squadron missions and tactics

Evaluate pilots' flying, leadership, and management skills

Manage a squadron department, such as maintenance, training, or safety

Manage combat missions, planning target selections and personnel utilization

Command Pilot

Excellent flight leaders who have broad experience in flying operations and who are outstanding leaders may advance to senior positions. At this level, they:

Command a squadron, flight operations group, or air facility

Direct flight operations of a major flying unit

Fly missions to maintain expert flying skills

Advise headquarters commanders on squadron operations

Civil Engineers

Army
Navy
Air Force
Marine Corps
Coast Guard

Civil engineers are the military's builders. In their varied careers they may: build air strips in the jungle; direct construction or maintenance of military bases; or work alongside combat troops, physically altering the battlefield to help them advance or hold their positions. You begin your career managing construction contracts, directing base utility and maintenance services, or leading a group of enlisted combat engineers. As you gain experience, you will serve in positions of increasing responsibility. There are opportunities to become director of engineering at a military base or to command a battalion of combat engineers.

Duty Assignment

Civil engineers work primarily in engineering offices or temporary construction facilities on military bases in the U.S. and overseas. Civil engineers assigned to combat engineering units may spend much time in the field during combat exercises and field maneuvers. Most have opportunities for overseas assignment, particularly in Europe and the Pacific Islands.

Specialization

Civil engineers typically spend their career developing expertise in several areas. Major areas include combat engineering, contract management, and public works. In each assignment, civil engineers use their engineering background, career experience, and increasing leadership ability.

Related Military Occupations

If you are interested in a career as a military civil engineer, you may also want to consider a career in another technical field. See the Engineering, Science, and Technical Occupations cluster in the Military Officer Occupations section of this book for descriptions of these occupations.

Advancement

To perform their wide range of duties, military civil engineers must be flexible, excellent leaders, and have superior analytical and communications skills. They may come from any of several engineering backgrounds. They apply their education and abilities to solve problems, supervise contractors, lead troops, and give advice on contracts and designs.

To advance, civil engineers must have excellent professional skills and managerial abilities. To build a record of excellent performance, they must win the confidence of the people for whom they work and those who work for them. As they gain experience, they serve in positions of greater responsibility. They manage larger contracts, lead more people, and direct projects of increasing complexity. An excellent performance record is essential to success. An advanced engineering or management degree may increase chances for promotion.

Engineers compete with their peers for promotion and career enhancing assignments. Only the best-qualified personnel are selected for advancement, and competition intensifies with each increase in rank.

Training

Initial training for civil engineers is a combination of classroom and field training. Courses are taught in: managing contracts, budgeting, combat engineering techniques, and leadership. To prepare for their next assignment, some engineers receive specialty training in such areas as environmental protection, fire prevention/protection, or mapping (cartography).

Advanced training is available in leadership and combat engineering. Civil engineers may earn a graduate engineering degree in a program funded by their service. Many others obtain degrees on their own time.

Civil engineers are also given opportunities for professional military education to prepare them for senior officer positions. These programs include study of military subjects such as strategy, tactics, and planning large scale operations. They may be completed by correspondence or full-time study.

Typical Career Path (with time line)

Civil Engineer (4 years)

After initial training, civil engineers are given their first duty assignment. Here they may:

Direct military and civilian personnel in maintaining and constructing buildings

Lead combat engineers in missions such as building fortifications, assembling mobile bridges, or preparing mine fields

Monitor contractors to ensure their work meets contract specifications

Lead and train enlisted personnel in construction techniques

Senior Engineer (9–11 years)

Civil engineers who have performed well in their first assignments may advance to become senior engineers. At this level, they:

Command combat engineering companies of 65 to 200 enlisted personnel

Plan and manage programs to maintain utilities, buildings, or roads on a military base

Train new civil engineer officers

Review plans and designs for engineering projects

Engineering Staff Officer (15–18 years)

Senior engineers who show excellent leadership and technical ability may advance to become engineering staff officers. At this level, they:

Analyze and recommend design specifications for buildings, bridges, roads, and other structures

Determine construction project costs

Lead other civil engineers in managing construction and maintenance contracts for a military base

Advise senior commanders on combat engineering and related matters

Director of Engineering

Engineering staff officers with outstanding records of leadership and technical expertise may be selected to direct major engineering activities or units. At this level, they:

Command combat engineering or construction battalions of 500 to 750 military personnel

Direct civil engineering operations at a military base

Advise base or area commanders on civil engineering matters

Evaluate construction bids submitted by civilian contractors

Direct planning and management of major engineering projects

Infantry Officers

Army
Marine Corps

Infantry officers lead their troops through rigorous training and maneuvers. As an infantry officer, you will make sure your men are in top shape, well trained, and properly equipped. You begin your career leading a platoon of 30 to 50 infantrymen. As you gain leadership and tactical experience, you will serve in positions of increasing responsibility. There are opportunities to become battalion commander.

Duty Assignment

Infantry officers serve in infantry units at military bases in the U.S. and overseas. They work in offices and spend much time in the field. The new officer's first assignment is to train and lead a platoon of 30 to 50 soldiers. Later in their career, infantry officers command a company of 100 to 200 soldiers and perhaps a battalion of 500 to 1,000 soldiers. There are excellent opportunities for overseas assignment in Europe and the Pacific Islands.

Specialization

Infantry officers may specialize in amphibious warfare (attacking land from the water), airborne operations (parachuting into battle), special operations, or Ranger operations. (Rangers are special units skilled in combat in many different geographical areas.) Infantry officers may also develop secondary career specialties through advanced education or special experience.

Related Military Occupations

If you are interested in a combat career, you may also want to consider a career as an artillery, tank, missile systems, or special operations officer. See the Combat Specialty Occupations cluster in the Military Officer Occupations section of this book for descriptions of these occupations.

Advancement

Infantry officers must be quick-thinking, aggressive leaders to be able to train and motivate the soldiers they command.

To be successful platoon leaders, infantry officers must master infantry operations and weapons and show outstanding leadership abilities. To advance to company commander, they must master all tactical aspects of the infantry, and demonstrate ability to coordinate combat actions with artillery, armor, airlift, and air strike support units. To advance to senior command positions, they must have successfully commanded and demonstrated potential at the company level. Outstanding performance in every duty assignment is essential for advancement. Officers with the broadest range of infantry skills and best records of leadership have the best chance for promotion.

Infantry officers compete with their peers for promotion and career-enhancing assignments. Only the best-qualified personnel are selected for advancement, and competition intensifies with each increase in rank.

Training

Initial training for infantry officers includes up to 6 months of training in the classroom and in the field. Training covers infantry weapons, combat tactics, infantry organization, and military leadership. Many officers also receive specialized training to prepare them for their first assignment. They may be trained in combat skills such as parachute jumping, Ranger training, or amphibious landings.

Advanced training is provided to prepare infantry officers for more senior leadership roles. Courses are taught primarily in coordinating infantry and mechanized infantry with other combat units.

Infantry officers are also given opportunities for professional military education to prepare them for senior officer positions. These programs include study of such military subjects as strategy, tactics, and planning large-scale operations. They may be completed by correspondence or full-time study.

Typical Career Path (with time line)

(This career is open only to men.)

Platoon Leader (4 years)

After initial training, infantry officers are assigned to lead a platoon. Platoon leaders:

Train and lead an infantry platoon of 30 to 50 soldiers

Inspect troops, barracks, and equipment

Plan daily conditioning programs for the platoon or the entire company

Lead the platoon on combat training exercises

Direct the care and maintenance of weapons, radios, and other equipment assigned to the platoon

Company Commander (9–11 years)

Platoon leaders who have shown leadership ability may advance to become company commanders. At this level, they:

Command an infantry company consisting of several platoons

Develop and carry out battle plans to support battalion objectives

Develop, schedule, and carry out training plans and field exercises

Explain battle plans and assign objectives to platoon leaders

Infantry Staff Officer (15–18 years)

Company commanders with demonstrated leadership skills may advance to become infantry staff officers. In this position, they:

Assist their battalion commander in administration and management duties

Manage a specialized function such as logistics or operations for a battalion or headquarters staff

Teach infantry courses

Resolve unit supply, maintenance, or personnel problems

Advise senior commanders on infantry operations and readiness

Battalion Commander

Outstanding officers with a broad range of infantry experience may advance to senior officer positions. At this level, they:

Command an infantry battalion of 500 to 1,000 men

Plan training exercises or missions

Instruct company commanders on mission assignments and objectives

Coordinate battle plans with armor, artillery, and air support units

INTELLIGENCE OFFICERS

Army
Navy
Air Force
Marine Corps
Coast Guard

Intelligence officers are the eyes and ears of the military. The information they deal with is vital to our national security. As an intelligence officer, you will analyze information on the military forces, governments, and people of other countries. You begin your career collecting and giving combat commanders briefings on information from sources such as satellite and aerial photographs, intercepted communications, and observers in the field. As you gain experience, you will serve in positions of increasing responsibility. There are opportunities to become intelligence operations director of an intelligence-gathering unit or of a large combat force on land or sea.

Duty Assignments

Most intelligence officers work at military bases in the U.S. and overseas. Many work in electronic data processing and evaluation centers or photographic interpretation labs. Some work aboard ships or airplanes with sophisticated intelligence gathering equipment. Many intelligence officers have an opportunity to work in Washington, DC, where much intelligence planning and evaluation takes place. Intelligence officers have good opportunities for overseas duty.

Specialization

Intelligence officers typically specialize in one area of intelligence early in their careers. They expand on the foundation as they advance. Areas of specialization include communications intelligence (information from intercepted radio voice communications), signals intelligence (data from non-voice coded radio and radar signals), imagery intelligence (information from satellite and aircraft images), combat intelligence, and human intelligence (information provided by agents and other individuals in the field).

Advancement

Intelligence officers serve in positions of great sensitivity. They analyze information vital to national security and prepare it for combat commanders around the world. Intelligence officers must be aggressively resourceful and analytical, and have excellent speaking and writing ability. In perhaps no other occupation is so much trust placed in individuals so early in their careers. After mastering the basic analytical skills, intelligence officers apply them in positions of increasing responsibility.

To advance, intelligence officers must have a record of consistently superior performance. Because military operations depend on accurate intelligence, there is no room for mistakes. Intelligence officers must win the respect and trust of their commanders and prove themselves as good leaders. They must often learn computer and related skills.

Intelligence officers compete with their peers for promotion and career-enhancing assignments. Only the best-qualified personnel are selected for advancement, and competition intensifies with each increase in rank.

Training

Initial training for intelligence officers includes up to 6 months of intensive classroom study. Officers learn how to analyze data and prepare briefings. They are trained in techniques for gathering intelligence and learn the kinds of information combat commanders need to make decisions in battle. They also are briefed on world situations. Intelligence officers may receive specialized training in areas such as electronics, communications, or satellite photographic intelligence gathering.

Advanced training is available, usually to prepare intelligence officers for a specific assignment. Other advanced courses may be in special analysis of intelligence information from many sources.

Intelligence officers are also given opportunities for professional military education to prepare them for senior officer positions. These programs include study of military subjects such as strategy, tactics, and planning large-scale operations. These military courses may be completed either by correspondence or full-time study.

Typical Career Path (with time line)

Intelligence Officer (4 years)

After initial training, intelligence officers are assigned to specialized intelligence units or to air, sea, or ground combat units. Here they may:

Research enemy force locations, size, and capability

Analyze weaknesses and strengths of enemy forces

Brief combat commanders or air crews on research results

Direct a small team of enlisted personnel intercepting and analyzing voice or other radio signals

Interpret aerial and satellite photographs

Debrief air crews or ground combat teams returning from missions or patrols

Senior Intelligence Officer (9–11 years)

Intelligence officers with an excellent performance record may advance to become senior intelligence officers. At this level, they may:

Analyze information from many sources of intelligence and prepare briefings or reports

Gather information to support combat exercises and maneuvers

Analyze potential security problems

Train new intelligence officers in job duties

Intelligence Staff Officer (15–18 years)

Senior intelligence officers with excellent records of performance and leadership ability may advance to become intelligence staff officers. Typically, they:

Brief senior-level staff and combat commanders on activities of enemy forces

Direct a team of officers and enlisted personnel, compiling and analyzing intelligence information from all sources

Confer with intelligence officers from other services and nations to share information

Teach military intelligence courses

Intelligence Operations Director

Outstanding intelligence staff officers may advance to become intelligence operations directors. Here they:

Direct intelligence services for air, land, or sea commands

Coordinate their intelligence with other military and civilian intelligence agencies

Determine the intelligence needed to support large combat forces

Evaluate intelligence sources for accuracy and usefulness

Brief top-level military leaders in areas of personal expertise

Lawyers

Army
Navy
Air Force
Marine Corps
Coast Guard

Military lawyers, known as Judge Advocates General's (JAG) Corps officers, work for the largest "legal firms" in the world. As a military lawyer, you will prosecute or defend military personnel in courts-martial, counsel personnel on legal problems, and advise commanders in matters of law. You begin your career handling trials and providing legal services. As you gain experience, your assignments will become more challenging. There are opportunities to become a legal services director or a judge in a military court.

Duty Assignment

Most military lawyers work in legal offices and courtrooms on military bases in the U.S. and overseas. Some serve aboard large ships at sea or on the flagship of a fleet commander. Legal services officers and directors normally work at major command headquarters, on large military bases, or in Washington, DC. There are good opportunities for overseas assignments.

Specialization

Lawyers may gain special expertise through experience or advanced education. They may specialize in contract, labor, international, maritime, or criminal law.

Advancement

Military lawyers must speak and write with ease and authority. They must be familiar with civilian and military law, as well as courtroom strategy. Creativity and perseverance are essential to research complex legal rulings and use them in court cases.

To advance, lawyers must continue to increase their knowledge of military, criminal, and civil law. They should have excellent legal performance and leadership records. Most lawyers obtain advanced degrees or specialties. However, they are also encouraged to broaden their experience through a variety of assignments. In later assignments, lawyers lead junior JAG officers as well as enlisted legal personnel.

Lawyers with a legal specialty and outstanding records of performance in a variety of assignments have the best opportunities to advance to senior positions. Only the best-qualified personnel are selected for advancement, and competition intensifies with each increase in rank.

Training

Lawyers entering the military must be graduates of an accredited law school. Initial training for lawyers is conducted by the service JAG school. Courses include introduction to military law, the military justice system, and officer leadership and management responsibilities. New lawyers train on the job in courtrooms and legal service offices.

Lawyers are expected to keep up with changes in laws, regulations, and legal procedures. They must continue to study and attend symposiums, conferences, and seminars throughout their careers. Many lawyers have opportunities to acquire specialties and advanced degrees.

Advanced training typically opens up a range of assignments that would otherwise be unavailable.

Lawyers are also given opportunities for professional military education to prepare them for senior officer positions. These programs include study of military subjects such as strategy, tactics, and planning large-scale operations. These military courses may be completed by correspondence or occasionally by full-time study.

Typical Career Path (with time line)

Lawyer (4 years)

Following initial training, lawyers are assigned to JAG offices. Here they:

Prosecute and defend military personnel in courts martial

Research cases using law libraries and computerized references

Interview defendants and witnesses

Prepare wills, adoption papers, and other personal legal documents

Senior Lawyer (9–11 years)

Lawyers who demonstrate the ability to interpret and work with law may advance to become senior lawyers. At this level, they:

Advise commanders and senior staff officers on general legal issues

Make sure policies and procedures comply with civil and military law

Investigate liability claims

Advise military personnel on legal matters

Legal Staff Officers (15–18 years)

Outstanding senior lawyers may advance to become legal staff officers. At this level, they may:

Advise commanders on specific legal topics (contract, labor, maritime, or international law)

Defend or prosecute personnel in courts-martial that require lawyers of senior rank and expertise

Direct lawyers and enlisted legal specialists in providing services to military personnel and their dependents

Review contracts to determine if they meet legal requirements

Legal Staff Director

Legal staff officers with outstanding records of leadership and legal expertise may advance to become legal services directors. Here they may:

Direct all activities of a legal services JAG office supporting local operational commands

Set up prosecution or defense in courts-martial

Advise senior staff and combat commanders on legal matters

Serve as a judge on courts-martial

Meteorologists

Navy
Air Force
Marine Corps

Accurate weather forecasts can save lives and equipment in military operations. As a meteorologist, you supervise enlisted weather observers and forecasters and advise operational commanders on changing weather conditions. You begin your career directing data collection and interpreting weather maps, observation data, and satellite information. As you gain leadership and forecasting skills, you will serve in positions of increasing responsibility. There are opportunities to become director of a major meteorological center in charge of a group of weather stations.

Duty Assignment

Most meteorology officers work in weather stations or weather support units at military bases in the U.S. and overseas. Some work in global weather centers. Others work in command and control centers aboard ships at sea. There are good opportunities for overseas assignment to military bases and outposts throughout the world, from the tropics to the North and South Poles.

Specialization

Meteorologists may specialize in the field in which they have an advanced degree. Specialties include oceanography, astrophysics, geophysics, and computer science. Typically, meteorologists serve in a variety of assignments, returning periodically to their specialty.

Related Military Occupations

If you are interested in a career as a meteorologist, you may also want to consider a career in oceanography or some other scientific or technical occupation. See the Engineering, Science, and Technical Occupations cluster in the Military Officer Occupations section of this book for descriptions of these occupations.

Advancement

Meteorologists must be able to forecast the weather accurately and to apply their expertise to research, military exercises, and strategic planning. Meteorologists begin by practicing short-term and extended forecasting, briefing flight crews, and directing enlisted weather observers. After mastering these skills, they work in larger weather stations serving more people and missions. In the Navy, meteorologists will also apply their knowledge to the field of oceanography.

To advance, meteorologists must make consistently accurate forecasts and show excellent leadership and management skills. Most senior meteorologists have an advanced degree in areas such as math, geophysics, astrophysics, oceanography, meteorology, and computer science. Outstanding performance and advanced education are keys to advancement in meteorology.

Meteorologists compete with their peers for promotion and career-enhancing assignments. Only the best-qualified personnel are selected for advancement and competition intensifies with each increase in rank.

Training

Initial training for meteorologists includes up to 12 months of classroom instruction in weather observation, analysis, and forecasting. Instruction is also given on the impact of weather on military operations and the information needed by combat commanders. Military leadership is an important part of initial training.

Advanced training is given in such areas of specialization as interpreting satellite weather data and computer applications to forecasting. Most meteorologists earn advanced degrees in areas such as meteorology, oceanography, geophysics, astrophysics, or computer science. They may specialize in such fields as environmental effects on electronic equipment, solar forecasting, or

acoustics in water. Some attend schools in programs funded by their service, while others obtain degrees on their own time.

Meteorologists are also given opportunities for professional military education to prepare them for senior officer positions. These programs include military subjects such as strategy, tactics, and forecasting requirements for planning large-scale operations. They may be completed by correspondence or full-time study.

Typical Career Path (with time line)

Meteorologist (4 years)

After initial training, new meteorologists are assigned to base weather stations or outlying weather support facilities. Here they:

Direct enlisted personnel gathering weather data from surface instruments, balloons, radar, and satellites

Analyze data and information from charts and other weather stations

Prepare short-term and long-range weather forecasts

Brief air crews on weather conditions

Senior Meteorologist (9–11 years)

Meteorologists who have excellent technical and leadership skills advance to become senior meteorologists. At this level, they may:

Command a small weather station or outlying weather facility

Train and evaluate new meteorologists and enlisted personnel

Send hazardous weather warnings

Direct preparation of weather forecasts and local advisories

Meteorology Staff Officer (15–18 years)

Senior meteorologists with records of excellent performance may advance to become meteorology staff officers. They may:

Command large weather stations

Advise scientists and technicians designing, developing, and testing new weapons systems

Direct weather computer centers

Confer with oceanographers to support operations at sea

Advise combat commanders and their staffs on weather conditions

Meteorology Director

Meteorology staff officers with superior technical expertise and leadership ability may advance to direct meteorological centers. At this level, they may:

Direct personnel predicting and monitoring global weather patterns

Advise top-level military commanders on weather conditions

Manage staff and weather planning for large geographic areas (such as northern Europe)

Inspect weather facilities under their command

NUCLEAR ENGINEERS

Army
Navy
Marine Corps

Career nuclear engineers conduct research and develop projects using the most advanced technology. As a nuclear engineer, you may work with lasers, particle beams, weapons effects, or space environments. Your contributions will be vital to maintaining the nation's defense. You begin your career in a laboratory. You will work with and learn from some of the world's foremost nuclear engineers. As you develop your knowledge and leadership abilities, you will take on greater responsibilities. There are opportunities to advance to director of a military research laboratory.

Duty Assignment

Nuclear engineers work in laboratories, offices, and sometimes in the field. During a typical career, a nuclear engineer performs and directs research and serves with military staffs. Almost all assignments are in the United States. However, there are a few opportunities for assignment abroad.

Specialization

Nuclear engineers specialize in military applications of nuclear energy. They conduct research, direct design and development projects, and manage purchasing contracts. Most seek to become an expert in one area of the field. Some areas of research are:

Nuclear reactor design for ships, submarines, or land (safety, performance, theory, and testing)

Nuclear reactor operation

Nuclear safety (storage and handling of fuel, reactors, and weapons)

Nuclear effects on electronic and other equipment

Technical aspects of nuclear weapons policy

As nuclear engineers advance to senior officer positions, they maintain their specialized knowledge and increase their general knowledge of the field.

Advancement

Nuclear engineers conduct research, design weapons and related systems, and manage projects critical to the nation's defense. They must understand the fundamental principles of physics, math, and other areas of science. They must master the most recent advances of an incredibly complex technological profession. They also need to become excellent leaders and managers.

To advance, nuclear engineers must develop their research skills. They must be able to design research programs, tests, and experiments. They work constantly to keep abreast of innovations in the field. It is essential for nuclear engineers to have an advanced degree (master's or doctorate), and there are many opportunities for fully-funded education to achieve this career milestone. Nuclear engineers must also develop their leadership skills to advance to the most senior levels in the profession.

The Air Force is the only service with a distinct career path in nuclear engineering. In the Army, Navy, and Marine Corps, officers typically enter nuclear engineering after qualifying in another occupation. They most often enter the field after 6 to 10 years of service and attending graduate school for a nuclear engineering degree. In these cases, nuclear engineering is a secondary occupational specialty and not a career, although officers may periodically return to assignments related to nuclear engineering.

Related Military Occupations

If you are interested in a career in nuclear engineering, you may also want to consider a career as a physicist, computer systems engineer, electrical and electronics engineer, or chemist. See the Engineering, Science, and Technical Occupations cluster in the Military Officer Occupations section of this book for descriptions of these occupations.

349

Training

Initial training for most nuclear engineers is on the job at a military-run laboratory. Nuclear engineers typically enter the service with a master's or bachelor's degree in physics, nuclear engineering, or a related field. After one or two tours in a laboratory, most nuclear engineers attend graduate school funded by their service. They earn a Ph.D. or a master's degree. The course work for their degree usually includes research in an area of direct interest both to them and to the service.

Nuclear engineers are encouraged to complete professional military education programs to prepare them for senior officer positions. These programs involve study of military subjects such as leadership, strategy, tactics, and planning large-scale operations. They may be completed by correspondence or full-time study.

Typical Career Path (with time line)

Nuclear Engineer (4 years)

Following initial training, new nuclear engineers are assigned to research and development laboratories, test sites, or nuclear reactor prototypes. Nuclear engineers:

Work with experienced research scientists on projects such as effects of the outer space electromagnetic environment on people and electronic equipment, laser and particle beam technology, weapons design, or effects of nuclear weapons on military equipment

Develop professional research skills

Give technical support to projects demanding knowledge in nuclear engineering

Senior Nuclear Engineer (9–11 years)

Nuclear engineers who have demonstrated technical proficiency and the potential to become excellent researchers and leaders may advance to become senior nuclear engineers. At this level, they may:

Conduct basic and applied research in a laboratory

Complete a master's degree or Ph.D. in an area of nuclear engineering

Teach courses in their field or specialty

Provide technical direction for research performed by contractors, universities, or government research laboratories.

Nuclear Engineering Staff Officer (15–18 years)

Senior nuclear engineers who have excellent research and managerial skills may advance to become nuclear engineering staff officers. Here they:

Manage research projects, directing civilian and military scientists. Provide senior military staffs with expert advice on matters concerning nuclear weapons

Assist scientists from many other disciplines in solving shared research or production problems

Conduct independent research in a special area of expertise

Laboratory Director

Outstanding nuclear engineering staff officers with career-long records of top performance as leaders, managers, and expert nuclear engineers may advance to become laboratory directors. At this time in their career, they:

Command a research laboratory, monitoring research, directing research, and leading teams of scientists and technicians

Develop and consult on military service research and development strategy

Provide expert advice to national-level staffs

Manage government weapons acquisition programs

Physicians and Surgeons

Army
Navy
Air Force
Coast Guard

Military physicians and surgeons lead health care teams in the field and in military hospitals and clinics around the world. As a physician or surgeon you will diagnose and treat military personnel and their family members. You begin your career treating patients under the direction of an experienced staff doctor. As your knowledge and skills increase, you will specialize in a medical field. There are opportunities to become medical director of a hospital or clinic.

Duty Assignment

Most physicians and surgeons work in clinics, hospitals, and medical centers at military bases in the U.S. and overseas. Some work aboard naval vessels or hospital ships. Many serve temporary duty assignments in field hospitals during combat exercises and maneuvers. The military services strive to provide doctors with a stable work environment. As a result, physicians and surgeons often serve extended duty assignments at a single hospital in the U.S., Europe, or the Pacific. Positions for physicians and surgeons in the Coast Guard are filled by U.S. Public Health Service Officers.

Specialization

Physicians and surgeons specialize as they gain experience and education. For physicians, typical specialties include family practice, pediatrics (providing care from birth to adolescence), and endocrinology (treating disorders caused by imbalances and diseases of the body's system of internal glands). Surgeons begin in general surgery and typically specialize in neurosurgery (surgery involving the brain and central nervous system), heart surgery, or cosmetic/reconstructive surgery.

Advancement

Military physicians and surgeons must have outstanding stamina, perseverance, and a desire to serve others. They must be scientifically astute and able to communicate well in speaking and writing. They are expected to learn and train continually throughout their career.

To advance, physicians and surgeons must be superb medical practitioners. They must be expert observers to diagnose illness or injury. They need excellent skills in gathering, organizing, and analyzing information to make accurate diagnoses and plan treatments. Their professional skills must continue to develop, and they must demonstrate their ability to lead and train younger doctors. When assigned to teaching hospitals, doctors are evaluated on their ability to instruct in both classroom and patient situations.

Physicians and surgeons who have excellent records of performance, leadership, and continuing education may advance to senior positions. Only the best-qualified personnel are selected for advancement, and competition is intense for promotions and career-enhancing duty assignments.

Related Military Occupations

If you are interested in a medical career, you may also want to consider other military medical occupations. Seethe Health Diagnosing and Treating Practitioner

Occupations cluster in the Military Officer Occupations section of this book for descriptions of these occupations. The nursing career is also described in the next military officer career path description.

Training

Initial training for physicians and surgeons includes basic orientation in military medical service administrative, professional, and military policies. Throughout their careers, physicians and surgeons are expected to keep pace with advances in medicine by attending professional symposiums and seminars and by reading technical literature.

Almost all physicians and surgeons will attend fully funded programs to obtain advanced medical specialties. Physicians specialize in a non-surgical branch of medicine, and surgeons in a branch of surgery. Specialty education may take place in military or civilian teaching hospitals. Programs may require 1 or more years to complete.

Physicians and surgeons are also given opportunities for professional military education to prepare them for senior officer positions. These programs include study of military subjects such as strategy, tactics, and planning large-scale operations. These courses are usually completed by correspondence, but a few doctors attend full-time courses.

Typical Career Path (with time line)

Intern (1–2 years)

Medical school graduates who have not completed their internship training serve as interns in a supervised program of medical practice training. Here they:

Work in a teaching hospital, diagnosing and treating patients

Accompany resident and staff doctors on medical "rounds" to evaluate patient condition

Help train medical students

General Medical Officer (2–4 years)

Doctors who complete their internships are usually assigned to hospitals, clinics, or, possibly, large ships as general medical officers. They:

Examine patients, and diagnose and treat illnesses

Order X-rays, tests, and medication

Conduct medical "rounds"

351

Resident Doctor (9–11 years)

General medical officers with 1 to 3 years of excellent performance return to military or civilian teaching hospitals to gain medical specialties. As residents, they may:

Complete rigorous programs of study in a specialty

Instruct interns and medical students

Conduct medical "rounds" to supervise interns and students and care for their own patients

Meet with hospital staff to discuss cases and procedures

Staff Doctor (15–18 years)

Resident doctors who complete specialty training may become staff doctors. At this level, they may:

Practice in their specialty

Supervise and advise residents, general medical officers, interns, and students

Serve as chief of a clinic or medical department

Evaluate resident doctors

Medical Director

Staff doctors with outstanding medical or surgical ability and outstanding records of leadership may advance to become medical directors. Typically, they:

Direct medical services at a military hospital or large clinic

Conduct a limited practice to maintain their skills

Direct training of interns and residents

Confer with staff doctors to verify diagnoses and treatments

Evaluate staff doctors

Registered Nurses

Army
Navy
Air Force
Coast Guard

Military registered nurses care for the sick, injured, and wounded. They are a vital part of the military health care team. As a military nurse, you begin your career administering medications prescribed by doctors, monitoring patients' progress, and training and directing enlisted medical technicians. As you gain experience and your skills increase, you will serve in positions of increasing responsibility. There are opportunities to become director of nursing care activities at a hospital or clinic.

Duty Assignment

Most military nurses work in clinics, hospitals, and medical centers at military bases in the U.S. and overseas. Some work aboard naval vessels and hospital ships. Many are assigned to temporary duty in field hospitals during combat exercises and field maneuvers. Others serve in ambulances, evacuation helicopters, or medivac transport planes. There are good opportunities for overseas assignments, particularly in Europe and the Pacific Islands. Positions for registered nurses in the Coast Guard are filled by U.S. Public Health Service Officers.

Advancement

Military registered nurses must want to serve others. They must be able to deal with their patients' emotional well-being as well as their medical needs. They also need to develop leadership and training skills. Initiative is needed to maintain a high level of patient care.

To advance, nurses must be highly skilled professionals. They must master basic nursing and leadership skills quickly. Seeking varied assignments will increase their professional expertise. Almost all nurses specialize, either by acquiring an advanced degree or through specialty training programs. An excellent performance record, combined with specialization and a variety of increasingly responsible positions, is the key to advancement.

Nurses compete with their peers for promotion and career-enhancing assignments. Only the best-qualified personnel are selected for promotion, and competition intensifies with each increase in rank.

Training

Initial training for nurses includes orientation in military medical administration, nursing programs and procedures, and leadership. Nurses continue to attend seminars, short formal courses, and conferences throughout their careers to improve their nursing and patient care skills. In addition to these programs, they study on their own to stay abreast of advancements in the field.

Almost all nurses have opportunities to obtain nursing specialties and advanced degrees, often in fully-funded programs. Clinical programs educate nurses in anesthesiology, pediatric nursing, or other clinical specialties. Educational specialties enable nurses to teach other nurses, patients, or enlisted medical technicians. Special programs in administration train them to manage nursing and hospital programs. Many military nurses will have the opportunity to pursue an advanced degree in a nursing specialty.

Nurses are also given opportunities for professional military education to prepare them for senior officer positions. These programs include study of military subjects such as strategy, tactics, and planning large-scale operations. They are usually completed by correspondence.

Specialization

After gaining experience as staff nurses, registered nurses may specialize in such fields as mental health, anesthesiology, operating room nursing, nursing education, pediatrics, or nursing administration.

Related Military Occupations

If you are interested in a medical career, you may also want to consider other military medical occupations. See the Health Care Occupations cluster in the Military Officer Occupations section for descriptions of these occupations. The career of physician and surgeon is also described in the previous military officer career description.

Typical Career Path (with time line)

Staff Nurse (4 years)

After initial training, registered nurses are as signed to patient care duty at a clinical service ward of a hospital or medical center. Typically, staff nurses:

Take and record "vital signs" of patients, such as temperature, pulse, and blood pressure

Administer medication prescribed by doctors

Observe patient condition and reaction to drugs

Assist doctors during examinations and treatments

Change or direct the changing of bandages and dressings

Direct enlisted medical and nursing technicians in routine patient care

Charge Nurse (9–11 years)

Staff nurses with excellent patient care skills who show leadership ability may advance to become charge nurses. They are responsible for all nursing activity on a hospital ward. At this level, they:

Discuss patient conditions and nursing activities during change-of-shift meetings

Assign staff nurses to patients

Consult with the patient care coordinator on unusual nursing problems

Participate in nursing orientation and training programs

Evaluate performance of staff nurses

Patient Care Coordinator (15–18 years)

Charge nurses who have excellent managerial skills may advance to coordinate nursing services for wards or clinics. Here they:

Assign nurses to shifts and wards

Determine the adequacy of nursing care

Inspect rooms and wards

Accompany doctors on medical "rounds" to keep informed of special orders

See that drugs, solutions, and equipment are ordered and records are maintained

Investigate problems of patients, nurses, and enlisted medical technicians

Director of Nursing Care

Nurses with outstanding performance records and managerial skills may become directors of nursing care activities at hospitals or other medical treatment facilities. At this level, they:

Manage all nursing services at their hospital or facility

Advise medical staff and hospital administration on nursing services

Direct nursing staff in maintaining approved standards of patient care

Direct nursing orientation and training programs

353

Ship and Submarine Officers

Army
Navy
Coast Guard

Ship and submarine officers sail the world's most powerful vessels, from fast-attack submarines to huge aircraft carriers. As a ship or submarine officer, you will lead highly trained enlisted specialists in maintaining and operating the ship's systems. You begin your career leading a team of 10 to 50 enlisted personnel. You may be responsible for maintaining and operating the ship's power plant, missiles and guns, or radar. You will learn to navigate the ship in all weather, day and night. As you gain experience, you will serve in positions of increasing responsibility. There are opportunities to become captain of a surface ship or submarine.

Advancement

Ship and submarine officers direct the sailing and combat operations of their vessels. They must complete extensive qualifications programs, learning to navigate and operate their ships in all weather, in any area of the world's oceans. They direct enlisted specialists who maintain and operate the ship's radar, power plants, or weapons systems. Ship and submarine officers must be aggressive, self-motivated, and excellent leaders.

To advance, ship and submarine officers must complete all shipboard qualifications and have outstanding leadership and management records. They must also develop special skills. They may get training in a warfare specialty, such as hunting submarines, or they may pursue an advanced degree.

Ship and submarine officers compete with their peers for promotion and career enhancing assignments. Outstanding performance in every assignment is the key to success. Only the best-qualified personnel are selected for advancement, and competition intensifies with each increase in rank.

Only the Navy offers a career in submarines. In the Army there are duty assignments involving directing units of landing craft and tugboats. However, there is no typical career path for ship officers.

Duty Assignment

Ship and submarine officers live and work in their vessels at sea. While in port, they spend the workday aboard their ships. They may travel to locations around the world, and some ships and submarines have "home ports" in the Pacific Islands or Scotland. At regular points in their careers, officers are assigned to a job on shore, usually in offices. Ship and submarine officers typically serve a number of tours on sea duty throughout their careers.

Specialization

Officers of surface ships must have a broad knowledge of their vessels. In addition, they usually focus on one specific area of their ships, such as engineering (power plants, pumps, or fuel systems), combat systems (weapons or electronics operation and maintenance), or operations (tactics and navigation). Some ships are nuclear-powered and require officers trained in nuclear reactor operation. All submarine officers are nuclear qualified. As they advance to senior-level assignments, ship officers are expected to learn about more areas in greater depth.

Because a submarine is a smaller self-contained unit, submarine officers must have a detailed knowledge of their vessels and all its systems.

When assigned ashore, officers often specialize in areas that will help them in senior staff positions later in their careers. These "second careers" may be in personnel management, fleet operations planning, or management of programs to develop or buy large weapons systems.

Training

Initial training for ship officers includes 15 weeks of classroom instruction. Training covers ship operations, naval tactics, navigation, and the responsibilities of each department aboard ships. After they attend "Surface Warfare Officer School," officers may be further trained for their first assignment aboard ships such as cutters, destroyers, battleships, or aircraft carriers.

Training for submarine officers begins with 12 months of courses on nuclear power. Following nuclear power school, they attend submarine basic school to learn submarine operations and tactics.

Both ship and submarine officers receive advanced training throughout their careers. They often get technical training in such areas as sonar, radar, missile systems, and power plants. They may attend graduate school for advanced degrees.

Ship and submarine officers also have opportunities for professional military education to prepare them for senior officer positions. These programs include study of military subjects such as strategy, tactics, and planning large-scale operations. They may be completed either by correspondence or full-time study.

Related Military Occupations

If you are interested in a career as a ship or submarine officer, you may also want to consider a career in transportation management or some other transportation occupation. See the Transportation Occupations and Executive, Administrative, and Managerial Occupations clusters in the Military Officer Occupations section of this book for descriptions of these occupations.

Typical Career Path (with time line)

Division Officer (4 years)

After initial training, new ship and submarine officers are assigned to their first vessels as division officers. Here they:

Lead a division of 10 to 50 sailors

Stand watches in the engine room, ship's bridge, or ship's weapons systems control center

Plan daily and long-term work schedules

Plan and monitor the training of sailors in their division

Evaluate performance of enlisted personnel

Department Head (9–11 years)

Division officers who show leadership potential in several ship divisions may advance to become department heads. Department heads:

Manage a major department such as engineering, navigation/operations, or combat systems

Train new officers in seamanship and leadership

Plan and coordinate the department's activities

Conduct drills to evaluate the department's performance in emergency or combat situations

Evaluate the performance of division officers

Executive Staff Officer (15–18 years)

Department heads with broad experience and outstanding leadership abilities may advance to second in-command (executive officer) of a ship or submarine. At this level, they:

Issue orders and instructions to assist the ship's captain in daily operations

Manage administrative and maintenance activities

Command the ship or submarine in the captain's absence

Plan fleet exercises as part of a naval staff

Ship Captain

Executive officers who have consistently shown outstanding leadership and technical ability may be selected to be ship or submarine captains. At this level, they:

Command the operations of a ship or submarine and crew

Study orders and plan exercises and maneuvers to carry out missions

Direct daily operations and plan tactics

Direct the planning of fleet operations exercises as part of a naval staff

Supply and Warehousing Managers

Army
Navy
Air Force
Marine Corps
Coast Guard

No military force can function without supplies. Supply and warehousing managers make sure our military units around the world have the food, weapons, uniforms, trucks, airplanes, fuel, and spare parts they need to fulfill their missions. As a supply and warehousing manager, you will buy, store, issue, and keep track of vast quantities of equipment and material. You begin your career leading a small group of enlisted specialists in one type of supply such as food, petroleum, or parts. As you gain experience, you will serve in positions of increasing responsibility. There are opportunities to become the supply and warehousing director of a large military base or major command area.

Duty Assignment

Most supply and warehousing managers work in offices, warehouses, and material-handling facilities at military bases in the U.S. and overseas. They work in facilities similar to wholesale, retail, and warehouse operations in the civilian world. Some supply and warehousing managers are assigned to ships or air units. Many serve temporary duty assignments in the field during combat exercises and maneuvers. There are significant opportunities for overseas assignments, particularly in Europe and the Pacific Islands.

Related Military Occupations

If you are interested in a career as a supply and warehousing manager, you may also want to consider a career in purchasing and contract management, transportation management, or a related field. See the Executive, Administrative, and Managerial Occupations cluster in the Military Officer Occupations section of this book for descriptions of these occupations. The career path of a transportation manager is described in the next military officer career path description.

Advancement

Supply and warehousing managers are vital to every military operation. They must be excellent planners, organizers, and leaders. From the first, they are entrusted with large quantities of valuable materials. They must become expert at using the supply system. Basic skills include purchasing, storage, and accounting for supply items.

To advance, supply and warehousing managers must have excellent records of performance. Their accounting skills must be outstanding, supplies must arrive at the right places at the right time, and they must show excellent leadership. As they master the supply system, they are assigned to positions of greater responsibility. They manage larger areas and lead more supply personnel. To advance to the most senior positions, supply and warehousing managers must seek out, and do well in, leadership and command positions. An advanced degree is helpful when combined with a record of outstanding performance.

Supply and warehousing managers compete with their peers for promotion and career enhancing assignments. Only the best-qualified personnel are selected for advancement, and competition intensifies with each increase in rank.

Specialization

Supply and warehousing managers may specialize in such areas as bulk petroleum storage and handling, aerial delivery of supplies, or supply and material management. With an advanced degree, they may also specialize in such areas as computer science, financial management, or weapons and material contracting and purchasing.

Training

Initial training for supply and warehousing managers includes 3 to 6 months of intensive classroom instruction.

Officers are trained to use and manage their services' supply system. Budget management, ordering, storage, distribution, and leadership are some of the subjects they study. Depending on their assignment, supply and warehousing managers may also be trained in petroleum management, food management, or aerial cargo delivery.

Advanced training prepares supply and warehousing managers for more responsible positions. Officers may be trained to operate computerized inventory and planning systems, to manage large warehouses and storage depots, or to prepare and manage major contracts with companies supplying the armed forces.

Almost all supply and warehousing managers earn advanced degrees. Some attend schools in programs funded by their service, others obtain degrees on their own after duty time. Degrees in computer sciences, industrial management, and business administration are particularly helpful.

Supply and warehousing managers are also given opportunities for professional military education to prepare them for senior officer positions. These programs include study of military subjects such as strategy, tactics, and planning large-scale operations. They may be completed either by correspondence or full-time study.

Typical Career Path (with time line)

Supply Officer (4 years)

After initial training, new supply officers are assigned to a supply unit where they gain experience in supply and warehouse operations. At this level, they:

Direct civilian or military personnel in ordering, receiving, and issuing equipment and supplies

Direct task assignments and prepare duty assignment and management reports

Inspect storage facilities, giving instructions on material handling and safety

Evaluate the performance of personnel working under their leadership

Senior Supply Officer (9–11 years)

Supply officers who do well in a variety of supply assignments advance to more demanding supply management duties. At this level, they:

Manage a supply or warehouse operation, directing other officers and enlisted personnel

Train new supply officers

Advise commanding officers of supply requirements

Inspect their supply facilities

Supply Staff Officer (15–18 years)

Senior supply officers who have demonstrated leadership in a series of assignments may advance to become supply staff officers. At this level, they:

Assist the supply and warehousing director in administrative and management duties

Help headquarters staff officers plan supply requirements for operational missions

Analyze purchasing and distribution patterns

Direct and evaluate studies to improve supply methods

Supply and Warehousing Director

Supply staff officers with outstanding records may advance to direct major supply and warehousing activities. At this level, they:

Command a supply facility or direct the supply operations at a military base

Advise senior service commanders on logistics and supply management

Evaluate bids and proposals submitted by suppliers

Conduct inspections of supply units

Transportation Managers

Army

Navy

Air Force

Marine Corps

Coast Guard

Transportation managers run the trucking, air, rail, and sea transportation system that moves military equipment, supplies, and personnel all over the world. As a transportation manager, you will direct a part of that system. You begin by leading a team of trained enlisted specialists. You may direct heavy trucking, landing craft, or air terminal operations. As you gain experience, you will serve in positions of greater responsibility, directing larger operations. There are opportunities to become director of transportation for a group of military bases or a major command area.

Duty Assignment

Transportation managers work in a variety of locations at military bases in the U.S. and overseas. Their "office" may be the deck of a large landing craft or the flight line of an air cargo terminal. They may also work in an office at a port or a truck motor pool. Many transportation managers support troops in the field during combat exercises and maneuvers. Some managers work in Washington, DC, where most of the military's logistics planning takes place. There are good opportunities for overseas assignments, particularly in Europe and the Pacific Islands.

Related Military Occupations

If you are interested in a career in transportation management, you may also want to consider a career in transportation maintenance or supply and warehousing management. See the Executive, Administrative, and Managerial Occupations cluster in the Military Officer Occupations section of this book for descriptions of these occupations. The career in supply and warehousing management is also described in the previous military officer career description.

Advancement

Transportation managers must be excellent leaders, planners, organizers, and problem solvers. They must understand military and civilian air, land, and water transportation systems. Good judgment and careful coordination are needed to avoid costly and time-consuming "bottlenecks" in the system.

To advance, transportation managers must have an outstanding performance record in positions of increasing responsibility. They must get people and cargo to the right destination at the right time. As they master the transportation system, they are assigned positions directing larger and more diverse transportation units. Many transportation managers obtain advanced degrees. An advanced degree, when combined with excellent performance, increases the chances for promotion.

Transportation managers compete with their peers for promotion and career-enhancing assignments. Only the best qualified are selected, and competition intensifies with each increase in rank.

In the Navy and Coast Guard, there are duty assignments involving transportation management. However, there is no true career path for transportation managers in those two service branches.

Specialization

Some transportation managers specialize in a particular mode or type of transportation operation. Specialties include ground and rail transportation; air, marine, and sea terminal operations; and traffic management.

Training

Initial training for transportation managers includes up to 5 months of both classroom and field instruction. Training covers transportation policy, maintenance and operation of vehicles and equipment, planning, and leadership. This instruction prepares officers for their first assignments.

Transportation officers have opportunities for advanced training to prepare them for future assignments. Courses may include budgeting, combined transportation specialty operations, or management development. Many transportation managers also receive specialty training in areas such as marine terminal operations, air transportation management, or truck transportation.

Most transportation managers earn master's degrees. Some attend school in a program funded by their service; others obtain degrees on their own after duty time. Degrees in transportation management, computer sciences, logistics management, and systems analysis are particularly helpful.

Transportation managers are also given opportunities for professional military education to prepare them for senior officer positions. These programs include study of military subjects such as strategy, tactics, and planning large-scale operations. They may be completed either by correspondence or full-time study.

Typical Career Path (with time line)

Transportation Officer (4 years)

After initial training, transportation officers are as signed to truck, air, boat, port (harbor), or terminal units. Typically, they:

Direct enlisted personnel in operating and maintaining transportation equipment

Schedule equipment use

Train personnel in transportation procedures

Prepare reports showing the use and costs of operations

Senior Transportation Officer (9–11 years)

Transportation officers who perform well and who are good leaders may advance to become senior transportation officers. At this level, they:

Inspect transportation, maintenance, or operations facilities

Command companies of trucks, landing craft, or tugboats

Plan missions and operations to support base and field operations

Evaluate the performance of transportation officers and senior enlisted personnel

Transportation Staff Officer (15–18 years)

Senior transportation officers with leadership experience and excellent records of performance may advance to become transportation staff officers. Here they may:

Coordinate with other military services to transport supplies from air, sea, or land bases to troops in the field

Develop long-range plans for use of transportation equipment and personnel

Evaluate new transportation procedures and equipment

Advise combat commanders on transportation matters

Teach transportation courses

Transportation Director

Outstanding transportation staff officers may advance to become transportation directors. At this level, they may:

Command a truck or boat transportation battalion

Direct an air transport terminal at a major air base

Advise major base and senior area commanders on transportation matters

Direct inspection programs for transportation activities they command